REWORKING THE PAST

—

Hitler, the Holocaust,
and the Historians' Debate

Edited by Peter Baldwin

—

Beacon Press Boston

Beacon Press
25 Beacon Street
Boston, Massachusetts 02108-2800

Beacon Press books
are published under the auspices of
the Unitarian Universalist Association of Congregations.

97 96 95 94 93 92 91 90   8 7 6 5 4 3 2 1

Text design by Linda Koegel

Library of Congress Cataloging-in-Publication Data
Reworking the past : Hitler, the Holocaust, and the historians'
  debate / edited by Peter Baldwin.
     p.   cm.
  Includes bibliographical references.
  ISBN 0-8070-4302-8
  1. National socialism—Historiography.   2. Holocaust, Jewish
(1939–1945)—Historiography.   3. Hitler, Adolf, 1889–1945.
I. Baldwin, Peter.
DD256.5.R436   1990
943′004924—dc20   89-46055

Reworking the Past

Contents

Acknowledgments

Edited volumes are by their nature cooperative efforts. And yet some cooperate more than others. Special thanks are due in this case to Deborah Johnson, the editor at Beacon who made this volume possible, and to Anson Rabinbach, who edited the issue of *New German Critique* in which a number of the chapters here first appeared. Acknowledgment is also gratefully made to Dan Diner and the Fischer Verlag, whose anthology *Ist der National-sozialismus Geschichte?* provided the original idea for this English edition and from which the essays by Saul Friedländer, Dan Diner, Hans Mommsen, Hagen Schulze, and Wolfgang Benz have been translated.

Part One

Introduction

1. The *Historikerstreit* in Context

Peter Baldwin

The *Historikerstreit*—the Historians' Debate—is but one of many recent controversies and events that serve to remind us how close the fascist past lies under the surface of European and especially German politics.[1] Others include the Bitburg debacle, particularly Reagan's virtual homage to graves of the SS; the Frankfurt staging of Fassbinder's play, *Der Müll, die Stadt und der Tod*, with its anti-Semitic overtones; the rediscovery, with Victor Farias's book, of Heidegger's Nazi past; Imhausen Chemie's connections to the Libyan chemical plant; Philipp Jenninger's resignation over his Kristallnacht anniversary speech; the victories in Berlin and Frankfurt municipal elections during the winter of 1988/89 by Franz Schönhuber's far-right Republican party; the mass exodus from East to West Germany the following autumn; the opening of the Berlin Wall. In a more general sense, the trial of Klaus Barbie, the Waldheim affair and the controversy over Paul de Man's early collaborationist writings have added fuel to such debates. Even when this particular disagreement has been forgotten, other related issues are certain to thrust such problems into the limelight anew.

The *Historikerstreit* is an unilluminating, almost tautological, designation for an unfortunate, but in many senses necessary, dispute. Historians are constantly fighting among themselves, although rarely over topics or in ways that spill out of the academy and into public view, onto the op-ed and, occasionally, front pages of the popular press. That this heated controversy has drawn in a wider circle of participants, that it has gone beyond the usual niceties of academic dialogue and taken on a polemical edge, is the case not only because it concerns the Nazi regime and the Holocaust— subjects that mercifully still evoke strong emotions, topics that have not yet been relegated to the conferences, proceedings and periodicals of scholars, but remain burning issues also for a much wider audience. More importantly, controversy has flared up in this case because the debate has gone beyond the immediate question at hand to embrace broader problems of historical methodology and, what is of even greater significance, to assume a clearly political character. The *Historikerstreit* in its narrow sense is but the currently visible tip of a much larger confrontation across the political divide between Left and Right within West German politics. Moreover, it is also to some extent evidence of a "nationalist" division between Germans and Jews and between erstwhile Axis and Allies, as Reagan discovered at Bitburg when it was revealed that, in much American editorial opinion at least, the anticommunist alliance of the Cold War did not yet fully outweigh (or, with prospects of reform in Eastern Europe, no longer did so) the antifascist enmities of the World War. Such cross-cutting cleavages, some of which are sorted out below, have added to the complexity of an already fragmented and multifarious debate.

The *Historikerstreit* in the Narrow Sense

The course of the controversy, well summarized in the introductory chapters below and elsewhere, requires only a brief orientation here.[2] The *Historikerstreit* was sparked during the summer of 1986 when Jürgen Habermas, the well-known Frankfurt social philosopher, challenged a series of assertions made by two historians in particular, Ernst Nolte and the since deceased Andreas Hillgruber.[3] In a small volume that paired two essays, Hillgruber had juxtaposed an account of the Nazi genocide against the Jews with an examination of the fate of the German army on the Soviet Front and that of the civilian population in the easternmost German territories at the hands of the Red Army during the last months of the war. This format and the title of his book (*Zweierlei Untergang* [Two kinds of destruction]) suggested an equivalence between what, in the second case, was the predictable outcome of the Germans' own war policies and, on the other hand, the actively pursued mass murder of the Jews. Moreover, the respective tone and approach taken in the two essays seemed to indicate that Hillgruber's concern lay primarily with the Germans in the East. In the essay on the East, he insists that the present-day historian empathize with the dilemma then confronted by the German soldiers, who faced a choice between the contradictory demands of humanity and patriotism, between protecting the homeland (thus allowing the crimes perpetrated in its name to continue) and succumbing to the invading forces. This concern contrasted with the tone of detached impartiality Hillgruber assumed with respect to the fate of the Jews. The controversy set ablaze by Hillgruber was partly the outcome of his unsophisticated attempt to evoke an historicist empathy with the actors of the past, a blurring of the line between understanding what it was that had motivated Hitler's contemporaries and justifying their actions, and partly a problem of the book's packaging (its awkward combination of topics best treated either separately or in some other manner, its tendentious dustcover blurbs).

No such circumstantial factors, however, moderated Habermas's provocation at the claims put forth, in turn, by Nolte.[4] Most generally, Nolte suggested that now, forty years after the German capitulation, the time had come for the Nazi regime to be undemonized, to be reevaluated as a period that may have been unusually, perhaps unprecedentedly, horrible, but not one that stood outside the course of historical development, nor one that could not be understood in the terms applicable to other eras and other political systems. This concern to place the National Socialist period within the framework of "normal" twentieth-century history he then applied more specifically to the Holocaust, that aspect of the regime which seems least explicable using the conventional historical categories and causes. Other and comparable genocides have been committed, Nolte argued: the Turkish massacre of the Armenians or Pol Pot's extraordinary crimes. Mass murder, it seemed in this perspective, was a regrettable, but not unusual, aspect of recent history. The Final Solution was but one example.

Moreover, he insisted, the Bolsheviks had been the first to carry out a form of mass or group extermination, based in this case on the distinguishing features of class—a form of aggression that was later copied by the Nazis, although now phrased in terms of race. Where the Soviet communists, in their persecution of the kulaks, for example, had sought to eradicate the bourgeoisie as a class, the Nazis sought to exterminate the Jews as a race. What united both acts was their shared ambition to rid the world of a particular group as a group. The members of the enemy category were targeted not because of what they had done, but because of who they were. Central to Nolte's argument is the causal tie he attempted to establish between the Bolshevik and Nazi mass murders. The Soviet killings were, in Nolte's terminology, both *Vorbild* and *Schreckbild*, both an example that was followed and a horrifying precedent. Hitler, he claimed, feared that the Bolsheviks would try something similar against the nations of Western Europe and therefore, in some very nebulous and unspecified manner, was provoked to commit an analogous, but race-based, act against the Jews. In particular, Hitler feared the method of torture, allegedly practiced by the Soviets and given its most widely known exposition in Orwell's *1984*, in which the head of a prisoner was placed in a cage with a starving rat. Finally, and most specifically, Nolte suggested that it was not wholly fanciful for Hitler to regard the Jews as the enemy, along with the Bolsheviks, against which Germany had to defend itself. To make Hitler's murderous anti-Semitism comprehensible, Nolte cited Chaim Weizmann's declaration at the Zionist World Congress in 1939 that the Jews would fight on Britain's side against Germany.

Habermas was incensed by at least two aspects of Nolte's arguments: first, by his attempt to relativize the Nazi regime, to portray it as worse than, but not essentially different from other authoritarian or totalitarian systems in the twentieth century and, second, by his claim that National Socialism was ultimately caused by the Bolshevik challenge, that the Gulag had been more "an origin" (*ursprünglicher*) than Auschwitz and that the Bolshevik class murder had been "the logical and real precondition" of Hitler's crimes. Nolte and Hillgruber were only two among a group of historians (one that included also Michael Stürmer, a professor with close ties to the Kohl government) whom

Habermas accused of wanting to resuscitate a form of German national identity that was not embarrassed by the Nazi crimes, a revitalized patriotism that would allow the Federal Republic to be proud of a German past not irredeemably tainted by National Socialism—of wanting to write what Charles Maier has called "Bitburg History."[5] These historians were attempting to reestablish a continuity of German history that need not negotiate an otherwise unbridgeable hiatus from 1933 to 1945. They were seeking to create a nationalist pedigree for the Federal Republic which would not be prevented by the Nazi interlude from reaching back to the glories of the Imperial period. By divesting the Nazi crimes of their singularity and by making them at least partially understandable as a response to the Bolshevik threat, Nolte and others like him—Habermas charged—were participating in a nationalist revival that was the historical profession's counterpart to the conservative political turn taken in 1982 with the formation of Kohl's Christian Democratic–led government.[6]

From these beginnings the debate spread out to engulf scores of other scholars in a hailstorm of *Feuilleton* and op-ed pieces. At its peak, even the president of the Federal Republic, Richard von Weizsäcker, intervened with a major speech, delivered at the convention of the German Historical Association in 1988. There he attempted to bring the controversy to an end by insisting that the Nazi past could and would not be normalized out of existence.[7] Much of the dispute has centered on Nolte, who is by choice a figure of controversy and provocation. Since he alone among the major contenders has brought forth new work to elaborate on his initial arguments (written after the pieces collected here) it is worth indicating the limited extent to which his position has actually evolved from the stance he first took.[8]

In 1987, Nolte published two books: a large work, *The European Civil War, 1917–1945: National Socialism and Bolshevism*, in which he fleshed out the ideas he had earlier cast in only skeletal form, and a volume of assorted texts to bolster and clarify his arguments.[9] In these, Nolte expands on his assertion of the causal connection between the Bolshevik regime and the Nazis. He treats the interwar period as one of war between Left and Right in terms of domestic politics and between the Soviet Union and the bourgeois democracies of Western Europe in terms of foreign policy. Fascism, in his hands, becomes understandable less as an extension and exacerbation of prewar currents on the far Right than as a response to communism. In this way, Nolte shifts the central and most important point about National Socialism away from its criminal tendencies or its fatally obsessive anti-Semitism to its relationship with Marxism and Soviet communism. Fear and loathing of Bolshevism were the driving forces behind Hitler's actions and, in this way, he only expressed with exaggeration what many of his contemporaries also dreaded "in a comprehensible and to a certain extent justified fashion."[10] Even though the transposition was not rational, it was nevertheless the German bourgeoisie's horror of Bolshevism which caused it eventually to turn against one part of itself, against the Jews.[11] Anti-Semitic genocide is thus regarded not primarily as an initiative taken for their own reasons by the Nazis, but as a partially understandable, although ultimately irrational, reaction to the Bolshevik threat.

The logic of Nolte's position is therefore this: Bolshevism represented a world-historical novum, the first time that a party had seized control of a major modern state with the intention of changing the entire world, in particular of eradicating its enemies *en masse*. By being the first to take such a step outside the usual course of political action, the Soviets cleared the path for the Nazi antithesis. The German response was therefore both prompted by an abhorrence of the Bolsheviks' actions and yet also imitated them. Lenin and Hitler are therefore not regarded as "normal" politicians, the products of their respective national circumstances, but rather as embodiments of this historical hiatus created by their ideologies. Hitler was not a German statesman in this sense, but the anti-Lenin. More pointedly, it was Lenin and then Stalin, not Hitler, who first sought the eradication of an entire group, the benchmark of the new form of politics based on "a collective attribution of guilt" that would eventually culminate in Auschwitz.[12]

When Nolte turns to the Holocaust itself, the consequences of his approach become clear. He undercuts the distinctiveness of the genocide against the Jews by emphasizing the cruelty and terror that have become increasingly characteristic of modern warfare.[13] In addition to the genocide that took place on the margins of the First World War against the Armenians, Nolte viewed many common features of war in the twentieth century, especially the violence now borne also on the home front, as genocidal. The attack on the citizens of Guernica had the trappings of mass murder, while the Allies' bombing of civilian targets during the Second World War was clearly genocidal. He even claims to detect genocide in the expulsion of the Germans from formerly east German territories with the shift westwards of the Soviet and Polish borders. Having thus hollowed out the concept, Nolte is nonetheless willing to admit that the Holocaust was an act of genocide of a different nature. The annihilation of the Jews was not simply another element of the war, but an end in itself, a goal dictated by the Nazis' ideology. And yet, the Holocaust was but the most specific and exaggerated aspect of their anti-Bolshevik ambitions. The Holocaust was "the exact counterpart" to the Bolsheviks' extermination of a class and was "a biological copy of the class-based original."[14] Hatred and persecution of the Jews was a "concretization" of the search for Germany's enemies, an immediate example of the threat that, in a broader sense, was posed by the Bolsheviks.[15] Nolte has thus in fact added little to the argument he originally advanced beyond a great deal of historical narrative of events during the interwar years.[16] His claim remains that the Nazi dictatorship and the Holocaust should be understood first and foremost as reactions to the Bolshevik threat.

Much of the disagreement Nolte has provoked hinges on his rather peculiar methodology. Nolte was trained as a philosopher at Freiburg under Heidegger's influence, and this has left a determining mark on his writings. He has consistently sought universal essences to historical phenomena, striving to free them of their time-bound specificity and to regard them in light of their supposedly general attributes. In his first and most famous book, *Three Faces of Fascism*, such concerns played only a secondary role to a fairly straightforward elaboration of three political traditions (Action Française, Italian Fascism, and National Socialism) whose similarities had, until then, not been systematically worked out. Yet, even here, those parts of the book which raised questions were precisely the most "philosophical"—the concluding sections that portrayed fascism as a "metapolitical phenomenon," as a movement in reaction to what Nolte called "transcendence," as an ideology that sought to reverse the Enlightenment and undo the process of human emancipation.

In his next major work, *Germany and the Cold War*, Nolte tipped the balance between philosophy and history even further. Although he included plenty of standard-issue historical narrative, the *Fragestellung* of the book strove for a greater degree of universality. In the introductory chapters, Nolte dealt with the historical antecedents of geopolitical division in general, he drew parallels to other divided nations through the ages and showed less interest in the specificity of the postwar confrontation between East and West than in the larger issues of political division and ideological antagonism. Here, he foreshadowed the civil war metaphor that would later become so important, the Cold War as a clash of *Weltanschauungen*. Such progressive etherealization of Nolte's concerns has now reached a peak in his most recent work. In this, he reduces an era that other historians see fraught with economic, political and social problems, as well as questions of ideology, to a simple, though titanic, battle of worldviews. The process of historical development becomes the logic of ideas unfolding in their mutual relations. Why Nazism actually came to power, as an example of the more mundane questions pursued by other scholars, is a matter of little concern to Nolte. For an answer, he is content with an allusion to Hitler's ability to play on popular longings: revision of the Versailles Treaty, German nationalism.[17] Hitler's true significance, in Nolte's scheme, is as the ideological riposte to Bolshevism, the anti-Lenin in this secular Manichaeanism.

Nolte's reasoning is based on a very abstract conception of intellectual causation in historical development that seeks to define the essence of particular events by pursuing their most extreme conclusions, what Carl Schmitt called the "ultimate" or "final" distinctions, by pressing them conceptually to the limit.[18] Bolshevism represented a historical novelty because it was the first to draw the consequences of group-based attributions of guilt in tangible terms. Nolte explains the perversion of the Nazi reaction to Bolshevism to the point of mass murder with a purely philosophico-historical argument: extreme exaggeration is the fundamental nature of all ideologies, especially those brought forth as counter-ideologies to other systems of thought.[19] Nolte's own reasoning is thus itself ideological in the sense that his fellow Heideggerian, Hannah Arendt, defined it: ideology as the logic of an idea.

"The ideology treats the course of events as though it followed the same 'law' as the logical exposition of its 'idea.'" [20]

Nolte tends to elide between scientific knowledge, insights into the nature of the world that, having once been won, can no longer (barring a Dark Ages–like experience of wholesale amnesia) be rolled back or passed over, and the opinions and attitudes, the ideologies and worldviews that vary among nations and epochs for reasons that can be accounted for in social and economic terms, but that are not necessary in any intellectual sense. Whether humans are inherently good or bad, whether the individual or the community is most important: such are the socially determined ideas in which philosopher-historians like Nolte are interested. Nolte seems to assume that such conceptions are similar to scientific knowledge, that, once the idea of destroying the enemy as a group (to take his primary example) has been broached or, in a sense, discovered, it can no longer be ignored any more than can the discovery of fire or the invention of the atom bomb. There is, in other words, a logic of historical development, an intellectual patrimony to which this insight now belongs and in ignorance of which human development can no longer take place. For this reason, Nolte argues that the very fact of introducing a concept, its first formulation or its first realization, represents a decisive step in the evolution of world history. [21] At other times, in contrast, he retreats to analytical and merely definitional equivalences whose significance as applied to the past can scarcely be more than trivial: the Gulag as more "an origin" than Auschwitz in the sense that counterrevolution presupposes revolution. [22]

Much of the disagreement with Nolte's views stems from his peculiar notion of causation, his insistence on tying a causal link between Bolshevism and Nazism where most historians find only insufficient evidence. The group-based notion of guilt and therefore enmity that was allegedly first realized in political practice by the Bolsheviks he identifies as a "precondition" for the Nazi genocide, not a "direct cause." [23] Nevertheless, despite this distinction, it is clear that Nolte is asserting some form of causal connection between the "original" class-based annihilation and the Holocaust. As Eberhard Jäckel has demonstrated, however, there is no evidence that Hitler actually feared the Bolshevik threat to this extent or that it in any specific way prompted the genocidal aims he pursued once in power. [24] According to Richard Löwenthal, information concerning the persecution of the kulaks reached the West only during the Second World War, in other words, after that which it was supposed to have prompted had, in fact, already begun. [25] Nolte is therefore left arguing that in some nebulous sense there is a connection at the level of the concepts, if not at that of the facts. [26] Nolte's inclination to theorize at this altitude also explains his attempt to present the Nazis' anti-Semitism as a clash of principles. Jews represented modernity and progress and the Nazis, despising this, were determined to counter it. Their hatred of the Jews was a concrete substitution for an intellectual battle of ideologies: revolution versus counterrevolution, the Enlightenment tradition versus reaction.[27] Visceral hatreds powerful enough to motivate mass murder are donnishly elevated to a contradiction of worldviews. The provocativeness of Nolte's position is due also to the overinflated Hegelianism of his intellectual technique. He relies in large measure on a form of portmanteau dialectics that allows him to embrace simultaneously what would otherwise be contradictory positions without needing to make a choice between them: Bolshevism and Nazism as similar yet different, as *Vorbild* and *Schreckbild;* fascism as "radically opposed and yet related" to Marxism, using "almost identical and yet typically modified methods."[28]

Much of the debate Nolte has sparked stems, of course, also from the political implications of his approach. In his most recent writings, he has made unmistakable the exculpatory ambitions of these attempts at revisionism. It is time, Nolte insists, to rethink the Nazi period without refusing a priori to consider claims and assertions which until recently have been voiced only in the apologist literature of the far Right—although, he hastens to add, only to the extent that they are sanctioned by historical research. Moreover, he goes so far as to claim that the collective attribution of guilt—that which he regards as having once been the core of the Nazi and the Bolshevik crimes—has now been turned against the Germans, who, after Auschwitz, are considered culpable as a group.[29] It is in this connection that Nolte's repeated description of the Bolshevik class murder as an "Asiatic" act so patently reflects his efforts to hold at arm's length the barbarities at which the Western world is only all too adept.[30] In a similar attempt at distancing, Nolte suggests that there was something un-German about Hitler's ideas, that their worst aspects were but imitations of features better exemplified by other peoples: the British who conquered empire without scruple, the Americans who exterminated the Indians, the Jews with their consciousness of race.[31]

Behind and Beyond the *Historikerstreit*

The *Historikerstreit* in the narrow sense has thus been the debate that broke out between, on the one hand, Nolte (as its most distinct formulator), Hillgruber and various others who voiced a similar position (Stürmer, Joachim Fest, Klaus Hildebrand, Hagen Schulze) and the opposing camp, spearheaded by Habermas and soon joined by historians like Hans-Ulrich Wehler, Jürgen Kocka, Eberhard Jäckel, Hans Mommsen, and Wolfgang Mommsen. The immediate conflict identified two groups. One side suggested that the Nazi regime, although reprehensible, had been far from unique when seen in the broader perspective of the twentieth century. This group claimed that the time had come to assimilate historically the dictatorship within an extended continuity of German development so that it no longer remained as an insurmountable barrier to the past, distorting national self-identity, and preventing contemporary West Germans from appreciating the positive aspects of the Federal Republic's Weimar and Imperial antecedents. The other side included those historians who argued that such integration and relativization represented an unvarnished nationalist attempt to gloss over the horrors of the Nazi period and to glorify the Imperial tradition whose peculiarities and weaknesses, as inherited by Weimar, had played a crucial role in allowing Hitler to power.

At this level, the dispute took place along fairly direct political lines, with those arguing for a nationalist position based on a relativization of the Nazi past being scholars associated with the Christian Democrats, while their opponents tended to be members of the Social Democratic or at least Liberal camp. Nevertheless, this simple polarity does not do justice to the complexity of the themes intertwined with the *Historikerstreit*. Along with this particular dispute, other issues of contention have also affected the various stances assumed during the course of intellectual jousting. Several ongoing debates prompted by various aspects of German history have intersected with the *Historikerstreit* to produce a welter of possible and sometimes cross-cutting positions.

The first among these other debates that have also been caught up in the *Historikerstreit* concerns the Holocaust and its genesis. In this dispute, "intentionalists" oppose those referred to either as "structuralists" or "functionalists."[32] Intentionalists argue that the Holocaust is sufficiently explained by looking at the leading Nazis' anti-Semitic hatreds and their eventual ability to carry out plans for extermination. For these historians, the obvious congruence between Hitler's murderous designs on the Jews, expressed in his earliest writings, and the eventual outcome allows an uncomplicated causal coupling between intent and effect. Functionalists, in contrast, admit that beginning and end bear undeniable similarities, but argue that the road from ambition to execution was, in fact, so meandering, at times doubling back on itself, at others forking in different directions, that no easy lines can be drawn from what Hitler said he intended to what was actually accomplished. This functionalist approach is closely coupled to a view of the Nazi regime, now largely accepted by most scholars, that, far from being an example of totalitarian control, with Hitler issuing orders that were carried down a clear chain of command to the point of implementation, the system was, in reality, a motley, centrifugally disorganized, contradictory collection of competing offices, institutions and centers of power, loosely held together by their loyalty to the Führer. In this chaotic or polycentric regime, few decisions were arrived at coherently, and fewer still were implemented with any degree of consistency.

The extermination of the Jews was, from this angle, but one among the most important examples of the regime's ambivalent process of policy making. The Holocaust thus becomes the outcome of a partially haphazard and, to some extent, chance set of concatenating circumstances, not a policy clearly determined early on by Hitler and eventually implemented under the cover of war. Functionalists do not deny that Hitler set out to persecute the Jews mercilessly, but they tend to argue that the actual decision to begin the organized annihilation was not an inevitable result of the Nazis' anti-Semitism alone (although without this, the Holocaust would obviously neither have been possible nor even conceivable). They regard the Final Solution as more immediately the outcome of various contingencies during the early months of the war against the Soviet Union. The decision to exterminate, in this perspective, came as the Nazis faced the problem of dealing with the Jews being deported. Once the advance on the Russian front had bogged down, the Jews could no longer be pushed ever further eastwards and a new decision on their fate was required.

A second dispute among historians of Germany that also has implications for the *Historikerstreit* concerns a much broader question. This controversy, summarized by Jürgen Kocka in the final chapter, pits those scholars who regard German history as having followed a *Sonderweg*, a special path of evolution, against those who deny this particularity. Members of the first of these camps, which includes not only Kocka but also Hans-Ulrich Wehler among those represented here, have explained Germany's historical development in terms of its detour from the course blazed in France, Britain, and, less dramatically, North America. France and Britain passed from their aristocratic, feudal stages to become liberal democracies by means of an act of bourgeois revolution during which the middle classes wrested power from the elites of the Old Regime and asserted their own control. America, for its part, avoided the problem altogether through virgin birth, without the taint of a feudal past. Germany, in contrast, did not follow suit. Her aristocratic classes remained firmly in the saddle, the bourgeoisie was weak and failed to assert its own interests, kowtowing instead to its social superiors. Parliamentary democracy was accordingly a late and weak development.

The ultimate point of this *Sonderweg* argument is to explain why Germany fell to the Nazis. Germany was subject to the same sorts of difficulties that also bedevilled other nations during the 1920s and thirties (the effects of World War One, the Depression) and yet it succumbed to a fascist temptation that Britain and France were better able to resist. The *Sonderweg* approach maintains that it was the peculiar traditions inherited from the Wilhelmine Empire which left Weimar Germany unable to cope with the interwar crises. The continuing power of the aristocratic classes meant that the Junkers were among the main actors behind the downfall of the republic and Hitler's appointment to the chancellorship. The tradition of authoritarian and supposedly unpolitical government made the German middle classes willing to accept extraparliamentary solutions during the turbulence of the early 1930s. The practice—inaugurated by Bismarck—of excluding the working class from a proportional share of political power meant that the socialists were radical, on paper at least, and that the bourgeoisie was accordingly inclined to accept fascist rule in hopes of avoiding the revolution it otherwise feared from the Left.

The opposing position, put most forcefully by Geoff Eley, is that—despite appearances—Germany did not differ appreciably from other European nations.[33] In part, France and Britain did not themselves undergo the sort of bourgeois revolution previously assumed. In part, Germany, when examined more closely, actually seems successfully to have accomplished more of the changes required to fit the Western model than historians had earlier realized. Although the middle classes did not take control politically, if one looks at economic development or the evolution of civil law, it is clear that, even in Germany, the bourgeoisie had become the dominant class by the late nineteenth century. Conversely, the strong paternalist state, that is often used as an example of the continuing influence of premodern tendencies here, can equally well be seen as a precocious step toward contemporary forms of statutory intervention that Germany was able to achieve earlier and with greater facility than either France or Britain. The welfare state, for example, although it may have begun in Bismarck's hands as a conservative attempt to tame an otherwise unruly proletariat, quickly evolved to become a tool socialists used to further working-class interests. Germany, in this respect, took the lead in a modern development that its European neighbors only belatedly followed.

Finally, among the controversies that have become intertwined with the *Historikerstreit*, there have been the debates (discussed in the chapter by Mary Nolan, p. 224) that set historians who pursue a history of high politics, leaders, and decision-makers against those who seek to reconstruct from the bottom up the experience of the common people, the history of everyday life or what is known in German as *Alltagsgeschichte*.

Historicization

The manner that these different debates among historians of Germany have intersected during the course of the *Historikerstreit* to produce cross-cutting and occasionally conflicting positions is well illustrated by the problem of historicization, the question of fitting the Nazi regime into the broader sweep of German development. Historicization was an issue first broached by Martin Broszat before the outbreak of the *Historikerstreit* in the narrowest sense, but it quickly became a central point of contention and is one of the themes best represented in this volume.[34]

Historicization raises in the most general sense the problem of locating the Nazi era within the course of German development: what is its place in the longer sweep of the past, what connections extend backward to earlier times or continue forward into the present? One interpretation from the immediate postwar period saw the Hitler regime as essentially unmoored in the stream of German evolution. In books like Friedrich Meinecke's *The German Catastrophe*, the Nazi dictatorship was regarded as an irrational eruption of demonic forces into history, an event with neither a heavy anchor in the era preceding it, nor strong mooring to the years after 1945. Clearly, such a view could not last. The historian's professional preoccupation with continuities, together with a commonsense search for more convincing causes of the Nazi regime, helped undermine this approach.

In its place, there have developed at least three alternative solutions to the problem of locating Nazism in German history. These are in many respects quite different; some concern methodological issues of interest primarily to historians, others are prompted by moral or political motivations. The first was a reaction to historians' early attempts at saving previous eras from implication in Hitler's reign. In this perspective, long-term continuities were uncovered between the Second and Third Empires, continuities transmitted largely unchanged by the Weimar Republic, that help explain why Nazism was possible. This approach belonged to the *Sonderweg* school (that has now been questioned, although far from refuted), and elaborated the idea that peculiarities of German development were significantly responsible for the disaster of the years after 1933. Continuities along the Imperial, Weimar, and the Nazi periods were explored in order to show that Hitler's chancellorship and subsequent dictatorship had been partially the outcome of trends with an unfortunately venerable pedigree. Traditions of militarism, strong authoritarian leadership, a lack of political liberalization, the continued power of the aristocratic elites were, in this view, among the factors characteristic of the Wilhelmine Empire whose continued importance helps explain why Germany was particularly responsible for the outbreak of the First World War and, subsequently, why the Weimar Republic failed.[35]

The second approach to Nazism's historical place, that broached by Nolte, practiced by Hillgruber, and described above, might best be called an attempt at normalization. It is less a methodological than a political issue and aims to integrate the Nazi years seamlessly into the broader course of German history, treating them as a period that, although unusually barbaric, was not qualitatively different from contemporary experience elsewhere. Where the first approach tends to view German history before 1933 through the lens of the Nazi era, seeking antecedents and causes, normalizers regard the Hitler dictatorship in light of other contemporaneous regimes that are alleged to be equally totalitarian, searching for relativization and comparative normalcy. Nolte's attempt to portray the Holocaust as a response—exaggerated beyond all bounds, but nonetheless a reaction and not an independent initiative— also shifts the cause of the regime and its most grotesque aspects away from long-term factors, indigenous to German history, and on to the immediate life-or-death challenge supposedly thrown down by the Bolsheviks.

Third and finally, there is historicization in the sense that Martin Broszat uses the term in his chapter (p. 77). Broszat is a scholar who earned a reputation first as a leading formulator of a functionalist interpretation of Nazism and, second, as a practitioner of *Alltagsgeschichte*, of an everyday life approach to the regime. His concern with historicization has been colored by this background. From a functionalist point of view, Broszat has been interested less in Hitler as a person and his role than in the overarching structures of the regime, with their roots in the pre-1933 period and their continuities into the postwar era. As an historian of everyday life, he has focused on the moral ambiguity of most Germans' experience of those years—the manner in which the normal citizen could live in comparative peace amid and as part of a criminal regime, the fact that there was more, seen from the average German's perspective, to the Nazi period than Auschwitz. His call for an historicization asks that the regime be accepted as something that was not wholly demonic, that for many was a period of relative normality. The Nazi era was an ineradicable part of the broader continuity of German history, a time when changes that had begun earlier continued unabated. It was a time in which seeds of evolution were planted that would later blossom during the Federal Republic and—finally and most controversially—a period when not every development was necessarily tainted by the horrors and bestialities also committed at the same time.

Broszat's example of this last claim is taken from the realm of social policy. The Nazi Labor Front (DAF) proposed changes in the social insurance system that, by including all and treating in an egalitarian fashion at least those Germans who met the regime's racial definition of citizenship, resembled the Beveridge Plan in Britain and other contemporaneous attempts at welfare policy change elsewhere that have been regarded as evidence of progressive reform. Broszat argues that the Nazis' social policy plans were also forerunners of reforms instituted later during the Federal Republic and should therefore not be dismissed as merely another of Hitler's propaganda ploys.

In fact, Broszat's example is ill chosen. There were, of course, superficial resemblances between the Nazi and the British plans, but it was precisely these similarities that condemned to failure postwar attempts in Germany at instituting reform like Beveridge's. Proposals that the Left advanced after 1945 to change the German social insurance system so as to resemble the British (with an all-inclusive membership and flat-rate, allegedly egalitarian benefits) failed in large part because of this bastard pedigree. In turn, the 1957 pension reform in the Federal Republic, which Broszat regards as similar to the Nazi plans, deliberately avoided the characteristics shared by the Nazi and the Beveridge proposals.[36] Nonetheless, Broszat's point could be well sustained with other examples. A better illustration of his argument that "not all those historically significant developments which occurred in Germany during the Nazi period merely served the regime's goals of inhuman and dictatorial domination," might be the *Kraft durch Freude Wagen*—the *Volkswagen*. The Volkswagen, the people's car, was intended as the automotive answer to the Nazi *Volksgemeinschaft*, the national community of Aryan Germans. The car—cheap, functional, and attractive in its own way—was, to corrupt Churchill's wartime phrase, an attempt to harness the magic of mass production for the millions. In fact, although begun by the Nazis, it did not achieve its undeniably laudable goals until long after the war and then did so in America and elsewhere as successfully as in Germany: a positive continuity with an otherwise despicable past.

What Broszat has done with his call for an historicization is to reemphasize a concern with the Nazi era's impact on developments after 1945 that has long occupied students of the period.[37] Historians have sought to determine what effect both the regime as such and, more generally, the experience of war, occupation and dismemberment had on the viability and stability of the postwar republics in the East and West. The division of the Reich equilibrated the population religiously and demographically and turned the east Elbian regions of Germany most in need of change over to those occupiers with the clearest reforming agenda. The Nazi regime's centralization and the migrations, expulsions, and displacements at the end of the war reduced the sway of old regionalist affiliations. The National Socialists successfully sought to reduce the importance of the collar line in the workforce.[38] The officer caste in the military was diluted by more democratic recruitment.[39] The old elites, once so powerful, were increasingly shunted to the side, finally directly attacked after July 1944. The parallel hierarchy of Nazi institutions undermined the inherited rank ordering of German society.[40] Most overarchingly, as Ralf Dahrendorf has portrayed it, the Nazi regime was the functional equivalent in Germany of what used to be considered the bourgeois revolution elsewhere.[41] Broszat has built on such themes to suggest that one reason why Hitler's appeal was so wide, why it cannot be reduced merely to manipulation or misunderstanding, was that he managed to articulate the wishes of significant social groups for change, for a revolution (what Broszat calls a "delayed bourgeois revolution") that was not only backward-looking, but one that also promised to sweep old elites from their customary positions and open channels of social mobility and advancement previously closed off by the traditional rigidities of German class structure.[42]

It is the anticipation that these various approaches to integrating the Nazi regime historically outlined here might be inadmissably confused and elided that informs Saul Friedländer's reply to Broszat and their ensuing exchange of letters below. Does historicizing the regime entail regarding Nazism as a "normal" part of the recent past? Friedländer fears that Broszat's preoccupation with the (at times positive) continuities between the Nazi Empire and Federal Republic and his concern with the morally neutral ordinariness of the average German's experience during the years after 1933 may help propel examinations of National Socialism down a slippery slope of normalization. By reducing the moral distance at which the historian would otherwise approach the regime, historicization threatens to encourage the sort of relativization for which Nolte speaks as well as the misplaced attempts at historicist empathy with the actors of the period practiced by Hillgruber.[43]

Friedländer does not deny that there are connections to be traced between the National Socialist and the postwar eras, but he worries that such a focus on the regime's position in a longer flow of development—a seeing it as but one, however unsure and faltering, step along an extended road of gradually modernizing evolution—will lead to a masking of the period's most horrifying features under the innocuous mantle of historical continuity. Can, he asks, the worst aspects of the regime be bracketed out from its "normal" evolution, or are the two sets of events intrinsically linked? If it were possible in any untroublesome sense to claim that modernizing tendencies were inherent in the Nazi regime, or at least that such developments with positive implications for the post-1945 era were an outcome of the war, then the controversy Broszat might have sparked would have differed little from that which has already been debated with respect to Italian fascism. Partly, the questions posed in the Italian case have been economic in focus and concern the role Mussolini's regime played as a developmental dictatorship, a period of forced industrialization that allowed the country to draw abreast of its more developed neighbors.[44] More analogously to Broszat's concerns, however, such debates in the Italian case have also dealt specifically with political issues and were given their most extreme expression in Renzo de Felice's claim that Mussolini, although perhaps its black sheep, nonetheless belonged to the family of Western revolutionaries, that fascism was at least partially an act of emancipation from the Old Regime.[45]

Friedländer objects that such parallels do not hold because the Italian case produced nothing like the Holocaust. Ultimately, it is the genocide committed by the Nazis that prevents us from regarding the regime, even from the most Olympian heights of comfortable retrospection, as but a turbulent phase in a larger and ongoing process of German development. Had the Nazi regime been like the Italian, or like other comparatively straightforward fascist or authoritarian systems, such a perspective might be justified. The Holocaust, however, being irreducible to any such overarching developmental perspective, obstructs attempts at an historicization.

The Politics and Methodology of the Issues

It is at this point that simple polarities of Right versus Left, nationalist relativizers versus *Sonderweg* continuity theorists, fail to do service any longer; it is here that the divergently intersecting angles of the positions taken in the *Historikerstreit* and in the other debates current among historians of Germany come to view. Friedländer fears that Broszat's call for historicization too closely approximates Nolte's attempt at normalization, a charge parried by Broszat in their exchange below. Broszat thus, in this perspective, ends on the same side of things as the conservative nationalist historians, including Hillgruber, who claimed that his attempt to empathize with the civilians and soldiers of the East was similar to the aim of *Alltagsgeschichte* historians in reconstructing the everyday experience of average Germans during the regime. In a similar manner, Otto Dov Kulka notes that Broszat and others like Hans Mommsen are critics of Nolte and yet at the same time take positions that tend to deemphasize the singularity of the Final Solution or the importance of anti-Semitism for the Nazis. It is, moreover, true that functionalist approaches to the Holocaust and attempts at historicization, although first and most prominently formulated by scholars with a left-of-center bent, have also been welcomed by unabashedly right-wing historians as a step toward a more differentiated view of the Nazi regime that promises to help unburden Germans of their collective guilt.[46]

Conversely, historians who think that the Holocaust can be compared without being lessened ask of those like Friedländer and Kulka how the singularity of the Jewish genocide fits into a broader view of German developments. As Hans Mommsen suggests below, emphasizing the uniqueness of the Nazi experience undercuts insights into the common fascist proclivities of European interwar regimes. How can one explain something which is truly singular? Is not a juxtaposition of some sort necessary to understand the Nazi horror? Historians interested in comparing the Third Reich to other regimes are concerned by the prospect of placing the Holocaust on a moral pedestal, thus saving it from being trivialized through comparison, and yet also preserving it in what may seem a rather fruitless purity: ineffable, but also impotent in its significance for others than the victims and survivors. They argue that the singularity of the Hitler period, if framed too consequentially, may lead to a denial both that Nazism was fascism, and therefore part of a broader movement characteristic of many nations, and also that it was a product of German historical development, except in a one-time, irreproducible and therefore safely quarantined sense. And yet, however well intentioned and compelling, such hopes of deriving salutary lessons and insights from the Holocaust also pose the possibility of ultimately cheapening what they seek to study. Dan Diner, in the first of his two chapters, provides a powerful statement of the tension between singularity and comparability created by the Final Solution, the degree to which the perspectives of perpetrators, victims, bystanders and retrospective observers may be inherently disjoint. Clearly, the respective demands and aspirations of scholarship, remembrance and politics are far from being easily reconcilable when looking back on the Holocaust.

When the *Historikerstreit* is phrased in terms of the singularity or comparability of Nazism, the lines of dispute belie the simple political polarities between Left and Right along which the controversy has otherwise appeared to unfold. Mommsen and Broszat are associated along the methodological axis of comparison with historians whose political motives they reject and with whom they disagree on other matters as well. They share nothing in common with Nolte, for example, when it comes to analyzing the causes of the Holocaust. Nolte, with his fixation on Hitler's ideas, is of necessity an intentionalist who never questions that the Nazi leadership wanted and directly caused the Final Solution. At the same time, on the opposite side of this particular divide, historians like Friedländer and Kulka who tend to treat the Holocaust as a singular phenomenon are also methodologically associated with scholars whose political intentions they would question. Precisely because an insistence on uniqueness can deprive comparisons of their force, many conservative historians have (until recently at least) embraced a view of the singularity of Nazi anti-Semitism and the Holocaust. They did so less because they sought to preserve a sense of its unprecedentedness or to resist any trivialization than because they wished to argue against attempts from the Left to portray Nazism as but one example of fascism, which, in turn, was an outgrowth of capitalism. If National Socialism with its radical anti-Semitism were *sui generis*, then the argument that capitalist systems, faced with the challenges of the interwar years, reacted by embracing fascism would be weakened. Emphasizing the importance of Nazi anti-Semitism was thus a way of being consistently anti-Marxist.[47] Moreover, portraying the Nazi era in this sense as unique interrupts continuities between it and the Imperial past or the Republican present and isolates it in a broader stream of otherwise unspoiled German history.

In a similar way, the lines that run between scholars who accept or reject the notion of a German *Sonderweg* also cut at various angles to those that have determined sides in the *Historikerstreit*, narrowly framed. The attempt by conservative historians to integrate the Nazi regime into the broader course of German development has been helped by attacks on the very idea of a *Sonderweg* that, in turn, were first broached by other scholars with quite different political agendas. Criticism of the *Sonderweg* was launched first and most prominently by two British historians, Geoff Eley and David Blackbourn.[48] To the extent motivated by political intentions, they were prompted less by a desire to "normalize" Germany than by a concern to undercut whatever claims ailing Britain could stake in the 1970s to represent the ideal model of Western development. Blackbourn and Eley's efforts aimed to lessen the necessary force of past development on the events of 1933: the *Sonderweg* did not lead willy nilly to Hitler's chancellorship. If Germany's evolution had not been peculiar, then its misguided historical trajectory could not be the issue. And yet, the problem Blackbourn and Eley faced was that, having disposed of the factors which distinguished Germany from those nations not as prone to political extremism, they were hard put to explain why, then, fascism was especially successful here. Having smoothed out differences among European nations during the nineteenth century, they were suddenly confronted with the need to reintroduce them in the twentieth.[49] The anti-*Sonderweg* historians thus agree with Nolte in at least their periodization. Nolte looks to foreign policy while Eley examines the economic crises of the era, but they are at one when looking for the origins of Nazism in their focus on the interwar years, rather than on longterm continuities inherited from the Empire.

The political implications of the anti-*Sonderweg* approach within the context of German history have been ambiguous at best. Michael Stürmer, one of the scholars attacked by Habermas, who has advocated the creation of an acceptable historical pedigree for the Federal Republic, fully agrees with Blackbourn and Eley that Bismarck's Empire, at least partially modern, served as a model in many respects for Europe's allegedly more advanced bourgeois democracies.[50] Seeking an historical fundament for present-day Germany, he is hardly averse to exploring those respects in which the Empire served as an exemplar, emulated by its European neighbors. In a similar manner, Hagen Schulze, in his chapter here (p. 185), gives evidence that an attack on the *Sonderweg* idea is well suited to hopes of normalizing German history in a conservative sense. He denies the peculiarity of German development before 1933 and suggests that the *Sonderweg* thesis was largely a creation of whiggish British historians seeking to legitimate their nation's goals in the First World War. To explain why, despite a development similar to that of other countries, Germany nevertheless eventually turned fascist, he focuses on the geopolitics behind the interests held by rival nations in German division, weakness, and instability. The 1848 revolution might well have succeeded, he claims, giving Germany its bourgeois upheaval, had the rest of Europe not intervened. Having first denied German peculiarity, he escorts it in again through the back door, now blaming it on Germany's neighbors, rather than on self-willed or self-caused factors.

Normalization is, however, not an aim pursued exclusively by conservative historians. There is also a version of this approach fostered by scholars to the left-of-center. In recent studies of the Holocaust, for example, historians who are prominent in the everyday life school tend to examine it as though it were but the wildest consequence of eugenic thought. Since such a racialist viewpoint was common to all European nations during the interwar years and since eugenic conceptions were not focused especially on the Jews, both the specificity of the Holocaust and the particular place of Jews in it tend to be undermined.[51] In her chapter, Mary Nolan discusses the perspective that the new focus on history from below gives the regime, a flattening out of the moral peaks and valleys, the danger of reducing the unusual and unprecedented to the ordinary.

The politics and methodologies that intersect at the *Historikerstreit* have thus cut at different angles, producing multiple and sometimes self-contradictory groupings. At the most obvious level, Stürmer has long been seeking to make the Federal Republic a "normal" member of the Western alliance, one equipped with historical memory and not just nightmares of the past, one with the requisite brightly colored patriotic bunting, not merely the ashen pallor of collective guilt. At the same time, Habermas, his opponent in terms of relativization and rejuvenated German nationalism, is also uncomfortable with the neo-neutralism and "third way" ideology that has become increasingly prevalent on the Left within the Green Party and hails the opening of the Federal Republic to the political culture of the West as the great intellectual achievement of the postwar period. Both Stürmer and Habermas, for all their differences, in turn stand in contrast to the implicitly anti-Western sentiments expressed by Hillgruber, who accuses the Allies of having planned to dismember Germany even before they knew about Auschwitz and who thereby rejects German responsibility for the two world wars as sufficient justification for the wartime coalition to have sought a bisection of Bismarck's Empire.

More overarchingly, it is clear that singularity and comparison, relativization and normalization can be sought or accomplished for different purposes and different ends, from Left as from Right, as accusation and as excuse. There is little inherent in these various approaches that determines the ideological spin put on them. The question is not methodological in a narrow sense, but political. As with so many debates that have political overtones, the important thing is less what is said than why. Comparison of the Nazi system both with other contemporaneous regimes and with the German past can serve different aims. The Left relativizes and compares with the past to show continuities, to draw Bismarck into Hitler's maelstrom; it compares with other countries to argue that all bourgeois regimes contain such inherently dangerous potentialities. The Right compares to show similarities with other nations and periods, to dilute the bestialities of the Nazi period in an unpleasant but mutually shared heritage. A singularizing approach, for its part, can be intended either to keep the memory of the Holocaust sacred or to isolate the genocide as an aberration.

In a similar way, different national and nationalist agendas have been accommodated among the themes raised during the *Historikerstreit*. Some West German historians have sought to submerge the crimes of the Nazi past in a common totalitarian age. They hope to salvage a positive national identity for their country after Auschwitz and after Potsdam—comparability as the first step toward respectability and normality. Israeli historians like Friedländer and Kulka, in turn, clearly also have interests of national identity in what would otherwise be a tepid scholarly quibble over methodology. The singularity of the Jewish suffering adds to the moral and emotional claims that Israel can make on her citizens and on other nations. The memory of the Nazi horror concerns "the question of roots, the question of faith of an entire society. . . . The recent past remained and still remains a massive justification," as Friedländer writes.[52]

Why the Controversy?

Having traced the outlines of the *Historikerstreit* there remains the question, why has it broken out at all? Clearly, the controversy is only partly explicable in terms of the ideas advanced. Nolte's latest assertions, the ones that so provoked Habermas, are extreme and untenable, to be sure, but they are hardly without precedent. Certainly, the idea that fascism was, at least partially, a reaction to communism, the revenge of the bourgeoisie for the Russian revolution, was not new and had long been put forth by significant elements on the moderate Left.[53] "A campaign of destruction [*Vernichtungsfeldzug*] against communism," was how Nazism was described shortly after Hitler's chancellorship.[54] Mussolini said that "fascism arose as the logical, legitimate and human retaliation against socialist extremism. Fascism answered violence with violence." On trial in Munich in 1924, Hitler described himself as the leader of the revolution against the revolution.[55]

Nolte himself insists that most of the arguments now put forth were foreshadowed in his previous books and laid out explicitly, although without prompting dispute, in an earlier article.[56] In large measure, he is right. These works demonstrate his longstanding preoccupation with the mutual threats of annihilation advanced by antagonistic groups, their dialectic of destruction.[57] Already in his best-known book, *Three Faces of Fascism* (1963), Nolte had described fascism as an ideology of anti-Marxism, one for which Marxism was accordingly a precondition. In another work, he claimed that the Bolsheviks were the first to seek the extermination of their enemies as a group and suggested that the formation of fascist parties had been prompted by a fear of the consequences.[58] Moreover, Nolte has long been claiming that Marxism contained characteristics which made it comparable to fascism and had also earlier argued that the Holocaust was a reaction to the threat of Bolshevik group annihilation.[59] Long before the *Historikerstreit,* one of his early reviewers caught the theme that would become a leitmotiv of his later work: "The European Civil War."[60]

Nolte has for many years been arguing that the Nazi regime was comparable to similarly authoritarian eras in the histories of other nations, what he has called the "plurality of the Hitler period."[61] It is also the case that Nolte has not performed quite the volteface of which some accuse him: from regarding fascism as a collectively distinct set of phenomena to comparing and relativizing between extremist regimes of both Left and Right along the lines suggested by the theory of totalitarianism. Nolte insists that it was never his intention completely to substitute for the theory of totalitarianism an account of the specificity of fascism and that he now seeks to combine the two approaches, to locate not only the parallelism between Stalinism and Nazism, but also the alleged causal relationship between the two.[62] He has been saying something similar for at least the last decade.[63]

Other scholars have also made claims similar to Nolte's, again without raising a storm. Stanley Payne, an authority on Franco's regime in Spain, writes in a widely read work on fascism: "Truly large scale genocide or mass murder is a prototypical development of the twentieth-century. . . . The unique Nazi tactic was to modernize the process, to accomplish the mass murder more efficiently and surgically than other great liquidators in Turkey, Russia or Cambodia have done."[64] With a closer echoing of Nolte's terminology, Domenico Settembrini has argued that, because Italian socialists were not sufficiently organized either to seize power themselves or to defeat the fascists, "This implies, objectively speaking, that on revolutionary socialism rests, not only the dual responsibility of engendering fascism and infecting it with totalitarianism, but also the responsibility of having made its decisive victory possible." He also describes communism and facism with a term much like Nolte's *Vorbild* and *Schreckbild* as "brother-enemies."[65] H. R. Trevor-Roper defines fascism as, above all else, anticommunist.[66] Even the Soviets, in this current era of reform, have been asking Nolte's question: "Would there have been Hitler without Stalin?"[67]

More generally, it should be clear that the charge of comparing and relativizing for ulterior political purposes is not one that can be leveled against

Nolte or German historians of his ilk alone. These sorts of juxtapositions can serve widely different aims: some exculpatory, others accusatory. From the very first, fascist systems have been compared with others, both communist and liberal democratic, in attempts to besmirch that with which they were paired. The Comintern's theory of fascism identified an essential continuity among all capitalist regimes, regardless of their specific political expression. Capitalism was judged inherently repressive and fascism was proclaimed but the most extreme form of a system whose more innocuous incarnation was liberal bourgeois democracy. Bourgeois society produced and was therefore solely responsible for fascism. Fascism was not, in this view, a reaction to or in any sense caused by the Bolshevik challenge.[68] Conversely, the theory of totalitarianism put the issue the other way around. Although it has roots extending back to the 1920s and 1930s, the concept of totalitarianism first gained wide popularity as a Cold War tit-for-tat, paying back the Comintern in the same coin for its attempt to damn the liberal democracies by association.[69] Comparison, it now became clear, was a double-edged sword. Where the Left had asserted similarities among capitalist regimes, the theorists of totalitarianism insisted on comparabilities of technique and effect between fascist and communist systems that otherwise claimed to be polar opposites.

It is also worth pointing out that revising the Nazi past to make it seem more a part of the "normal" history of the twentieth century and thereby an event in which the Allied nations, too, were implicated, is a longstanding tendency of which the *Historikerstreit* is only the latest example. Moreover, such revisionism has been as eagerly pursued by foreign as by German scholars. Hellmut Diwald, a conservative historian and former colleague of Stürmer at the University of Erlangen, caused a stir a decade ago by seeking to reduce Auschwitz to insignificance, but similar and earlier attempts to unburden the Germans and displace much of the blame for the war and even some of its worst horrors have come equally from British and American observers.[70] The sufferings of the Germans in the eastern territories, for example, that so concerned Hillgruber have long been the subject of a revisionist literature in both America and Germany.[71] David Irving, a British historian, has made a career of seeking to shift culpability for the worst atrocities from Hitler and to draw also the Allies into proximity with the outrages of the war.[72] On the far fringe of such tillers in the vineyard of right-wing revisionism has been the Harvard Ph.D. and former Berkeley faculty member, David Hoggan, whose books (published mainly by an obscure but similarly inclined press in Germany) have progressed from an attempt to relieve Hitler of the blame for the beginning of the war in 1939 to a massive and bizarre critique of the course of American history from a racialist and wildly anti-Semitic perspective.[73]

Foreign policy has, in general, been that aspect of the Nazi regime most accessible to this sort of revision. A narrow, but hardy, strain of Anglo-American historiography has long concerned itself with the problem of apportioning responsibility for the two world wars. Starting with distinguished scholars like Sidney B. Fay and (in an indirect sense) John Maynard Keynes on the First World War, it has since progressed—leaking accuracy, prestige, conviction, and resonance along the way—to the Second.[74] Historians of the second conflagration have rightly explored the extent to which the temptations of anti-Bolshevism, the indecision and vacillation of appeasement, and the inaction of isolationism among the Western powers gave Germany the chance to provoke hostilities. They have thereby implicated the Allied nations in the creation of those general circumstances that made it possible for a Hitler to run amok.

And yet, the comparative clarity of the immediate responsibility for the outbreak of events and the all but total monopoly on aggressive designs held by the Nazis have allowed fewer of the ambiguities inherent in the First World War to trouble the historiography of the Second. Revisionists in the latter case have therefore been forced to take stances that are much more extreme and untenable—ones often prompted by unabashed political motives. The high point of such tendencies, at least in terms of academic respectability, came with A. J. P. Taylor's successful attempt to play *enfant terrible simplificateur* by arguing that Hitler had not sought the war he started in 1939.[75] From there, war guilt revisionism applied to the Second World War has degenerated, going on, with widely varying political motives and claims to exactitude, to blame the Western Allies for the outbreak of hostilities in 1939 and Stalin for Hitler's decision to launch the Barbarossa campaign against the Soviet Union in 1941.[76] Harry Elmer Barnes, for example, a former Smith professor and onetime historian with a respectable reputation, placed himself on the extreme edge of such rewriting, pushing matters further than Nolte, by insisting that the bombing of civilian Germany was as depraved as anything committed by the Nazis and that the Morgenthau Plan for the pastoralization of postwar Germany was comparable to the Holocaust.[77] At the time of the *Historikerstreit*, a minor dispute on the far Right of the historical spectrum was proceeding in tandem, prompted by observers who claimed that Hitler had started what was in effect a preventive war in 1941 and that Stalin was therefore in some sense the true aggressor.[78] The revision debated during the *Historikerstreit* has in this perspective been neither novel, nor a German invention.

To put the *Historikerstreit* in context, it must also be said that Nolte and his nationally revisionist colleagues represent the extreme and ill-considered end of a broader trend in the historiography of modern Germany that has been gaining strength over the last decade. Nolte and the like-minded have given such tendencies one particular political inflection, but there is no inherent necessity that such new approaches be interpreted in one manner or the other. A clear example of these developments has been the gradual shift in emphasis apparent among recent accounts of the Nazi regime from a focus primarily on anti-Semitism and the genocidal persecution of the Jews to a broader concern with the war in the East, of which the Holocaust was one part.

This shift began at the latest with the recognition, elaborated in Eberhard Jäckel's classic study of Hitler's worldview, that the war against the Soviet

Union and the Holocaust had been closely linked.[79] Since then, the debate between intentionalists and functionalists concerning the Holocaust has provided an arena for the working-through of this change. Functionalists have in no sense denied the viciousness of the Nazis' anti-Semitic beliefs, but they have attempted to revise our understanding of the process by which these general anti-Jewish ambitions were actually implemented. In so doing, their focus has shifted from the intentions expressed already in Hitler's earliest utterances to the manner whereby the war (especially the campaign in the East and that in particular after the attack on the Soviet Union) allowed conditions in which the Holocaust was possible.

These historians have tended to concentrate their aim not on anti-Semitic hatreds per se, which remain as a necessary but insufficient condition of the Final Solution, but on the actualities of wartime barbarities, many of which were first inflicted on groups other than the Jews and only gradually extended to become full-scale genocide. At the same time, recent studies have increasingly been concerned with the nature of hostilities on the Eastern front, the barbarization of warfare there, the staggering losses inflicted on the soldiers, the exertions demanded of them and the connection of these extraordinary circumstances to the atrocities committed against the civilian population—the manner, for example, in which German attempts to suppress partisan warfare became a cover for much greater horrors.[80] Attention in such studies has been paid to the way the army was won for the policy of genocide by a gradual escalation of the victims, from the Red Army Commissars (comparatively easy to portray as military enemies who had to be liquidated) through civilians of the Slavic nations and finally ending with the Jews. The army's anticommunism was, in this sense, the thin edge of the wedge that eventually permitted its participation in the Holocaust.[81] Close ties have been identified between the nature of the war against the Soviet Union and the extermination of the Jews, with the Holocaust increasingly depicted as unlikely to have been realized except within the context of that war and possibly therefore in a meaningful sense caused by it.[82]

The clearest expression of this new focus is provided by Arno Mayer's recent book, *Why Did the Heavens Not Darken? The "Final Solution" in History* (New York, 1988), a work that in many respects is similar to Nolte's *Der europäische Bürgerkrieg*, while being motivated by wholly different intentions. First, the differences: Mayer is in no sense concerned to argue for the comparability or even relative "normality" of the Jewish genocide, but in fact seeks to portray it as the unique and culminating point of what he calls the Thirty Years' Crisis of the twentieth century, the turbulent and troubled decades that spanned the two world wars. At the same time, his search for similarly horrifying events in the crusades of the Middle Ages and the Thirty Years' War of the seventeenth century denies Nolte's premise, that the group annihilation first realized by the Bolsheviks was unprecedented in history and therefore an event of a kind and quality able to provoke an analogous, but conversely directed Nazi response. Mayer is partially a functionalist, partially an intentionalist and does not locate the source of the Holocaust wholly in Hitler's aims. With the functionalists, he argues that the actual implementation of the genocide was decided in a largely ad hoc manner in some connection with the beginning of the Soviet campaign.[83] At the same time, the causal force behind the Holocaust in his presentation is not the functionalists' self-accelerating logic of competing bureaucratic initiatives, but a spiraling ideological crusade against what the Nazis called Judeo-Bolshevism. The motives behind the Holocaust are therefore, in Mayer's analysis, of a sort that intentionalists would find familiar.[84] The war was prompted from the German side by anti-Judeo-Bolshevism and strivings for *Lebensraum* and was not, as Nolte describes it, largely a preemptive reaction. The reader is offered a crusade instead of a civil war as the organizing metaphor.[85]

Ultimately, the politics of Mayer's book are diametrically opposed to Nolte's. Mayer seeks to portray the war that led, in some sense incidentally, to the Holocaust as motivated more immediately by anti-Bolshevik ambitions than by a pursuit of the Jews. The genocide against the Jews became the second best substitute for a victory over communism once the course of the war put the Soviets out of reach. The disaster wrought by the Nazis was only secondarily concerned with the Jews. Mayer and Nolte are therefore at one in shifting the focus to the Soviet Union and Germany's war against this alleged arch-rival, but wholly at odds in their evaluation thereof. For Nolte, the Bolsheviks were the main aggressors, for Mayer, the primary victims. And yet, there remain significant similarities of approach. Most importantly, for both of them the war was first and foremost one between fascists and Bolsheviks, not between Germans and Jews; it was a titanic struggle of ideologies. For both, the emphasis has shifted away from the Jews to the Soviets. For both, Hitler's enemy was ultimately the modern world, for which the Jews stood in as convenient scapegoats.[86]

Nolte's views and those of like-minded observers are indefensible exaggerations of positions that in more moderate formulations are becoming increasingly accepted by historians. Few historians would deny that pitched battles between Left and Right were a characteristic feature of European interwar politics, both domestically and in terms of foreign policy. Nor is there much question that a fear of Bolshevism helps explain the willingness of some in Britain and France—faced with the alternative of cooperating externally with the Soviet Union and domestically with the parties of the Left against the threat posed by the fascist dictators—to appease Mussolini and then Hitler in the twenties and thirties: better Hitler than Blum, as the extreme Right in France put it.[87] Fascism was, to some extent, a reaction to the fear of Bolshevism, however misfounded and exaggerated it may eventually have become. To insist on the general interrelations between communism and fascism during the interwar years is hardly a controversial position. The *Historikerstreit* has therefore been provoked in a scholarly sense by the further step that Nolte and others have taken in making a specific causal connection here.[88]

Yet, since even Nolte's extreme formulations were not new in 1986, there remains the question, Why, then, the dispute? Why now? There would be little point in paying attention to Nolte's views had they not helped provoke such a storm. Without the escalation into a Debate, Nolte would have trod his course alone, spinning out increasingly outré opinions in diminishingly influential megavolumes, gradually becoming the William Shockley of the historical profession and dimming what would otherwise have been a still luminescent reputation. Other historians would not have been swept into the maw of controversy. Certainly, the debate does not owe its existence to intellectual provocation alone. It must be admitted, as Hans Mommsen points out below, that in scholarly terms there is little new at stake in the *Historikerstreit*. Few of the points rehearsed here on the alleged comparability of the Stalinist and Nazi killings, for example, have not already been put through their paces in the critical literature on the theory of totalitarianism.[89] The reasons for the *Historikerstreit* as a dispute lie elsewhere. Partly, they are a matter of timing. One article by Nolte does not a debate make. In this case, however, Nolte's position was apparently seconded by Hillgruber—a well-respected historian of a sober mien whose earlier work gave little inkling that he might be prone to such tendencies—and given backing by the well-known writer and editor Joachim Fest at the influential conservative newspaper, the *Frankfurter Allgemeine Zeitung*, where many of the original writings that provoked the controversy first appeared.[90]

More importantly, the *Historikerstreit* came as but one element in a broader political dispute over questions of national identity and the role of the Nazi past in the democratic present. An important aspect of the wider context of the *Historikerstreit* was Chancellor Kohl's attempt to draw a line under the Hitler era, exemplified in the Bitburg affair and in the speech held during his 1984 visit to Israel in which he insisted that "the grace of late birth" had absolved his generation of direct implication in the horrors of German history. The disputes given vent at about the same time over the proposed construction of two historical museums in Bonn and Berlin and the nature of the presentation their exhibitions should strive for were yet further examples of similar concerns. Falling on such well-marled soil, the initial spores of the *Historikerstreit* quickly grew into a squabble of prize proportions.

The *Historikerstreit* is, from this perspective, an outcome of the larger political shift in a conservative direction that Germany has undergone along with other European nations and the United States—what is known as the *Wende*, which, beginning here in the late 1970s, was cemented with the formation of the Christian Democratic-Liberal coalition government in 1982. In the broadest sense, the controversy has been political, not intellectual or scholarly.[91] At heart, the debate has revolved around the nature of the Federal Republic's historical and therefore national identity, its self-understanding. Should Germany, as Franz Joseph Strauss, the late Bavarian Christian Socialist leader, demanded during the 1987 election campaign, "emerge from the dismal Third Reich and become a normal nation again"?[92] Nolte and his allies have accused scholars to the left-of-center of starting the debate in dismay at the political and intellectual shift rightwards, in response to their inability to continue dictating the historical agenda.[93] These historians have, in turn, attacked conservatives for fostering a form of guilt-free nationalism that is no longer possible for a post-Nazi Germany.

By seeking to normalize the past, the German Right has attempted to overcome the dilemma in which the end of the war left it. Conservatives, who had traditionally been the advocates of German nationalism, were now—during the first postwar decades—associated with a bankrupt tradition that was obliged to accept a large share of the blame for Germany's present predicament, divided and despoiled of her sovereignty. In response, the Center and Right became ardent Westernizers and Europeanists, riding the tide of postwar peace and prosperity under the auspices of the Atlantic community, the Common Market, and NATO.[94] At the same time, as Andrei Markovits discusses in his chapter (p. 262), the Left in Germany, especially its Newer and Greener factions, began to appropriate elements of a certain strain of German nationalism, evoking a neutralist "third way" for Germany between East and West.[95] When this tendency was sharpened in conjunction with the decision to station the Pershing missiles during the early 1980s, the Right responded by seeking to brook the contradictions of German nationalism in the Federal Republic: an anti-European sentiment within the West European camp. Bitburg, the clumsy political choreographing of the claim that the anticommunist coalition of the Cold War was more important and compelling than the antifascist union of the hot war, was among the attempts made by the Right to reconcile the respective demands of being good patriotic Germans who did not have to shy back from their past and yet also reliable partners in the Western alliance.[96] At the same time, the German Center-Right has also been pressured on its other flank from a groundswell of unabashed neonationalism from the far Right, the Silesian *bleibt unsers* being among the most visible examples.[97] The *Historikerstreit* was prompted by the academic end of this attempt at a synthesis of nationalism and NATO. This general political context is explored in the introductory chapters by Charles Maier and Anson Rabinbach.

At its most immoderate, the *Historikerstreit* has given evidence of a resurgence of German patriotism and, less innocuously, of a desire to rewrite and whitewash the past. On the extreme Right, within a thin and powerless fringe far beyond the Noltes, Hillgrubers, Hildebrands, Stürmers, and Fests, there are those who have welcomed the controversy as the first step toward a major revision of German history, a repudiation of the historical *nostra culpa* for the Nazi regime that they claim was imposed by the victorious Allies. Hitler did not start the war alone; equally horrible atrocities were committed by all sides in the conflict; 1945 did not mark the liberation of Germany from Nazism, but the imposition of the Soviet-

American yoke; the reunification of the country should take precedence over the commitment to any transnational alliances.[98] Such are the themes sounded by the most dyspeptic sort of conservatism—themes that encourage a description of the *Historikerstreit* with a slight reformulation of Oscar Wilde's definition of foxhunting: the pursuit of the ineffable by the unspeakable.[99] Yet, despite such unrepentant tub-thumping, it seems clear that Hans-Ulrich Wehler is correct in claiming below that little of the new approach advocated by some in the *Historikerstreit* has won much of a hearing among scholars or the public at large. After the initial flourishes, the revisionist camp—with the exception of Nolte—has been notable for its avoidance of further debate.[100]

Nonetheless, the *Historikerstreit* is not without a broader significance. The most important theme that it raises concerns the inevitability of a new coming to terms with Germany's recent past, for Germans and for others alike. As the Nazi regime recedes into historical view, as the accretions of the postwar period multiply to fill the retrospective foreground, it is unavoidable that the emotional and moral thrust of the Hitler era be dulled, that the perspectives of the victim and the participant cede pride of place to those of the observer and the descendant. As the two halves of the former Reich unify, Germans will search for a degree of historical normalcy, a present less freighted with the past, than has been possible until now. The Nazi era and its horrors will not change, the past will not be rewritten. Despite all understandably concerned alarm, that sort of revisionism has never found any sure foothold. But the perspective on the Hitler era will evolve. As the historical distance on Nazism lengthens and as interpretations grow more sophisticated, it is foreseeable that the regime and the Holocaust will be placed in increasingly broad contexts, ones that will—superficially at least—serve to dilute their specificity and partially to historicize them. And yet, as the *Historikerstreit* has shown, there is no automatic process by which the past recedes, by which the searing memories of contemporaries become the footnotes of dispassionate scholarship. When and how an event becomes History is a political decision.

One thing, however, seems clear. The fears of Jews and others among the regime's victims, the hopes—in turn—among the most conservative Germans and their foreign allies, that the Nazi era will at some point be subsumed without trace into a seamless continuity of the past, that it will become a diminishing blip on larger secular oscillations, that its bestialities will disappear at the vanishing point in the *longue durée* of historical retrospective— these fears are baseless, these hopes are in vain. There is no historical statute of limitations after which a "normal" perspective will set in once again. The question is not when will Nazism finally be viewed as part of history as usual, for that day is unlikely ever to come, but how will this period, with all its anguish and inexplicability, be situated within our collective memory. How the history of this era will be written is the issue over which the dispute has been fought, a question that will continue to prompt controversy. Given the eventual inevitability of a distancing of perspective, the *Historikerstreit* and especially its polemical edge, the swath it has cut outside the academy, should not be feared as a foretaste of how the unprecedented will be normalized, the barbaric domesticated. Instead, the debate should be welcomed as evidence that Nazism and its horrors are far from having been swallowed up by forgetfulness.

Notes

1. I am grateful to Elazar Barkan, Andrei Markovits, Aron Rodrigue and Anjana Shrivastava for readings and criticism of earlier drafts.
2. Overviews may be found in Charles Maier's chapter (p. 38) and the penultimate section of Anson Rabinbach's (p. 45). There are also excellent surveys of the dispute in Richard J. Evans, "The New Nationalism and the Old History: Perspectives on the West German *Historikerstreit*," *Journal of Modern History* 59 (December 1987); Evans, *In Hitler's Shadow: West German Historians and the Attempt to Escape from the Nazi Past* (New York, 1989); Ian Kershaw, *The Nazi Dictatorship: Problems and Perspectives of Interpretation*, 2d ed. (London, 1989), chaps. 8, 9; Geoff Eley, "Nazism, Politics and the Image of the Past: Thoughts on the West German *Historikerstreit* 1986–1987," *Past and Present* 121 (November 1988).
3. Habermas's gambit has been translated into English as "A Kind of Settlement of Damages (Apologetic Tendencies)," in *New German Critique* 44 (Spring/Summer 1988). The writings that initially prompted the controversy and the first round of responses have been published in a German volume (*"Historikerstreit": Die Dokumentation der Kontroverse um die Einzigartigkeit der nationalsozialistischen Judenvernichtung* [Munich, 1987]) and are scheduled for an English-language edition by Knopf. These pieces are referred to as *Historikerstreit* without specific page numbers throughout the rest of this volume and may eventually be consulted in either edition.
4. The texts in question were Nolte, "Vergangenheit, die nicht vergehen will," in *Historikerstreit* and "Between Myth and Revisionism? The Third Reich in the Perspective of the 1980s," in H. W. Koch, ed., *Aspects of the Third Reich* (London, 1985). A version of the latter essay is also in *Historikerstreit*.
5. Charles S. Maier, *The Unmasterable Past: History, Holocaust and German National Identity* (Cambridge, Mass., 1988), chap. 1.
6. On Habermas and the dispute, see John Torpey, "Habermas and the Historians," *New German Critique* 44 (Spring/Summer 1988). Habermas has collected his pertinent political writings in *Eine Art Schadensabwicklung* (Frankfurt am Main, 1987), forthcoming in an English translation from MIT press.
7. "Nachdenken über die Geschichte: Ansprache des Bundespräsidenten zur Eröffnung des 37. Historikertages in Bamberg," 12 October 1988, Presse- und Informationsamt der Bundersregierung, *Bulletin* 131 (Bonn, 14 October 1988), 1185–88.
8. Hillgruber published a collection of essays after the main thrust of the *Historikerstreit*, but these have only indirect bearing on the debate. Andreas Hillgruber,

Die Zerstörung Europas: Beiträge zur Weltkriegsepoche 1914 bis 1945 (Frankfurt am Main, 1988).

9. *Der europäische Bürgerkrieg 1917–1945: Nationalsozialismus und Bolschewismus* (Frankfurt am Main, 1987); Nolte, *Das Vergehen der Vergangenheit: Antwort an meine Kritiker im sogenannten Historikerstreit* (Frankfurt am Main, 1987).
10. *Bürgerkrieg*, 16.
11. Nolte, *Vergehen*, 74–75, 103.
12. *Bürgerkrieg*, 185.
13. Ibid., 499ff.
14. Ibid., 517.
15. Ibid., 122.
16. Empirical novelties, even were they possible given the thesis Nolte wants to prove, would be unlikely from a historian who has never made use of materials other than easily accessible published sources and who considers the act of obtaining a newspaper from the Hoover Institution in Stanford a research effort worthy of being described in a footnote. Ibid., n. 41, 558.
17. Ibid., 17.
18. Carl Schmitt, *The Concept of the Political* (New Brunswick, 1976), 26. See also, Maier, *Unmasterable Past*, 86.
19. *Bürgerkrieg*, 17.
20. Arendt, *The Origins of Totalitarianism* (New York, 1973), 469.
21. The significance he attaches, for example, to having found what he claims is the earliest suggestion to perform mass annihilation through the use of gas in a pamphlet by a British Malthusian in 1838. "Bürgerliche Gesellschaft und Vernichtungspostulat," in his *Was ist bürgerlich?* (Stuttgart, 1979), 227–28.
22. *Vergehen*, 79. See also Maier, *Unmasterable Past*, 14.
23. Nolte, "Between Myth and Revisionism," 35.
24. Eberhard Jäckel, "Die elende Praxis der Untersteller: Das Einmalige der nationalsozialistischen Verbrechen lässt sich nicht leugnen," in *Historikerstreit*.
25. Josef Joffe, "The Battle of the Historians: A Report from Germany," *Encounter* 69, 1 (June 1987): 74. It is worth noting, however, that one objection to Nolte's argument (that Hitler's anti-Semitism is well known to have predated the Russian Revolution and cannot therefore have been caused by it) does not answer the logically possible, but historically inaccurate, assertion made by Nolte that not Hitler's anti-Semitism as such, but the decision to exterminate the Jews was prompted by the Bolshevik threat. Wolfgang Mommsen, "Nazi War Crimes Were Unparalleled," *Independent*, 5 November 1988; Maier, *Unmasterable Past*, 31.
26. Take, for example, the merely asserted causal connection in the following: "Hitler's 'destruction of the Jews' was, at root, not 'genocide,' but rather the most radical and, at the same time, most desperate form of anti-Marxism. *Because* he could not seize his actual enemy [Bolshevism], he sought to eliminate it by attacking its alleged cause [the Jews]. *Thereby*, he was forced to leave the social level and enter that of biology [and racial distinctions]." Nolte, "Bürgerliche Gesellschaft und Vernichtungspostulat," in *Was ist bürgerlich?* 235, emphasis added.
27. See, among many examples, Nolte's "Philosophische Geschichtsschreibung heute?" *Historische Zeitschrift* 242, 2 (April 1986): 273–74. That Jews in popular opinion represented modern currents and that anti-Semitism was in some sense a displaced attack on modernity is, of course, an insight of long standing, elaborated in its best-known form by Peter Pulzer, *The Rise of Political Anti-Semitism*

32   *Peter Baldwin*

in Germany and Austria, rev. ed. (Cambridge, Mass., 1988). Yet Nolte's version is different since it deals not with popular conceptions or perceptions, but with a clash of concepts in the abstract. His approach here is largely an extension of the method he earlier applied to defining fascism in metaphysical terms as a "resistance to transcendence," as a form of counter-Enlightenment and counter-emancipation. Nolte, *Three Faces of Fascism* (New York, 1969), part 5.

28. *Three Faces of Fascism*, 40.
29. *Vergehen*, 91, 105. A similar lament is to be found in Nolte's charge that the sorts of questions he raises are considered controversial only because he is a German. Nolte, *Was ist bürgerlich?* 65–66.
30. The adjective was used by the biographer of Max Erwin von Scheubner-Richter, a mentor of Hitler's and earlier a German diplomat in Turkey, in reaction to the massacre of the Armenians.
31. Nolte, "Über Frageverbote," in *Was ist bürgerlich?* 65.
32. Good surveys may be found in Kershaw, *The Nazi Dictatorship*, chap. 5; Michael R. Marrus, *The Holocaust in History* (New York, 1987), chap. 3. A sampling of the various positions is in François Furet, ed., *Unanswered Questions: Nazi Germany and the Genocide of the Jews* (New York, 1989).
33. David Blackbourn and Geoff Eley, *The Peculiarities of German History: Bourgeois Society and Politics in Nineteenth-Century Germany* (Oxford, 1984). Recent surveys include several of the essays in Richard J. Evans, *Rethinking German History: Nineteenth-Century Germany and the Origins of the Third Reich* (London, 1987), and Jürgen Kocka, "German History Before Hitler: The Debate about the German 'Sonderweg,'" *Journal of Contemporary History* 23 (1988).
34. There is also an excellent discussion of the issue in Kershaw, "'Normality' and Genocide: The Problem of 'Historicisation,'" chap. 8 in his *The Nazi Dictatorship*.
35. A classic statement of this approach in Hans-Ulrich Wehler, *The German Empire, 1871–1918* (Leamington Spa, 1985). There is also a variation on this approach that draws long-term continuities in intellectual terms, ones reaching back beyond the Wilhelmine Empire. George L. Mosse, *The Crisis of German Ideology: Intellectual Origins of the Third Reich* (New York, 1964).
36. Hans Günter Hockerts, *Sozialpolitische Entscheidungen im Nachkriegsdeutschland: Alliierte und deutsche Sozialversicherungspolitik 1945 bis 1957* (Stuttgart, 1980); Eckart Reidegeld, *Die Sozialversicherung zwischen Neuordnung und Restauration: Soziale Kräfte, Reformen und Reformpläne unter besonderer Berücksichtigung der Versicherungsanstalt Berlin (VAB)* (Frankfurt am Main, 1982); Peter Baldwin, *The Politics of Social Solidarity: Class Bases of the European Welfare State, 1875–1975* (Cambridge, 1990), chap. 3.
37. This was one of the main concerns of David Schoenbaum's aging, but as yet unsurpassed, classic, *Hitler's Social Revolution* (New York, 1966).
38. Michael Prinz, *Vom neuen Mittelstand zum Volksgenossen: Die Entwicklung des sozialen Status der Angestellten von der Weimarer Republik bis zum Ende der NS-Zeit* (Munich, 1986); Jürgen Kocka and Michael Prinz, "Vom 'neuen Mittelstand' zum angestellten Arbeitnehmer: Kontinuität und Wandel der deutschen Angestellten seit der Weimarer Republik," in Werner Conze and M. Rainer Lepsius, eds., *Sozialgeschichte der Bundesrepublik Deutschland* (Stuttgart, 1983), 216–28.
39. Bernhard R. Kroener, "Auf dem Weg zu einer 'nationalsozialistischen Volksarmee': Die soziale Öffnung des Heeresoffizierkorps im Zweiten Weltkrieg," in Martin Broszat et al., eds., *Von Stalingrad zur Währungsreform: Zur Sozialge-*

schichte des Umbruchs in Deutschland (Munich, 1988); Reinhard Stumpf, *Die Wehrmacht-Elite: Rang- und Herkunftsstruktur der deutschen Generale und Admirale 1933–1945* (Boppard am Rhein, 1982).

40. Ronald M. Smelser, "Nazi Dynamics, German Foreign Policy and Appeasement," in Wolfgang J. Mommsen and Lothar Kettenacker, eds., *The Fascist Challenge and the Policy of Appeasement* (London, 1983).

41. Ralf Dahrendorf, *Society and Democracy in Germany* (New York, 1967), chap. 25.

42. Broszat is here drawing on a wider literature that is surveyed in the penultimate section of Peter Baldwin, "Social Interpretations of Nazism: Renewing a Tradition," *Journal of Contemporary History* 25, 1 (January 1990).

43. An example of the regrettable extremes to which such an elision can go may be found in Detlev Peuckert's wholly fanciful suggestion, following an examination of how German youth expressed their dissatisfaction with the regime through various ordinary sorts of rebellious activity, that young Germans were equivalent victims of Nazism to the more obvious candidates: "As long as the Nazis needed armament workers and future soldiers, they could not exterminate German youth as they exterminated the Poles and the Jews." Note also the order of priority among the actual victims. Peuckert "Youth in the Third Reich," in Richard Bessel, ed., *Life in the Third Reich* (Oxford, 1987), 35. This is Reagan's Bitburg fallacy of the SS as victims, this time committed from the Left.

44. The literature here is vast. Representative examples include: A. James Gregor, *Italian Fascism and Developmental Dictatorship* (Princeton, 1979); Henry A. Turner, "Fascism and Modernization," *World Politics* 24, 4 (July 1972); Arnold Hughes and Martin Kolinsky, "'Paradigmatic Fascism' and Modernization: A Critique," *Political Studies* 24, 4 (December 1976). Similarly for Germany, Horst Matzerath and Heinrich Volkmann, "Modernisierungstheorie und Nationalsozialismus," in Jürgen Kocka, ed., *Theorien in der Praxis des Historikers* (Göttingen, 1977: *Geschichte und Gesellschaft*, Sonderheft 3).

45. An overview of the debate is in Michael A. Ledeen, "Renzo de Felice and the Controversy over Italian Fascism," in George L. Mosse, ed., *International Fascism* (London, 1979). A similar approach is taken in Gino Germani, *Authoritarianism, Fascism and National Populism* (New Brunswick, 1978).

46. Rolf Kosiek, *Historikerstreit und Geschichtsrevision* (Tübingen, 1987), 36–38.

47. Maier, *Unmasterable Past*, 89–91.

48. See n. 33 above.

49. It is Eley's need to account for the reasons Germany, but not France or Britain, turned fascist, that explains why, having attacked the *Sonderweg* for the Imperial period, he is much less dismissive and seeks to integrate it in a "deep historical" approach to the origins of the Nazi period in his "What Produces Fascism: Pre-Industrial Traditions or a Crisis of the Capitalist State?" in his *From Unification to Nazism: Reinterpreting the German Past* (Boston, 1986).

50. For example, Stürmer, *Das ruhelose Reich: Deutschland 1866–1918* (Berlin, 1983), 113–19.

51. This approach is well represented in Thomas Childers and Jane Caplan, eds., *Re-evaluation of the Third Reich: New Controversies, New Interpretations* (New York, 1989). Also Detlev J. K. Peukert, *Inside Nazi Germany: Conformity, Opposition and Racism in Everyday Life* (New Haven, 1987), chap. 12.

52. Freidländer, *When Memory Comes* (New York, 1979), 63. Also, Maier, *Unmasterable Past*, 160–68.

53. The idea of fascism as testimony to the strength of the bourgeois order and its ability to defend itself that Klara Zetkin was at pains to denounce. Zetkin, "The Struggle Against Fascism" (1923), in David Beetham, ed., *Marxists in the Face of Fascism: Writings by Marxists on Fascism from the Inter-War Period* (Manchester, 1983), 102–4. This was also a theme pursued by the New Left: Manfred Clemenz, *Gesellschaftliche Ursprünge des Faschismus* (Frankfurt am Main, 1972), chap. 5: "Fascism as Bourgeois Counterrevolution."
54. Theo Pirker, ed., *Komintern und Faschismus: Dokumente zur Geschichte und Theorie des Faschismus* (Stuttgart, 1965), 169–71.
55. Leonid Luks, *Entstehung der kommunistischen Faschismustheorie: Die Auseinandersetzung der Komintern mit Faschismus und Nationalsozialismus 1921–1935* (Stuttgart, 1984), 49.
56. *Vergehen*, 11, 13. The earlier article was "Die negative Lebendigkeit des Dritten Reiches," *Frankfurter Allgemeine Zeitung*, 24 July 1980, a version of his "Between Myth and Revisionism?"
57. Nolte, *Marxismus und Industrielle Revolution* (Stuttgart, 1983), 280–85, 525.
58. Nolte, *Deutschland und der Kalte Krieg* (Munich, 1974), 118–19, 132–34.
59. Nolte, *Marxismus und Industrielle Revolution*, 460–66; Nolte, "Bürgerliche Gesellschaft und Vernichtungspostulat," in *Was ist bürgerlich?* esp. 234ff.
60. George Lichtheim, "The European Civil War," in *The Concept of Ideology and Other Essays* (New York, 1967).
61. Nolte, *Deutschland und der Kalte Krieg*, 601; also Nolte, *Was ist bürgerlich?* chap. 6.
62. *Vergehen*, 72, 101. He has also recently expanded his definition of fascism as the resistance to transcendence to include Marxism as well in this embrace, both philosophies in this way equally opposed to liberalism. Nolte, "Philosophische Geschichtsschreibung heute?" 285–86.
63. *Totalitarismus und Faschismus: Eine wissenschaftliche und politische Begriffskontroverse: Kolloquium im Institut für Zeitgeschichte am 24. November 1978* (Munich, 1980), 28–30.
64. Stanley G. Payne, *Fascism: Comparison and Definition* (Madison, 1980), 98.
65. Domenico Settembrini, "Mussolini and the Legacy of Revolutionary Socialism," in Mosse, *International Fascism*, 97, 99. The *Vorbild* and *Schreckbild* terminology is also echoed in Pirker's description of fascism as "reaction" to and "copy" of communism, in addition to his use of the "civil war" concept. Pirker, *Komintern und Faschismus*, 9.
66. "The Phenomenon of Fascism," in S. J. Woolf, ed., *European Fascism* (London, 1968), 25.
67. The title of an article in *Sputnik* 10 (October 1988): 135, which (admittedly) deals not with the themes raised here, but with the Comintern doctrine of social fascism and the resulting split on the German Left that helped the Nazis to power. The degree of revision implicit here was apparently too much for the East Germans, who banned the issue.
68. Luks, *Entstehung der kommunistischen Faschismustheorie*, 209.
69. On the early origins of the theory, see Walter Schlangen, *Die Totalitarismustheorie: Entwicklung und Probleme* (Stuttgart, 1976), chaps. 1, 2.
70. Hellmut Diwald, *Geschichte der Deutschen* (Frankfurt am Main, 1978), 163–65. A survey in Kosiek, *Historikerstreit*, chap. B.
71. The American Alfred M. de Zayas is a key figure in this respect. See de Zayas, *Nemesis at Potsdam: The Anglo-Americans and the Expulsion of the Germans* 3d ed.

(Lincoln, 1989); idem, *Anmerkungen zur Vertreibung der Deutschen aus dem Osten* (Stuttgart, 1986); idem, *Die Wehrmacht-Untersuchungsstelle: Deutsche Ermittlungen über alliierte Völkerrechtsverletzungen im Zweiten Weltkrieg*, 4th ed. (Munich, 1980); idem, *Zeugnisse der Vertreibung* (Krefeld, 1983). See also Heinz Nawratil, *Die deutschen Nachkriegsverluste unter Vertriebenen, Gefangenen und Verschleppten* (Munich, 1986); idem, *Die Vertreibungsverbrechen an Deutschen: Tatbestand, Motive, Bewältigung* (Munich, 1982).

72. Among his many works, David Irving, *The Destruction of Dresden* (New York, 1963); idem, *Hitler's War* (New York, 1977).

73. David L. Hoggan, *Der erzwungene Krieg* (Tübingen, 1961); Hoggan, *Frankreichs Widerstand gegen den Zweiten Weltkrieg* (Tübingen, 1963); idem, *The Myth of the "New History": The Techniques and Tactics of the New Mythologists of American History* (Nutley, N.J., 1965); idem, *Der unnötige Krieg* (Tübingen, 1974); Hoggan, *Das blinde Jahrhundert*, 2 vols. (Tübingen, 1979–84). *Der erzwungene Krieg* has now appeared in an English translation after many printings in German: *The Forced War: When Peaceful Revision Failed* (Costa Mesa, Calif., 1989). Hoggan's dissertation (by far the most moderate and scholarly of his efforts) preceded A. J. P. Taylor's similar attempt at revisionism by a decade, but his first book (based on the dissertation) appeared six months after Taylor's work (See n. 75 below). Hoggan, *The Breakdown of German-Polish Relations in 1939: The Conflict Between the German New Order and the Polish Idea of Central Eastern Europe* (diss., Harvard University, 1948).

74. On the First World War: Sidney B. Fay, *Origins of the World War* (New York, 1928); J. S. Ewart, *The Roots and Causes of the Wars, 1914–1918* (New York, 1925); Harry Elmer Barnes, *The Genesis of the World War* (New York, 1929); Frederick Bausman, *Let France Explain* (London, 1922), and more generally, John Maynard Keynes, *The Economic Consequences of the Peace* (London, 1919).

75. A. J. P. Taylor, *The Origins of the Second World War* (New York, 1961). On Taylor, Roger William Louis, ed., *The Origins of the Second World War: A. J. P. Taylor and His Critics* (New York, 1972); Gordon Martel, ed., *The Origins of the Second World War Reconsidered: The A. J. P. Taylor Debate After Twenty-five Years* (Boston, 1986).

76. On the first, Max Klüver, *War es Hitlers Krieg? Die "Irrtümer" der Geschichtsschreibung über Deutschlands Aussenpolitik 1937–1939* (Leoni am Starnberger See, 1984).

77. Harry Elmer Barnes, *Revisionism: A Key to Peace and Other Essays* (San Francisco, 1980), 67.

78. Victor Suvorov, "Who Was Planning to Attack Whom in June 1941, Hitler or Stalin?" *RUSI: Journal of the Royal United Services Institute for Defence Studies* (June 1985), and responses in the June 1986 issue; Viktor Suworow, *Der Eisbrecher: Hitler in Stalins Kalkül* (Stuttgart, 1989); Max Klüver, *Präventivschlag 1941: Zum Vorgeschichte des Russland-Feldzuges* (Leoni am Starnberger See, 1986); Joachim Hoffmann, "Die Sowjetunion bis zum Vorabend des deutschen Angriffs," in Horst Boog et al., *Der Angriff auf die Sowjetunion*, vol. 4 of *Das deutsche Reich und der zweite Weltkrieg*, (Stuttgart, 1983), 38–75; Ernst Topitsch, *Stalin's War: A Radical New Theory of the Origins of the Second World War* (London, 1987). The apologetic intent of this last book comes out most baldly in the postscript to the English edition: what is important is "an understanding of the deep-rooted political implications of the Second World War as a part of the Soviet long-term strategy for the subjugation and destruction of the noncommunist world. The enormity of the crimes ordered by Hitler or committed in his name should not be used

to divert attention from this fact" (141). Generally, see also Wolfram Wette, "Über die Wiederbelebung des Antibolschewismus mit historischen Mitteln oder: Was steckt hinter der Präventivkriegsthese?" in Gernot Erler et al., eds., *Geschichtswende? Entsorgungsversuche zur deutschen Geschichte* (Freiburg i. Br., 1987).

79. Eberhard Jäckel, *Hitler's World View* (Cambridge, Mass., 1981; original ed. 1969), chap. 3.

80. Omer Bartov, *The Eastern Front, 1941–45, German Troops and the Barbarisation of Warfare* (London, 1985).

81. Christian Streit, "The German Army and the Policies of Genocide" and Jürgen Förster, "The German Army and the Ideological War against the Soviet Union," in Gerhard Hirschfeld, ed., *The Policies of Genocide: Jews and Soviet Prisoners of War in Nazi Germany* (London, 1986).

82. Christian Streit, *Keine Kameraden: Die Wehrmacht und die sowjetischen Kriegsgefangenen 1941–1945* (Stuttgart, 1978), 9–24.

83. Much of the controversy sparked by his book stems simply from the fact that a larger audience first learned through it of the long-debated functionalist position that Hitler did not necessarily premeditate the Holocaust all along.

84. Which is why some of the reviews of the book, focusing on the technicalities of the timing of the decision, although perhaps correct on the details, miss the larger point Mayer is making about the connection between the war and the Holocaust. For example, Daniel Jonah Goldhagen, "False Witness," *New Republic,* 17 April 1989.

85. It has been pointed out that the idea of a European civil war presupposes the idea of a European polity within which struggle took place. In this perspective, the idea of a crusade or holy war works better, since the all-consuming hatred that Nolte makes a cornerstone of his account seems to undercut any sense of a common political order, now disrupted by civil strife. Donald C. Watt, "The European Civil War," in Mommsen and Kettenacker, *The Fascist Challenge and the Policy of Appeasement,* 5.

86. *Heavens,* 94, 107; *Bürgerkrieg,* 514.

87. Charles Micaud, *The French Right and Nazi Germany* (Durham N.C., 1943).

88. Maier, *Unmasterable Past,* 68.

89. See, for example, A. J. Groth, "The 'Isms' in Totalitarianism," *American Political Science Review* 58 (1964); Martin Greiffenhagen, "Der Totalitarismusbegriff in der Regimenlehre," in Greiffenhagen et al., *Totalitarismus* (Munich, 1972); Dieter Albrecht, "Zum Begriff des Totalitarismus," *Geschichte in Wissenschaft und Unterricht* 26, 3 (March 1975); Martin Greiffenhagen, "Totalitarismus rechts und links: Ein Vergleich von Nationalsozialismus und Kommunismus," *Gesellschaft-Staat-Erziehung* 12, 5 (1967).

90. Hillgruber died in 1989. He was known for his studies of foreign policy, which did not deny Germany's role in the origins of the two world wars or the centrality of Hitler's actions against the Jews. For example, Andreas Hillgruber, *Germany and the Two World Wars* (Cambridge, Mass., 1981); "Die 'Endlösung' und das deutsche Ostimperium als Kernstück des rassenideologischen Programms des Nationalsozialismus," *Vierteljahrshefte für Zeitgeschichte* 20, 2 (April 1972).

91. One of the main points made by Hans-Ulrich Wehler in *Entsorgung der deutschen Vergangenheit? Ein polemischer Essay zum "Historikerstreit"* (Munich, 1988), English edition forthcoming.

92. Quoted in Anson Rabinbach, "German Historians Debate the Nazi Past: A Dress Rehearsal for a New German Nationalism?" *Dissent* (Spring 1988): 192.

93. See for example, Imanuel Geiss, *Die Habermas-Kontroverse: Ein deutscher Streit* (Berlin, 1988), which examines the debate from a relatively moderate right-of-center position.

94. One aspect of this shift is discussed in Jerry Z. Muller, *The Other God That Failed: Hans Freyer and the Deradicalization of German Conservatism* (Princeton, 1987).

95. See also Andrei S. Markovits, "Was ist das 'Deutsche' an den Grünen? Vergangenheitsaufarbeitung als Voraussetzung politischer Zukunftsbewältigung," in Otto Kallscheuer, ed., *Die Grünen—Letzte Wahl* (Berlin, 1986).

96. Joffe, "The Battle of the Historians," 75–76. On Bitburg in general there is Geoffrey Hartman, ed., *Bitburg in Moral and Political Perspective* (Bloomington, 1986).

97. Hans-Georg Betz, "*Deutschlandpolitik* on the Margins: On the Evolution of Contemporary New Right Nationalism in the Federal Republic," *New German Critique* 44 (Spring/Summer 1988).

98. Kosiek, *Historikerstreit und Geschichtsrevision.*

99. That definition, readers will recall, concerned the pursuit of the inedible by the unspeakable.

100. Which is why, despite all editorial desires to be impartial and fair in the selection, the pieces collected here represent the antirevisionists best. For the revisionist position, the *Historikerstreit* volume is the most detailed source, along with Geiss, *Die Habermas-Kontroverse.*

2. Immoral Equivalence: Revising the Nazi Past for the Kohl era

Charles S. Maier

Germans have long understood that history matters. For much of the postwar period their historical scholarship pondered, if imperfectly, the breakdown of democracy in the 1920s and 1930s, and the lessons of National Socialism. But now a new coalition of historians regrets that the obsession with the traumas of Nazism, the lost war, and the division of the country have denied Germans the chance to work through a less problematic, longer run national history; or so these historians allege. They appear preoccupied with the idea that those who define a people's history structure its sense of community and politics. As one of their number, Michael Stürmer, a professor at Erlangen and a speechwriter for Chancellor Kohl, has argued, today's West Germans seem hungry for usable history: "Whoever supplies memory, shapes concepts, and interprets the past will win the future."

The recent campaign of these German historians to interpret the past has proved profoundly disturbing, however, as they have sought not to deny Nazi crimes but to remove their special nimbus of horror. For obvious reasons the search for a usable past in present-day Germany is a difficult one. Indeed, the catchword that Germans have applied, quite appropriately, to the Nazi experience has often been "the unmastered past." It is not clear how such a past should be mastered, how historical consciousness comes to terms with a national experience that remains the standard for collective brutality. History has a twofold mission: it is analytic and imaginative. It is supposed to provide a convincing explanation, to answer, why did it happen? or, how could it happen? But history is also expected to convey some sort of lived resonance. Obviously it cannot convey the experience itself, but at least an echo of the experience may reverberate in the reader's imagination. How, then, can history ever really "master" the murder factories that curved in a crescent of death from Auschwitz in Silesia, east to Belzec, then north to Majdanek, to Sobibór and Treblinka—killing pens for Slavs, for Gypsies, and above all for the Jews?

If it is not apparent how historians should "master" this past, it is quite clear how they can evade it. Call it Bitburg history, when historians of mass murder relativize the Holocaust, search for alternative horrors that other peoples have perpetrated, link slayers and slain in a dialectic of victimhood. The trivialization of memory was exemplified by Bitburg: at first glance, only a public relations botch by two leaders with a woefully deficient sense of history. For Helmut Kohl, however, Ronald Reagan's gesture was politically important. If the NATO allies were determined to commemorate their wartime comradeship, then full accreditation of a Christian Democratic Federal Republic required that Germany's wartime sacrifices also be enshrined in the brotherhood of arms—a reconciliation that had been denied it at the D-day anniversary of June 1984. Unfortunately, Bitburg, it turned out, was the resting place for forty-seven SS soldiers. Only forty-seven next to so many thousands of ordinary soldiers—and in any case not representatives of the SS *Einsatzgruppen* charged with exterminations, but youth from more honorable elite combat units. Still, Valhalla was tainted, Reagan embarrassed, and Kohl confused. The remedy was for Reagan to compensate by visiting Bergen-Belsen. Perhaps if Bitburg had harbored the remains of one hundred SS dead, Buchenwald, too, might have been included in this parody of equal time.

The German reaction to Bitburg revealed how widespread was the feeling that remorse was being demanded for too long. When would the new generation of Germans no longer have to atone for the sins of their fathers? Had not the Federal Republic paid large reparations to Israel? Was it not among the most stable democracies, the most loyal of NATO partners? Only a few spokesmen, most eloquently the Federal president, Richard von Weizsäcker, admitted that Germany's sort of debt is never really acquitted.

Recently the controversy about the normalization of German history moved from Bitburg to the academy. Early in 1986 Andreas Hillgruber, a respected Cologne University scholar who has written extensively on Hitler's strategies during the Second World War, produced a small volume that was published by the conservative publisher Siedler. Entitled *Two Sorts of Destruction: The Shattering of the German Reich and the End of European Jewry*, it did not seem destined for notoriety until Jürgen Habermas, Germany's leading contemporary philosopher and critic on the Left, attacked the volume as an ominous portent of conservative trends under the Kohl government. By bracketing the defeat of Hitler's regime (honored in Hillgruber's title with the label "German Reich," the designation that the German nation-state, including the Weimar Republic, had claimed since unification) with the genocide carried out by that very regime, Hillgruber's work seemed "scandalous." For Habermas, and others, common decency should have forbidden that the two developments be juxtaposed. In its "apologetic tendency" to depict the German nation as having been as much a victim as the Jewish people, Hillgruber's book allegedly typified the attempt of conservative intellectuals and historians to allow West Germans to normalize their past and claim a national history. Moreover, Hillgruber's book seemed designed to revive the sort of nationalist anticommunism for which there are no enemies to the right.

What did Hillgruber intend with his 100-page essay? The major chapter in the book concerns the collapse of the eastern front in the winter of 1944–45. Evoking the Wehrmacht's terrible mission in the winter of 1945, Hillgruber has written, is among the most difficult challenges a historian can face. He refers to the harrowing winter flight before the Russians. Hitler had given orders for impossible defenses of fortress cities; Soviet troops arrived with apparent license to rape and assault. Millions of German civilians and soldiers waited for occasional trains in bombed-out stations, caravanned through the Prussian forests, or precariously sailed across the Baltic to Jutland, often harassed by their own fanatic Nazi officials. Hillgruber's purpose in depicting these conditions is to defend the German army against the charge that by fighting against the Soviet troops they were abetting Hitler's work of massacring the Jews, despite the fact that historians have not taxed the Wehrmacht with defending East Prussia so that Hitler could keep massacring Jews. In the end Hillgruber demands that his German readers identify neither with the Nazis' victims, not even with the German resistance, but with the tragically beset soldiers:

> If the historian gazes on the winter catastrophe of 1944–45, only one position is possible [and that is that] he must identify himself with the concrete fate of the German population in the East and with the desperate and sacrificial exertions of the German army of the East and the German Baltic navy, which sought to defend the population from the orgy of revenge of the Red Army, the mass rapine, the arbitrary killing, and the compulsory deportations.

Hillgruber goes on to claim, moreover, that Stalin, Roosevelt, and above all Churchill had long harbored designs to dismember Germany. It does not seem relevant to Hillgruber's way of thinking that German aggression might indeed have led the Allies to contemplate partition; in any case the notion was rejected in theory, and partition came about only as a result of circumstances when the war ended. Hillgruber's historical contribution to "winning the future" thus amounts to the old Prusso-German lament, dusted off and refurbished, that the Machiavellian British were always conspiring to encircle the Reich. Predictably enough, the essay closes with a lament that after 1945, Prussia and Germany would no longer be able to fulfill their mediating role between East and West. But precisely what sort of "mediating role" had brought all those German soldiers to Stalingrad in the first place?

Unfortunately this is vulgar *Historismus* at best. It is not the job of the historian to identify with one group of contending personalities and interests; it is to allow each to speak for itself, and then to explore the alternative perspectives from which their decisions might be viewed. It is no wonder that Hillgruber's second (and brief) chapter on the extermination of the Jews might seem pallid after the emotional exercise in "identification" that precedes it. No depiction of sealed freight cars, purposeful starvation, degradation, and the final herding to the gas chambers parallels Hillgruber's vivid evocation of the East Prussian collapse. Not that Hillgruber minimizes the crimes of the SS (though he ignores the massacres of Red Army prisoners by his heroic Wehrmacht). He understands that German anti-Semitism was periodically virulent before the Nazis, and he suggests that even a traditionally authoritarian regime would have instituted at least the equivalent of the Nuremberg laws. Hillgruber's is not an evil book, but it is badly balanced; and its particular imbalance opens the way to apologia.

Certainly Hillgruber's slim volume was less egregious than the essay by Ernst Nolte that appeared in the eminent center-conservative daily the *Frankfurter Allgemeine Zeitung* in June. *Vergangenheit die nicht Vergehen will*—"The Past That Will Not Pass Away"—was originally intended as an address to a prestigious annual conclave of public figures and intellectuals in Frankfurt, but Nolte's invitation was suddenly withdrawn. Nolte is arguably one of the most brilliant, and certainly the most brooding, German thinkers about history. He calls himself the last practitioner of "philosophical history." Trained in Heideggerian metaphysics, he made his mark as a historian of political ideas with his *Three Faces of Fascism*, which appeared in 1963. That study examined the protofascism inherent in French reactionary thought, the paradigmatic Italian movement, and then its radicalized German "fulfillment." Thus no "apologetic tendency," no ambiguity in the judgment of the fascist phenomenon, was really predictable from this suggestive, almost Hegelian magnum opus, in which fascist political practice emanated ineluctably from ideological premises and a logic of history. More problematic was Nolte's murky rumination of 1976, *Germany and the Cold War*. Its target was the strident left-wing German student movement of the late 1960s ("the party of the GDR"), whose attacks scarred Nolte at the University of Marburg before he moved to Berlin. He also seemed curiously obsessed with Israel—the nation of the former victims, whose army had won territory and statehood while Germany had lost both. Germany was fated to be torn between the two competing ideological visions that together had defeated Nazism: communism and democracy. Nolte called for a historical sense that could rehabilitate the reputation of the old Bismarckian Reich and recognize that every major nation (Britain and the United States excepted) has had "its own Hitler era, with its monstrosities and sacrifices."

Nolte's notorious essay of June elaborated these hints of a decade ago. Germans remain preoccupied with their Nazi past, Nolte implies, in an almost neurotic and ahistorical manner. Isn't there some justification for calling a halt to further obsessive reexamination? Isn't the talk about "the guilt of the Germans," he explicitly asks, all too reminiscent of Nazi charges about "the guilt of the Jews"? It is a startling deficiency of the literature on Nazism, Nolte charges, that it will not recognize that, with the exception of poison gas, every atrocity of the Nazis was committed by the Bolsheviks in the early 1920s:

Did the Nazis carry out, did Hitler carry out, an "Asiatic" deed [the term that one of Hitler's later advisers supposedly used in horror at the 1915 Armenian massacres] perhaps only because they regarded themselves and their ilk as the potential or real victims of an "Asiatic" deed? Wasn't the Gulag Archipelago more an origin than Auschwitz? Wasn't class murder on the part of the Bolsheviks logically and actually prior to racial murder on the part of the Nazis?

Nolte was seconded in August by Joachim Fest, editor of the *Frankfurter Allgemeine Zeitung* and author of a major study of Hitler and a useful collective biography published in English as *The Face of the Third Reich*. Fest's main concern was to criticize Habermas's attack on Hillgruber and Nolte. How could Habermas have overlooked Nolte's chief concern, the connection between Bolshevik and Nazi mass murder? To drive home the notion that genocide was a widespread occurrence, Fest illustrated his essay with a photograph of skulls accumulated by the Khmer Rouge and quoted a Toheka leader's exhortation that the bourgeoisie had to be exterminated as a class. Not only were the Nazi and the Bolshevik murders equivalent, Fest suggested, but it is very likely that Hitler was influenced, in the panicky condition of Germany of 1919, by admittedly exaggerated reports of atrocities from Russia. In post–World War I Germany, the core of truth in these reports gave Hitler's "extermination complexes a real background." Fest claims, moreover, that Nazism got the worse press largely because it was more visibly "mechanized." He does not acknowledge that mechanization and bureaucratic arrangements horrify not because squeamish historians prefer pastoral mass murder as in Cambodia, but because "mechanization" testifies to intent and pathological planning.

Comparative genocide has turned out be a capacious bandwagon. Fest's outrage, not at genocide but at Habermas's assault on the fudging of the distinctions between genocides, was endorsed in a pompous defense of the historian's lofty search for science by Klaus Hildebrand, historian of Nazi foreign policy at the University of Bonn. Distinguishing between planned genocide and war crimes in the field or pogromlike outbursts, Hildebrand admits that the former was carried out only by Hitler's Germany "under the sign of racial domination, and Stalin's Soviet Union under the sign of class domination." Genocide evidently loves company. What *Wissenschaft* demonstrates is that Germany only followed the Slavic lead.

Why isn't the Holocaust relative? It would hardly seem necessary to answer the question, but these German historians require an answer. Of course numbers are important. The more innocents killed, the worse. And the number killed in the Soviet Union—even excluding the reprisals of the civil war— may well have exceeded the toll taken by the SS. "The Armenian Holocaust" alone probably cost over a million lives. And the historian Richard Lukas has now asked that Polish gentiles be recognized as covictims of the Nazis in a "forgotten holocaust." There are tears enough, in short, in the histories of many peoples.

Still, the Final Solution was different. Years ago Raymond Aron answered the question posed by Nolte and Fest: "Hostility based on the class struggle has taken on no less extreme or monstrous forms than that based on the in-compatibility of race," he wrote. "But if we wish to 'save the concepts,' there is a difference between a philosophy whose logic is monstrous, and one which can be given a monstrous interpretation." The Holocaust was no mere wave of killing. It was a systematic effort to exterminate *all* the Jews under direct German control, and to pressure German allies or occupied governments to surrender the Jews temporarily beyond the reach of the SS. That effort at ethnic round-up and total extermination still separates the *furor teutonicus* from Stalinist terror. Granted, the Soviets, too, periodically targeted their terror on those, such as bourgeois parents or kulaks, bearing ascriptive char-acteristics that could not easily be cast aside. But they never aspired to destroy physically every individual who bore those stigmata. Destroying a class might mean disposessing its members, not slaying them all. In addition, Soviet camps were never exclusively dedicated to extermination, no matter how cynically they were programmed to encourage brutality and the destruction of their inmates.

Indeed, terror played different roles in the two regimes, a difference often overlooked after Hannah Arendt and others focused on terror's common func-tion in all forms of totalitarian control. If one was compliant and quiet and Aryan in the Third Reich, life could go on. Terror established the perimeter of the racial community, confirmed membership for the obedient within, warned them not to resist, and surrendered those without to lawless brutality. Under Stalin, terror raged precisely to shatter any predictability. No citizen could be sure he or she had not betrayed the revolution. The Nazis staged only two "judicial" purges as such, each probably removing no more than 1,000 to 1,500 "conspirators": the 1934 decimation of the Storm Troops, and the 1944 reprisals against the resistance. The Soviet purges of the 1930s un-leashed terror against millions. But precisely this strategy of "random" bru-tality meant that Soviet murder did not amount to a Final Solution.

What purpose does the claim of comparable genocides serve for the Ger-man intellectuals who insist upon it? Nolte seems to be the only scholar to whom one may attribute, if not an anti-Semitic agenda, at least a love-hate preoccupation with Israel. But neither Jews nor Israel are the real stake in this controversy. The question, as Stürmer recognized, is who shall master the German present and the German future.

In 1983, at a major conference of historians in Berlin's Reichstag building, those who repeatedly returned to the uniqueness of Nazi anti-Semitism and the unparalleled radicalism of Hitler's Jewish policies were the more centrist and conservative German historians; their objective seemed to be to discredit a historiography of the Left (but not only of the Left) that has tried to group Mussolini's movement and German National Socialism as species of a com-mon fascism. During the 1960s the comparison of different fascist regimes and their alleged commonality with capitalism had become a historical leit-motiv of the leftist student movement. As the final speaker of the symposium baldly charged, the late 1960s had witnessed "the ideological and political transformation of the debate over fascism into a means of delegitimizing the political system of the Federal Republic." It had become subversive.

Thus the conservative historians' insistence on the integral role of Nazism's anti-Semitism helped them roll back the cliches of Marxist historiography. But now it appears that victory was not enough. With the battle against the Marxist "fascism theory" won, and a militant student movement no longer menacing, the conservatives can proceed to tackle the normalization of national consciousness: the need to instill West Germany with as much nationhood as its partitioned existence permits. In today's world, this project is probably no longer dangerous; Stürmer has insisted that it entails emphasizing the Federal Republic's loyalties to the West, not hankering for a neutralist reunification. Still, this revisionism can be offensively forgetful. It also forges a curious alliance that some historians may well have reason to repent. For it brings together those who claim to care about history with the beer-hall crew who want nothing more than to forget it.

To their credit, West Germans have usually been willing to face up to the past, even if as individuals they did not want to confront it. As a society, at least, they have consistently elected representatives who negotiated reparations with Israel and boundaries with Poland. Unlike the Austrians, it is doubtful that they would have allowed a Waldheim to climb to the state presidency (even though some of their politicians do not have immaculate pasts). Chancellor Kohl, in any event, is young enough not to bear that burden. But unburdened, Kohl is insensitive in ways that most of his older predecessors could not have been. He, too, claims to be a student of history. But whose history will he learn?

3.   The Jewish Question in the German Question

Anson Rabinbach

Bitburg and the *Historikerstreit* are the most recent reminders that the Nazi past continues to resonate in contemporary West German politics. The topos of the "singularity" of the Holocaust in these highly public confrontations with the past demonstrates, moreover, that the "Jewish Question" in today's Germany is simultaneously a sovereignty question. Since 1945, every expansion of German sovereignty has, at least symbolically, been linked to a particular image of the Nazi past. The symbolic value of the "Jewish Question" in the history of the Federal Republic of Germany is to hold German sovereignty in escrow. Conversely, each reevaluation of the past on the part of Germans opens for Jews a new chapter in the equally permanent link to their own collective nightmare. Since 1945 there has been what Dan Diner, writing in the first Jewish-German intellectual journal since Weimar, *Babylon,* described as a negative symbiosis between Germans and Jews, a "kind of opposing commonality." [1]

Yet in all the furor over the new historical revisionism, the deeper reasons for the emergence of a new "strategy of oblivion" have largely escaped critical scrutiny. It is not sufficient to moralize about the "misuse" of comparisons, or to invoke the phrase "relativization" to impart a sense of their injustice vis-à-vis the victims. [2] The attempt to eradicate the burden of the past by means of a casuistry of comparative genocide, the symbolic reconciliation of the German and American "fallen" over Waffen-SS graves, or even the failed parliamentary attempt to promote a national "day of mourning" for all "victims" of the Nazi era, cannot simply be attributed to a calculated effort to close the door on a history that has now entered its fifth decade. It is an oversimplification to point to the deep division between "the Jewish desire to remember and the German desire to forget," to explain this state of affairs.

The *Historikerstreit* demonstrates that the Nazi crime against the Jews has always belonged to the political discursive topography of the postwar Federal Republic, and that a closer examination of this persistence of the Jewish Question reveals that every stage in the emergence of West German sover-

eignty has been linked to the question of responsibility for the German past.
There have been three major turning points in the postwar German confrontation with the legacy of Nazism. The first occurred in September 1951,
when Konrad Adenauer delivered his famous declaration on reparations to
the Parliament, a prelude to the financial reparations treaty (*Wiedergutmachung*) concluded between the Federal Republic of Germany and representative Jewish organizations both inside and outside Israel and ratified by the
Parliament on March 18, 1953. The second occurred in 1958/1959 and coincided with the SPD's turn towards NATO at a time when public displays of
anti-Semitism demonstrated the apparent failures of the very limited denazification of the postwar era. The third occurred at Bitburg, and reflected
the Kohl government's attempt to counter a Green variant of German nationalism and symbolically "normalize" political relations with the U.S. and the
Western alliance. Bitburg raised a series of crucial issues for the Kohl government's strategy of overcoming the past, which subsequently took the public
form of the *Historikerstreit* in the fall of 1986.

Each of these turning points coincided with a major shift in the domestic
and international situation of the Federal Republic. The first took place when
the Adenauer government, in light of the intensification of the Cold War and
the "hardening" of the postwar settlement, abandoned the hope of reunification and the "provisional" character of the Federal Republic in favor of integration in the Western Bloc. The second came at the end of the Adenauer era
and, in the context of *détente*, prepared the way for a broader coalition government including the Social Democrats and the subsequent opening of *Ost-
politik*. The third phase, which is hardly over, marks both the acceptance of
the consequences of the East treaties, and an attempt to create for the first
time a German national identity whose ultimate character—e.g., whether it is
pro- or anti-American, West German, German, or Middle European—still
remains open to question.

Guilt Questions

The German confrontation with the past in the immediate postwar
years recently became the subject of an intense debate provoked by Hermann
Lübbe, a prominent neoconservative philosopher. Lübbe challenged the conventional view that the absence of a moral renewal so desired after 1945 by
German intellectuals like Karl Jaspers, and so frequently met with by indifference or hostility among the populace, was traumatic for the subsequent
history of the Federal Republic. His rationale is that "a certain silence was the
social-psychological and politically necessary medium for the transformation
of our postwar population into the citizenry of the Federal Republic of
Germany."[3]

If old Nazis quietly returned to their old jobs, careers, and positions of authority in the governing elite, this "continuity of personnel" was, he asserts,

only part of the necessary work of breaking with the past politically. The restoration of normalcy did not require an "explanatory and analytic overcoming of National Socialism" but rather a practical tolerance of individuals, an "asymmetrical discretion," e.g., mutual acceptance of one another's past.[4] Despite the silence of the postwar epoch, there was a "complete discrediting of National Socialist ideology, in particular in its racist *Lebensraum* expansionist core ideas."[5] The positive side of this decision for "integration" over "exclusion" was a fundamental consensus in the FRG about the anti-Nazi nature of the new state and its democratic foundation.

While Lübbe is not completely wrong, his overly optimistic version of the events in question is nevertheless intended to justify some of the worst aspects of the postwar era and deliver a rationale for the moral vacuum that this "silent mastery of the past" produced. There *was* a practical and political decision for "integration" over "denazification" in the first years of the Federal Republic, a political process that also involved the triumph of a view of Nazism which emphasized its criminal aspects at the expense of its broad popular basis and deep social roots in German history and tradition. Even in the wartime debates among German émigrés, we can see the formation of this deep division between the advocates of the "outlaw theory" of the Nazi criminal elite, and the antifascist view of Nazism as a broadly supported social system.[6] The Nuremberg trials, which were the institutional analogue of the outlaw theory, did not challenge the "continuities" of personnel in postwar German society, whereas the antifascists supported a thoroughgoing denazification, coupled with a reconstruction of German society. In its official Stalinist variant, antifascism became the ideology of the SBZ (Soviet Zone of Occupation). In the West, the antifascist option was linked to the political "road not taken," Kurt Schumacher's attempt to create a unified socialist and democratic Germany independent of the superpowers.[7] The actual denazification process was unsystematic and often unjust, punishing lesser functionaries while more serious criminals and corporate elites were courted. It gave rise to much cynicism, and was powerfully parodied in Ernst von Salomon's famous novel, *Der Fragebogen*, of 1951.

There can be no doubt that the moral no-man's-land experienced by Germans after 1945 also reflected, to no small degree, the real difficulties of drawing lines of demarcation between different kinds of participation in the Nazi system of domination, between different social strata, between different kinds of acts, and ultimately between different levels of motivation. Hans-Ulrich Wehler has argued plausibly that given the large number of potentially guilty individuals who might or might not have been caught in the net of a general "purge" of anyone who collaborated with the Nazis, or who, without the "party book," still sympathized with their aims, the price of denazification in the immediate postwar era might have been nothing short of a social and cultural civil war.[8] Even if one does not accept Lübbe's questionable characterization of the postwar course of events as a positive contribution to the political stability of the FRG and the integration of the Nazi "fellow travelers" into the political culture of postwar democracy, the difficulties that would have arisen from a general denazification cannot be minimized. Gustav Heinemann's remark that if the finger points at one's contemporaries, the other fingers point at oneself, is sadly apt.[9] Even before the end of the war, Hannah Arendt reflected with astonishing prescience on the moral dilemma that such a general confrontation with the past might entail:

Just as there is no political solution within human capacity for the crime of administrative mass murder, so the human need for justice can find no satisfactory reply to the total mobilization of a people for that purpose. Where all are guilty, nobody in the last analysis can be judged.[10]

Relegated to the limited justice of Nuremberg, by the end of the 1940s, German guilt became, to borrow Jaspers' words in *Die Schuldfrage*, largely a "metaphysical question." For Jaspers metaphysical guilt referred to an injury to the "solidarity of human beings with other human beings," which occurs "when I am present where injustice and crime occur."[11] Hannah Arendt's 1946 letter to Jaspers further articulated the difficulty with that conception:

It appears to me that in what you call metaphysical guilt not only is the "unconditional" ("*das Unbedingte*") located, where in fact no earthly judge can be recognized any longer, but also that solidarity which (in the words of Clemenceau, "*l'affaire d'un seul est l'affaire de tous*") is the political basis of the Republic.[12]

Jaspers's desire for what he later called "a moral-political revolution" remained unfulfilled. At best, it was a matter of individual remorse, subject to the inner justice that Jaspers's existentialism superbly executed. At worst, it was subject to the exorcism of the popular ethics of the *Stammtisch*. To be sure, there were efforts to realize Jaspers's ideal, for example, in the attempt of Protestant theologians and leaders like Martin Niemöller and Gustav Heinemann to provide a "self-accusation before God" in the *Stuttgarter Schuldbekenntnis* of October 1945.[13] But Heinemann himself bemoaned the lack of resonance produced by these noble—though by contemporary standards extremely mild—efforts when he wrote in 1950 that that "which we experienced in hubris and catastrophe, in judgment and grace, was not an occasion for a reversal and renewed reflection."[14] More characteristic was the tortured rhetoric with which returned émigré intellectuals were received, as when the mayor of Frankfurt greeted Max Horkheimer's ascendancy to the rectorship of the university as "the crowning of our own duty of reparation [*Wiedergutmachungs-Pflicht*]."[15] Lübbe's arrogant observation that the moral critique of the Nazi past was "elitist and intellectual" has a ring of truth, especially to the extent that it participates in the very moral expatriation of the guilt question to the province of the spirit that it condemns. Little wonder the majority of the population lived, so to speak, in a state of moral amnesia between "criminal" and "metaphysical" spheres of guilt.

Wiedergutmachung

In this context, the Reparations Treaty of 1953 assumed inordinate importance. It is often overlooked that the single most important consequence of the reparations debate in the new Republic was discursive: it distinguished between war crimes, crimes against humanity and the crimes committed against Jews, and so retroactively created a moral hierarchy. It should be recalled that the Nuremberg tribunal distinguished only crimes against humanity (murder, slavery, extermination, deportation) from other "war crimes" (reprisals, political murder or acts of individual murder in the last phase of the war). As late as the mid-1960s, German courts often did not distinguish "war crimes" from Nazi crimes per se.[16] Moreover, in the cultural climate of the immediate postwar years, the crime against the Jews was almost never mentioned and, if it was, then euphemistically and metaphorically. The strong taboo against any descriptive phrase was broken by Theodor Heuss, the Republic's first president, when, speaking to the Gesellschaft für christlich-jüdische Zusammenarbeit in Wiesbaden in December 1949, he said: "it makes no sense to talk around these things: the horrible injustice that has been done to the Jewish people must be brought to speech."[17]

For Adenauer, *Wiedergutmachung*—achieved despite the opposition of many in his own party, much of the Left, the occupation powers (including the United States), and within Israel—represented the most potent symbol of regained German respect in the world. Although by 1951 West Germany had already become a partner in the Western Bloc, Adenauer saw in the reparations treaty a fundamental precondition for any further extension of West German sovereignty.[18] Adenauer's persistent and successful efforts to negotiate a reparations treaty with the Jewish World Congress and with Israel was clearly undertaken in the hope of "overcoming the unimaginable bitterness which the National Socialist crimes against the Jews has called forth in the world and among all those of good will."[19] The desire for such a tangible symbol was not one-sidedly German. Herman Gray, chairman of the foreign affairs bureau of the American Jewish Committee, noted at the time: "Germany is about to become a member of the Western world, while the Jews still wait for an almost dramatic event, for a symbolic act."[20]

At the same time, however, the universally lauded reparations declaration and the accompanying statement of responsibility, which Adenauer delivered to the German Parliament on September 27, 1951, also coincided with the progressive decriminalization of Nazism in the early years of the Federal Republic. Adenauer's promise that anti-Semitism and "racially inflammatory propaganda would be met with heavy sanctions," was an act of state without popular support (as public opinion polls demonstrated, only 11 percent favored the treaty, more than half rejected it).[21]

The reparations question linked—inextricably it now seems—the "German Question" to the "Jewish Question" for the first time. The symbolic significance of the reparations issue was not only that the material settlement indicated the willingness of the new German state to assume direct responsibility for the Nazi crimes against the Jews, but—and this was a source of the Communist opposition at the time—it created a normative precedent restricting the issue of responsibility to the Jewish crime alone, bracketing out all other claims of reparations.

Efforts to compensate other victims of the Nazis, Gypsies, subjects of medical experimentation, eugenics, and especially those who had been in concentration camps as a result of resistance activities were largely thwarted (with the singular exception of the 20 July plotters).[22] The reparations treaty served a dual purpose: internationally, it demonstrated the Federal Republic of Germany's desire to participate in the community of nations as an independent, militarily strong, post-Nazi state. Domestically, it focused the Nazi past on the singular crime against the Jews which could be accentuated and pursued in the present, thereby consigning all other questions of the Nazi era—especially the issue of former Nazis—to the periphery.

Adenauer's genius was to find the Jewish Question useful, where his political colleagues saw only a permanent source of embarrassment. Almost overnight, the crime against the Jews was transposed from a taboo to a politically overloaded symbol of the entire Nazi complex. Even more important, the permanent postponement of the question of reunification was compensated for by the permanent postponement of the Nazi question. The settlement of the "Jewish Question" was a presupposition for a crucial decision concerning the German Question, the primacy of West-integration over reunification. Indeed, the debate on reparations coincided with Adenauer's decision not to accept the famous Stalin note of 1952 offering to exchange unification for a declaration of neutrality.[23]

Adenauer was able to carry off this masterstroke in the face of negative public opinion and a divided elite, because he made the confrontation with the past a precondition for the expansion of German sovereignty. The reparations treaty was also a social contract *among* Germans: the abandoned Nazi question was replaced by the new "consensus" on the Jewish Question about which there could be no statute of limitations (this was implicit) or public debate.[24] Ironically, it was conservative political elites who did not permit the *Schlußstrich* to be drawn under the Nazi epoch, despite their recognition that this was ardently desired by the vast majority of Germans in that era. The discovery of the Jewish question as a way of distancing the present German government from the past created a peculiar situation which necessitated that German leaders be *more* philosemitic than their constituents, legislate political morality and prohibit anti-Semitism by strict sanctions, perpetuating a deep disjuncture between public professions of responsibility and popular attitudes. If the famous paragraph 131 permitted the reintegration of former Nazis into the civil service, the reparations declaration sanctioned the substitution of the Jewish Question for the Nazi question.[25] The implicit power accorded to the Jewish Question (the reverse side of the taboo, we might say) also produced what Saul Friedländer described as a negative form of Jewish power in contemporary Germany: the power of absolution.[26] That this power would eventually become the source of resentment was not hard to predict.

The reparations settlement circumscribed the discourse of National Socialism within a version of "metaphysical guilt" in which the state assumed moral responsibility for its legal predecessor. On the other hand, the antifascist concept of political responsibility broadly defined (in the 1950s addressed by left intellectuals like Grass, Böll, Andersch) was exiled to West German literary culture.

Politically, the antifascist alliance of 1945 was broken by the imperatives of the Marshall Plan and the Cold War. The moral substance of the antifascist critique of the "fascist," e.g., populist, dimension of National Socialism was instrumentalized in the official ideology of the East which substituted the doctrine of capitalist conspiracy for a recognition of popular support. The Cold War further undermined the "antifascist" option: In the eyes of the majority of citizens, the Stalinist dictatorship in the SBZ/GDR mirrored the Hitler dictatorship, while for the KPD and the SED the continuity of personnel apparent in the West confirmed the diagnosis of no decisive break with the past. To the extent that these mutually exclusive perceptions were subsequently concretized in alternative historical narratives, totalitarian theory and fascism theory, future historiographical controversies were already anticipated.

Jews in the Jewish Question

It is important to recognize that from the "Jewish standpoint," the reparations treaty and Adenauer's speech to the Bundestag were key moments of recognition for the generally underplayed and often ignored reality that the Jews were in fact "different" from other victims of National Socialism by virtue of the sheer number of Jews exterminated, and the special status afforded them in the apparatus of mass murder. If the antifascist option was defeated politically, its more lasting achievement may have been the premature leveling of distinctions among the victims of National Socialism— sometimes even (especially in the GDR) to the exclusion of Jewish victims. From the "Jewish point of view," therefore, the reparations treaty restored a proper perspective to National Socialist criminality, but not without consequences. Moreover, as Saul Friedländer points out, from the founding of the State of Israel, the "catastrophe" was coupled with images of "redemption"/"rebirth"/"heroism." But the official commemoration of the *Shoah* as part of Israeli national politics only began shortly after the reparations demand was put forward.[27] In this sense, the "singularity" postulate of the Holocaust implicit in the reparations treaty served *both* West German and Israeli legitimation purposes—but for different reasons.

The reparations treaty also greatly enhanced the importance of the newly founded West German Jewish communal organizations which were soon enlisted for symbolic purposes. During the occupation, the German-Jewish presence in Germany was a community in the process of dissolution—"living on packed suitcases." [28] Even the new arrivals from the East considered themselves a community in transit. Until 1949–50, the international Jewish organizations like the American Jewish Joint Distribution Committee still saw the existence of Jews in Germany as temporary, providing material relief and assistance in relocating the displaced persons (DPs) abroad, mostly in Israel. [29] Only after 1952 was there growing recognition that Germany, rather than becoming a "land without Jews," was instead becoming the destination of a surprising number of Jews, with the majority (two-thirds) not originally of German origin. [30] The post-reparations climate not only favored a higher profile for the Central Council of Jews in Germany, founded as the umbrella organization of the Jewish communities in 1950, but increasingly placed official Jewish representatives in the position of attesting to the positive efforts of the CDU/CSU state in fulfilling its moral obligations and offering a concrete testimonial of tolerance. [31]

The attitude of these Jewish communities remained ambivalent. Linked by religion and an orientation toward Israel, their relation to the German environment was largely reserved for ritualistic events like the "Brotherhood Weeks" organized by the "Society for Christian-Jewish Cooperation." [32] The conservatism of these official Jewish organizations, especially in regard to the various scandals involving former high-level Nazis in the political hierarchy of the FRG, attests to their dependence on the political patronage of the West German "consensus."

The Crisis of *Vergangenheitsbewältigung:* 1958/59

By the late 1950s, the unexpected popular resonance of the dramatization of the *Diary of Anne Frank* and other cultural events dealing with Nazism, and the spontaneous Bergen-Belsen pilgrimages organized by the Hamburg journalist Erich Lüth in 1957, were among the first signs that a new confrontation with the Nazi past was taking shape. The desecration of Jewish cemeteries and synagogues in December 1959 seemed to underscore the multiple sins of the Adenauer years. Significantly, the CDU/CSU proposed that the Federal Republic should respond with new laws against "popular incitement" (*Volksverhetzung*), but the SPD opposed granting any "special protection" to German Jews, a situation ultimately resolved by a political compromise in favor of a national program of political enlightenment. [33]

The crisis of *Vergangenheitsbewältigung* (mastering the past) in 1958/59 occurred, like the reparations treaty, against the backdrop of a crucial turning point in the global situation of the Federal Republic. The reopening of the German Question was at first the consequence of a brief moment of "estrangement" between Germany and the United States. By mid-1958, Adenauer's domestic popularity had peaked and new divisions emerged among the Western powers, especially in regard to European fears of the American "nuclear guarantee." Adenauer reacted negatively to the American view of

Germany as a "shield" against the Soviet threat (the Radford Plan). He reso-lutely opposed a proposed four-power conference in Geneva on the German Question backed by Britain and France, fueling renewed domestic debate on the future of Germany. The SPD sided with the Western Europeans in their support for a policy of "nuclear-free zones" and "disengagement," creating new anxieties of a return to Schumacher's vision.[34] But the end of 1959 saw first the collapse of the Geneva Conference, Khrushchev's ultimatum un-leashing a new Berlin crisis, and in November, the decisive turn of the SPD toward NATO and the Western alliance at Bad Godesberg. By the end of the year, reunification was no longer on the agenda.

The breakup of the Adenauer epoch, coupled with the "hardening" of the German situation into a permanent reality, required a more extensive con-frontation with the past acceptable to the SPD as a member of the new na-tional consensus. Especially for those SPD leaders who, like Willy Brandt, had been part of an antifascist tradition, the narrow mastery of the past achieved by the CDU/CSU in the early 1950s was inadequate. The Adenauer consensus on the Jewish Question was not overturned. But the fifteen-year public evasion of Nazism was terminated, and historical efforts to confront Nazism were restored to the national (and educational) curriculum. In Febru-ary 1959, Adenauer himself spoke of the need "to devote particular attention to historical education about the recent past," and, in response to the widely perceived "educational emergency" German school authorities attempted to eradicate the scourge of "historical illiteracy."[35] The question of guilt was superseded by the discourse of repression. If reparations substituted policy for pedagogy, the *Vergangenheitsbewältigung* turned pedagogy into national policy.[36]

The cultural mastering of the past which took place after 1959 was also accompanied by a juridical dimension which began when West Germany empowered a Ludwigsburg agency (Zentrale Stelle der Landesjustizver-waltungen zur Verfolgung national-sozialistischer Gewaltverbrechen) to pros-ecute Nazi "crimes of violence." (Though the Ludwigsburg center was set up in 1958, the Eichmann trial in 1961 was the real impetus.) By the time of the Auschwitz trials in the mid-1960s, the juridical process served a double pur-pose. It demonstrated the government's resolve—in the face of strong op-position from the "grace lobby" in Parliament—to prosecute the most se-rious Nazi offenders. At the same time, however, it further narrowed the definition of criminal acts to those committed against Jews and certain other victims (most recently, the euthanasia victims), but still largely excluded all political victims, Gypsies, and homosexuals. The juridical process paralleled the reparations precedent in confirming the distinction between the Holo-caust and other (apparently lesser) Nazi crimes, a distinction affirmed on the Israeli side by the Eichmann trial which prosecuted him solely for "crimes against the Jews." Much of the public debate in the 1960s concerned the stat-ute of limitations (*Verjährung*) on Nazi crimes which was scheduled to expire in 1960, but was extended (only for first-degree murder), first to 1965, and subsequently to 1979, when the statute itself was finally abolished.[37] The narrow definition of Nazi crimes in the courts further accentuated the detachment of the crime against the Jews from the general complex of Nazism in the 1960s.

When, in 1959, T. W. Adorno published his famous essay, "Was bedeutet: Aufarbeitung der Vergangenheit?" ("What does coming to terms with the past mean?" first given as a lecture to the Gesellschaft für christlich-jüdische Zusammenarbeit), he articulated a principle that motivated much of what was said in the decade to follow: "I consider the persistence of National Socialism *in* democracy as potentially more threatening than the persistence of fascist tendencies *against* democracy."[38] The relation of the past to the present in Germany is marked by pathological evasions, euphemisms, by "a loss of history." "The eradication of memory" was a defense against "the superior power of unconscious processes." For Adorno, the broad popularity of the Nazi regime was rooted in a "national vanity beyond measure," the "collective narcissism" of the masses, while its false "working through" was an "empty and cold forgetting." The past, Adorno concludes, can only be mastered when "its causes in the present are overcome."

The great evasion of the postwar years revealed a deep psychic debility, the inability to work through or "master" the past, a pathological time bomb, which Alexander and Margarete Mitscherlich later diagnosed in *The Inability to Mourn* as a latent explosive potential for irrational behavior.[39] Denial and "flight from memory" characterized one aspect of the syndrome of repression, while social and behavioral continuities with an illiberal past marked the other aspect. Above all, the social-psychological potential hidden in an authoritarian character structure, the latent persistence of anti-Semitism and antidemocratic attitudes—these are, in Adorno's often quoted *summae*, the tropes of the new democratic and antifascist consensus that emerged in the late 1950s and early 1960s.

To be sure, none of this seriously challenged the Adenauer consensus on the subject of the personal histories of former Nazis in government service, nor did it attempt to reintroduce the issue of denazification. The object of this critique was the repression of the first decade and a half, a "capitulation before history."[40] The model of a psychoanalytic "overcoming" of a historically situated repression distinguishes the new antifascist discourse of the 1960s from the moral and judicial preoccupations with "guilt" in the late 1940s and early 1950s. The repression is double: on the one side, the repression of the antifascist tradition and the Nazi Question, on the other, the persistence of deep structures of psychological identification with authority, resentment toward the Jews, or a regressive subservience to outmoded national ideals.

The renewal of the antifascist discourse in the early 1960s shifted the emphasis to the subjective elements of the Nazi past which resonated in the present—anti-Semitism, authoritarianism and (to a far lesser extent) nationalism. In marked contrast to the narrow juridical emphasis on the criminal side of Nazism, the new *Vergangenheitsbewältigung* highlighted its more quotidian aspects.

If the reparations issue placed guilt in German hands, so to speak, the new antifascist discourse internationalized it. Writing in 1957, the historian Martin Broszat pointed to this aspect of the discussion when he noted, "National Socialism cannot be understood solely as a consequence of German history."[41] A 1963 colloquium on the problem of education and the Nazi past under the title "Autoritarismus und Nationalismus: Ein deutsches Problem?" for example, carried the subtitle "*Der Hitler in uns*" and saw authoritarianism and nationalism as "two particularly easy to observe symptoms" which in "milder form, have a tendency to resonate in Germany."[42] This emphasis on the continuities with the past often overemphasized universal characteristics present in, but hardly specific to, Nazism (including anti-Semitism) at the expense of the uniquely radical elements of Nazism. Most of the contributors to the symposium, with the exception of the historian K. D. Bracher, failed to distinguish between Nazi authoritarianism and authoritarianism *tout court*. Horkheimer, for example, oversimplified the thesis of Hellmuth Plessner's *Die verspätete Nation*, claiming that National Socialism "did a series of things, which were done earlier in other countries and only because they occurred too late [in Germany], were they bound up with so much awfulness."[43] Horkheimer argued that recognizing the psychological and social affinities between pre- and post-Nazi realities would expose the hypocrisy of "indignant talk of demonic forces which secretly serves as apology: that which has irrational origins is removed from rational penetration, and is magically turned into something that simply has to be taken for granted."[44] Rejecting the "metaphysical guilt" of the 1950s existentialists was meant to remove Nazism from the sphere of impenetrability, but at the risk of domesticating it and minimizing its horror.

The core of postwar critical theory was a therapeutic model of historical discourse—it was both enlightenment about the past to redeem the present, and enlightenment about the present to redeem the past. As early as 1960, the historian Hans Tietgens questioned the consequences of directly linking historical memory to a psychoanalytic model of repression and cure, "history as panacea, as *medicina mentis*."[45] Even though this course appears necessary as a reaction to the repression of the preceding decade and a half and contributed to a remarkable change in the intellectual makeup of an entire generation, its overarching image of Nazism did not adequately establish those aspects of Nazism which were *not* present in the present. If "barbarism," as Adorno wrote in his "Erziehung nach Auschwitz" (1966), "persists as long as the conditions which produce that regression also persist to a significant degree," how can we distinguish between barbarism and the persistence of its possibility?[46]

Adorno always insisted that the categorical imperative of contemporary civilization is to prevent the recurrence of Auschwitz. But the therapeutic model of redeeming the past by transforming the present constituted a symbolic displacement of the past *into* the present. Ultimately (and it would be a gross exaggeration to blame Adorno for this) the struggle against contemporary "fascisms," e.g., in the Federal Republic, Greece, Mozambique, or Israel, became a surrogate for the missing antifascism of the postwar generation. Along with the distinction between past and present, those between the personal and the political, the psychological and the historical also became blurred. In the dark night of the Freudian-Marxist critique, all fascists are black.

The New Left: Belated Antifascism

The German New Left, with its characteristic antiauthoritarianism, obsessive focus on pedagogy, and alienation from parents, made the "theory of fascism" part of the cultural style of a generation. A psychoanalytically informed antifascism, in contrast to the state ideology of orthodox Marxism in the East, challenged the moralizing attitudes of the Adenauer era, characterized in an influential book by Wolfgang Fritz Haug as "helpless antifascism." [47] The antiauthoritarian movement accomplished a sustained demolition of the postwar Federal Republic's deeply embedded conservatism (as well as a kind of cultural integration with the West). But the antifascism of the 1960s also further extended the dissociation of the Nazi Question and the Jewish Question constructed by the Adenauer consensus. The antifascism of the 1960s displaced the Jewish Question by a largely unconscious strategy of marginalization:
1. by emphasizing the "repression" of those elements of fascism *not* included in the "singularity" postulate: especially anticommunism, antiliberalism and authoritarianism;
2. by emphasizing the continuities of the authoritarian personality in the pre- and postfascist epoch;
3. by emphasizing the elements of continuity between the structures of fascism and contemporary capitalism;
4. by establishing a historically valid lineage for the New Left with the overwhelmingly Jewish antifascist (and non-Stalinist) intellectuals of the 1920s and 1930s, a kind of ersatz genealogy to a generation of resistance;
5. by reducing fascism to a set of universal characteristics, and by subsuming anti-Semitism under a variety of possible ideological prejudices, e.g., racism, anticommunism, etc.

Rudi Dutschke articulated the fundamental principle of this complex when he wrote that the "character basis of fascism was not overcome by the external defeat of fascism in Germany, but was transformed, essentially unbroken, into anticommunism." [48]

Until the 1967 Arab-Israeli war, the 1968 generation was largely sympathetic to Israel, and, in their rejection of the blackout of history that was the underside of the official *Wiedergutmachung*, shared the Frankfurt School's view of Auschwitz as emblematic of the horrors of Nazism. Not long after the Six Day War, the situation was reversed: German conservatives, previously cool toward Israel, warmed to recent military successes, and old enthusiasms were reignited by the new "desert fox," Dayan. The Left did a *volte-face*, identifying with the Palestinians and viewing the State of Israel as the consequence, not of Nazi genocide, but of "the political economy of imperialism."[49] For the German New Left in the 1970s, racism and fascism were omnipresent, Nazism and anti-Semitism anachronistic and historically obsolete forms of these universal evils. The tragic theater of the 1977 Deutsche Herbst with its hypernervous state apparatus and its ascetic and self-denying radical martyrs was an all too real enactment of the "missing" antifascist moment in the culture of postwar Germany (also evident in Italy and Japan). The macabre dance of death in the early 1970s was not a consequence of any "new fascism," but of the illusions of a postfascism which played itself out "behind the backs" of the protagonists. The identification of the West German Left with the Palestinian cause was motivated less by authentic solidarity with the oppressed than by the "giant exculpation" derived from a symbolic displacement of blame onto the victims.[50] This tragic course reached its apotheosis in the absorption of the West German RAF in the machinery of Arab terrorism and the infamous "selection" of Jewish passengers in the airplane hijacking at Entebbe in 1976.

Totalitarianism vs. Fascism

To sum up, by the 1970s the divided legacy of 1945 had created an extraordinary situation. On the one side, there was an official policy of Jewish reparations and prosecuting crimes against the Jews as a sign of the anti-Nazi consensus of the postwar era. On the other, a belated antifascism emphasized the failures of the postwar state to confront both past and present manifestations of "fascism." This divided legacy of German post-Nazi history was reflected in the explosion of research and scholarship that emerged after the crucial turning point of 1958/59.[51] The intense conflicts over the problem of fascism versus totalitarianism "divided the spirits" over the Nazi past in the 1960s. The proponents of totalitarianism theory were the quasi-official guardians of the cultural imperatives of the Cold War—an interpretation officially mandated by the German *Länder* for educating students "in the characteristics of totalitarianism and the chief aspects of Bolshevism and National Socialism."[52] The theorists of fascism, on the other hand, with few exceptions (notably the Heideggerian Nolte) were concerned with demonstrating the "contingent relations between fascism and capitalism"; the class basis of fascist systems of power; and the "primacy of politics," e.g., the temporarily detached (*verselbständigt*) character of the dictatorship within the overall structure of "bourgeois hegemony."[53] The theorists of totalitarianism saw in the concept of "fascism" an "attempt to repress completely the anticommunist critique of dictatorship through antifascist argumentation"; the theorists of fascism saw in "totalitarianism" a category of "comparative techniques of power," which "unified the new with the one-time, but at this stage, politically and globally extinct, enemy."[54] Ironically, in both versions the present (totalitarianism/communism—fascism/authoritarianism) was encapsulated in the past, and in both versions the Nazi past was "relativized" by comparison to a contemporary political reality.[55]

By the mid-1970s, there was a good deal of dissatisfaction with the fascism/totalitarianism controversy even on the part of its protagonists. The dispute dissipated into a more genteel debate on historical method: the problem of elites versus structures (intentionalists versus functionalists), or the "history of everyday life" versus more social scientific, quantitative history. By the 1980s at least a *modus vivendi* among historians in West Germany seemed to be emerging: traditionalists pursued more orthodox themes, e.g., political history, diplomatic history with conventional methods, while more liberal social historians pursued newer directions, e.g., women's history, labor history, regional history with more innovative methods. Yet as the *Historikerstreit* demonstrated, this division of labor also revealed serious elisions on both sides.

The emphasis on the *singularity* of the Nazi regime and its destructiveness became increasingly significant for the traditionalists, while, for social historians, the blander, more quotidian, and private aspects of life in the Nazi era became more salient.[56] The "everyday" historians saw the problem of resistance not in terms of isolated acts of public opposition, as did historians in the 1950s, but as a continuum of behaviors which ranged from private griping to sabotaging the economic and military efforts of the regime.[57] If for the traditionalists the events that followed mirrored Hitler's view of the world, the social historians saw Nazism through the mirror of those who experienced it as participants, each with their respective distortions. This set the stage for a decisive confrontation between these two competing "historical pictures": Hitler and his personal rule without the social dimension of Nazism; the social history of the Third Reich in which Hitler and his policies play only a peripheral role. That a major historical debate erupted at precisely the moment this bifurcated vision of the past reached a crisis point is no coincidence.

The Jewish Question in German Politics in the 1980s

A new orientation toward the "Jewish Question" in the German politics of the 1980s began, not with the Kohl government's "*Wende*" of 1982/83, but with that of Helmut Schmidt in 1980. The government of Schmidt and Hans-Dietrich Genscher was the first to abandon the symbolism of guilt in its dealings with Israel and to pursue a policy of "normalization" in the Middle East. According to Michael Wolffsohn, Schmidt's confrontation with Menachem Begin over arms sales to Saudi Arabia in May 1981, more a matter of style than substance, was the first real break with the symbolism of the Adenauer (and Brandt) eras.[58] It was Helmut Schmidt, not Helmut Kohl, who, on a return flight from Israel in April 1981, said that "German foreign policy can and will no longer be overshadowed by Auschwitz."[59]

The Schmidt government's acceptance of the 1979 NATO "double decision" to station Cruise and Pershing missiles in Europe, rallied large parts of the German Left and the peace movement around the antimissile campaign, strengthening neutralist overtones, especially among the Greens (although the actual demand for immediate withdrawal from NATO did not occur until May 20, 1986). The peace movement created a deep anxiety among many European conservatives (and some liberals as well, especially in France) about the emergence of a "Rapallo Complex"—the nightmare of a neutralist, nationalist, pacifist, and *mitteleuropäisches* Germany untethered from the West and "wandering between two European worlds."[60] Although it is not true that the German peace movement was a movement for national reunification by other means, as some critics have argued, it contributed to a renewal of "middle-European thought" at all points on the German political spectrum, from Peter Glotz in the SPD to the neonationalist Right.[61] The Greens are above all a generational phenomenon, offering a new West German cultural identity unencumbered by the past, and an affront to the political style of the old governing elites. Significantly, the Greens have also been highly ambivalent on the Jewish issue: the "embarrassments" of the 1985 Green Israel trip and the anti-Peres demonstrations, both characterized by "negative cliché-thinking," contrast sharply with Joschka Fischer's generally excellent *Zeit* articles and speeches and the Green parliamentary proposal for a national survey of anti-Semitism in 1986.[62] Nevertheless, in light of the Fassbinder affair and the "lack of inhibition" evident in a number of periodicals on the "alternative scene," it was the West German Left that first expressed a new attitude toward the "Jewish Question" in the mid 1980s.[63]

Normalization über Alles

The Bitburg affair linked the Jewish Question to the German Question as intensely as only the Adenauer reparations treaty had done before in the history of the Federal Republic of Germany—with reversed symbolism. The reparations treaty placed the Jewish Question *above* the German Question insofar as it singled out the uniqueness of the Holocaust as opposed to all other crimes and insofar as it declared it to be apart from all other aspects of Nazism. Thus, it became part of the collective conscience of the Federal Republic. The Bitburg wreath—despite, and perhaps even more intensely, because of the last-minute Belsen visit (interpreted as a mere concession to American Jews)—demonstrated that the Kohl government was the first to abandon the *singularity* postulate and to publicly relativize the Holocaust in relation to all other suffering inflicted by "the war." At Bitburg, the German Question (the NATO partnership) was placed *above* the Jewish Question. It was now world Jewry that persisted in "memorializing" the Holocaust, when three-fourths of all Germans favored the visit. Germans were reacting against their "victimization" by the Jewish monopoly on the moral capital of suffering which held the present hostage to the past. The Greens, to their credit, were the only party in Parliament to oppose the visit, a reversal of their previous ambivalence toward this aspect of Nazism.

The triumph of the Kohl government consisted not only in forcing an American president into an embarrassing choice between an ally and a (largely Democratic) American constituency, but in further isolating and *Judaizing* the memory of the Holocaust. If this symbolism was not clear at the time, the chancellor reemphasized it a few days later when he said that reconciliation "is achieved when we are able to mourn for human beings, independent of whatever nationality the murdered, the fallen, the dead once belonged." [64] If the postwar world inverted "victims" and "perpetrators," subordinating the guilt of Germans to the power of the Jews over atonement and sovereignty, the only solution, he proposed, was full equality for both.

The road to Bitburg was paved with a series of calculated fiascos, carefully planned situations in which the German chancellor proved his identification with German public opinion by getting attacked in the liberal and international press. During his 1984 visit to Israel, for example, Kohl astonished Israelis with a plethora of well placed *faux pas*, which the *FAZ* described alternatively as "disgraces," "blunders" and "embarrassments." [65] Speaking with pride of his "grace of belated birth" (*die Gnade der späten Geburt*), he asserted the independence of his generation from the moral obligations of previous German generations toward Israel. The second prelude to Bitburg was Kohl's summer 1985 appearance at a convention of *Heimatvertriebene,* a group of ultraconservative exiles from Silesia (he was the first German chancellor to do so), where he spoke under a "revanchist" banner proclaiming "Silesia Remains Ours." With these more spectacular events, the wider CDU/CSU campaign to reassert traditional "typical German virtues" was personified by the Parliamentary chairman Alfred Dregger's 1984 speech which condemned the Nazis for undermining the "spiritual substance" of the German nation and creating "a trauma of self-evaluation" through their "revolutionary attitudes." [66] The reopening of the "German Question" on the Left created new anxieties about a neutralist Germany governed by a left coalition hostile to the United States and produced a strong sentiment in CDU/CSU government circles that the moment was opportune for their own public ritual. Combined with fears of a party to the "right of the CDU," as occurred with the emergence of the populist Bavarian *Die Republikaner*, the Jewish Question once again provided a convenient occasion for a reassertion of West German sovereignty. [67]

For Kohl's loyalty to Reagan in the missile debate, and for signing on to SDI, the chancellor requested and received Reagan's support for the visit to a military cemetery at Bitburg where there were forty-nine Waffen SS graves (it is still unclear whether Kohl knew of them at the time). At a political level, the visit was a quid pro quo. At a symbolic level, the Bitburg visit was intended to demonstrate the end of the German guilt requirement, and at the same time (perhaps less intentionally), to contribute to the "Napoleonization of the Wehrmacht"—the myth of a positive, anti-Soviet German military effort on the Eastern front. As Dregger highlighted in his letter to the congressional opponents of the visit, "he had defended the . . . town of Marklissa in Silesia against attacks by the Red Army" and his brother, a "decent young man," had died on the Eastern front in 1944.[68] Peter Glotz, SPD general secretary, summed up Dregger's (and Kohls) intentions when he wrote: "Your letter is infused by the idea that the Americans would do well to forget the past, because we are now allies and support the policies of the present American administration. That idea is morally corrupt."[69] An important ideological pillar of the German Right for decades, the last phase of the German defeat (the defense against red barbarism) was incorporated *ex post facto* into the first phase of the Cold War.

For the Reagan administration, the Bitburg visit was a public relations debacle ("he who lives by the photo opportunity, dies by the photo opportunity").[70] For the Kohl government, the real meaning of the event was expressed by President Reagan, not at the graveside ceremonies, but some weeks earlier on April 18, 1985 when he said that those buried there were no less "victims of Nazism, even though they were fighting in the German uniform. . . ."[71] This is exactly what Mr. Dregger embellished several months later, when he delivered his even more important parliamentary speech on behalf of a national holiday for "victims" of the Third Reich, which in its idiom (*Volkstrauertag*) recalled the era it wanted to forget. Bitburg was a return to what Raul Hilberg called "a nebulous collective innocence."[72]

Less than a week after Bitburg, President Richard von Weizsäcker delivered his now famous speech to the German Parliament, a speech widely praised for its refusal of any gesture of normalization: "Whoever closes their eyes to the past, will be blind to the present."[73] It was not only the far Right but the *Frankfurter Allgemeine Zeitung* that was "uncomfortable" with the frequent unflattering contrasts between Kohl's and von Weizsäcker's performance. As *Die Zeit* pointed out, von Weizsäcker's view of history was closer to Willy Brandt's in its emphasis on the connection between "May 8, 1945 and January 30, 1933" than to Kohl's condemnation of "the dictator."[74] Given Bitburg's highly charged public reversal of the reparations postulate, it is not at all remarkable that precisely these issues were raised in the *Historikerstreit*: (1) the German "desire" for normalcy and equal partnership in the Western alliance versus the "abnormality" of German history and limited sovereignty; (2) the place of the singularity of the Holocaust in German, and in global history; (3) the distinction between "victims and executioners," between "*schlußstrich* and remembrance." As Hans Mommsen noted, the government was on the right course "to open the Pandora's box and provide a free space for apparently obsolete nationalist strivings, without being in the position of being able to control the spirits that it evoked." [75]

The *Historikerstreit*

The extraordinary controversy which erupted in the summer/autumn of 1986 was the first atmospheric test of the fallout from Bitburg. Unlike scholarly debates which sometimes rise to the level of public scrutiny, this one originated in, and was conducted between, two of Germany's major newspapers, the conservative *Frankfurter Allgemeine Zeitung,* and the liberal Hamburg weekly *Die Zeit.* Eventually, hardly any German periodical with serious pretensions failed to comment on it, and most major West German intellectuals weighed in on one side or the other. No historical controversy in the entire postwar period—including the famous debate on Germany's role in the First World War in the 1960s—produced such ferocious polemics. Nolte's public musings on how "the so-called annihilation of the Jews during the Third Reich was a reaction or a distorted copy and not a first act or an original" became a scandal because they brought to public discourse what had previously been beer hall fare and sanctioned these views in one of Germany's leading newspapers. Nolte himself acknowledged that he had bridged the gap between the German *"pays légal"* and the *"pays réel."* To make matters even clearer, the argument was taken up and extended by one of the *FAZ*'s leading editors, and Hitler biographer, Joachim Fest.

The course of events is by now familiar. The *Historikerstreit* was provoked by the appearance in the *FAZ* in June 1986 of Nolte's infamous article, where he wondered in print why "more than anything else it was the memory of the 'Final Solution' which contributed to that past which would not go away." [76] Nolte also wondered if there were not "interests" at play here, like those of the "persecuted and their descendants in a permanent status of select [*herausgehobenen*] and privileged existence." But the most "original" aspect of Nolte's by now well-known new "questions" about the past concerned the historical origins of the Nazi crime against the Jews:

Did not the National Socialists, did not Hitler perhaps commit an "Asiatic" deed only because they regarded themselves and those like them as potential or real victims of an "Asiatic" deed? Was not the Gulag Archipelago more original than Auschwitz? Was not the "class murder" of the Bolshevists the logical and factual *prius* of the "racial murder" of the National Socialists?

Nolte provided a more detailed version in an article entitled "Between Myth and Revisionism," which appeared in English in 1985. [77] There he traced the various "annihilation therapies" that led to the Holocaust from the French Revolution. But his main argument is that

Auschwitz is not primarily a result of traditional anti-Semitism. It was in its core not merely a 'genocide' but was above all a reaction born out of the anxiety of the annihilating occurrences of the Russian Revolution. . . . It was more horrifying than the original because the annihilation of men was conducted in a quasi-industrial manner.[78]

Fest contended that Nolte never challenged the "singularity of the National Socialist annihilatory action," but he took up the cudgel against the singularity argument even more emphatically.[79] For Fest, the singularity argument rested on four claims: (1) that Hitler committed crimes against "guiltless" victims; (2) the abstract, mechanical, and administrative character of the crime against the Jews; (3) that the crime against the Jews occurred against the backdrop of a highly developed culture, and "a century long growing German-Jewish symbiosis"; (4) that Hitler's motives were radically different from the humanist aspirations that could be traced to the foundations of communism, despite the sufferings and death which it produced. None of these, he claims, constitute "uniqueness": (1) what distinguished a Nazi victim from a communist victim is that in the one "a biological rather than a social being" is determined to be worthy of death; (2) Stalin's crimes were not realized in any less administrative fashion; the "shot in the nape of the neck" is not qualitatively different from gas; (3) the cultural argument "perpetuates the old Nazi distinction, according to which there are higher peoples and people at a more primitive level"; (4) there is little to be gained from distinguishing a "corrupt humanity" from a "rotten worldview." Fest concludes: "the thesis of singularity . . . stands on weak ground."

We cannot here examine all of Fest's claims in which truth, half-truth, and nonsense congeal. Eberhard Jäckel provided an eloquent refutation, above all that it astonishingly excludes Hitler's often repeated desire to exterminate the Jews as "race" from the list.[80] "I maintain," he writes,

that the National Socialist murder of the Jews was unique because never before did a state decide and proclaim with the authority of its responsible leader that a specific human group should be killed . . . and then translate this decision with all the possible means at the disposal of the state.

It should simply be said that in Fest's "generalized balance sheet," the obsessive desire to overthrow the singularity postulate with comparisons to Cambodia, Algeria, Vietnam, and "millions of dead of this century" cannot but throw the limelight on the suspicion that, as Fest himself seems to admit, "this is nothing but an effort to derive exoneration for oneself from crimes everywhere in the world."[81] The point, however, is not that the "relativization" of the Holocaust pursued by Nolte and Fest should absolutely be refuted on scholarly grounds, but rather to understand what it proposes in terms of the legal and historical consensus established around the singularity postulate in postwar German politics. Nolte and Fest proposed, for the first time, a discursive strategy for reversing the reparations precept established in the Adenauer era, and this is why their efforts caused a public uproar.

Nolte's essay coincided with the publication of a small volume consisting of two essays by the Cologne historian Andreas Hillgruber, entitled *Two Kinds of Collapse: The Destruction of the German Reich and the End of European Jewry.*[82] Hillgruber never explicitly relates the two essays, which deal with the collapse of the German Army on the Eastern front and with the "Final Solution" in the East. Nevertheless, the effect of their juxtaposition is strikingly clear: the first essay laments the final days of the German Army and the consequences of the Russian conquest as a German national "catastrophe," the second is a dry and ascetic account of the Nazi crime against the Jews in light of recent historical works on anti-Semitism.[83] Placed together, it is difficult to escape the conclusion which appears on the book jacket, "that the amputation of the Reich in favor of a greater Poland was a war aim of the Allies long before Auschwitz." The destruction of the German Army, the terror unleashed by the Soviet Army, and the complicity of the Allies in dismembering the eastern part of Germany are all tragic consequences of the blind anti-Prussianism of the Allies, independent of Hitler's crimes.

Several weeks after Nolte's essay appeared, Jürgen Habermas reacted in *Die Zeit* under the title, "A Kind of Settlement of Damages."[84] In addition to Nolte and Hillgruber, Habermas charged two other historians, Klaus Hildebrand of Bonn, and Michael Stürmer of Erlangen, with "apologetic tendencies in German historical writing." Professional historiography, Habermas claimed (quoting Stürmer), was "driven forward by collective and largely unconscious desire for the provision of inner-worldly meaning." Hillgruber's book is an example of such an enterprise, especially insofar as he believes that the historian "must identify with the concrete fate of the German population in the east and with the desperate and costly struggle of the German eastern army and of the German navy. . . ." Nolte, however, as Habermas recognizes, "is made of different mettle than Hillgruber." Via a laudatory review by Hildebrand, who praised Nolte for removing the history of the Third Reich from its "seemingly unique character," Habermas discovered Nolte's earlier essay. There Nolte repeated one of the most scurrilous neo-Nazi propaganda clichés (first propounded in historical circles by David Irving), the alleged September 1939 "declaration of war" by Chaim Weizmann, then president of the Jewish Agency, calling for Jews to support Britain and the democracies, which, according to Nolte, "might justify the consequential thesis that Hitler was allowed to treat the German Jews as prisoners of war and by this means intern them."[85] "In this context of terror," Habermas adds, "the destruction of the Jews appears then to be only the regrettable result of a nevertheless understandable reaction to that which Hitler must have perceived as a threat of destruction."[86] Habermas does not deny that there are good grounds for a historicizing distance. But what the new historical revisionism—along with the plans laid by the Kohl government for two new historical museums, a German Historical Museum in Berlin and a House of the History of the Federal Republic in Bonn—promises is "to *shake off* the debts of a successfully de-moralized past."

Much of the attention paid to the historical debate has been focused on Nolte's strategy of "relativization." Several critics, like the liberal historians

Heinrich August Winkler and Jürgen Kocka, have underscored this aspect of the debate, pointing out, as Kocka writes, that a comparative approach "should not repress the singularity of German development through comparison with Stalin and Pol Pot; it remains important, dangerous and shameful." [87] At the same time, there has been considerably more sympathy for Hillgruber and Stürmer than for the "eccentric" Nolte and Fest. [88] As Winkler noted, despite Hillgruber's "pronounced sympathies for the Prussian Junkers and the military," he and Stürmer are "no relativizers à la Nolte, and don't deserve to be thrown into the same pot with him." [89]

Given the particular symbolism of the singularity postulate in postwar German political discourse, the reversals enunciated by Fest and Nolte take on special significance. Moreover, if we include Stürmer's appeal for a positive historical continuity in the construction of German identity and Hillgruber's clever dissociation of the postwar fate of Germany from the crimes of National Socialism, the divergent strands in the conservative assault on previous attempts to find a postwar consensus is apparent. The *Historikerstreit* is a departure from *both* the metaphysical guilt and the antifascist discourses.

I would, however, take issue with Winkler's conjecture that "the deeper reasons for the national apologetic wave" can be found in the "call for German reunification." There is, of course, a distinction between the "identity creating" purposes of Stürmer and Hillgruber and the moral-political exonerations of Nolte and Fest. Hillgruber does not relativize the crime against the Jews, but changes its contextual meaning. The argument of *Two Kinds of Collapse* is directed against the West for its role in destroying the continental status of Germany as a nation; it is an appeal to consider the German claim to its eastern territories independent of Hitler's crimes. The novelty in Hillgruber's approach, and what few commentators on the debate have noticed, is that he is among the first to openly criticize the Western alliance for the fate of postwar Germany, and to restate the German Question in new terms. Hillgruber introduces the novel thesis that since the decision to divide Germany and "dismember" East Prussia was a Western capitulation to Stalin, and since the terms of the Allied defeat of Germany might only be justified as a response to the crimes against the Jews, postwar Germany is the victim of wartime power politics. After the myth of Yalta, the myth of Teheran.

Hillgruber argues that the division of Germany and its loss of global political status as a "failed world power" (*gescheiterte Grossmacht*) was a consequence of anti-Prussian (not expressly anti-Hitler) war aims of the Allies. In World War II, the legitimate "core" of the desire for revision (of Germany's eastern borders and its *Untertan* role in world affairs) in the Weimar Republic was perverted by the "Hitler Reich." [90] The German catastrophe is the end of a "power politically fully sovereign great power German empire," and the "unconscious retreat of the majority of Germans in the postwar years from their nation." [91] The "German Question," in short, has to be separated from its subversion by Hitler. The defense of the nation is divorced from the catastrophic policies of the leader.

Conclusion

The German historical controversy has revealed two new strategies of mastering the past: one which relativizes and denies the singularity of the Holocaust by reducing it to a phenomenon of the "age of tyrants," and a second, far more sophisticated strategy which places the burden of responsibility on Hitler, does not deny his crimes, but relegitimizes German "national identity" and the role of Germany as a continental Middle European power (Stürmer/Hillgruber). This distinction between the relativizers and the proponents of a new historical paradigm for German national identity also seems to conform to the divisions within the Kohl government. The more conservative elements of the CDU/CSU, Strauss, Dregger, and Co. have been absolutely "uninhibited" about removing Germany from "the shadow of Hitler and his crimes," as Strauss put it.[92] But the neoconservative and modernizing thrust of the CDU/CSU is more concerned with marginalizing the Right Wing and thus offers, in the vein of Hillgruber and Stürmer, a new and "positive" image of German history which does not pretend to historicize the crimes of Hitler out of existence, but rather reasserts the continuities between the political "*kleindeutsch*" aims of Bismarck and the Middle European status of Germany as a world power, despite its subversion by Hitler's "grasp for world domination." Indeed, this view of German history is not concerned with the old dreams of reunification or reconquest, but rather with establishing, at least "in the realm of dreams," as Heine put it, a revindication of the historical status of Germany as a European power, in the face of a realistic assessment of its contemporary political possibilities. As Hans Mommsen has pointed out, much of what has occurred in the recent debate on national identity has been part of an attempt to expand German economic and military sovereignty within the parameters of NATO.[93] In fact, one legacy of Bitburg is not necessarily a strengthening of conservative aspirations toward Middle Europe, but rather their abandonment, and the recognition that the chances for any reopening of the German Question are far brighter on the Left than on the Right. The CDU/CSU has had to abandon the claim to reunification without saying so, and, in this situation, has chosen the return to the symbol of nationhood—national history—in the absence of its potential for realization. When Stürmer argues that "no people can in the long run live without historical identity," it is this compensatory nationalism, and not a return to the old conservative motifs of the past, that is at stake.[94] The Jewish Question has once again emerged as the implacable object in the path of this newly constructed identity.

The *Historikerstreit* was, as Charles Maier put it, "a dispute over the controlling public discourse of the Federal Republic."[95] It demonstrated the extent to which the writing of history in West Germany has been part of a broader cultural and political discourse on the past. The controversy has also brought about a number of important reversals. As Mary Nolan shows, one consequence has been to call into question some of the arguments of the "history of everyday life," especially in its more "normalizing" aspects.[96] As Saul Friedländer and Dan Diner argued, the attempt of everyday life history to rehabilitate the German "private sphere" during the Third Reich created an "innerworldly" habitus which brackets out the larger world—and its crimes.[97] To the extent that younger, more liberal historians have emphasized the normality of daily existence, they have no doubt fueled the claims of those, like Hillgruber, who insist that only the Nazi elite or Hitler personally should bear sole responsibility for Germany's postwar fate. The *Historikerstreit* has frequently reversed conservative and liberal arguments: whereas in the past the Left generally focused on the continuities of German elites and traditions, conservatives have now emphasized the continuities between pre National Socialist and post-1945 German culture. The so-called *Stunde Null* of 1945 has migrated from Right to Left. Habermas, for example, reinterprets 1945 as a potentially positive moment of "release from a past centered on national history," and in departure from the traditions of the German Left of 1968 has argued for the positive ramifications of this caesura in German identity. Habermas's explicit praise for the "unreserved opening of the Federal Republic to the political culture of the West" as "the great intellectual achievement of the postwar period" is directed against the nebulous politics of "*Mitteleuropa*" which enjoyed a brief but significant popularity on the left in the mid-1980s. His appeals to the moral dimension of politics as an antidote to nationalist nostalgia owe more to Arendt and Jaspers than to Marx and Horkheimer. In light of the prominent Greens Joschka Fischer and Otto Schily's recent cautious turn toward the Western alliance, the *Historikerstreit* may signal a change on the Left as well.

To judge by the chorus of negative responses to their joint venture, Nolte and Fest have suffered what might be described as a significant defeat.[98] The "vulgar relativization" they proposed has not become *salonfähig*. Politically, the Kohl government has taken a far less adventurous tack. For the time being, conservatives have retreated to a different arena for assertions of "normalcy." As Manfred Wörner, the new German secretary general of the North Atlantic Treaty Organization said of his ascension to the post, "it is my impression that from the outside this is regarded as a slice of normality. And it is important to us that it means that we are a normal nation like any other."[99]

However, the opening of public discourse to the arguments of the neonationalist Right is not insignificant.[100] The creation of a national historical tradition in which Hitler and the crime against the Jews no longer occupies a prominent place cannot be discounted for the future. Whether Jürgen Habermas is right that Germans can be satisfied with a "post-conventional identity," or whether, as Wehler argues, the vast majority is less than preoccupied with questions of identity, cannot be decided with any certainty.

The *Historikerstreit* has demonstrated that the Jewish Question will not easily disappear from the landscape of West German politics. It underscores a central fact of the postwar history of the Federal Republic of Germany: every expansion of German political sovereignty has been accompanied—at least subjectively—by a debate about the Jewish Question. The linkage between Hitler's crimes and German sovereignty continues to be paramount in the cultural construction of German identity. Since 1945, the German Question and the Jewish Question have been inseparable.

Notes

1. Dan Diner, "Negative Symbiosis: Germans and Jews after Auschwitz," in this volume, p. 251.
2. Judith Miller, "Erasing the Past: Europe's Amnesia about the Holocaust," *New York Times magazine*, 16 November 1986, 30.
3. Hermann Lübbe, "Der Nationalsozialismus im Deutschen Nachkriegsbewusstsein," *Historische Zeitschrift* 236 (1983): 585.
4. Lübbe, "Der Nationalsozialismus," 587.
5. Lübbe, "Der Nationalsozialismus," 584.
6. Peter Steinbach, "Nationalsozialistische Gewaltverbrechen in der deutschen "Öffentlichkeit nach 1945," *Vergangenheitsbewältigung durch Strafverfahren? NS-Prozesse in der Bundesrepublik Deutschland*, ed. Jürgen Weber and Peter Steinbach (Munich, 1984), 18.
7. Peter Brandt and Herbert Ammon, eds., *Die Linke und die Nationale Frage* (Hamburg, 1981), 36, 37. See the discussion of this option in Ferenc Feher and Agnes Heller, "Eastern Europe under the Shadow of a New Rapallo," *New German Critique* 37 (Winter 1986): 20–23.
8. Hans-Ulrich Wehler, "30. Januar 1933—ein halbes Jahrhundert danach," *Aus Politik und Zeitgeschichte* 4–5 (1983): 45.
9. Quoted in Martin Hirsch, "Anlaß, Verlauf und Ergebnis der Verjährungsdebatten im Deutschen Bundestag," *Vergangenheitsbewältigung durch Strafverfahren?* 40.
10. Hannah Arendt, "Organized Guilt and Collective Responsibility," *The Jew as Pariah: Jewish Identity and Politics in the Modern Age*, ed. Ron H. Feldman (New York, 1978), 230.
11. Karl Jaspers, *Die Schuldfrage: Zur politischen Haftung Deutschlands* (Munich, 1946), 48.
12. *Hannah Arendt–Karl Jaspers Briefwechsel 1926–1969*, ed. Lotte Köhler and Hans Saner (Munich, 1985), 91.
13. A. Boyens, "Das Stuttgarter Schuldbekenntnis vom 19. Oktober 1945—Entstehung und Bedeutung," *Vierteljahreshefte für Zeitgeschichte* 4/19 (1971): 374–97; Karl Jaspers, Die Schuldfrage, 31–40.
14. Cited in Diether Koch, *Heinemann und die Deutschlandfrage* (Munich, 1972), 45.
15. Rolf Wiggershaus, *Die Frankfurter Schule: Geschichte, theoretische Entwicklung, politische Bedeutung* (Munich, 1986), 497.
16. Cf. Heinz Arzt, "Zur Abgrenzung von Kriegsverbrechen und NS-Verbrechen," *NS-Prozesse: Nach 25 Jahren Strafverfolgung*, ed. Adalbert Rückerl (Karlsruhe, 1971), 164.
17. Theodor Heuss, "Wir dürfen nicht vergessen," *Neue Zeitung* 9 (December 1949).
18. Hans Keilson, "Die Reparationsverträge und die Folgen der Wiedergutmachung," *Jüdisches Leben in Deutschland seit 1945*, ed. Micha Brumlik et al.

(Frankfurt am Main, 1986), 125. As Michael Wolffsohn points out, it is a historical legend that Adenauer was pressured by the United States to adopt the treaty. Michael Wolffsohn, *Ewige Schuld? 40 Jahre Deutsch-Jüdische-Israelische Beziehungen* (Munich, 1988), 22–23.

19. Konrad Adenauer, *Erinnerungen 1953–1955* (Stuttgart, 1965). Cited in Keilson, "Die Reparationsverträge," 125.

20. "Die Tat wird die Probe sein," *Berliner Allgemeine*, 28 September 1951.

21. Wolffsohn, *Ewige Schuld?* 27; *Deutschland und das Judentum: Die Erklärung der Bundesregierung über das deutsch-jüdische Verhältnis*, ed. Presse- und Informationsdienst der Bundesregierung (Bonn, 1951), which includes press summaries and the text of Adenauer's speech.

22. Alfred Grosser, *Western Germany from Defeat to Rearmament* (London, 1955), 214.

23. Adenauer believed that were he to postpone the treaties negotiated with the occupying powers for a consideration of the Russian offer, he would not be permitted to reopen the negotiations. On the Stalin note and its connection to the debates on foreign policy, see Hans-Peter Schwarz, *Adenauer: Der Aufstieg: 1877–1952* (Stuttgart, 1986). See also Andreas Hillgruber, *Deutsche Geschichte 1945–1982: Die "Deutsche Frage" in der Weltpolitik* (Stuttgart, 1984), 52.

24. Andrei S. Markovits, "Germans and Jews: An Uneasy Relationship Continues," *Jewish Frontier* (April 1984): 15.

25. Jack Zipes, "The Vicissitudes of Being Jewish in West Germany," *Germans and Jews since the Holocaust: The Changing Situation in West Germany*, ed. Jack Zipes and Anson Rabinbach (New York, 1986), 32.

26. Saul Friedländer, "Some Present-Day German Struggles with Memory," lecture, Jewish Museum, New York, 31 March 1986.

27. Saul Friedländer, "Die Shoah als Element in der Konstruktion israelischer Erinnerung," *Babylon: Beiträge zur jüdischen Gegenwart* 2 (July 1987): 13.

28. Monika Richarz, "Juden in der Bundesrepublik Deutschland und in der Deutschen Demokratischen Republik seit 1945," *Jüdisches Leben in Deutschland* 15.

29. Richarz, 16, 17.

30. Richarz, 18, and Zipes, 28.

31. See Hans Jakob Ginsberg, "Politik danach—Jüdische Interessenvertretung in der Bundesrepublik," *Jüdisches Leben in Deutschland* 110, 111; and Y. Michal Bodemann, "Staat und Ethnizität: Der Aufbau der jüdischen Gemeinden im Kalten Krieg," in *Jüdisches Leben in Deutschland* 62.

32. Bodemann, "Staat und Ethnizität," 63.

33. Hans-Peter Schwarz, *Die Era Adenauer 1957–1963* (Stuttgart, 1983), 210.

34. Hillgruber, 70, 71.

35. Konrad Schilling, "Beitrag zur Behandlung von Judentum und Antisemitismus im Oberstufenunterricht," *Geschichte in Wissenschaft und Unterricht* 11 (1960): 135. Occasionally the language of the past pokes through even when its very opposite was intended, as when Erich Lüth wrote of how some knowledge on the part of the "young primitives" who desecrated the cemeteries "might have immunized them against the bacillus of anti-Semitism and made them unfit to carry the anti-Semitic infection." Erich Lüth, "Anti-Semitism," in *The Politics of Postwar Germany*, ed. Walter Stahl (New York, 1963), 194.

36. A study of the impact of the anti-Semitic vandalism on public opinion conducted by the Institute for Social Research in Frankfurt confirmed that anti-Semitism

and indifference accounted for a high proportion of public opinion (16 percent openly anti-Semitic; 41 percent indifferent). See Peter Schönbach, "Reaktionen auf die antisemitische Welle im Winter 1959/60," *Frankfurter Beiträge zur Soziologie* (Frankfurt am Main, 1961).

37. Hirsch, "Verjährungsdebatten," 40–50. Significantly, Karl Jaspers's campaign—documented in his *Wohin treibt die Bundesrepublik?*—in the mid-1960s for a distinction, not recognized by German jurisprudence, between "ordinary" murder and crimes against humanity, was unsuccessful, a testimony to the popularity (revealed by the polls) of a statute of limitations on *all* wartime crimes. See Karl Jaspers, "Für Völkermord gibt es keine Verjährung: Gesprach mit Rudolf Augstein (1965)," Karl Jaspers, *Provokationen: Gespräche und Interviews,* ed. Hans Saner (Munich, 1969), 122–46.

38. Theodor W. Adorno, "Was bedeutet: Aufarbeitung der Vergangenheit" in *Erziehung zur Mündigkeit,* ed. Gerd Kadelbach (Frankfurt am Main, 1972), 10–28. An English translation appears as "What Does Coming to Terms with the Past Mean?" in *Bitburg in Moral and Political Perspective,* ed. Geoffrey Hartman (Bloomington, 1986), 114–29.

39. Alexander and Margarete Mitscherlich, *The Inability to Mourn: Principles of Collective Behavior,* trans. Beverley R. Placzek (New York, 1975), xvii.

40. Hermann Heimpel, *Kapitulation vor der Geschichte* (Göttingen, 1956).

41. Martin Broszat, "Aufgaben und Probleme zeitgeschichtlichen Unterrichts," in *Nach Hitler: Der schwierige Umgang mit unserer Geschichte,* ed. Hermann Graml and Klaus-Dietmar Henke (Munich, 1986), 16.

42. *Autoritarismus und Nationalismus—Ein deutsches Problem? Bericht-über eine Tagung veranstaltet vom Institut für staatsbürgerliche Bildung Rheinland-Pfalz,* Politische Psychologie 2 (Frankfurt am Main, 1963), 11.

43. *Autoritarismus und Nationalismus,* 64. Significantly, Adorno's unpublished contribution to the conference was a reprise of *The Authoritarian Personality.*

44. Max Horkheimer, *Vorträge und Aufzeichnungen 1949–1973, Gesammelte Schriften* 8 (Frankfurt am Main, 1985), 127.

45. Hans Tietgens, "Unbewältigte Vergangenheit—Auseinandersetzung mit der Zeitgeschichte als Aufgabe der Erwachsenenbildung," *Kulturarbeit* 4 (1958): 73–76; Hans Wenke, "'Bewältigte Vergangenheit' und 'Aufgearbeitete Geschichte'—zwei Schlagworte, kritisch beleuchtet," *Geschichte in Wissenschaft und Unterricht* 11 (1960): 66–70.

46. Theodor W. Adorno, "Erziehung nach Auschwitz," *Erziehung zur Mündigkeit* (Frankfurt am Main, 1972), 88.

47. Wolfgang Friz Haug, *Der hilflose Antifaschismus: Zur Kritik der Vorlesungsreihen über Wissenschaft und NS an deutschen Universitäten* (Frankfurt am Main, 1967); reprinted in W. F. Haug, *Vom hilflosen Antifaschismus zur Gnade der späten Geburt* (Berlin, 1987).

48. Uwe Bergmann, Rudi Dutschke, Wolfgang Lefèvre, Bernd Rabehl, *Rebellion der Studenten oder die neue Opposition* (Reinbek bei Hamburg, 1968), 58.

49. See, for example, Horst Stemmler, Walmot Falkenberg, "Der Konflikt im Nahen Osten," *Neue Kritik* 42/43 (August, 1967): 68. A notable exception is the remarkable "Joint Declaration by 20 Representatives of the German Left, Concerning the Middle East Conflict" (1967), drafted by Ernst Erdös and Michael Landmann, and signed by Ernst Bloch, Irving Fetscher, Helmut Gollwitzer, Walter

Jens, Alexander Mitscherlich, Uwe Johnson, Martin Walser, Günter Grass, Ludwig von Friedeburg, and others.

50. Susan Heenen, "Deutsche Linke—Linke Juden und der Zionismus," in *Die Verlängerung der Geschichte: Deutsche, Juden und der Palästinakonflikt,* ed. Dietrich Wetzel (Frankfurt am Main: 1983), 109.

51. On the early confrontation with Nazis, see Jean-Paul Bier, "The Holocaust, West Germany, and Strategies of Oblivion, 1947–1979," in *Germans and Jews Since the Holocaust,* 191.

52. On this point, see Pierre Ayçoberry, *The Nazi Question: An Essay on the Interpretations of National Socialism,* trans. Robert Hurley (New York, 1981), 137.

53. For a survey of this approach, see Anson Rabinbach, "Towards a Marxist Theory of Fascism: A Report on Developments in West Germany," *New German Critique* 3 (1974), 127–54.

54. Cited in Eike Hennig, *Bürgerliche Gesellschaft und Faschismus in Deutschland: Ein Forschungsbericht* (Frankfurt am Main, 1977), 56–59.

55. Both conceptions are largely indifferent to the victims of the "annihilatory impulses" of the regimes in question. Saul Friedländer, "Nazism: Fascism or Totalitarianism?" in *The Rise of the Nazi Regime: Historical Reassessments,* ed. Charles S. Maier, Stanley Hoffmann, and Andrew Gould (Boulder, 1986), 25–34.

56. See, for example, Martin Broszat, "Alltagsgeschichte der NS-Zeit," in *Nach Hitler,* 131–39.

57. For an extended discussion, see Mary Nolan, "The *Historikerstreit* and Social History," in this volume, p. 224. See also Martin Broszat, "Widerstand: Der Bedeutungswandel eines Begriffs der Zeitgeschichte," *Süddeutsche Zeitung* 22/23 November 1986, 7.

58. Wolffsohn, 42.

59. Ibid.

60. For a detailed examination of all aspects of this problem, see *New German Critique* 37 (Winter 1986), "Special Issue on the German Question," especially Sigrid Meuschel, "On the Eruption of the German Volcano," 127–35.

61. Peter Glotz, "Ein Instrument der Entspannung," *Rheinischer Merkur/Christ und Welt* 45, 31 October 1986, 3; Karl Schlögel, *Die Mitte liegt ostwärts: Die Deutschen, der verlorene Osten und Mitteleuropa* (Berlin, 1986), and Hans-Georg Betz, "'Deutschlandpolitik' on the Margins: On the Evolution of Contemporary New Right Nationalism in the Federal Republic," *New German Critique* 44 (Spring/Summer 1988).

62. On the Greens and the Jewish issue, see Andrei S. Markovits, "Was ist das 'Deutsche' an den Grünen? Vergangenheitsaufarbeitung als Voraussetzung politischer Zukunftsbewältigung," in *Die Grünen: Letzte Wahl?* ed. Otto Kallscheuer (Berlin, 1986), 146–64; Joschka Fischer, "Wir Kinder der Kapitulanten," *Die Zeit,* 10 May 1985; "Grosse Anfrage des Abgeordneten Ströbele und der Fraktion Die Grünen zum Antisemitismus in der BRD," 27 February 1986, Drucksache 10/5551; and the commentary by Klaus Hartung in the *Tageszeitung,* 28 February, 1986, which criticized the Greens for their "saturated anti-anti-Semitism and routinized concern."

63. On the Fassbinder Controversy, see *Die Fassbinder-Kontroverse, oder das Ende der Schonzeit,* ed. Heiner Lichtenstein (Königstein, 1986); Special Issue on the German-Jewish Controversy, *New German Critique* 38 (Spring/Summer 1986); and on

72   *Anson Rabinbach*

the German Left and the Jews, Jessica Benjamin and Anson Rabinbach, "Germans, Leftists, Jews," *New German Critique* 31 (Winter, 1984), 183–95.

64. Cited in Carl-Christian Kaiser, "Für den Schaden ist gesorgt," *Die Zeit* 19, 10 May 1985, 4.

65. Y. Michal Bodemann, "Die 'Überwölbung' von Auschwitz: Der jüdische Faktor in der Mythologie der Wende-Republik," *Ästhetik und Kommunikation: Beiträge zur politischen Erziehung* 56 (1984): 45.

66. Ibid., 44.

67. See Hans-Georg Betz, "Deutschlandpolitik on the Margins: On the Evolution of Contemporary New Right Nationalism in the Federal Republic," *New German Critique* 44 (Spring/Summer 1988).

68. Cited in *Bitburg and Beyond: Encounters in American, German and Jewish History,* ed. Ilya Levkov (New York, 1987), 95.

69. Ibid., 104.

70 .Witticism attributed to Fred Siegel.

71. *Bitburg and Beyond*, 39.

72. Raul Hilberg, "Bitburg as Symbol," *Bitburg in Moral and Political Perspective*, 19.

73. *Eine Rede und ihre Wirkung: Die Rede des Bundespräsidenten Richard von Weizsäcker vom 8. Mai 1985*, ed. Ulrich Gill and Winfried Steffani (Berlin, 1986), 180. Less frequently acknowledged is the negative reaction to the speech within CDU/CSU circles, especially among the rightist organizations of *Heimatvertriebene* who interpreted the speech as a public declaration of disinterest in their "legal rights" in the East. Herbert Czaja, "Recht auf die Heimat—für alle? Kritische Fragen zur Rede—ein Jahr danach," *Eine Rede und ihre Wirkung*, 94.

74. Gunter Hofmann, "Der Präses und der Populist," *Die Zeit*, 31 May 1985, 3.

75. Cited ibid.

76. Ernst Nolte, "Vergangenheit, die nicht vergehen will," *Frankfurter Allgemeine Zeitung*, 6 June 1986, in *Historikerstreit*.

77. Ernst Nolte, "Between Myth and Revisionism? The Third Reich in the Perspective of the 1980s," *Aspects of the Third Reich*, ed. H. W. Koch (London, 1985), 17–38.

78. Ibid., 36.

79. Joachim Fest, "Die geschuldete Erinnerung: Zur Kontroverse über die Unvergleichbarkeit der nationalsozialistischen Massenverbrechen," *Frankfurter Allgemeine Zeitung*, 29 August 1986, 23, in *Historikerstreit*.

80. Eberhard Jäckel, "Die elende Praxis der Untersteller: Das Einmalige der nationalsozialistischen Verbrechen," *Die Zeit* 38, 12 September 1986, 3, in *Historikerstreit*.

81. Fest, "Die geschuldete Erinnerung," 23.

82. Andreas Hillgruber, *Zweierlei Untergang: Die Zerschlagung des Deutschen Reiches und das Ende des europäischen Judentums* (Berlin, 1986).

83. The second essay was an expanded version of his concluding remarks at the 1984 International Congress "Mord an den europäischen Juden im Zweiten Weltkrieg" in Stuttgart.

84. Jürgen Habermas, "Eine Art Schadensabwicklung," *Die Zeit* 29, 11 July 1986; English translation in *New German Critique*, 44 (Spring/Summer 1988) and *Historikerstreit*.

85. Nolte, "Between Myth and Revisionism?" 28.

86. Habermas, "Eine Art Schadensabwicklung"

87. See Jürgen Kocka, "Hitler sollte nicht durch Stalin und Pol Pot verdrängt wer-

den," *Frankfurter Rundschau*, 23 September 1986, 10; and Heinrich August Winkler, "Auf ewig in Hitlers Schatten: Zum Streit über das Geschichtsbild der Deutschen," *Frankfurter Rundschau*, 14 November 1986, 20, in *Historikerstreit*.

88. See, for example, Gordon Craig, "The War of the German Historians," *The New York Review of Books*, 15 January 1987, 16–19.

89. Winkler, 20.

90. Andreas Hillgruber, "Deutschland und die Deutschen—'Gescheiterte Grossmacht'—gescheiterte Nation?" In *Die Last der Nation: Fünf Beiträge über Deutschland und die Deutschen* (Düsseldorf, 1984), 17.

91. A clue to Hillgruber's attitude can be found in an earlier essay when he cites the *"finis/Germaniae"* verdict of the World War I General Groener, and quotes revealingly, "Unconsciously we strove for world domination . . . before we secured our continental position." Andreas Hillgruber, " 'Revisionismus'—Kontinuität und Wandel in der Aussenpolitik der Weimarer Republik," in *Die Last der Nation*, 59.

92. *Der Spiegel*, 5 January 1987, 25.

93. Hans Mommsen, "Suche nach der 'verlorenen Geschichte'?" *Merkur*, September/October 1986, 865, in *Historikerstreit*.

94. Michael Stürmer, "Was Geschichte Wiegt," *FAZ*, 26 November 1986, 1, in *Historikerstreit*.

95. Charles Maier, *"Jenseits des Historikerstreits:* The Significance of the *Historikerstreit,"* in *German Politics and Society* 13 (February 1988), 5.

96. See Nolan, "The *Historikerstreit* and Social History."

97. See Saul Friedländer, "Some Reflections on the Historicization of National Socialism," p. 88; Dan Diner, "Between Aporia and Apology: On the Limits of Historicizing National Socialism," in this volume, p. 133.

98. See Hans-Ulrich Wehler, *Entsorgung der deutschen Vergangenheit? Ein polemischer Essay zum "Historikerstreit"* (Munich, 1988). Nolte unrepentently defends himself in *Das Vergehen der Vergangenheit: Antwort an meine Kritiker im sogenannten Historikerstreit* (Berlin, 1987).

99. James Markham, "The New NATO: A Pronounced German Accent," *The New York Times*, 1 August 1988, A4.

100. See Betz, "Deutschlandpolitik."

Part Two

Historicization: Placing National Socialism in History

4.   A Plea for the Historicization of National Socialism

Martin Broszat

How "historical" is National Socialism forty years after the capitulation of the Third Reich? Does Hitler still block access to the rest of German history? What does "bygone history" mean? Such questions, which could easily be multiplied, are not directed at historians alone. They are equally relevant to the issues of individual and collective memory, legal judgments about the past, political education, and the media's approach to contemporary history. Yet even to raise these questions immediately arouses suspicion, for in the conceptual world of the present, National Socialism functions as a kind of indispensable negative standard for civic education and as the anti-model for a political order based on freedom, peace, and the rule of the law.

It is also true, however, that the moral impact of the Nazi past has progressively exhausted itself. The Nazi era has lost much of its singularity in light of new catastrophes and atrocities, and we are left with a set of convictions, as safe as they are vague, that no longer carry any moral force. Phrases like "the National Socialist reign of terror" have become tired stereotypes, and only a new, more nuanced historical analysis can make them morally useful again. The key to the question of how "historical" National Socialism has become lies in the shifting relationship between morality and historical understanding.

The Nazi Shock Continues

"Someday, perhaps, the popular and scholarly fascination with a few insane years of Germany's history will fade away, but that day is not yet in sight." This is the remark not of a German observer of the contemporary media scene in the Federal Republic, but of the American historian Istvan Deak. It was provoked by the imposing quantity of specialist literature that continues to appear in English on National Socialism (*New York Review of Books*, May 31, 1984). For Deak, the obvious reason for this astonishing scholarly production is that "we have not yet succeeded in mastering the shock" provoked by the mass criminality of National Socialism. This is true not only of

Israel, but also along the East Coast of the United States, where hundreds of thousands of émigrés and survivors of the Nazi period from central and eastern Europe found refuge.

But it is not the victims alone who keep the memory alive. Nazi Germany's unequalled powers of influence, mobilization, and achievement as well as the fear of old or new fascism's potential for success are still very much with us. The legacy of National Socialism also includes a sensitivity or hypersensitivity to any hints of fascism in the present. In light of the many related forms of totalitarian manipulation, ideological legitimation through violence, and irrational protest movements, the impression persists that "still, the thing exists" (Istvan Deak).

The contradictory nature and apparent irreconcilability of many aspects of National Socialism have helped keep both the discussion surrounding it and its influence alive. The confusing linguistic and intellectual character of that "righteously persecuting innocence," which made its appearance in the spring of 1933 with the activists of the Nazi takeover, called up in Karl Kraus's mind the image of a witches' sabbath, a "third *Walpurgisnacht*." The pseudo-religious fervor with which the "nonperson" Hitler entranced large segments of the German people, including its most educated elements, drove many postwar historians in Germany and elsewhere toward demonic interpretations with little explanatory power. Syberberg's distressing cinematic recreation of the Third Reich using a phantasmagorical montage of words, images, and music was inspired by the regime's irrational incongruities. In the intellectual sphere, a mixture of moral revulsion and fascination with violence has led to the concept of a "fascist aesthetic" (Susan Sontag), while in the area of popular culture an international pulp literature on the Third Reich and the new genre of "Nazi adventure films" have sprung up. In *this* way as well, the cultural shock has taken on a life of its own with the mass production of a distorted picture of the Third Reich against which historians, with their marginal influence, can do little.

The Germans have not been the only ones concerned with the National Socialist period, nor should they be the only ones to dictate its characterization. What is peculiar to the German situation is the necessity and difficulty of fitting the Nazi period into the overall course of national history. Forty years' distance has not helped this enterprise very much. No matter which history book one opens, the tone becomes cold and distant as soon as the author broaches the Third Reich. The ability to feel one's way empathetically into the web of historical interconnections evaporates along with the pleasure of narration. The history of National Socialism is no longer repressed; it has instead degenerated into dreary required reading.

One thing has become clear, however: the Hitler period and the agony of Weimar that preceded it, though they may appear short in retrospect, represent a particularly dramatic and crowded chapter in German history. Their meaning and impact cannot be measured either by their short duration or through their contrast with the much longer, stable, successful, and in many ways "cleansing" history of the Federal Republic since that era. One suspects that the colorless character of the historiography on the Third Reich does not correspond to the intensity of people's memories of the period, whether positive or negative, or to the importance of those memories—their historical consciousness—for German nationalism and the German state.

However painful the Nazi period proved to be for many Germans, the experience of the National Socialist "community of fate" still shapes historical consciousness. Its influence remains especially strong since it was the last instance of a shared national history. The attempts to replace the legacy of the Nazi era with a historical consciousness for the Federal Republic run into difficulties because the postnational experience of the FRG is very different, less emotional as well as less singular, from the experience of National Socialism. West Germany is a provisional entity that resulted from a break with national history. The affirmation it has gradually won from the majority of its people has expressed itself less in outspoken declarations and manifestations than in quiet, positive habituation to a pleasant community of material well-being, law, and civilization.

It has been said that the National Socialist past is to blame for the blocking of a more forceful historical consciousness in the Federal Republic. In a certain sense the opposite is also true: precisely because the FRG is integrated into Western political culture and can only become an object of national identification to a limited extent, the memory of the last days of a united Germany has remained alive at a deeper level of the collective consciousness. Its existence at some level explains the feelings of solidarity with East Germans, who share with West Germans (but not with Austrians) an entire past history as a single nation-state as well as the terrible second half of the Hitler era.

Forty Years of Research on National Socialism

Historians' confrontation with National Socialism took place under special conditions in the Federal Republic. West Germany could not, like the German Democratic Republic, simply place itself in the tradition of the antifascist vanguard of the working class and fancy itself the heir to the "other Germany." In fact, West Germany relied to a great degree during postwar reconstruction on the old elite functionaries who had previously served the National Socialist regime. As a result, it was necessary for the Federal Republic to take a clear official distance from its Nazi past as a compensatory gesture toward the occupying powers and later allies. On the one hand this gesture took the form of an indulgent forgiveness for—or silence about—concrete personal responsibility during the National Socialist period; on the other hand, it meant requiring any representative of the new state and society to reject Nazism unconditionally. However little willingness there may have been to confront the Nazi past in an honest way, open violations of this last norm were met with sharp sanctions.

Within this overall framework, the German historical profession began to reorient itself. Leadership devolved almost of necessity on those contemporary historians whose university careers had been interrupted after 1933 for political or racial reasons, who had been forced to emigrate, or who had gone into "internal exile" during the Nazi period (Friedrich Meinecke, Hans Rothfels, Gerhard Ritter, Ludwig Dehio, Ludwig Bergsträsser, Hans Herzfeld, Franz Schnabel et al.). Most of these historians were of a Christian-conservative or liberal-conservative orientation.

The new research did not limit itself to the documentation and description of the German resistance in order to defend against accusations of collective guilt. It also undertook a general revision of the prevailing historicist tradition, thanks in part to representatives of the new "democratic" discipline of political science (Heinrich Otto v.d. Gablentz, Theodor Eschenburg, Arnold Bergsträsser, Hans Rosenberg, Dolf Sternberger et al.). Since the 1950s this discipline had exercised a strong influence on the emerging research on National Socialism and the Weimar Republic. This development was enhanced through familiarity with work already begun by German émigrés in the United States (Franz Neumann, Ernst Fraenkel, Hannah Arendt) and above all by several Anglo-Saxon historians (Alan Bullock, Wheeler-Bennett, Trevor-Roper, et al.). Finally, the extensive documentation assembled for the Nuremberg trials and the successive release of large caches of documents previously confiscated by the Allies enabled the Weimar and Nazi periods to emerge as a principal battleground and object of study in a worldwide wave of research on contemporary history.

By the beginning of the 1970s, with increasing German participation, such research had exposed all politically and morally sensitive areas of National Socialist rule to scrutiny, if not to exhaustive exploration. In the foreground stood the documentation of the specifically National Socialist philosophy and political views. Only gradually, with increasing "academization," did other topics receive more attention, among them the internal structure and dynamics of the regime, economic and social conditions, literature, art and entertainment, popular opinion, and everyday life in the Third Reich. Under the influence of research on comparative fascism and of leftist, neo-Marxist interpretations of fascism, German history was also subjected to a general, comparativist, and sociological level of observation.

All in all, the growing autonomy of research over the course of time has brought about an increasing historicization of the questions asked. The resulting changes in perception can be illustrated with regard to several areas of history. The development of ideas about the historical preconditions for National Socialism is a convenient place to start.

The typical reaction to the contemporaneity or temporal proximity of the recently ended Third Reich has been to adopt the broad perspective of national history and to trace a line of development reaching far into the past—from Luther to Hitler, or at least from the German Romantics to National Socialism. This perspective viewed the catastrophe of 1945, which seemed to have utterly destroyed all the hopes and achievements of the recent German past, as the clogged mouth of a river fed by all the polluted and polluting currents of German history. Friedrich Meinecke recommended that Germans examine their history not with loving understanding but with great "firmness" in the search for the cause of the catastrophe.

The questionable elements of such a perspective are well known: among them the many stages and forms of German defensiveness toward Western humanist culture and the Enlightenment, beginning in the seventeenth and eighteenth centuries; the rigorously overblown or mythologized ideas of a "German cultural nation" and *Volksgeist* that arose under conditions of national political frustration after the Napoleonic wars; and finally, most significantly, political development influenced (especially in the nineteenth century) far too weakly by a liberal bourgeoisie and far too strongly by monarchist authority and preindustrial elites. The retrograde and stagnant constitution of the Bismarckian-Wilhelmian nation-state is another such element.

These and other elements have become in a certain sense commonplaces of the post–National Socialist revision of modern German history. Every historian knows his Plessner, and the idea of the "latecomer nation" has firmly established itself within the repertoire of conceptual instruments used to analyze Germany's special path of development.[1] In the 1960s, the concept of a narrowly circumscribed "prefascist" era appeared in place of a long-term national (and strongly intellectual) derivation of National Socialism. This era was seen as the period of the imperial nation-state with its internal "dislocations" in the midst of the general crisis of liberalism and modernization—a crisis that took place in turn within the context of the capitalism, imperialism, and threat of socialism that were shared by all European countries at the time.

The most recent discussion surrounding Germany's "special path" of historical development has, thanks to substantial contributions from non-German historians, significantly reduced the hypotheses concerning the prefascist potential of Wilhelmine government and society. From a comparative perspective (between Germany and Great Britain), this discussion has raised questions about whether the *weight* of the internal tensions that were especially explosive in Germany was great enough to render integration impossible except through war or fascism.

In the meantime, a broad international consensus has emerged. The real prelude to National Socialism and the "epoch of fascism" (Ernst Nolte) in general was the First World War and the new threat posed by the Bolshevik Revolution that arose in its wake. The result was aggressive antirepublican and antisocialist protest movements, ones that were no longer merely ideological, but now motivated by activist, pseudo-revolutionary energy and determination. Such movements appeared first and foremost as a by-product of the depressing social and political conditions in countries that had lost the war or fared badly in it (Italy and Hungary, for example). Despite the enormous burdens inherited by the Weimar Republic (which this essay will not recapitulate), one can offer a heuristic hypothesis similar to theories about the

Wilhelmine nation-state. The German elites and bourgeoisie adjusted gradually to the Republic during the brief period of consolidation between 1924 and 1929. This process could have created the necessary conditions for success had it not been cut short by the Depression and the ensuing political crisis of Weimar.

Forty years of intensive research on the historical preconditions for National Socialism have left few traces of the determinism with which they began, but have substituted something quite different: the restoration of historicity to both the imperial and Weimar periods. Releasing these two eras from the role of mere "preludes" was only possible after historians had become sensitive to the long-term determinants of National Socialism. Only then was the reduction of whole epochs to "forerunner" status no longer necessary. This development was not, as some have claimed, the result of a "neoconservative shift in direction" within the historical profession, but a turn toward authenticity and concreteness with regard to moral issues in history.

A Plea for a Historicization of National Socialism

The question of the historicity of National Socialism, of whether historical understanding must halt helplessly in the face of the Nazi phenomenon, has become more and more important. Hitler's fatally false answer to the fundamental questions posed by his time and by the course of German development—his accelerating flight into egocentric, aggressive, expansionist philosophy and policy as he misjudged the domestic and international limits of his rule—none of this will be altered or masked by a reinterpretation of history. What will be viewed with a new understanding are the many misguided motives, longings for change, and attempts at problem-solving that went on below the level of ideologically driven politics and that help to explain the great attractiveness of National Socialism to so many. It is difficult to historicize the Nazi regime because of the need to view its two sides both together and separately: the proximity and interdependence of its capacity for success and its criminal energy, of its mobilization for achievement and for destruction, of people's participation and dictatorship. It is here, above all, that the current overall picture of the Nazi period clashes with the actual results of detailed historical studies.

Such studies have analyzed and illuminated the countless inner contradictions of National Socialism. One of these is the discrepancy between the nominal political order and the real one; between the harmonizing and organizing pretensions of the Führer-principle and its polycratic, disorganizing effects. Other complex and contradictory features of the regime include the different areas and levels of administrative, legal, economic, social, and cultural development in the Third Reich with their varying degrees of independence, their own inner logics, and their creative transmutations of Nazi ideology; the complex, improvisatory process of decision-making; the qualitatively distinct phases in the structure and politics of the regime and its heterogeneous potential for success and domination; populist sensitivity side by side with brute force; the manifold ways that inherited representatives and institutions with their established interests, traditions, and beliefs were assimilated; and so forth.

The results of the last twenty years of detailed research have not yet been translated into a "new objectivity" with regard to the overall picture and historical presentation of the Nazi past. No history of the National Socialist *period* has yet emerged from the histories of the National Socialist *dictatorship*. The historiography is still dominated by the overwhelming impact of the catastrophic end and final condition of the regime. This impact is used as a golden thread to explain a posteriori the motives, methods, and stages of National Socialism. The dominant view of the Nazi era stresses its systematic character, its calculated stages of evolution and goal-oriented worldview, and its control by a Machiavellian system of division of labor under Hitler's leadership. In order to highlight the contradiction and tension between a retrospective approach that aims at drawing conclusions and one that is prospective and historicizing, we must now turn to a discussion of specific examples.

The large number of local and regional studies now available on the emergence of the NSDAP as a mass movement before 1933 provide a much more nuanced picture of this process and render the motives that drew the "masses" to the Nazi party more clearly recognizable. Among other things, the following becomes apparent: what in retrospect appears to have been a "massive earthquake" in the political landscape, a "catastrophic collapse" of political liberalism, or "drastic radicalization" of political confrontations (including a marked rise in political violence) looks far less dramatic from the vantage point of the provincial and rural areas where the NSDAP first made its big advances. For example, "liberalism" in the countryside, which originally took the form of farmers' associations (in Schleswig-Holstein, for instance), had long been in decay and had disappeared almost everywhere by the time the agrarian crisis in 1928 began, to be replaced by nervous farmers' parties.

It is also clear that the National Socialist "infiltration" or "takeover" of many formerly liberal provincial interest organizations was often accompanied by the replacement of older functionaries, by the rejuvenation of the leadership, and by the representation of previously underrepresented social groups (e.g., small farmers, rural craftsmen, etc.). It is now much more evident just how different the political-social profile of the NSDAP was in each individual case, and how much it adjusted itself to particular surroundings. The will of the leadership from above could only set in motion those below who were already strongly motivated by an impatience for change and by long pent-up social anxieties which the economic crisis had pushed closer to the surface. The manipulative abilities of Nazi propaganda could only address that potential mobility, the latent desire to break out of encrusted social relations and to cease submitting to traditional authority, that was already present.

To generalize for a moment, these facts mean that during the Depression

National Socialism was able to rally behind itself nearly all those discontented individuals who for reasons of confession or tradition were immune to the appeal of either Marxist socialism or political catholicity. As the latest research has shown, such people were to be found not just among the lower middle classes and rural population, but also to a considerable degree among unorganized workers and the upper middle class. Disenchantment among these groups was evidence that many needed social reforms had failed to materialize during Weimar. It was a reaction to the strong social stratification of German society that had existed since the imperial period, and hence was a kind of delayed bourgeois revolution fuelled by a backward-looking ideology.

All of this also suggests that the vague populist attractiveness of National Socialism carried more weight than the ideological indoctrination of its mass base. And it was in large part thanks to this populist appeal that the Nazis were able to triumph during the last phase of the Weimar Republic. From the standpoint of many of its voters and supporters, National Socialism was not a radical movement directed against the Weimar welfare state, but rather a middle way between democracy and the old authoritarian state which Brüning and von Papen still favored but which had now become obsolete.

The views expounded above contradict the common image (itself a creation of Nazi propaganda) of the German "masses" held under the spell of political irrationality and fanaticized by the hypnotic powers of Hitler. Both before and after 1933, mass support for National Socialism only partly expressed agreement with Hitler's worldview, one never entirely discernible to his contemporaries and one whose consequences could not be foreseen. Widespread backing for the Nazi regime derived rather from the simultaneous (though logically and politically contradictory) need among the middle classes both for protection and for participative mobilization. With its slogans stressing upward mobility, recovery, and renewal, National Socialism represented a source of conservative legitimation as well as an impetus for action.

Finally, thanks to the thousands of mini-"Führer" positions it could dispense, the Third Reich offered very real opportunities for dynamic young forces from the middle classes to prove themselves. Through competition with the "old" elites, these people could deploy their energies and improvisatory skills while at the same time enjoying the security and insurance against risk provided by the regime. Ideology, even in the form of the racial theory of the survival of the fittest, was often nothing more than a superstructure to provide legitimacy. More important and historically effective was a newly cultivated type, the National Socialist "special leader" [*Sonderführer*], the prototype for the politically protected and dependent entrepreneur who nevertheless possessed wide-ranging powers. Special leaders spread during the Third Reich to all areas of society, could be used for practically any task, and brought with them good qualifications for facing new challenges during the primitive capitalist period of reconstruction and economic boom that followed the currency reform in the Federal Republic.

In viewing the catastrophic consequences of the Nazi regime's ideological policies and their correspondence to Hitler's insane racial and geopolitical ideas with the benefit of hindsight, it is tempting to explain the dynamics of the Third Reich in a primarily ideological fashion. In answer to this perspective, which is actually less plausible than it seems, detailed studies of the society and mentality of the period have emphasized not only the great importance of social forces, but also their pre-1933 origins and post-1945 effects. To illuminate the social dynamism of National Socialism is not to cover up the moral consequences of the system of norms derived from the Nazi ideological worldview, but rather to integrate elements that seem to pertain only to the Nazis into a broader view of long-term changes within German society.

Let us take for example the subject of resistance and persecution in the Third Reich. The didactic need to create unequivocal standards and images, especially with regard to this topic, has often led to unhistorical monumentalization and to the avoidance of taboo subjects. The "legacy" of the conservative resistance movement to Hitler, readily appropriated for legitimizing purposes even by West German political forces outside of the labor movement, has often masked the fact that the resisters' ideas about constitutional, domestic, and foreign policy issues had little in common with the modern self-understanding of the Federal Republic. The "discovery" of this fact has almost always led to controversies in which the contrast between authentic historical reconstruction and the use of the resistance movement for pedagogical purposes has revealed itself in exemplary fashion. To clarify this point, we will examine a recent example which is especially well suited to illustrate the pattern.

The former lord mayor of Leipzig, Carl Goerdeler, has long been considered a leading representative of the conservative opposition to Hitler. Gerhard Ritter's impressive biography is an imposing monument to him. Ritter claims that Goerdeler resigned his post as mayor in 1937 in protest over the cultural desecration occasioned by the removal of the Mendelssohn statue from the front of the Gewandhaus concert hall. In a recently completed study of the reaction of the German resistance to the regime's Jewish policies, the historian Christof Dipper has incontrovertibly shown that during the first years of the Third Reich, Goerdeler was in basic agreement with the limited legal measures designed to eliminate Jews from public life and even with the fundamental idea of the 1935 Nuremberg laws. Like many national conservatives in Germany and elsewhere, Goerdeler did not seem to condemn the revision of the principles of equality before the law and the reduction of the rights and freedoms of the Jewish minority as wrong. The documentation of these facts, disseminated with overtones of moral outrage, was greeted by leading opponents of National Socialism and admirers of Goerdeler with a storm of indignation and was perceived as a defamation of his character.

This example shows that for the "official" moral-political memory, which wishes to promote exemplars and must therefore monumentalize, the distinction between the National Socialist and the "other" Germany cannot easily be dispensed with. From a historical perspective, however, this black-and-white picture becomes blurred. From this point of view it is clear that almost all resistance during the Nazi period was, strictly speaking, only temporary and limited. Often it went hand in hand with passive tolerance or partial affirmation of, even active participation in, the ends of the regime. In light of the later development of National Socialist Jewish policy, the early, temporary, and moderate anti-Semitism of a man like Carl Goerdeler must be seen as one of those typical, decisive, and no longer revisable failures of the early conservative partners of Nazism. From a historical perspective, then, Germans' inability during the first years of the Third Reich to foresee the murderous radicalization of anti-Jewish measures and the growing arbitrariness of the Führer's absolutism represents an important moment in understanding the faulty judgments and faulty reactions of that time. Goerdeler's subsequent moral achievement, for which he paid with his life, was founded precisely upon an ability to work through his mistakes.

Finally, a last example to help characterize our problem. In recent years, social historians have shown a markedly increased interest in the social problems of the Third Reich. Their research has left behind the old institutional analysis of the German Labor Front (DAF) and its social policy–related propaganda, which concentrated mainly on the techniques of domination. In her book on Nazi social policy during World War II, Marie-Luise Recker has expounded in detail the plan for a universal social insurance system that was drawn up at the behest of the DAF in 1941/42. It was only a plan, to be sure, but one containing some of the fundamental ideas (e.g., state-guaranteed pensions indexed to the level of national wealth) that appeared in the 1950s as significant accomplishments of the FRG's social legislation. It is also noteworthy that the DAF plan appeared at almost the same time as the Beveridge Report, which laid the groundwork for the British Labour government's postwar social welfare reforms. The authors of the DAF plan, among them experts from the Labor Research Institute (founded in 1935) who had joined the NSDAP only after 1933, certainly helped pursue the goal of preserving the National Socialist system. Yet in the final analysis they also responded to the social-political exigencies of war—ones that were not specific to National Socialism and that were already familiar from the period 1914–18. In related areas of social legislation (improvements in the protection of minors, equalizing the status of white- and blue-collar wage earners), the Second World War brought with it in Germany a series of social policy innovations in spite of the largely manipulative and repressive function of the DAF.

This example shows that not all the historically significant developments that occurred in Germany during the Nazi period merely served the regime's goals of inhuman and dictatorial domination. The tendency has been to interpret all changes that took place during the Third Reich—in the economic and legal spheres, for example—from the perspective of their function in stabilizing the regime. This tendency still persists within the historical profession. This approach forces all pre- and non–National Socialist elements of German history under the aegis of the Nazi period and hermetically seals off those twelve years from both front and back. The fact that this epoch was in general one of infamy should not mean that its many social, economic, and civilizing forces and efforts at modernization must be deprived of their historical significance solely because of their connection with National Socialism.

Instead of a complete moral quarantine of the Hitler period, what is needed is a purging of our routinized conceptual and linguistic apparatus in order to free many perspectives on people and events from the straitjacket of the notion that the Nazi Regime was simply the all-encompassing rule of force. Above all, a new, long-term view of the arena of modern German history in which National Socialism played itself out must be developed. When this is done, the place of Nazism within that history will have to be reassessed in many respects. A clearer focus on long-term modernizing tendencies and social pathologies that exploded into extreme violence when legitimized and combined under the Nazis will become possible. From such a new perspective historians will also be able to examine critically, but without across-the-board denunciations, many of the influences exerted by the Nazi period on the social and legal constitution of the Federal Republic—a task that has hitherto been taboo.

One cannot bemoan the blockade imposed on the German historical consciousness by National Socialism and at the same time insist that the Hitler regime be kept under lock and key, inaccessible to historical understanding. The "normalization" of our historical consciousness cannot in the long run exclude the Nazi period, nor can it succeed by bypassing it. A total distancing from the Nazi past is still a form of repression, the creation of a taboo. It can create the impression, and the longer it goes on the more this is the case, of serving as a compensatory alibi for the restoration of historicism to the "healthy" areas of the past lying before 1933 and after 1945. Lifting this blockade in favor of a moral sensitivization of history, itself inspired by the experience of National Socialism—that is the aim and hope of this plea for the historicization of the Nazi period.

Note

1. Helmuth Plessner formulated the idea that much of Germany's supposedly peculiar development stemmed from the late timing of her evolution, compared to France and Britain. See H. Plessner, *Die verspätete Nation* (Stuttgart, 1959)—ED.

5. Some Reflections on the Historicization of National Socialism

Saul Friedländer

The "Historians' Debate," which drew considerable attention within the German intellectual world as well as outside Germany, was, in essence, a political-ideological confrontation which crystallized around the writing—or rewriting—of the history of the Nazi period. This confrontation can be analyzed on the political-ideological level; it can also be considered in terms of diverging attitudes toward the issue of German identity—a level which tallies in large part with the former, but is not identical with it; finally, it must be considered from the historiographical point of view, i.e., in terms of the specificity or nonspecificity of Nazism and its crimes, particularly as far as the extermination of the Jews is concerned.

Independent of this debate, however, though in relation to it, a concept was also employed which had first been brought to wider attention by the Munich historian Martin Broszat in an article published in *Merkur* in May 1985: the "Historicization of National Socialism."[1] Martin Broszat's article was, in fact, an overall presentation of some converging aspects of German historiography of the Nazi era which developed, in part, beginning in the late 1960s, and, much more significantly, during the late 1970s and the 1980s, and which, *if considered as a whole*, represent an important transformation of the historical conception of the Nazi era. In fact, two different reelaborations of the history of National Socialism are taking place simultaneously: they need to be clearly distinguished.

The historiographical arguments used by Ernst Nolte and those who share his views leave little to a genuine scholarly debate. When "Between Myth and Revisionism: National-Socialism from the Perspective of the 1980s" appeared in 1985 and "Eine Vergangenheit die nicht vergehen will" in 1986,[2] the arguments Nolte advanced in these essays seemed to many untenable. These arguments, familiar by now, need not be repeated here.

The problem of historicization, on the other hand, as presented in Martin Broszat's *Merkur* article and in other writings, belongs within the realm of a fundamental scholarly-scientific dialogue, a dialogue between historians who may indeed have differing ideological positions and different scientific out-looks, but who nonetheless share some basic concerns as far as the attitudes towards Nazism and its crimes are concerned.

When, for instance, Martin Broszat published his "Hitler and the Genesis of the 'Final Solution': An Assessment of David Irving's Thesis" in 1977, and when, in 1982, Hans Mommsen continued the same line of thought in his "The Realization of the Unthinkable: The 'Final Solution of the Jewish Question' in the Third Reich,"[3] these two contributions—which certainly aimed at changing the traditional presentation of the genesis of the "Final Solution"—led to significant controversies; yet for all concerned, these con-troversies belonged to the realm of genuine historiographical debate.

One postulate, however, is shared by all: "Both with the demand to in-tegrate National Socialism into a larger historical framework and with the warning against pedagogically motivated taboos, Ernst Nolte and more pro-gressively inclined historians agree," wrote Hans Mommsen in the course of the recent debate.[4] Nobody disagrees, I would think, with the necessity of eliminating taboos or any kind of didactic history. The ways part after all ta-boos are eliminated.

At the very outset, let me present as clearly as possible the core of the thesis which will be developed here. For any historian, historicization, understood in its most general sense as the approach to the Nazi era with all the methods at the disposal of the historian, without any forbidden questions, is self-evident. However, what gives rise to a possible problem is the open-ended-ness of the process which does not offer any clear conceptual alternative. In such a situation, as we shall see, the process itself can, *particularly within the current ideological context,* lead to unexpected results.

First of all, I will attempt to analyse the meaning of historicization as such on a purely conceptual level; I will then show how the indeterminate nature of historicization, mainly because of the context in which it appeared, can lead to various shifts in meaning; finally, I intend to venture some thoughts about the critical discourse which could accompany this approach to the his-tory of Nazism and about its limits as well.

I

In his "Plea" and other writings, Martin Broszat has not offered any precise definition of historicization; on the one hand, he indicated what the traditional approaches to the Nazi past were which the process of historiciza-tion aimed at reconsidering and, on the other hand, what the new modes of historical understanding of that period were which historicization was gener-ally attempting to attain.

The traditional views of the Nazi period which historicization questions are easily defined: "The greater the historical distance becomes," writes Martin Broszat in *Nach Hitler: Der schwierige Umgang mit unserer Geschichte,*

the more important [it is] to understand that the act of separating out the Hitler period
from the broader scope of history and of historical thought takes place in a certain
sense already when the Nazi regime is treated in a largely political-moral sense and not
with the same differentiated historical methodology used for other epochs, when it is
subjected to less thoroughly weighed judgments that are delivered in a coarser, less
nuanced language than is customary, when, in other words, for good didactic reasons,
the historical presentation of the National Socialist regime is given a kind of special
treatment [*Sonderbehandlung*] in methodological terms.

Whether today the main thrust of historical writing about Nazism can still be
defined in terms used by Martin Broszat is a moot question. But what is implied is that the traditional paradigm still somehow weighs on the historian's
vision of the past. The characteristics of this traditional vision are, one may
assume, an emphasis on the ideological, political, and criminal aspects of the
Nazi phenomenon, i.e., on the destruction of the democratic system, the expansion of state control over society and of terror over those considered enemies of the regime or outcasts, emphasis on the "conquest of *Lebensraum*,"
on racial policies and global struggle against the Jews, as well as other massive
expressions of the criminality of the system. This paradigm, which indeed implies a fundamental moral distancing from the epoch and which—because of
the political, ideological, and moral issues raised by the Nazi era—considers the period 1933–1945 as a clearly identifiable field of enquiry, would be
recognizable, for instance, in Karl-Dietrich Bracher's classic *The German
Dictatorship*.

  Whatever progress has already been made in terms of historicization from
the 1960s on, the implicit presence of this paradigm still leads, according to
Broszat, to an almost ritual attitude on the part of the historian approaching
the Nazi era:

What is peculiar to the German situation is the necessity and difficulty of fitting the
Nazi period into the overall course of national history. Forty years' distance has not
helped this enterprise very much. No matter which history book one opens, the tone
becomes cold and distant as soon as the author broaches Third Reich. The ability to
feel one's way emphathetically into the web of historical connections evaporates along
with the pleasure of narration. The history of National Socialism is no longer repressed;
it has instead degenerated into dreary required reading.

The definition of historicization is less precise than the definition of what historicization aims at changing. It seems nonetheless possible to sum up its ob-
jectives under four major points:
1. The study of the Nazi era should be similar to that of any other historical
phenomenon: it must avoid any limitation either in the questions posed or the
methodological approaches used.
2. The political-ideological-moral framework which still dominates the interpretation of the epoch should be replaced by a much more complex picture,
one in which the role of social continuities would find its proper place; the
black-and-white picture of the era should be replaced by a presentation of all

its contradictory aspects. It should be understood that the Nazi era cannot be judged only from the viewpoint of its catastrophic end, and that many aspects of life and social development during that era were not necessarily linked to bolstering the regime and its aims.

3. Both previous points and the very relativization of the centrality of the political perspective means a decisive relativization of the "1933–1945" framework and the reinsertion of the Nazi era within wider trends of historical evolution, common both to German history and to the history of the Western world.

4. The abrogation of the self-imposed distancing between the historian and the Nazi epoch as whole, i.e., the abrogation of the "imposed lesson" syndrome created by moral judgment on the Nazi era in its totality. The very presentation of the complex and contradictory aspects of that era will be the only possible basis for anchoring a renewed moral evaluation of history in general in light of the lessons drawn from the historicization of National Socialism: "A total distancing from the Nazi past is still a form of repression, the creation of a taboo. . . . Lifting this blockade in favor of a moral sensitivization of history, itself inspired by the experience of National Socialism— that is the aim and hope of this plea for the historicization of the Nazi period."

II

Differentiation and nuancing constitute the very essence of the historian's craft. However, the introduction into the picture of an ever-growing number of details, of ever-more subtle distinctions, without clearly aiming at a precise change of paradigm, may well create a fundamental transformation by itself, at least in so far as the dominant elements of the traditional picture disappear in what could well be a blurred juxtaposition of contradictory features. This in itself may well create a major problem for the historian of that era. Let me illustrate this by concentrating on precise dilemmas, directly linked to some of the characteristics of historicization as just defined.

The first dilemma is between upholding the traditional periodization "1933–45" or discarding it in favor of much wider perspectives. The relativization of the 1933–45 framework implies, almost by definition, the relativization of the essentially political-ideological-moral framework identified with the traditional approach to the epoch.

Since the 1960s, left-wing historians have been insisting on the basic continuity of the social structures and institutions which dominated the German scene since the end of the nineteenth century at least, and directly influenced the accession of the Nazis to power, provided Nazism with its necessary support and dynamism, and which did not disappear with the defeat of the Third Reich. On the other hand, they argued that—for conservative historians—to view Nazism as a temporary phenomenon imposed on Germany by Hitler and his party was supposedly an easy way to limit and circumscribe the damage and to cleanse German history—both before 1933 and after 1945—of any pernicious elements. One could argue that this ideological dichotomy is not entirely convincing: one can clearly perceive continuities, in particular between the pre-1933 period and the Third Reich, without discarding the decisiveness of the turning point represented by 1933 and, once again, by 1945. The new regime had a mobilizing and "potentializing" effect which made all the difference. The preexisting factors and social structures were the necessary breeding ground, but new political, social, and psychological circumstances gave the Third Reich its specificity. However, historicization as it is understood here goes one step further and draws the historian's attention to the necessity of including within the picture of the era any number of much more general, longitudinal processes. Many a "normal" social evolution could, indeed, in no way be encompassed within the twelve years of the Third Reich: such trends originated far before 1933 and continued to mark German society long after 1945.

Martin Broszat gives the interesting example of planning for overall social security, which started at the end of World War I, was developed through the 1920s and 1930s, presented as a full-fledged program by the research unit of the Deutsche Arbeitsfront in 1941/42 and was finally integrated in large part into the social security policies of the Federal Republic. Moreover, the plans presented in 1942 were very similar to the Beveridge Plan, prepared more or less at the same time, which became the basis of the British welfare state. We therefore have the example, within the Third Reich, of a longitudinal process very similar to one developing at the same time in an exemplary democracy. Let me suggest another example: the slow process of emancipation of the German woman during the Wilhelminian and the Weimar periods was considerably accelerated during the Nazi era—against all the ideological tenets of the regime—and, no doubt, it influenced even more rapid developments in the same direction within West German society since the end of the war.

One could add any number of similar long-term developmental processes, subject to acceleration or various transformations during the Nazi period, and this quite independently of the policies or ideology of the regime. Those various transformations would fall largely within the wider category of the impetus towards modernization linked to the National Socialist era. Over the past two decades, a considerable number of studies have brought to light the most varied aspects of this modernization: when considered as a whole, they show that the attention of the researchers shifts to the general problems of modernization, away from the specificity of National Socialism. The question, therefore, is one of relevance, or, more precisely, of the relative relevance of developments of this kind for an overall history of the Nazi era.

The specificity of the epoch seems to reside precisely in those new elements which were introduced in the realm of the ongoing and preexisting processes when Hitler came to power. Many trends which existed much before 1933 were then potentialized, concretized, instrumentalized for political purposes and for the transformation of society.

In the sphere of ideologies, anti-Semitism or eugenics certainly existed before 1933, as did theories about the expulsion of the Jews and even their eradication, as well as theories regarding the possible eradication of carriers of hereditary diseases, etc. However, within the vast field of theories, it is the appearance of the political conditions which made for the concretization of these theories, their transformation into policies—whatever the dynamics of these transformations may have been—which emerges as the essential factor: what was potential becomes reality. After all, no mentally ill patients were exterminated in England or the United States, notwithstanding widespread eugenic thinking, nor were they in any danger in the Weimar Republic either. The answer would probably be that concentrating on the specifically criminal dimension, one which indeed was potentialized by the accession of the Nazis to power, is precisely what is too simple in the traditional image, and that long-term, "neutral" processes should be considered along with the traditionally perceived developments. In this hypothetical exchange, the response would stress the issue of relative weight: any long-term process can be introduced into the picture; however, for the historian—notwithstanding the complexity and the additional layers so added—a choice of focus remains essential. Such a choice of focus seems practically impossible if the 1933–45 framework, with the potentializing effect it implies and the specific elements it contains, is relativized too much. This is not a purely theoretical discussion. If one moves from the level of the monograph to the general picture which historicization is explicitly aiming at, then one wonders if the Enabling Act or the law "for the reestablishment of the professional civil service," i.e., the formal end of the democratic system and the legal beginning of the antiSemitic measures, two landmarks of the year 1933, should not necessarily remain dominant elements in a landscape where there are many hills but a number of volcanoes as well. In short, how far can the new political dimension introduced by Hitler's accession to power be relativized without entirely changing the overall landscape?

The second dilemma is that of "distance." As mentioned, historicization aims at abrogating the syndrome of "required reading," the automatic distancing of the historian from his subject as soon as he reaches the Nazi era. No doubt, the intention is not to urge for empathy with the criminal aspects in this era, but rather to abandon the kind of generalized quarantine supposedly imposed up to now on the epoch as a whole.

Although the general thrust of such a plea is quite understandable and although it aims, one may assume, at establishing some kind of differentiation between keeping a distance from some aspects of the era and the abrogation of distance from other aspects of that period, this may indeed lead to inextricable problems once one again leaves the level of the monograph for that of the global picture. During the Nazi era, few domains—with the exception of direct criminal activities—can be considered as entirely abhorrent; on the other hand, very few domains can be considered as entirely untouched by some of the objectionable or even criminal aspects of the core. The most varied examples of this intertwining of normalcy and criminality come immediately to mind: industry, state bureaucracy, etc. The historical significance of these institutions within the Nazi era is, first and foremost, their system-supporting role. If one considers institutions from the angle of their system-supporting function, very few will appear as functioning independently of the regime or without any contribution to its ever more radical evolution. The problem of not maintaining distance then becomes quite apparent and seems acceptable, at first glance, only for the noninstitutionalized domains of life.

However, in a system whose very core is criminal from the beginning, passivity is, as such, system-supporting. This may lead, quite naturally, to maintaining distance even from what appears to be normal, noninvolved, etc. The local church community, which may have remained ideologically untainted, but which expels its non-Aryan members and allows them to be transported away without any protest, can hardly be considered without some distancing. Moreover, the urge to do away with the *overall distancing* from the epoch and to distinguish between various areas implies that this history can be written from a kind of "neutral," "objective" viewpoint which allows the establishing of clear criteria for distancing or nondistancing. It seems to me that distancing is a subjective value judgment which cannot be shared, one way or another. For instance, for the victims of the regime, whoever they may have been—and, after all, why should their viewpoint not be as valid as that of the majority to which they belonged until 1933?—the 1933–45 period as a whole certainly creates overall distancing as, for them, the mistreatment started at all levels with the accession of Hitler to power. However, let us take a more general viewpoint here: as we shall see further on, the relativization of distancing from the era can have unexpected results.

This leads, finally, to the third dilemma, a dilemma which, in a sense, encompasses most of the other aspects of historicization and which is an almost necessary corollary of the preceding two.

The aim of historicization is not, so it seems, to take up once again the discussions of the last three decades about one or another familiar interpretation of National Socialism. If the desired transformation was to be considered only within these well-known parameters, we would be back at a discussion of the respective merits of "totalitarianism" vs. "fascism," of Hitler-centrism vs. polycracy, and so on. Clearly, however, historicization aims at something more, something which would not be a simple re-presentation of arguments which are by now familiar and well known. The key formula may be: one should now be able, four decades after the end of the war, to consider the Nazi era *as any other era*, in terms of historical analysis. *The relativization of the political-moral framework implied in the delimination of the 1933–45 period and the relativization of distance-taking from the whole era are key elements in the approach to this period as any other.*

Such a plea does not really indicate where this program can lead and what its implications may be: it tells us what the image we should discard is, what

the framework is which we should break open; it does not indicate what results this *open-ended* attitude can achieve, as if new approaches would make
the facts speak for themselves, as if the "return to history," as understood
here, was not open to all possible interpretations and shifts of meaning, once
overall "distancing" and the "moral blockade" of those years are lifted. The
recent West German context has shown the manifold possible interpretations
of historicization.

III

If one considers historicization *in abstracto,* i.e., in purely conceptual
terms, outside of any concrete ideological-political context, then, indeed, the
problem becomes merely one of refining this or that theoretical issue. But,
in fact, no historical concept can be considered entirely out of the context in
which it is formulated. Martin Broszat himself pleaded for historicization in
view of the passage of time, i.e., on the assumption that temporal distance
should by now allow a new look at the Nazi era. What this meant within the
context of the mid-1980s, in the Federal Republic, was clearly expressed by
Karl-Heinz Janßen in an article in *Die Zeit.* As Janßen states, "Broszat hopes
that, through 'more strongly differentiated historical insight,' this epoch
'could be opened up again in a moral sense.' Was he aware of how ambigu-
ously he would end up straddling the fence in this way?" And he adds: "For,
in the meantime, the winds of the conservative change in Bonn now blew
against these bearers of enlightenment. Many now understand historicization
as relativization. For them, the epoch of National Socialism was to be but one
epoch among others."[5] Karl-Heinz Janßen could, for instance, have quoted
Klaus Hildebrand's comments on Ernst Nolte's "Between Myth and Revisionism: National Socialism from the Perspective of the 80s": "The article by
Ernst Nolte [deserves] particular attention. For, in a very stimulating and
suggestive manner, it manages to integrate in an historicizing fashion the crucial element of the genocidal capacity of National Socialism and the Third
Reich and is able to understand this totalitarian phenomenon in the mutually
related context of both Russian and German history."[6]

We will forgo any examination of historicization according to Ernst Nolte,
as it could be argued that his questions and constructs are in no way inherent
in the historicization process as understood here. Let us, therefore, consider
a different case of historicization, one which, to my mind, clearly illustrates
an aspect of ideological contextualization of what historicization does not—
and cannot easily avoid: the passage from historicization to some kind of
"Historismus," mostly when the narrative form is not discarded.

Martin Broszat clearly rejects the return to "Historismus," and indeed one
could argue that the train of historicization can stop at any station before
reaching the end of the track. But the context within which historicization is
now used may well encourage making the journey to the final station of "historicism," and this for basically the following reasons: (1) the relativization of

distance and of the overall moral quarantine in relation to the Nazi epoch as a whole, as already mentioned; (2) the stress put on the noncriminal, nonideological, and nonpolitical aspects of the epoch, that is, among other things, on the daily life (*Alltagsgeschichte*) and the ordinariness of many aspects of the Third Reich.

Although there are many approaches to the study of daily life and although some of the research groups which develop these approaches are well aware of the problem of distancing involved in such studies, this way of looking at the Third Reich must, almost by definition, draw attention to the nonpolitical dimensions of the epoch and to ever more nuanced attitudes within the population, creating thereby some kind of continuum which can stress the criminality within everyday life, but also the large spheres of normality within the overall criminal system.

Within an overall context encouraging the relativization and normalization of the Nazi era, within an overall effort to reconsider the traditional image, the tendency to follow the continuum toward one end rather than toward another cannot easily be dismissed. All this does not mean that any line of enquiry should be avoided, but some of the shifts of meaning which it may encourage should not be left unmentioned. Let us take one example.

The multivolume study of daily life in Bavaria during the Nazi era brought forth a concept much discussed since, that of *Resistenz*. It represents the conceptualization of an intermediate category of behavior, in between active opposition and total conformism and, in that sense, the new approach (*Alltagsgeschichte*)—by leading to important differentiations—illustrates one of the principal aims of historicization.

If one takes Hartmut Mehringer's definition of *Resistenz*—Mehringer was one of the main coauthors of the project on Bavaria in the Nazi period (*Bayern in der NS-Zeit*) within which this concept came strongly to the fore—then a category of understanding is presented, whereby the basic attitudes of the majority of the population in the areas of conflicting loyalties were determined by a mixture of conformism and nonconformism: "A close examination of the social and political zones of conflict within the Third Reich shows, however, that the general rule was [not outright resistance, but] conditional opposition and its association with temporary and partial acceptance of the regime, that it was the coexistence of conformity and nonconformity."[7] One could argue—and one indeed has—that *Resistenz* is much too amorphous a concept to be of any great use and there is no reason for excluding anyone who subscribed to the *Völkischer Beobachter* for opportunistic reasons and then threw the paper away without reading it from this vast field of blurred nonconformity. One could identify the concept with tacit acquiescence or passive acceptance of the worst crimes of the regime, notwithstanding whispered disapproval, etc.

In any case, if the mixture of conformism and nonconformism was a rule for many, it creates a conceptual bridge which allows the overcoming of the contradictory positions of the individual who does not approve of some of the aspects of the regime and who nonetheless actively participates in an institution which bolsters the regime. In other words, even if the Wehrmacht as a whole was system-supporting more than any other institution, many units fighting on one or another of the fronts were more or less immune to ideological considerations and were only doing their best to hold the line, as soldiers in any other army. In this sense, the attitude of these units, that is, also of most of the members, was a mixture of conformism and nonconformity and could be defined as *Resistenz*.

This kind of *Resistenz*, when added to fighting against a threat considered morally no less condemnable than Nazism and viewed as catastrophic from a German national perspective, namely the Soviet Union, may lead the historian from neutrality to empathy. This is, more or less, the position adopted by Andreas Hillgruber in his *Zweierlei Untergang: Die Zerschlagung des Deutschen Reiches und das Ende des europäischen Judentums*. As is by now well known, in Hillgruber's view, the historian has to find a point of identification in his subject, and he chose to identify with the fighting units of the Wehrmacht and the suffering German populations of the East, notwithstanding the fact that the resistance of the Wehrmacht allowed the continuation of the extermination process behind the lines. In an interview given to the *Rheinischer Merkur*, Andreas Hillgruber compared his description of the fate of the Wehrmacht on the Eastern front with the work on *Alltagsgeschichte* done in other fields:

In my essay on the defeat at the Eastern Front in 1944/45, I have, as an introduction, sketched the events from the point of view of the population and the fighting German army, not, that is to say, from the perspective of Hitler's watchtower or the victorious Red Army. . . . This attempt to portray matters from the view of those most directly affected meshes with efforts made by my colleagues (Hans Mommsen or Martin Broszat, for example) also to experience things along with the main part of the suffering population.[8]

Andreas Hillgruber's argument is not entirely untenable, as Hermann Rudolph pointed out in an article entitled "Falsche Fronten?": one could not, wrote Rudolph, be in favor of a historicization process on the one hand—a process of which he himself approves—and, on the other hand, impose some sort of moral blockade on the resistance of the Wehrmacht units on the Eastern front, because it enabled the continuation of the extermination behind the lines: "One cannot promote this process of differentiation," he added, "and at the same time simply look back at the past with abhorrence."[9]

At the end of his "Plea," Martin Broszat asks us to lift the blockade imposed on the 1933–45 period in order, among other things, to avoid the return to some kind of traditional *Historismus*, i.e., some kind of traditional identification and empathy with the periods considered "healthy," before and after the Nazi era. What is happening, ironically, is that the search for the "healthy" areas within the National Socialist period and the abrogation of the distance between the historian and this era as a whole, leads to a return of

Historismus, not only as far as the periods preceding and following the Third Reich are concerned, but in relation to the Third Reich itself. The constant juxtaposition and differentiation between the normal and everyday and the abnormal and criminal within the Third Reich itself, when not accompanied by sufficiently precise categories of differentiation and by a clear framework for analysis may, within the new ideological context, confront the historian who considers historicization as some kind of more "objective" approach to the Nazi era, with unexpected outcomes.

IV

Historicization, in short, implies many different things and within the present context it may encourage some interpretations rather than others. At this concluding stage, three very general problems should be raised.

First of all, one may argue with some measure of plausibility that historicization is, in itself, part of a wider and continuous process of construction (or reconstruction) of German memory of the Nazi period. There are also many others apart from historians who are constructing or reconstructing, on a collective level, the memory of this epoch. Historiography—although in principle the critical eye scanning the constructs of memory—is, in many ways, part of the general process, in one direction or another, since it is dealing with a past so massively present, a past that refuses to go away. In my view, to put it briefly, this past is still much too present for present-day historians, be they German or Jewish in particular, be they contemporaries of the Nazi era or members of the second and perhaps third generation, to enable an easy awareness of presuppositions and of a priori positions.

One may assume that, more often than not, the historian approaching the Nazi era has not made it entirely clear to himself on what specific basis, from what specific motives, within which specific ideological context, he wishes to deal with it. What, therefore, is necessary for any kind of historical analysis is a fundamental self-reflective process, one whereby the historian remains aware that—whatever his feeling of objectivity may be—he is still the one who selects the approach, determines the method, and organizes the material according to some kind of agenda. What is true for any historical writing is decisive for the study of such an era. Writing about Nazism is not like writing about sixteenth-century France. The possibly mistaken assumption in the idea of historicization as analyzed here may well be that forty years after the end of the Third Reich, Nazism can be dealt with more or less in the same way as sixteenth-century France.

The second issue which derives directly from the first is that of differential relevance. The history of Nazism belongs to everybody. Indeed, for Germans, it is an essential issue in terms of national self-perception and identity, in terms of understanding not only their own past, but their present-day society as well. For this reason, the historicization of the Nazi era may mean different things to different groups within the Federal Republic, according to their ideological and political choices. But the same past may mean something else to the victims of Nazism, whoever they may be, and for them, there are other, no less legitimate, modes of historicizing the era. For instance, if the growing centrality of the study of everyday life under the Third Reich may be of considerable importance within the historicization process for both conservative and left-wing German historians, albeit for opposite reasons, this same aspect of the history of the Third Reich may seem of less direct relevance for some historians outside of Germany, who may find the political and ideological aspects of the Third Reich in need of much more detailed research, since the relation between ideology and politics still remains extremely hazy, for instance, as far as the Final Solution is concerned.

Finally, one may wonder about the question of the possible limits to the historicization of National Socialism, limits in no way linked to any taboo, but inherent in the phenomenon itself. These limits are related to the way one approaches the issue of the specificity or nonspecificity of Nazi crimes. Although one may state and restate one's own interpretation of the facts, one is clearly facing a choice not between facts, but between interpretations anchored in value judgments not amenable to decisive proof or disproof.

Something essential in National Socialism is determined by the evaluation of the specificity or nonspecificity of its crimes. As the choice made by the historian determines the nature of the whole picture, as this kind of evaluation is hardly amenable to historical analysis, *historicization can be completed only if the crimes of the Nazi regime are entirely integrated within a complex historical context; if such integration does not take place, a decisive element for the historicization of the era may remain elusive.*

In 1972, Geoffrey Barraclough published a series of three articles in *The New York Review of Books* which already included some of the arguments for the historicization of National Socialism. Among other things, Barraclough criticizes what he calls the liberal approach to modern German history. He then quotes the historian of fascism Gilbert Allardyce, who wrote: "Our knowledge of what happened at Auschwitz has vastly increased, but not our understanding." Why is this so? asks Barraclough. His answer is worth quoting:

If the answers still elude us, the easiest assumption is that what is necessary is more fact, more information, more burrowing among the "roots" of National-Socialism. It is the obvious answer but not necessarily the right one. If the jigsaw puzzle does not work out, the reason may not be that some pieces are missing but that we have set it up wrongly. What is at issue, in other words, is the validity of the assumptions and methodology of the prevailing liberal approach to modern German history.[10]

Some fifteen years have elapsed since Barraclough's lines were published, and the liberal approach to modern German history has been seriously questioned, precisely by historians such as Martin Broszat, Hans Mommsen, and many others. The pieces of the jigsaw puzzle have been shifted around in all possible ways, an immense amount of new detail has been added; nonetheless, Martin Broszat pleaded in 1985 for the historicization of National Socialism. One year later, the debate among German historians about the specificity or nonspecificity of Nazi crimes erupted. These various phases need to be recalled to indicate that what appears to be the ever-recurring obstacle to the completion of the jigsaw puzzle is precisely and repeatedly the specificity and the historical place of the annihilation policies of the Third Reich. Therein lies the problem—and probably also the limits—of historicization.

V

In the concluding lines of her book, *Eichmann in Jerusalem,* Hannah Arendt may have unintentionally given us a clue as to what distinguished Nazi crimes from others. The Nazis, argued Hannah Arendt, tried to "determine who should and who should not inhabit the world." *This, in fact, is something no other regime, whatever its criminality, has attempted to do.* In that sense, the Nazi regime attained what is, in my view, some sort of theoretical outer limit: one may envision an even larger number of victims and a technologically more efficient way of killing, but once a regime decides that groups, whatever the criteria may be, should be annihilated there and then and never be allowed to live on earth, the ultimate has been achieved. This limit, from my perspective, was reached only once in modern history: by the Nazis. It goes without saying that one may try to compare Nazi annihilations to other annihilationist policies, that one may look for any number of comparable elements; all this does not exclude the identification of some differences. The aspect just mentioned is what gives the Nazi regime its specificity. According to my own criteria, such reasoning is of the realm of value judgments.

In the present ideological context, those historians who wish to relativize the significance of Nazism, and to historicize its "annihilating capacities," may instrumentalize the concept we discussed and utilize the open-endedness of the process and the lack of precision of some of its elements to arrive at what appears to them to be a long-postponed objective view of the past.

Historicization understood as more precise historical analysis is an ongoing and necessary process. However, the awareness of some of the problems raised here may eventually help to ensure the development of a historicization, which would not lend itself to being easily used for the relativization of the Nazi past and its banalization, and ultimately for the elimination from human memory of its criminality.

Notes

I wish to thank my colleagues and friends Dan Diner, Lutz Niethammer, and Shulamit Volkov for discussing with me some of the issues raised in this paper. Needless to say, they bear no responsibility for the final version or for any mistakes therein.

1. Martin Broszat, "Plea for a Historicization of National Socialism," in this volume, p. 77.
2. Ernst Nolte, "Between Myth and Revisionism: National-Socialism from the Perspective of the 1980s," in H. W. Koch, ed., *Aspects of National Socialism* (London, 1985); "Eine Vergangenheit, die nicht vergehen will," in *Historikerstreit*.
3. Martin Broszat, "Hitler and the Genesis of the 'Final Solution,'" *Yad Vashem Studies* 13 (1979); Hans Mommsen, "The Realization of the Unthinkable: The 'Final Solution of the Jewish Question' in the Third Reich," in Gerhard Hirschfeld, ed., *The Policies of Genocide: Jews and Soviet Prisoners of War in Nazi Germany* (London, 1986).
4. Hans Mommsen, "Suche nach der 'verlorenen Geschichte'? Bemerkungen zum historischen Selbstverständnis der Bundesrepublik," in *Historikerstreit*.
5. Karl-Heinz Janssen, "Als ein Volk ohne Schatten?" in *Die Zeit* 48, 21 November 1986.
6. Klaus Hildebrand in "Buchbesprechungen 20. Jahrhundert," *Historische Zeitschrift* 242, vol. 2 (April 1986).
7. *Alltagsgeschichte der NS-Zeit: Neue Perspektive oder Trivialisierung?* (Kolloquien des Instituts für Zeitgeschichte), Munich, 1984.
8. Andreas Hillgruber, "Für die Forschung gibt es kein Frageverbot," in *Historikerstreit*.
9. Hermann Rudolph, "Falsche Fronten?" in *Süddeutsche Zeitung* 4–5 (October 1986).
10. Geoffrey Barraclough, "Mandarins and Nazis: Part I," in *The New York Review of Books*, 19 October 1972; "The Liberals and German History: Part II," in *The New York Review of Books*, 2 November 1972; "A New View of German History: Part III," in *The New York Review of Books*, 16 November 1972.

6.   A Controversy about the Historicization of National Socialism

Martin   Broszat   and
Saul   Friedländer

I

September 28, 1987

Dear Mr. Friedländer,

On the occasion of the 40th anniversary of the end of Nazi rule in May 1985, I published an essay entitled "A Plea for the Historicization of National Socialism" ("Plädoyer für eine Historisierung des National sozialismus") in the magazine *Merkur*. As far as I know, you have voiced reservations about the concept and fundamental idea of this historicization postulate a number of times in various lectures and articles, more than any other of my colleagues in the field of contemporary history in Germany and abroad. Moreover, your apprehensions were also affected by the backwash of the *Historikerstreit* that erupted in 1986 in the Federal Republic, though this particular debate has been characterized in part by a quite different set of motives, emphases, and opposing camps. In my view, this dispute has certainly also led to some positive results. Yet the *Historikerstreit* was not particularly suited as a means toward furthering an objective discussion of the notions which I—for completely nonpolemical reasons—had put forward in my "Plea" a year earlier. Rather, a part of my arguments were extolled and applauded by the wrong camp, while in contrast, certain reservations and doubts surfaced where the basic ideas expressed therein (in my "Plea") had met open-minded interest and agreement before.

Due to such "distortions" of the objective discussion of the topic as a result of the *Historikerstreit*, I declined (as you are aware)—after giving the matter considerable thought—to accept an invitation by the Fischer Verlag to contribute to a paperback collection of essays that might have afforded me an opportunity in the fall of 1987 to respond, albeit briefly, to your critical "Reflections on the Historicization of National Socialism" ("Überlegungen zur Historisierung des National sozialismus") contained in that volume.[1] I decided against such a response and against a republication of my "Plea" in this paperback collection for one principal reason: because I did not wish to contribute a helping hand to yet another rather one-sided compilation of essays on the *Historikerstreit,* which had already generated a spate of publications.

You regretted that decision, but have fortunately agreed with my suggestion that we discuss the problem "among ourselves"—outside of such a context and within the more sedate forum of the *Vierteljahrshefte für Zeitgeschichte*—in the form of a dialogue consisting of three exchanges of letters. We trust the readers of this journal will take it upon themselves to read the two initial points of departure for this dialogue—my "Plea" and your "Reflections"—since, in the course of the following exchange of letters, I am sure that it will be possible to recapitulate the arguments developed by us there only in part and not in their full entirety. Moreover, we will be embarking here upon an experiment whose outcome is quite uncertain. Our agreement in regard to the dialogue remains, for the time being, only a token of our mutual good intentions to engage in a discourse which will not be simply polemical, but rather, so we hope, a fruitful and enlightening undertaking. Yet whether—and how well—we have succeeded in this task will not emerge until we are finished, and the readers of the journal will have to be the final arbiters of that.

In opening our dialogue, I would like to dwell on three questions: 1. The concept of the historicization of National Socialism which I make use of is ambiguous and can easily be misunderstood—in this I agree with you completely. In your critique, you proceed basically from the premise of the pervertibility of this concept, the ease with which it can be abused and misused, and not from what I indicated quite expressly as its objective and motivation. In my "Plea" I did not furnish any basis or "handle" for your fear that the concept of the historicization of National Socialism had provided a dangerous catchword for a false normalization of historical consciousness in the Federal Republic, and that a step had thus been taken down the path leading toward a moral leveling of perspectives on the Nazi period.

Due to the fact that misunderstanding and distrust can nonetheless apparently remain extremely powerful factors, I would like, at the outset of our discussion, to underscore quite clearly the following point. My concept of historicization was—and remains—bound up with two postulates which are mutually conditioning and thus indispensable: first, it is based on a recognition of the necessity that, in the final analysis, the Nazi period cannot be excluded from historical understanding—no matter how much the mass crimes and catastrophes which the regime perpetrated challenge one again and again to take a stance of resolute political and moral condemnation. Secondly, my concept of historicization is founded on a principle of critical, enlightening historical understanding [*Verstehen*]; this understanding, shaped in essential terms precisely by the experience of National Socialism and the nature of man as revealed by the Nazis, should be clearly distinguished from the concept of *Verstehen* in the frame of German historicism of the nineteenth century, with its romantic-idealistic basis and the one-sided pattern of identification bound up with this notion.

From my perspective, the concept of historical "insight" (*Einsicht*) appears more pertinent and to the point than that of "understanding" in regard to the ambivalence of post–National Socialist historicization. Insight in a double sense: seen, on the one hand, as a distancing explanation and an objectification to be achieved analytically; and, on the other, viewed as a comprehending, subjective appropriation and empathetic reliving [*Nachvollzug*] of past achievements, sensations, concerns, and mistakes. Historical insight in this dual sense is quite generally—and not only in respect to the Nazi period in German history—charged with the task of preventing historical consciousness from degenerating once more into a deification and idealization of brute facts of power, as exemplified by the Prussian-German historical thought of a Heinrich von Treitschke. A historicization which remains aware of this double objective in gaining and transmitting historical insight is in no danger whatsoever of relativizing the atrocities of National Socialism. Correspondingly, I attempted to make clear in my 1985 "Plea" that in trying to deal with National Socialism, what remains crucial is precisely the ability to endure the acute tension between the two components of "insight"—(a) the desire to understand and (b) critical distancing—and not to take refuge either in a *Pauschaldistanzierung,* a general and wholesale distancing, (which is morally likewise an all-too-simple option) or an amoral *Verstehen* predicated on "mere understanding."

For reasons which remain a mystery to me, all this was not able to dispel your fears and suspicions that a departure on the train of historicization supposedly constituted the beginning of a journey whose final destination was a relativism of values: a relativism where everything can be "understood" and "excused." To allay such apprehensions, I would like to cite a wise and historically knowledgeable journalist on the staff of the *Süddeutsche Zeitung,* Hermann Rudolph. In October 1986, Rudolph commented on the *Historikerstreit* in his paper in the following way: the historicization of National Socialism, in his view, is not only unavoidable, but rather is absolutely necessary if one wishes to comprehend the ambivalent connections between civilization and aggressivity in the effective history [*Wirkungsgeschichte*] of the Third Reich. In dealing with such interconnections, "a sense of judgment that has only been sharpened in moral terms gets nowhere, or merely lacerates itself." As Rudolph sees it, the danger that the singularity of National Socialism might be compromised by such a differentiation is "about the least likely eventuality." National Socialism, Rudolph contends, itself provided a sufficient guarantee against such an eventuality by the unprecedented magnitude of its crimes and devastation—in historical terms, these remain unforgettable.[2]

2. My polemic stance against a more declamatory, morally impotent general and wholesale distancing from the Nazi period provoked particular concerns and criticial objections on your part. I would like in the following to present a clarification regarding this—a classification drawn from the very evolution which "mastering of the past" [*Vergangenheitsbewältigung*] has undergone in the Federal Republic.

Initially, right after 1945, the number-one item on the agenda was the creation of an anti–National Socialist political and social order and a return, on the level of the discussion about constitutional norms, to the humanitarian values of a constitutional state. This renewal of norms and the associated necessity for a sharp verbal renunciation of the Nazi period were all the more unavoidable since (and although) at that time, during the Adenauer era, people were not particularly willing or indeed able, to a sufficient degree, to assume a morally convincing position of uncompromising condemnation in respect to the concrete individual cases of manifold entanglements in the former regime of injustice—and to engage in a detailed confrontation with this past. In other words, the official general and wholesale distancing from the Nazi past, despite its importance for the reestablishment of norms, compensated for (and yet simultaneously served to mask) the insufficient investigation and subsequent punishment of concrete individual involvement with respect to guilt and responsibility. Such investigations and punishment frequently did not occur, or were too limited in scope. The Nazi past was rejected in general terms, in declamatory fashion, also due to the fact that it was very awkward to weigh and ponder that past more precisely and in detail. Correspondingly, historical inquiry about the recent past in the 1950s and 1960s was dominated by a demonological interpretation of National Socialism, concerned more with bringing about a distancing exorcism of the demons than arriving at a historical explanation.

In the immediate postwar period, there were many weighty political and psychological reasons for this approach of declamatory general distancing. Yet these reasons lost much of their importance as time passed and the democratic order of government in the Federal Republic took on stability. Nowadays, when we have a situation where the field of history and historical studies is no longer represented by a generation whose members were contemporaries of National Socialism and became adults before 1945, but rather is represented, already in large measure, by the grandchildren of that generation, there is no longer a sufficient reason for the imposition of a general quarantine. Moreover, there is no longer any great need for the charging and prosecution of perpetrators, since at the present time there are very few left who might properly be accused of direct responsibility. In addition, the former distinctions of being differentially involved in and affected by National Socialism have, in the meantime, largely blurred and faded within the society of the Federal Republic. In contrast, the desire to understand this past has become all the more powerful, especially among younger people—a past with which they are repeatedly confronted as a special legacy and burden, a kind of "mortgage," yet a past which for them can only be experienced intellectually and in historical terms.

By no means—and let me repeat this once again—does this mean that the moral evaluation and condemnation of the crimes and failures of the Nazi period are passing from the scene. It does mean though that such evaluation and condemnation must be mediated by conscientious historical inquiry, and that they must be able to stand the test of a rational comprehension of this period. If one proceeds from these needs and from the necessarily transformed perceptions of the younger generation of Germans, then, for quite some time, the crucial matter has indeed not been whether historicization should be seen as a desideratum. Rather, what remains crucial today is only the necessity of making people conscious and aware of the unavoidability of this historicization—a process which has been in progress now for some time.

3. Of course, such a German-centrist perspective alone is not enough. I attempted in my "Plea" to make clear, if nothing else, that the history of the Nazi period cannot be determined by German historians alone. Rather, one of the special features of this period is that, in the wake of the incalculable persecution of millions of individuals of non-German nationality, any exclusive German claim to historical interpretation in regard to this period has been forfeited. Every German historian is well advised to keep this fully in mind, with all the consequences such an awareness entails. To the extent that the history of National Socialism has become a central chapter in the historical experience of those persecuted by the Nazis from all countries and nations, it holds to a particular degree that this period is by no means a dead past in historical terms for these persons and the generation of the bereaved. It is both absurd and presumptuous for Germans to demand that memory be submerged in the slough of such dead historicity. Among the special features of the scholarly-scientific investigation of this past is the knowledge that this period still remains bound up with many and diverse monuments of mournful and accusatory memory, imbued with the painful sentiments of many individuals, in particular of Jews, who remain adamant in their insistence on a mythical form of this remembrance.

German historians and students of history—and let me add this very expressly to my "Plea"—have the obligation to understand that victims of Nazi persecution and their bereaved relatives can even regard it as a forfeiture of the right to their form of memory if historical research on contemporary history, operating only in scientific terms, makes claims in its academic arrogance to a monopoly when it comes to questions and concepts pertaining to the Nazi period. Respect for the victims of Nazi crimes demands that this mythical memory be granted a place. Moreover, there is no prerogative here of one side or the other. Whether the juxtaposition of scientific insight and mythical memory represents a fruitful tension also depends, to be sure, on whether the former is able to provide productive images and insights, or whether it is based only on a coarsening—with the passage of time—of the data of history: on a process involving the forgetting of details still familiar to contemporaries and of the imponderable elements of genuine historical events. Among the problems faced by a younger generation of German historians more focused on rational understanding is certainly also the fact that they must deal with just such a contrary form of memory among those who were persecuted and harmed by the Nazi regime, and among their descendants—a form of memory which functions to coarsen historical recollection.

In your collection of essays entitled *Reflections of Nazism*, you dealt with various literary forms into which such mythical remembrance has been transposed. Perhaps you paid too little attention there to a fact which appears to me of great significance in this regard: namely, that, in their nonscientific way, many such literary, mythical images of the Nazi experience furnish us with insights. Such insights are, in the best sense of the term, "intelligent," and are thus quite compatible with the growing need for a better scientific understanding of this past.

II

Dear Mr. Broszat,

The present context is certainly a most adequate framework for a thoughtful clarification of the themes outlined in your "Plea" (as well as in some previous articles), and of some of the critical remarks expressed in my "Reflections." I am grateful to you for suggesting this possibility and to the editors of the *Vierteljahrshefte* for accepting the idea.

In the opening statement to our discussion, you may have given the impression that my criticism of your text was much sharper and less tentative than it was. But, we seem to agree on what explains part of the criticism, namely, that the concept of historicization, as you formulated it in the "Plea," was "ambiguous and easily misconstrued" and led thereby to some incomprehension and some misuse too, particularly within the context of the *Historikerstreit*. Some difficulties, however, seemed inherent in the concept itself. In any case, your statement put in focus some of the main issues and brought up at least one crucial new theme, possibly the most important of all.

1. The historical origins of the general and wholesale distancing from the Nazi era, within the postwar West German context, are clear to me. But our discussion is not about the general scene; it is about historiography. My impression was that, since the early 1960s at least—let us take K. D. Bracher's *Die Auflösung der Weimarer Republik* as a symbolic starting point—West German historiography and the historiography of the Nazi era in general adopted, all in all, a reasonably detached, nonmoralistic approach. As far as precise and detailed inquiry goes, this historiography was certainly as strictly scientific as that of any other period. You know the impact of your own work, as well as that of Hans Mommsen, for instance. Thousands of studies have dealt with all possible subjects, from all possible angles. Nowhere do I see "moralism" or, as a matter of fact, some kind of "overall blockade" which would have hampered the normal development of scientific inquiry. *Alltagsgeschichte* may have been criticized for conceptual reasons, but this did not stop it from becoming a flourishing field.

You were possibly right in pointing to the "monumental" presentation of the *Widerstand* and, in general, in stressing the existence of much more confusion and normalcy in many areas of life during the Nazi era, in emphasizing similarities more than clear-cut differences in attitudes of various groups (your examples in the literary field, for instance), etc. In short, you ask for a greater perception of complexity and ambiguity, but again, although this process of differentiation is still going on, and will by definition go on as long as historical inquiry itself, one cannot say that historians have been unaware of the complexities of the overall picture for the last twenty-five or thirty years. It so happens that, more than twenty years ago, I myself published a biography of Kurt Gerstein with the subtitle "Die Zwiespältigkeit des Guten" [The duality of the good] (Paris, 1967; Gütersloh, 1969), where the ambiguity of individual positions and roles, even within the SS, even within the annihilation machinery, was at the very core of my argument.

In short, all this being well known, one may wonder what blockade the "Plea" was trying to lift, what yet unopened door it wished to open. And, as your articles, those of 1983 and that of 1985, were somehow pleas for a massive change in historiographical attitudes toward the Nazi era, one could wonder what the boundary was which you wished to cross. Sometimes, you express your aim in general formulas, but these general formulas leave uncertainty about what you have in mind. For instance, you conclude your 1983 article "Literatur und NS-Vergangenheit" with the following lines:

Our reflection on this period from the vantage of a lengthy span of fifty years should finally also help us to disengage ourselves to a greater extent from the false notion of the dominant negative centrality of National Socialism in German twentieth-century history.[3]

You will understand that for those who are aware of the ongoing debates about the *Sonderweg*, who know that the place of the Nazi era within German history is the object of the most diverse and unhampered opinions, such a call, with the word *finally*, sounds puzzling. In short, how should one understand the "Plea" in relation to the historiographical work of the last decades? Why a "Plea?" Where is the "blockade?"

The discrepancy between the general state of the historiography of the Nazi epoch and the tone of urgency of your "Plea" can give the impression that you aim, in fact, at a very significant change of focus in considering the overall picture, along some of the lines which I tried to define in my "Reflections": relativization of the political sphere; cancellation of distancing; historical evaluation of the Nazi epoch as if it were as removed from us as sixteenth-century France . . .

2. Within the theoretical framework which you outline, you write that historical *Verstehen* cannot "come to a halt with the Nazi period." You suggest, as a possible approach, a critical understanding, that is, if I follow you correctly, a balanced "historical insight" based on the constant interaction of *Verstehen* and of "critical evaluation." The question is, What does it mean concretely?

The immediate problem is that of the limits. There is no reason to argue against your endeavor on any theoretical ground, but in practice you may indeed encounter the difficulty to which I pointed in my "Reflections." We both quote approvingly Hermann Rudolph's "Falsche Fronten?" and, indeed, it was one of the more original contributions to the *Historikerstreit*. But what is Rudolph's concrete point, the one relevant here? Historicization as you pursue it is necessary, he says, but one cannot praise it, as Jürgen Habermas did, and at the same time heavily attack Andreas Hillgruber's position in *Zweierlei Untergang:* "One cannot actively accelerate this process of differentiation," writes Rudolph, "and simultaneously continue to look back in disgust." There, really, lies your dilemma: Where are the limits of the *Verstehen?* Where does the critical distancing intervene? There is no difficulty as far as the overtly criminal domains are concerned, but what about the Wehrmacht units holding the Eastern front in 1944/45? I do not want to develop all the contradictions into which this, by now notorious, example could lead, in the light of your theoretical premises, but it would be extremely helpful if you agreed to comment on it, as it is almost a litmus test of the applicability of the widened historical insight you possibly have in mind.

3. I wonder, however, if one of the main reasons for your "Plea" and, therefore, part of the answer to my previous questions is not to be found in the third and last section of your statement. It is the perception of the NS-era held by "the victims" of the Nazi regime which could well be the main locus of the moralistic approach. Here is the problem that historiography—and you say "German historiography"—has to face. You express respect for what you consider as the specific memory of the victims, but you call it a "mythical" memory and you conclude:

Among the problems faced by a younger generation of German historians more focused on rational understanding is certainly also the fact that they must deal with just such a contrary form of memory among those who were persecuted and harmed by the Nazi regime, and among their descendants—a form of memory which acts to coarsen historical recollection.

I assume, first of all, that we do not speak here of popular *Geschichtsbilder*, but of the work of historians. In the "Plea" you mentioned that, after the war, the history of the Nazi era was essentially written by historians who had been forced to leave Germany for political or racial reasons, or had placed themselves at a strong critical distance from Nazism. This certainly influenced the image they had of this era. What you imply here is that the victims or their descendants continue, even after four decades, to hold to this kind of nonscientific, black-and-white "mythical" memory, creating in fact the problem you allude to.

This issue will, I think, be very central to our debate. It has not been openly dealt with up to now and it is important for all that it be brought to the surface and clarified. Let me therefore try to understand your point as well as possible and ask you, at the outset, who, more precisely, would be the historians belonging to the category of carriers of a "mythical" memory.

I assume that the Jewish victims (and their descendants) are the essential category you have in mind. It would be useful to know, however, if non-Jewish French historians for instance, belonging, let us say, to families involved in the Resistance, or just French historians, considered among many others, would be included in your category. And, if you limit the category to the Jews, who is included? Those who were direct victims of Nazism and their descendants only, or all the Jews? You once expressed your admiration for such pioneers of the analysis of Nazism, all of them Jewish émigrés, such as Ernst Fraenkel, Franz Neumann, and Hannah Arendt. Are they, retrospectively, included in your analysis? And what about Jewish historians who, later on, opened vistas which correspond to your own interpretation of the history of the Third Reich?

A second preliminary aspect of the issue seems to me no less important than the preceding one. You oppose the rational discourse of German historiography to the mythical memory of the victims. You mention younger German historians as the natural bearers of this rational discourse. Some of these younger historians are, it so happens, among the most sensitive to the moral issues raised by the history of the Third Reich. But why refer to the younger historians? The recent debates have all been conducted among a great majority of historians belonging, on the German side, to the "generation of Hitler Youth," at least, sometimes belonging to families considered as involved at the time, etc. Do not misunderstand me: I feel strong empathy with those bearing such difficult burdens, but wouldn't you agree that this German context creates as many problems in the approach to the Nazi era as it does, differently, for the victims? This point, which you seem to have disregarded, was a decisive argument in the "Reflections." Allow me to quote a few words from my text:

> This past [the NS era] is still much too present for present-day historians, be they German or Jewish in particular, be they contemporaries of the Nazi era or members of the second and perhaps third generations, to enable an easy awareness of presuppositions and of *a priori* positions. . . .

But, if we see things from your perspective, why, in your opinion, would historians belonging to the group of the perpetrators be able to distance themselves from their past, whereas those belonging to the group of victims, would not?

These are really preliminary issues. As for the historical place of the "Final Solution" (as a paradigmatic illustration of the criminal dimensions of the Nazi era) within an overall representation of that era which should not be "dominantly negative" [*übermächtig negativ*], we should, it seems to me, come back to it in our next exchange.

III

October 26, 1987

Dear Mr. Friedländer,

Your objections provide abundant material for our continued exchange of ideas. Naturally, they also point up all the difficulties entailed in a German-Jewish discussion on the presentation and remembrance of the Nazi period. Some time ago, you expressed the apprehension that a heightened move back to one's own historical experience and concerns among both Germans and Jews could serve to widen even further the gap in a contrastive and opposed presentation of this period. This danger certainly exists, and I would like later on to speak a bit about a few aspects in this regard which also disturb me. Yet perhaps one should view the situation with a certain sense of confidence. In view of the liveliness of the controversies—but also of the new kind of reflection being generated, as I see it, by the *Historikerstreit*—I wonder whether there might not indeed be new possibilities emerging here as well for German-Jewish dialogue, a dialogue which has to date been neglected.

One must ask: Did this dialogue—which Gershom Scholem even 25 years ago called a mere myth[4]—indeed ever take place as a public event? When it comes to this "dialogue," is not the same thing basically true with respect to the German side which I have criticized regarding the official German "mastering of the past": namely, that despite all its merits in setting the fundamentally correct political and moral tone, it has remained floundering for some time now in declamatory statements, devoid of any strength or imagination for historical reflection that might also be morally innovative? In German-Jewish discussions on recent history which have taken place in increasing numbers in Israel, the Federal Republic, and elsewhere for two decades, isn't it true that an open expression of a good many of the particularly sensitive, most opposed sentiments, feelings, and memories have been avoided—either consciously or unconsciously—because otherwise it would have been impossible even to initiate contacts for such a discussion in the first place? Consequently, is it really so terribly surprising if now, after the need on both sides (for whatever reasons) has grown stronger to give expression to such elements of memory, that this is quite naturally taking place associated with every possible kind of awkwardness, mutual offense, and counterreaction due to wounded feelings—because it is new and untried, and there is little fund of experience on which to draw? Yet I do not wish to see this simply as a reason for being discouraged. Please accept this thought, tentative as it is, also as my first response to the especially insistent and pressing questions you pose in the final section of your contribution. In the following, I do not intend to take up your important objections one by one. Rather, I wish once again to try to put forward my position in respect to several larger complexes.

It is a fundamental misunderstanding of the concept of historicization, as I have sketched it, to assume that it involves a *revision*—brought about consciously or by negligence—of the clear judgment on and condemnation of the dictatorial, criminal, inhumane aspects and measures of the Nazi regime, aspects and measures which have by now been researched and documented in detail and at length. That judgment has been firmly established within the historical sciences in West Germany for some time, and with almost 100% unanimity. This likewise holds true in fundamental terms when it comes to Ernst Nolte. Rather, the making conscious of the process of historicization—a process which in factual terms has been going on now for some time—or the plea for greater historicization of the Nazi period, aims more at a meaningful *continuation*, at a *new stage* in dealing with the Nazi past (in the discipline of history as well as in public discussion), *on the basis* of this evaluation of the essential political-moral character of Nazi rule. This is an evaluation which is now indeed quite firmly established.

Such a call for greater historicization proceeds from the assumption that despite the colossal expansion of detailed historical research on the Nazi period which you allude to, the total image of the period as reflected in public consciousness and in comprehensive historiographic treatments has remained strangely shadowy and insubstantial, precisely because of the "obligatory" and preeminent underscoring of the philosophical-political basic features. It is more often a black-and-white construct viewed in retrospect rather than a genetically unfolding multidimensional history; it is a landscape inhabited less by plastic, psychologically convincing figures than by types and stereotypes drawn from the conceptual vocabulary of political science. It is framed more by moral-didactic commentary than by historical report. It is formulated in the more-or-less emotional or abstract-academic language of historians whose embarrassment, disconcertedness vis-à-vis the history of National Socialism, also manifests itself in the fact that they refuse to grant that history the true and genuine means of communication employed by historical presentation—namely, narrative language.

What is basically meant by historicization is an attempt to break up and dissolve such stereotypes, embarrassment constraints, and overgeneralizations. It does not imply any softening of the political-moral judgment on the unjust character of the Nazi regime, even if it must work out the plurality of historical lines of action and historical subjects, not all of which can be categorized in terms of the political system and ideology of Nazism. In this sense, I spoke in 1983, within the framework of what was more some sort of ancillary observation on literature during the Nazi period, about the false conception, which ought "finally" to be overcome, "of a dominant and all-powerful negative, central position of National Socialism" in all areas of life during the Nazi period. Unfortunately, what you then did was to take this quote and place it in another context, thus giving it a misleading meaning.

Apparently, however, in the matter just alluded to we also have differing conceptions. In your "Reflections," you contend that because Nazism was fundamentally criminal, even those institutional and social spheres which were little contaminated by the Nazi ideology (industry, bureaucracy, the military, churches, etc.) should be viewed primarily from the perspective of whether—and how—they served to maintain Nazi rule. "Even nonparticipation and passivity" were "as such elements serving to stabilize the system."[5] From the perspective of the victims of National Socialist persecution—and, in particular, Jewish experience—in view of the large number of "bystanders," who *did not aid* the regime in its measures of persecution, this standpoint is certainly understandable. Formulated in absolute terms, however, it would serve to block important avenues of access to historical knowledge, and would also hardly satisfy the demands of historical justice.

I sense something similar when it comes to your strong reservations and doubts regarding almost all the newer perspectives of historical inquiry into the Nazi period, such as the study of *Alltagsgeschichte* (everyday history) or the social-historical approach, especially insofar as these approaches exceed the bounds of the political sphere and political period of 1933–45. You view this—and quite narrow-mindedly in my opinion—merely, or primarily, as an attempt to deflect interest from the political-ideological core of events. In my opinion, in arguing this way you fail to give proper consideration to the fact that only by the inclusion of such other perspectives do many aspects of the question as to how Nazi rule was able to develop become comprehensible. Only by including such perspectives can numerous "shearing forces," as it were, lying outside of ideology and politics be rendered visible for the first time. This in no way alters the judgment about the crimes of the Nazis; yet it helps make more comprehensible why such large segments of a civilized nation succumbed mistakenly—and to such a massive degree—to National Socialism and Hitler. Historicization in this sense also means, above all else, an attempt to remove some part of that barrier which would make this period in history appear to be a completely strange and alien phenomenon.

Christian Meier was correct in his recent reference to this point. For a long time, not only the Germans in the GDR but in the Federal Republic as well, which claims to be the successor state of the German Reich, were unwilling to accept this successor status, but rather had accustomed themselves to presenting German history prior to 1945 with distancing, like the history of a foreign people. We wrote about this history only in the third person, and not in the first person plural; we were no longer able to feel that this history was somehow dealing with ourselves, and was "our thing."[6] Historicization, which wishes to contribute to lifting this barrier, is not an attempt to place the Nazi period in some compartment reserved for dead history. Rather, its intention is to create the prerequisite for rendering it at all possible for this utterly depraved chapter in German history to become capable of being integrated once again as a portion of one's own national history.

What I comprehend least of all is your criticism regarding the intention and manner of "everyday history" of the Nazi period, as we have been endeavoring to develop the approach in the Institut für Zeitgeschichte in Munich since the mid-1970s within the framework of the long-term "Bavaria Project." What we have focused on here is the previously much-neglected task of rendering historical memories comprehensible and infusing them with life, an endeavor which quite specifically does not seek to exclude the political and moral elements, but tries rather to provide them with a new foundation by means of concretization.

One such example of concretization involved rendering the motives of erring small-time Nazi supporters more transparent via the detailed presentation of a specific local milieu during the emergency, thus divesting the concept "Nazi" of its character as a mere catchword. It was also achieved, when, through the plastic portrayal of individuals and cases of brave resistance on a small scale, the exaggerated concept of the basic resistance was once again imbued with fidelity to historical reality, thus opening up for the reader a new approach to the topic, both via the path of *Verstehen* and that of moral empathy [*Nachvollzug*]. Or it was accomplished in still another manner: for example, when the Jews, the "objects" of this persecution, often degraded to mere abstractions in the description of Nazi persecution, took on palpable form in their concrete local and social milieu, and it became possible— through the presentation of concrete exemplary instances—to make visible the so heavily poisoned relationship between Germans and Jews under the conditions prevailing during Nazi rule.

Documentation and studies focusing on local and everyday history, like those of the "Bavaria Project," were able to unearth a profusion of previously unknown facts for the first time, specifically in regard to what remains the central question in moral terms—namely, what degree of involvement in the murderous persecution of Jews by the Nazi regime the majority of our people can be accused of, and what manner of guilt they incurred, also by failing to provide assistance and sympathy. It is not enough that the treatment of the Nazi period express the retrospectively correct moral view of its more-or-less smug and self-satisfied authors. As little as history can ill afford to get along "without distinguishing between good and evil"—as Dolf Sternberger recently pointed out in a thoughtful reflective commentary on the *Historikerstreit*—it likewise cannot do without "a sympathetic and involved interest."[7]

In conclusion, I would like to take up once again the problem of German and Jewish historical memory and—at your special suggestion—the role of Auschwitz within this historical memory. I believe I made clear that what I mean by "mythical memory" is precisely a form of remembrance located outside the framework of (German and Jewish) historical science. However, such remembrance is by no means simply the negative opposite pole to scholarship and scientific method; it is not simply erroneous or coarsened historical memory. Precisely when confronted with the inexpressible events of the Holocaust, many Jews have indeed come to regard as indispensable a ritualized, almost historical-theological remembrance, interwoven with other elements of Jewish fundamental world-historical experience, alongside the mere dry historical reconstruction of facts—because the incommensurability of Auschwitz cannot be dealt with in any other way.

For this reason, there probably is no need to provide an answer to those additional and very artificial questions regarding any classification, as imputed by you, of various historians, Jewish and German. We certainly both agree that such great émigré German-Jewish scholars as Hannah Arendt, Franz Neumann, and Ernst Fraenkel achieved pioneering insights into the nature of National Socialism, viewed in part precisely from the vantage of a longer-range historical perspective—insights whose importance was not recognized and utilized by German research on recent history sufficiently until at best fifteen to twenty years later.

What remains for us a difficult problem—one that may lie at the very center of our differing conceptions, though it need not necessarily be a line of demarcation separating the perspectives of Jewish and German historians—is that the magnitude and singularity of the horrifying events of the destruction of the Jews call not only for a mythical interpretation; rather, they also necessitate a retrospective construction of diabolical causation in historical presentation which is comparable in scale. Consequently, this need has repeatedly come into conflict with the political-scientific discovery of the "banality of evil" by Hannah Arendt or with other historical treatments which demonstrate that the full magnitude of this crime was made up of a multitude of often very small contributing elements, and of frequently negligible portions of guilt.

A point is reached in confronting the singular event of Auschwitz where scientific comprehensibility and explicability are doubtless far outstripped by the sheer epochal significance of the event. For that reason, Auschwitz has in retrospect rightfully been felt again and again indeed to be the central event of the Nazi period—and this not only by Jews. Consequently, Auschwitz also plays a central role in the West German historical treatment of the Nazi period—in school books, for example—as can be readily shown. And in the face of the especially intense Jewish memory of the Holocaust, it may well be that such intensity causes other deeds and outrages perpetrated by the Third Reich to pale and fade away more and more in the memory of the world. Yet this potential of Holocaust memory also tends retrospectively toward the creation of new hierarchy and ordering of the factors shaping history, i.e., an attempt to unfurl the entire history of the Third Reich in reverse fashion backwards starting from Auschwitz, instead of unfolding its development in a forward direction, in keeping with historical methodology.

When viewed retrospectively, one historical fact must be juxtaposed to the centrality of Auschwitz: namely, that the liquidation of the Jews was only feasible during the period of time in which it actually was carried out specifically because that liquidation was not in the limelight of events, but rather could largely be concealed and kept quiet. Such concealment was possible because this destruction involved a minority which even many years before had been systematically removed from the field of vision of the surrounding non-Jewish world as a result of social ghettoization. The ease with which the centrality of the "Final Solution" was carried out became a possibility because

the fate of the Jews constituted a little-noticed matter of secondary importance for the majority of Germans during the war; and because for the allied
enemies of Germany, it was likewise only one among a multitude of problems
they had to deal with during the war, and by no means the most important one.

It is evident that the role of Auschwitz in the original historical context of
action is one that is significantly different from its subsequent importance in
terms of later historical perspective. The German historian too will certainly
accept that Auschwitz—due to its singular significance—functions in retrospection as the central event of the Nazi period. Yet qua scientist and scholar,
he cannot readily accept that Auschwitz also be made, after the fact, into the
cardinal point, the hinge on which the entire factual complex of historical
events of the Nazi period turns. He cannot simply accept without further ado
that this entire complex of history be moved into the shadow of Auschwitz—
yes, that Auschwitz even be made into the decisive measuring rod for the
historical perception of this period. Such a perspective would not only serve,
after the fact, to force totally under its usurped domination those non–
National Socialist German traditions which extended on into the Nazi period
and, due to their being "appropriated" by the regime, to a certain extent
themselves fell prey to National Socialism. Above all else it would fail to do
justice to the immense number of non-German and non-Jewish victims, who
also have their own—and different—monuments of memory.

IV

Dear Mr. Broszat,

Each exchange, indeed, opens many new vistas in our discussion. Let me,
at the outset, try again to clarify the reasons for the possible misinterpretation
of your "Plea" as a demand for some kind of revision of the traditional historical representation of the Nazi epoch.

In our first exchange of letters, we agreed that the ambiguity of the historicization concept led, by itself, to many misunderstandings, and I added
some remarks about the possibly problematic aspects of the concept as such,
even when correctly understood. But there is more to it. It seems to me that
the aspect of the "Plea" which raised most questions was the way in which
the sequence of your arguments ended in a generalization about the moral
evaluation of the Nazi epoch.

The sequence could be read as follows: after the war, a black-and-white
picture of the Nazi era was imposed by an essentially émigré-dominated
historiography, creating some kind of moralistic "countermyth," as Ernst
Nolte would put it. This stereotypical, simplistic representation seemed
to endure, notwithstanding the passage of time. Now, after several decades, a change became imperative and you outlined the methodological
aspects of that change, aspects which I myself analyzed in my "Reflections."

It is at this point that what seemed to be the logical outcome of your argumentation—and these were the concluding lines of your text—found its expression:

A total distancing from the Nazi past is still a form of suppression and the creation of a taboo. . . . Lifting this blockade in favor of a moral sensitivization of history, itself inspired by the experience of National Socialism—that is the aim and hope of this plea for the historicization of the Nazi period.

This conclusion was meant, I am sure, to overcome the moral paralysis, the declamatory and ritual aspect which you impute to much that was written about Nazism over the last three decades. But widening the moral perception of the Nazi epoch to the whole of history as such, that is, making it boundless and, therefore, hard to define and to apply, except for general formulas about good and evil, could easily be understood as a thrust toward some kind of overall relativization of the moral problems *specifically raised by Nazism:* this may have created the feeling that your idea of historicization as expressed in the "Plea" was quite far-reaching.

You criticized what you considered to be my rejection of new historical approaches. Obviously, I am not opposed to social history of the Nazi era or to *Alltagsgeschichte* as such. In my "Reflections," I stated several times that, for the historian, the widening and nuancing of the picture was of the essence. But the "historicization," as you presented it and as was already discussed here, could mean not so much a widening of the picture, as a *shift of focus.* From *that* perspective, the insistence on *Alltag* or on long-range social trends could indeed strongly relativize what I still consider as the decisive historiographical approach to that period, an approach which considers these twelve years as a definable historical unit dominated, first of all, by the "primacy of politics." If we agree that this is the core, every additional differentiation is not only important, but necessary. My methodological "traditionalism" should be understood only in the context of my initial reading of the sense of the "Plea." As far as *Alltagsgeschichte* is concerned, however, I am of two minds. Some of the criticisms expressed at the colloquium which you yourself organized around the Bavaria Project and which carried the pertinent title *Alltagsgeschichte: Neue Perspektiven oder Trivialisierung?* do not seem unconvincing to me. But, as an example will show further on, many insights can obviously be drawn from the *Alltag.*

It would be helpful to clarify one more methodological point: your insistence on the *narrative approach* as the only possible historical approach for the *Gesamtdarstellung* [total account] you have in mind. In the "Plea," you criticized the fact that up to now when the historian turns to the Nazi era, "the ability to feel one's way empathetically into the web of historical interconnections evaporates along with the pleasure in historical narration." In your second letter, you insist on the narrative approach and have hard things to say about conceptual history of the Nazi era. This was not your position when

118 *Martin Broszat and Saul Friedländer*

you wrote *The Hitler State*, and I assume that it is the constant awareness of the nuances of each specific situation, as brought to the fore in the Bavaria Project, which led you to change your theoretical approach.

One could argue about conceptual history versus traditional narrative until doomsday and come to no result. I am curious to see, however—and this is said without any irony—where, once we get the kind of total presentation you call for, the "pleasure in historical narration" will find its expression. It is not the "narrow" viewpoint of the victims I try to express, but something else. What created the distancing, what eliminated the normal historical empathy is not only the criminal dimension of the regime, but also the abhorrent vision of nationalist exaltation, of frenetic self-glorification which so rapidly penetrated practically all domains of public life and so much of private life, too.

Other regimes have demonstrated their capacity for criminality, but at their beginnings at least, in their official proclamations at least, they aimed at universal ideals, at changing the condition of man. We know what became of all this. Nonetheless, there can be a kind of ideologically free "pleasure in historical narration" when we think of "the ten days that shook the world," possibly even when we recall the first years of the Soviet experience, notwithstanding one's personal commitment to liberalism. The universalist dream is there in all its power. Nothing of that exists in Nazism. For other reasons, millions of people still feel historical understanding and empathy when they think of the Red Army crossing the borders of the Reich. For Andreas Hillgruber, this could be the viewpoint of the victims of Nazism only, and his "pleasure in historical narration" was awakened by the desperate resistance of the Wehrmacht. But for you, where could that domain be? Don't you think that, seen from the angle of narrative history and the "pleasure in historical narration," my argument about the possible reappearance of some kind of historicism is not entirely unfounded?

Let me now respond, very scantily, to what, in fact, would require much longer considerations: your thoughts about the place of "Auschwitz" within the *Gesamtdarstellung* of the Nazi epoch. First of all, when I speak of "Auschwitz" in this context, I refer to Nazi annihilation policies toward various categories of victims. As I mentioned at the end of my first letter, I consider Auschwitz as a paradigmatic expression of Nazi criminality. In that sense, the implicit meaning of the last line of your second letter does not correspond to my thinking.

You state—and we obviously agree—that for any historian of the Nazi epoch, Auschwitz is the salient "event," because of its specificity and incommensurability. It seems to me that Jürgen Habermas recently expressed this specificity and incommensurability in particularly strong terms:

Something took place here [in Auschwitz] which up until that time no one had even thought might be possible. A deep stratum of solidarity between all that bears a human countenance was touched here. The integrity of this deep stratum had, up until that time, remained unchallenged, and this despite all the natural bestialities of world history. . . . Auschwitz has altered the conditions for the continuity of historical life connections—not only in Germany.[8]

You write that this incommensurability of Auschwitz calls for a mythical creative memory to help in reaching any kind of understanding. Historiography, indeed, does not suffice. This being said, I agree with you that the historian, as historian, cannot consider the Nazi era from its catastrophic end only. According to the accepted historical method, we have to start at the beginning and follow the manifold paths as they present themselves, including numerous developments within German society which had little to do with Auschwitz, and this throughout the history of the era. But the historian *knows the end* and he shares this knowledge with his reader. This knowledge should not hamper the exploration of all the possible avenues and interpretations, but it compels the historian to choose the central elements around which his unfolding narrative is implicitly built. In short, we come back to the problem of the dominant focus. Nobody would argue that a whole chapter on social security cannot be included in a *Gesamtdarstellung*, but even if you show the normalcy of everyday life, even if you stress the split consciousness, the main thrust of your narrative progresses toward an end that you know very well.

All this leads to the two arguments outlined toward the end of your second letter and which seem to me to be central to your entire demonstration. Their validity would allow, up to a point, the integration of Auschwitz within the general framework of the historicization of the Nazi epoch, as outlined in the "Plea."

First, you indicate that the very singularity and incommensurability of Auschwitz not only leads to a necessary search for some kind of mythical interpretation, but that, on the level of historiography, it also leads (only for some historians, obviously) to a reconstruction of the chain of events, as if these had been initiated by equally singular, almost demonic, causes. This created, for scientific historiography, the kind of problem which you already mentioned in your first letter. In your opinion, the answer is to be found in Hannah Arendt's theory of "the banality of evil."

Secondly, you write that the centrality of Auschwitz, as we perceive it today, was not perceived during the events, as the Jews had been progressively isolated from the surrounding populations, the annihilation was kept totally secret, and even the Allies did not consider it a central issue.

Both the "banality of evil" and the nonperception of the events by German society are clearly essential for the historicization of National Socialism. Let me try to relate to both points, albeit in inverse order, and, necessarily, in the most schematic terms.

Let us start with what people knew or did not know. As far as Germany is concerned, the most recent studies of this problem—the one by Ian Kershaw in his revised English edition of *The "Hitler Myth": Image and Reality in the Third Reich*[9] and an excellent study in *Alltagsgeschichte*, H. and S. Obenaus's *Schreiben, wie es wirklich war!* . . .[10]—indicate that the general population was much more aware of what was happening to the Jews than we thought up to now. But why not quote your own texts, for instance your 1983 article, "Zur Struktur der NS-Massenbewegung," where you write, concerning what the population knew of the extermination policies against the Jews:

> The Nazi leadership was thus itself plagued by the strongest doubts as to whether the full knowledge of the crimes it had initiated would find popular support. Yet these persecutions were not so completely and totally evident and visible. And especially the antihuman basic conception from which they were derived—in particular, the fanatical hatred of the Jews—was repeatedly given expression by the leadership in public on almost every occasion. Thus, there was certainly a social basis of response for this.[11]

More telling even is the remark you make at the end of the same article concerning the possible reasons for the passivity of the German population, even as the end approached: "One factor involved here apparently was also the consciousness that one had a shared complicity in the excesses and crimes of the regime."[12]

In short, although the destruction of the Jews may have been a minor point in the perceptions and policies of the Allies during the war, it seems, more and more, that it loomed as a hidden but perceived fact in many German minds during the war itself.

If my point is correct, it has considerable importance in relation to the core thesis of your "Plea." Indeed, normal life with the knowledge of ongoing massive crimes committed by one's own nation and one's own society is not so normal after all. . . .

In your opinion, Hannah Arendt's "banality of evil" offers the historiographical answer to the kind of unacceptable constructs which you mentioned. Immense evil can result from a multitude of tiny, almost unperceived and more or less banal individual initiatives. There need not be an overriding evil design to achieve a totally evil result. But even Hannah Arendt used other concepts when dealing with Nazism and the "Final Solution." You may recall that she spoke of "radical evil," too, and that, in a famous letter to Karl Jaspers, she considered the actions of the Nazis as not to be comprehended in normal categories of guilt and punishment.[13]

I do not know, by the way, who the historians are who seek demonic causes to explain Auschwitz. I know of some Germans and others who put emphasis on ideology and on centrally directed policies: this has little to do with demonology, and I cannot understand why you impute this strange position to historians belonging to the group of the victims. Nobody denies the "banality of evil" at many levels within this annihilation process, but it possibly is not the only explanation at all levels.

In my opinion, part of the leadership and part of the followers, too, had the feeling of accomplishing something truly, historically, metahistorically, exceptional. We both know Himmler's Posen speech of October 1943 in its details. This is not the banality of evil, this is not, as far as the Jewish question is concerned, a pep talk to tired SS dignitaries; it is the expression of a *Rausch*, [exhilaration], the feeling of an almost superhuman enterprise. That is why I would tend to consider some important aspects of the Nazi movement in terms of "political religion," in the sense used by Eric Voegelin, Norman Cohn, Karl Dietrich Bracher, James Rhodes, Uriel Tal, and many others. If we speak of a political religion, we come closer again to the traditional framework, but from an angle which leaves ample space for new investigations. That is what I meant in the "Reflections" when I referred to the still nebulous relation between ideology and politics as far as, for instance, the "Final Solution" was concerned. And if we take this angle, then, indeed, we are somewhat at a distance from the *Alltag* in Schabbach, but not very far from the *SS Ordensburgen* or from the insistence of some of the commanders of the *Einsatzgruppen* to stay on duty, not very far either from that *Rausch* which penetrated so far and so deep and which was not just the result of a functionally useful "Hitler-Myth." All this, too, somehow has to be interpreted within the continuity of German history. Here, no doubt, we agree.

Finally, allow me some remarks about the German-Jewish dialogue, its difficulties and its possibilities. When Gershom Scholem, in the text you mention, spoke of this dialogue as a myth, he referred first of all to the pre-Nazi period, in which, possibly, the Jews in Germany carried on a "dialogue" with themselves. After what happened between 1933 and 1945, the idea of such a dialogue appeared to Scholem as a desecration of the memory of the dead. He may have changed his mind later on, and his stay in Berlin, shortly before his death, may have been an expression of this change of mind.

The fundamental difficulty of such a dialogue remains nonetheless, and is compounded by the layers of ritualized behavior and gross interests which cover it. You mentioned this difficulty in general terms, but you also referred to it in relation to the "pressing questions" which I asked you in the last part of my first letter. These were not "pressing questions:" it was an attempt to understand what you meant by opposing the rationally oriented German historiography to the more mythically oriented memory of the victims. In your answer, you give central importance to the mythical memory and, as for the difficulties of historiography in the face of unacceptable constructs, you present them with less emphasis, but present them nonetheless, as I have just tried to show.

In case the change of emphasis in your second letter was more the expression of a desire not to push too strongly a theme considered overly sensitive for our discussions, perhaps you would wish to reconsider. Some measure of openness belongs to our "experiment" and this openness, as you yourself noted, is the only possible basis for a true German-Jewish dialogue.

V

Dear Mr. Friedländer,

I have given a great deal of thought to the question of the element of constraint or openness in our exchange of ideas in the wake of your final remark in your last letter. The difficulty inherent in our dialogue—and this we both agree on—is probably also manifested in this respect. You yourself express it with a certain degree of reserve when you state that "some measure of openness" is necessary. In the concluding section of your first letter, as in your "Reflections," you had already warned about the danger of overestimating the possibilities of objective scholarly-scientific treatment of the Nazi period, since this period was still "much too present" and it was by no means an easy task for present-day historians to rid themselves of their prejudices or even to make themselves conscious to these prejudices. Of course, I wonder whether your skepticism necessarily has to burden our discourse with such a high degree of suspicion, which I repeatedly can sense behind your comments and remarks.

Thus, I find it very meaningful that in connection with the above-mentioned admonition you also conjecture that certain positions of the *Historikerstreit* in the Federal Republic may perhaps be bound up with the fact that the German historians involved in that debate "belong to the generation of Hitler Youth." In the context of our correspondence and what occasioned it, this remark should probably also categorize my plea for historicization as being a need of the generation of Hitler Youth. A few paragraphs before that, you challenge me in your first letter to apply the concept of "critical understanding" which I make use of to the example put forward by Andreas Hillgruber of the "German Wehrmacht units which held the Eastern front in 1944/45" (and thus also helped to maintain the concentration camps). You contend that that would constitute "almost a litmus test," and it is your belief I should not be spared that test. In your second letter, you broached the matter of Hillgruber's identification with the Eastern front and inquired as to whether my "delight in historical narration" might perhaps wish to seize upon this topic as well, or some other one.

Do you really believe, Mr. Friedländer, that such questions are merely pensive and reflective, rather than "pressing" and constraining, that they serve to promote the openness of our dialogue—and do not engender embarrassing constraint? Haven't you yourself staked out such definite positions in your suspicious distrust of possible tendencies toward trivialization and minimization in dealing with the Nazi period in the work of German historians, in particular those of the generation of Hitler Youth—as expressed in articles you have published and lectures you have given (specifically, for some time now, in the form of a critique of my "Plea")—that you are no longer able to break free from and abandon these positions, even here in this exchange of letters? Wasn't, for example, the dispute you had several years ago with Syberberg's and others' treatments of the Nazi period in films or imaginative literature[14]—in itself a quite fascinating confrontation—shaped and determined to an excessive degree by such a pessimistic, suspicious distrust? In so doing, haven't you also erected a fence around yourself, one which only permits you "some measure of openness"?

First I would like to say something about the topic of the generation of Hitler Youth, to which I belong (born 1926); these remarks are not only intended in reference to my own case, but are broader in implication. Initially, allow me a very personal comment: if I myself had not been a member of the generation of Hitler Youth, if I had not lived through its very specific experiences, then I probably would not have felt such a need after 1945 to confront the Nazi past so critically and, as we sensed back then, to do this at the same time with "solemn sobriety." As a member of that generation, one had the good fortune of not yet being drawn (or being drawn only marginally) into political responsibility for actions. Yet one was old enough to be affected emotionally and intellectually to a high degree by the suggestivity—so confounding to feeling and to one's sense of morality—which the Nazi regime was capable of, especially in the sphere of youth education, and this despite the counterinfluence stemming from parents, teachers, and acquaintances who were critical of the regime. An important portion of the potential for youthful dreams had been occupied, taken over by the world of Nazism; it was no longer possible to dream other, better dreams.

Only later on, in the period of retreat into the realm of private values during the final years of the war and the immediate postwar period, did we begin to make up avidly, greedily for what we had missed—with a growing feeling, and sense of anger, that we had been cheated out of important years of our youth. Affected, yet hardly burdened, the generation of Hitler Youth was both freer than those who were older, and more motivated than those who were younger, to devote itself totally to the learning process of these years. From the personal knowledge of many of my contemporaries—and this is, I believe, confirmed by the biographies of many others—I know that the majority of this generation of Hitler Youth after 1945 adopted with enthusiasm the values once denounced by the Nazis, and made them their own. An especially large number of committed democrats emerged from this generation, and that generation is indeed overrepresented in the ranks of those who are prominent in politics and culture in the Federal Republic today, as is shown by a report on contemporaries published on the occasion of the fortieth anniversary of the end of the World War II.[15]

I must try to maintain further openness, if only because, with the necessarily limited framework of our exchange of letters, this is, for the moment, the last opportunity I will have to come back to a few points in your argumentation which I do not wish to let pass without comment, lest the documentation of our exchange of ideas become defective by dint of omission.

First of all, I would like to deal with three clarifications regarding specific points. I then intend to return to several more complex issues that will lead back to the thematic substance of our discussion.

—In my first letter, I stated only that the *concept* of historicization as such was ambiguous and can easily be misused—not my presentation as contained in the "Plea." You thus went too far and were mistaken in contending in your first letter that we were both in agreement that I had expressed myself in a misleading way in this "Plea."

—Your version of the supposed motivation of my "Plea," as put forward in the third paragraph of your second letter, has no basis in what I have written. You yourself call your version a possible reading ("could be read as . . ."). I would have preferred you to have made reference to what I had actually written. I am also surprised that you then go on to embellish the motivation imputed by you to underlie my "Plea" with an imputed concept drawn from Ernst Nolte. This is reminiscent of your already characterized attempt, also contained in your "Reflections," to place my "Plea" in close proximity to Andreas Hillgruber's identification with the Eastern front.

—At the end of the second letter, you give rise to the impression, as you did in your first letter, that I had made a distinction between a rational German memory of the Nazi period versus an irrational Jewish memory of that time. In so doing, you completely reverse and misconstrue the train of thought which guided me and which I was trying to express. I already made clear reference in my first letter to two points, and did so with the expressed purpose of wishing to supplement my plea in this respect and to expand its initially German-centered perspective, as determined by the motivating occasion. My first point was that "any exclusive German claim to historical interpretation in respect to this period had been forfeited" as a result of the outrages of the Nazi regime; secondly, I pointed out that alongside the scientific-academic reconstruction of the Nazi period (by German and non-German historians), there was also a legitimate claim by the victims for other forms of historical memory (for example, mythical), and that there was "no prerogative of one side or the other."

You can appreciate that it was important for me to point out what I however alluded to above. Now, I would like to get back to several of the broader complexes touched on in our exchange of ideas. First of all, let me return once more to the questions of approaches in research and the focus in historical inquiry dealing with the Nazi period.

You concede that "everyday history" or looking at the Nazi period in terms of a longer-range social-historical perspective, is a positive development—as long as there is some guarantee that the most important aspect of the period, i.e., the Nazi world view [*Weltanschauung*] and the criminal dimension of the political system, remains within the center and focus of the approach. In contrast, I hold that the wish to prescribe what should or should not be done scientifically—and thus to juxtapose and contrast Broszat qua author of the study *The Hitler State* to Broszat qua author within the "Bavaria Project"—

leads us astray, forcing us into a constrictive narrowing of the possibility to ask scientific questions.

In research such as the "Bavaria Project," for example, what is crucial initially is to gain new experiences and impressions of the historical reality of the Nazi period as based on a specific new approach, in order to then be able to contrast these in fruitful and productive fashion with experiences garnered using other research approaches. Naturally, you are quite correct in stating that the focus of the "Bavaria Project" differs from the focus, for example, of my earlier studies over many years of German and National Socialist policy toward Poland, or work on the Nazi concentration camps. But a concentrated pursuit of a specific research perspective would be quite impossible if one constantly had to worry and fret nervously about whether the focus—which would naturally have to pay considerable attention to the political system and world view of National Socialism in the writing of any comprehensive treatment of the Nazi period—is also properly chosen within the framework of such a specialized study.

I also wish to contradict your view, expressed with such great eloquence, that a study of the *Ordensburgen* is a greater contribution to essential knowledge on the period than a study of the everyday history of Schabbach. If you take a good look at the findings of all six volumes of the series *Bayern in der NS-Zeit,* you will easily note that what has been documented there is by no means simply an unpolitical "normalcy" of everyday life under Nazism. Rather, one can see that the criminal dimension also extends to a considerable degree far out into the Bavarian province, and that it can even be illustrated in a very vivid and impressive manner instantiated in the local fates of individuals in this province. Take, for instance, the case documented in the sixth volume of this series: that of the Würzburg lawyer and wine dealer Obermayer, who was persecuted with especially rapacious vindictiveness by the Gestapo as a Jew and homosexual—for double ideological reasons, as it were; a man who nonetheless proved capable of resisting this persecution over many years, and with astounding bravery, until he finally met his death in Mauthausen. Yet, on the other hand, I see the function of a research endeavor such as the "Bavaria Project" precisely in its ability to render the side-by-side existence—to an extent without any linking connections—of (a) a relatively unpolitical "normal life" and (b) the dictatorial impositions and persecutions of the regime, a fruitful object for historical inquiry and further thought. In this regard, what can and should ultimately emerge is what you have justifiably stressed using the example of the "half-knowledge" of the German people regarding the crimes perpetrated against the Jews: namely, that under such conditions, everyday life in the Nazi period was probably not as normal after all as it might appear to have been on the surface.

Yet it is not only these political-moral key questions which are of concern here. Historicization of the Nazi period also encompasses the possibility of looking at the events of this time from the point of view of functionality as well: for example, within the framework of a social-historical theory of mod-

ernization. This certainly entails a shift in focus. But it is unlikely any historian who still has his wits about him will, as a result, forget the political aspects, and especially the criminal nature of the regime, or exclude these in an
overall treatment of the period.

A quite different aspect of historicization is the problem I raised—which
you apparently misunderstood—of the expressive powers of historiography
when confronted with the so "corrupt" historical segment of the Nazi period.
I had originally written about the lost "delight" in historical narration in another context prior to my "Plea" [16]—this is an article you were probably not
familiar with, and in that other context the word itself had an ironic meaning.
Actually, it is not a question of "delight"; rather, what is important is the
restoration of a plastic historical language even in dealing with the indeed
often quite sinister or mediocre figures of the Nazi period—in order to raise
these figures up from their shadowy existence as mere phantoms and make
them once more the subjects of emphatic (and this can also mean angry) retrospective reexperiencing, and thus likewise subjects of a new moral encounter. Perhaps it is only the plasticity of language which can finally determine
whether a figure or a pattern of action of the Nazi period can indeed be conceived of only in typological or symbolic terms, and can no longer be made a
living concrete reality within historical language.

I consider it extremely hard—and, in the final analysis, unfair—to justify
that you are willing to regard the erring Trotsky, if need be, as a worthy object for the language-based illustrative demonstration of history, but that, by
the same token, you would completely withhold the consideration of language from the erring petit bourgeois [*Kleinbürger*] of the Nazi era—a petit
bourgeois who voted for Hitler and followed him, but who otherwise profited
very little from this and understood even less; and who nonetheless unintentionally made a significant contribution to the efficiency of the regime—
indeed, a prototype who "made history" during the Nazi period. There will
continue to be spheres within the Nazi period which elude the grasp of plastic
historical language. But to deny this language to the Nazi period as a whole
appears to me similar to a denial of the historiographical method based on
criticism of sources—because what is at the heart of the project of infusing
history with life through the medium of language is an attempt to recover
authenticity.

In closing, I would like once again to address myself to the topic of
Auschwitz and several of the problems arising from this for history as a science and for historical memory. In your second letter, you stated that what
you meant by "Auschwitz" was, quite generally, the "Nazi annihilation policies toward various categories of victims." You say that you regard Auschwitz
as a "paradigmatic expression of Nazi criminality" as such. In my view, such
a far-reaching extension of the concept is problematic, also precisely because
it is no longer possible then readily to give reasons for and defend the singularity of Auschwitz. If Auschwitz is employed only as a synonym for the

"Final Solution," the problem I have alluded to remains: namely, that in connection with the "centrality of Auschwitz," which should be underscored for good reasons in any historical, retrospective view, one must also bear in mind just how many other, non-Jewish victims of Nazism there were.

I would like quite expressly to second your position when you emphasize that the "banality of evil" cannot by any means serve as a sole and exclusive explanation for the mass murder of the Jews. That was not what I meant, and I think what you say on this point is impressive; for example, as seen from the perspective of a negative "political religion," which I likewise regard as a possible way of trying to comprehend the fanatical hatred of the Jews based on the Nazi worldview. However, let me also point out that the older generation of German historians (Meinecke, Ritter, Rothfels, and others), a generation that initially played a dominant role in German historiography after 1945, very often resorted to writing about a "demonic" or "diabolical" Hitler and the like as a consequence of their inability to offer historical explanations. In contrast with this, there has long been a need for more rational explanation, and such metaphors tend in this connection to impede further questioning rather than furnish answers. When I myself stated that I considered it important, for example, to make clear that even the existence of such a murderous, racist ideology as that of the Nazis nonetheless did not necessarily have to lead automatically to genocide as a consequence—and that the historian therefore was charged with the task of investigating very carefully what the operative real conditions were, in the context of what structures of influence and power, etc., it became possible to translate such an ideology into practice—I saw this likewise as a contribution to historicization: namely, in the sense that the normal historical methods of inquiry and research should also be applied to the study of National Socialism. It should, however, be borne in mind that this is a plea for normalization of the method, not of the evaluation.

Let me come now to the final point that I regard as important in our discussion. My conception of historicization—and this certainly must be quite evident—is antithetically opposed to any presentation of the Nazi period in the form of frozen "statuary," and meant primarily for didactic purposes. As I see it, the danger of suppressing this period consists not only in the customary practice of forgetting, but rather, in this instance—almost in paradoxical fashion—likewise in the fact that one is too overly "concerned," for didactic reasons, about this chapter in history. As a result, what happens is that an arsenal of lessons and frozen "statuary" are pieced together from the original, authentic continuum of this era; these increasingly take on an independent existence. Particularly in the second and third generation, they then intrude to place themselves in front of the original history—and are finally, in naive fashion, understood and misunderstood as being the actual history of the time.

That danger is all the greater when historians themselves believe that they no longer need to make any special effort to present an authentic picture of this time—since that period has, in any case, been so totally corrupted by the

Nazis; and when historians are accommodatingly inclined to hand over and relinquish this period of history, without any regrets, to be utilized for purposes other than that of historical understanding.

I am firmly convinced that it is precisely the credibility of the didactic transmission of the Nazi period which would suffer immense damage over the longer term if it is not left sufficiently open to repeated feedback from the process of differentiated historical knowledge about this segment of history.

I can well imagine that, seen in this perspective, the centrality of Auschwitz—which lies so very much in the foreground of consciousness and which presses so compellingly for a paradigmatic view—can also pose a problem for the Jewish historical memory of the Nazi period and the transmission of this authentic memory to the following generation. The gigantic dictatorial and criminal dimension of the Nazi period also harbors within it the danger that the authenticity of this segment of history may end up being buried beneath monumental memorial sites for the Resistance—and indeed perhaps also beneath memorials for the Holocaust. In contrast with this, I would like, in closing this final letter, to quote a sentence of the great Israeli historian Uriel Tal, which he formulated in such impressive manner some years ago in Jerusalem at a German-Jewish discussion on the proper form which the historical presentation and treatment of the Holocaust should take. As I best recall, his exact words were: "We have not only or primarily to tell what had been done to the Jews, but what had been lost."

VI

December 31, 1987

Dear Mr. Broszat,

The inner tension, which, to various degrees, accompanied our exchange of letters, may have been, among other things, the expression of a fundamental commitment to the values which have prompted both of us to devote our entire professional lives to the study of the Nazi period. This tension does not stem from a divergence in basic values, but from differences in perspectives which, nevertheless, appear to us to be of major importance.

In this concluding letter, I shall attempt to clarify, first of all, an issue which you emphasized in your last response—the problem of generations. I shall then touch upon some of your more polemical remarks and finally attempt to sum up where, in my eyes, our differences in interpretation may lie, as well as where I feel our positions have come closer together as a result of this exchange.

Allow me, just incidentally, to correct a purely semantic misunderstanding, as you attached some importance to this question. My basic language is French and my English is often influenced by gallicisms: when I wrote "some measure of openness," I had automatically translated from the French "une certaine mesure de franchise," which, notwithstanding the apparent meaning, has no restrictive connotation. It simply means: openness. We have, I think, succeeded in large part in expressing ourselves in this spirit.

Let me now deal with the first issue, that of generations and, more particularly, the problem of the "Hitler Youth generation." As a matter of fact, these age-group distinctions and their impact on the memory of the Nazi epoch were clearly made by all the participants in a seminar organized at the *Wissenschaftskolleg* in Berlin on German historical memory of the Nazi period, which you, unfortunately, were unable to attend. In that context, all the German participants pointed to the crucial importance of the "Hitler Youth generation" and its diverse implications.[17]

My own thinking on this issue, however, led me to a comparative perspective, whereby this German age group has a significant counterpart among the victims. What is *common to both* is the fact that they are the *last* groups active on the public scene whose members carry a personal, clear memory of the Nazi period. Therefore, the members of these groups—be they Germans, Jews, or others directly involved—have to confront this personal memory with what they may perceive as a kind of shift of collective representations of that past in surrounding society in general. Furthermore, they have to face a possible growing dissonance between their own memories and what their counterpart group constructs in terms of collective memory (this is also true of the groups of Jews and Poles, for instance). The dissonance between personal memory and socially constructed memories, within one's own society as well as within the counterpart groups, is, I think, one of the reasons which give the present debates their peculiar intensity, aside from the various familiar political-ideological elements. This also holds true when it comes to the *Historikerstreit,* as the great majority of those involved are part of the age group just mentioned (although I am six years your junior, I am, nonetheless, part of the group's outer limit). Within this group, there may be attempts, quite differing and even antithetical, to fix the experience in some kind of final form.

The point of my argument has been and still is that we are all inextricably caught in a web composed of personal recollections, general social conditioning, acquired professional knowledge, and attempts at critical distancing. In point of fact, it is axiomatic that each and every historian, by definition, is confronted with such contextual problems, and yet is able to master these problems and resolve them to a considerable extent, mainly within the sphere of limited, small-scale research. However, if a total interpretation is what is aimed at, like in an extreme case such as ours, I do not believe, be it from experience, observation or from a theoretical point of view, that our generation can "jump out" of this context, much as it may wish to do so.

In relation to the historicization issue, this indeed means that for us a kind of purely scientific distancing from that past, that is, a passage from the realm of knowledge strongly influenced by personal memory to that of some kind of "detached" history, remains, in my opinion, a psychological and epistemological illusion.

The decisive question is that of the attitude toward the same epoch of age groups that come after ours. Is their existential involvement with this epoch lesser or possibly nonexistent, or will it be so in the future? Are the historians among them crossing the line between an existentially determined perspective and a detached scientific point of view? I do not believe that this, for the time being, is the case for many of them. Christian Meier expresses this well when he writes:

It is precisely this path leading beyond the threshold to the "merely historical and nothing more" which the twelve years from 1933 to 1945 apparently do not wish to tread. Instead of becoming shadowy, this past seems to be growing ever larger and more global, and it reaches in undiminished vitality into our own lives.[18]

The same impact of that past weighs, obviously, on parts of the younger generation belonging to the group of the victims. All this makes the correlation between the passage of time and the possibility of a detached historical view of the Nazi epoch, that is, its historicization, still problematic. As expressed by a younger historian, Wolfgang Benz:

Thus, an open and candid approach to National Socialism, and its treatment—solely for purposes of scholarly interest—as but one era of German history among others, does not as yet appear to be such an easy and ready option. An interval of only forty or fifty years is still not enough to make the Nazi period something historical.[19]

When it comes to the future development of perception and memory, however, I am not quite so confident about this prediction. Maybe things could turn out quite differently. . . .

Let me come to my second point and some polemical aspects of your last letter: in my "Reflections," as well as in my letters, I have constantly kept in mind that no basic values cause opposition between us, and that we are discussing matters of perspective, although historiographically of major significance. I had not forgotten the strong lines, so encouraging during the *Historikerstreit,* that you wrote in your "Wo sich die Geister scheiden."[20] If there remain some misunderstandings in our exchange, they can easily be clarified.

The opposition, raised at the end of your first letter, between the mythological memory of the victims and the more rational approach of German historiography, seemed quite clearly stated to me. In your last letter, you indicate that you had differentiated between the historians of both sides on the one hand ("German and non-German historians"), and the mythical memory of the victims, understood in a general sense, on the other. I am glad you have now put it this way.

I mentioned Ernst Nolte's "countermyth" in my last letter because, notwithstanding the total difference between the two of you in positions and argumentation—a difference I made crystal clear at the beginning of my "Reflections"—the postulate that a black-and-white, postwar-determined, moralistic history of the Nazi period had now to be approached without any forbidden questions and without any pedagogical aims, was indeed some kind of common starting point for both conservative as well as more progressively oriented historians. Hans Mommsen stated this unmistakably in his *Merkur* article "Suche nach der 'verlorenen Geschichte'?" and he made special mention there of Ernst Nolte.[21] In that sense, my remark was a purely factual one and, in any event, I agree with that view myself.

You reproach me for juxtaposing your position with that of Andreas Hillgruber's representation of events on the Eastern front in 1944–45. In my "Reflections" and my first letter, I referred to Hermann Rudolf's article "Falsche Fronten," an article we both praised, to point out the difficulty that he had underscored: one could not, on the one hand, be in favor of historicization and, on the other, distance oneself from Hillgruber's mode of representing the situation on the Eastern front, for moralistic reasons. *There* lies part of the difficulty of historicization, as far as the abolition of distance and moral judgments are concerned: it is within those "intermediate" situations that some major obstacles become, I think, evident. This is the only reason why I mentioned that text and indeed wrote that it was a kind of litmus test of the whole problem of distancing and moral positions. When I referred to Hillgruber for the second time, in relation to the "Lust am geschichtlichen Erzählen," I did not write that *you* found the "pleasure in historical narration" in the same area as Hillgruber, but, precisely, I asked *where* in that epoch one could find an expression for it.

Finally, you state that the *concept* of historicization was unclear, but not its application in the "Plea." The trouble is that the "Plea" could not be clearly understood if its basic concept was in itself unclear and open to misunderstanding. Much clarification, however, has been achieved by this exchange.

This having been said, there remain between us some differences concerning the historical representation of the epoch, though one should also bear in mind what we could regard as the product of our now improved understanding. Let me avoid repeating here the problem of the primacy of politics versus longitudinal social trends, etc. Let me skip the issue of periodization, and concentrate on distancing, narration, and different evaluations determined by different group contexts. I shall approach each issue from an angle thus far not strongly emphasized, to avoid mere repetition.

First, the issue of distance. There is, it seems to me, a fundamental difference between normality defined as long-term social processes, as the outward aspects of daily life, etc., and the *perception of normality*. If, within the context of objectively definable normal processes, wide strata of the population perceived the criminal aspects of the system, even in the nonmassive criminality of the early years and certainly in their massive criminality later on, and did not distance themselves outrightly from the system itself—whatever the expression of this distancing could have been—the nondistancing for the postwar historian remains something of an intractable problem. I can well appreciate your desire for differentiation and, thanks to our exchange, also the point you made in your last letter about the need to bring contemporary Germans to a recognition of their past by dissolving the traditionally determined, automatic reaction of general and wholesale distancing. Nonetheless, the difficulties entailed by such an undertaking are obvious, because this endeavor is Janus-faced, both on the level of reception and interpretation.

In my opinion, the possibility of a historical narrative reaching a high degree of plastic representation, in the sense of the "historical narration" as you explained it in a very interesting way in your third letter, is relatively easy to achieve within the realms of normality, but becomes a growing problem when you move to the other side of the spectrum. By the way, even within the realm of normality, the image of the common "fellow traveler" [*Mitläufer*] has become something of a stereotype, possibly the most widely used one in the representation of the Nazi era. In fact, stereotypization is very difficult to avoid when we approach this epoch, possibly because behind each specific case one tends to establish, implicitly or explicitly, the category of political-moral behavior to which the specific case may be linked, this in itself being imposed by the existence of an outer limit of criminality within this system. In any event, when one abandons the field of normality and seminormality and enters the manifold criminal dimensions of the regime, the plasticity of description becomes practically impossible. One may wish merely to produce the documentation: more would be untenable or obscene.

I recently read Günther Schwarberg's *Der SS-Arzt und die Kinder: Bericht über den Mord vom Bullenhuser Damm*, which describes how some twenty Jewish children, aged five to twelve, from all over Europe were brought together for the purposes of medical experiments which I will not specify here. After the experiments were completed, the children were hanged in the basement of the Bullenhuser Damm school near Hamburg. At this stage of horror, no descriptions are, to my mind, possible, and if you take this as one example among hundreds of thousands and work your way back toward normality, you immediately see the problem which a "total presentation" encounters.

At some stage, a new style has to be introduced for the purpose of historical description, something we have not yet encountered very much in historiographical work. One could say, in fact, that for the historian who chooses narration regarding the immense majority of topics covered by historical inquiry, the duty is, in a sense, to try to visualize as well as possible the events described in order to be able to render them with all the necessary plasticity: when we approach the immense domain of Nazi criminality, the duty of the historian may well be to forego the attempt to visualize, precisely so that he can fulfill his task in terms of documentary precision and rendition of the events. This paradox may reveal from an unexpected angle what may well be one of the difficulties of historicization as we understand it in our exchange.

Finally, the issue of the differing agendas. By stressing the normality of daily life, the continuity of social processes, etc., you are possibly not only following a purely theoretical historiographical path, but also—and this is quite natural—restoring for the readers, i.e., for German society, a continuity in historical self-perception, not at the level of political institutions, but at that of the permanence of social reality. Although that is quite understandable, this type of perspective necessarily will differ considerably from that belonging to another group—and above all from the perspective of the victims. Almost by definition, we have differing emphases, differing foci in the general description of that epoch. What might be viewed as a kind of "fusion of horizons" is not in sight.

Moreover, we have never as yet given proper consideration to what is a very new problem, namely that of the historical "boundary event." As I see it, Auschwitz constitutes just such a "boundary event"—a phenomenon that is not necessarily singular, but which remains unprecedented. To return to Habermas, whom I quoted in my last letter: "A deep layer of solidarity between all that bears a human countenance was touched here." For this reason, the problem of "focus," as we would term it, remains for me an unresolved theoretical aspect in regard to a total description of the era, an aspect extending far beyond what could be viewed as a differing group perspective.

Dear Mr. Broszat, we are coming to the end of our discussion on historicization as such. Let me repeat here that, obviously, I am all in favor of trying to understand the Nazi epoch in all its historical dimensions, as well as we can, with all the methods at our disposal and without any forbidden questions. Our difference of perspectives relates, I think, to diverging approaches after all this has been admitted as an obvious postulate. What the result of the historians' endeavors concerning this period will be in a few decades, neither of us knows. I mentioned previously the paradoxical effect of the passage of time as far as this period was concerned. Like you, I am also saddened by the enormous simplifications in the presentation of the Holocaust. Little can be done to counter this except to hold up one's own scientific-scholarly standards in contrast.

However, entirely opposite thoughts often cross my mind, as I mentioned above, and then I foresee that within a very short span of time, the erosion of that past will increase rapidly within collective consciousness. It occurs to me that under the detached gaze of the future historian, the normal aspects of the picture of the Nazi epoch will, of necessity, grow in dimension and importance. The *intermediate categories* of representation which contain just enough elements of the nature of the regime to make them plausible will become the dominant mode of perception, not because of any conscious desire to eliminate the horrors of the past, but because the human mind, by a natural tendency which has nothing to do with national circumstances, prefers to dwell on the normal rather than the abnormal, on the understandable rather than on the opaque, on the comparable rather than on the incomparable, on the bearable rather than on the unbearable.

Notes

1. Saul Friedländer, "Some Reflections on the Historicization of National Socialism," in this volume, p. 88.
2. Cf. *Süddeutsche Zeitung*, 4–5 October 1986.
3. Hermann Graml and Klaus-Dietmar Henke, eds., *Nach Hitler: Der schwierige Umgang mit unserer Geschichte. Beiträge von Martin Broszat* (Munich, 1986), 130.
4. Gershom Scholem, "Wider den Mythos vom deutsch-jüdischen Gespräch," *Judaica* 2 (Frankfurt am Main, 1970), 7ff.
5. Friedländer, "Some Reflections."
6. Christian Meier, *40 Jahre nach Auschwitz: Deutsche Geschichtserinnerung heute* (Munich, 1987), 42ff.
7. Dolf Sternberger, "Unzusammenhängende Notizen über Geschichte," *Merkur* 9 (1987), 748.
8. Jürgen Habermas, *Eine Art Schadensabwicklung* (Frankfurt am Main, 1987), 163, and *Historikerstreit*. In English in *The New Conservatism: Cultural Criticism and the Historians' Debate* (Cambridge, Mass., 1989).
9. Ian Kershaw, *The "Hitler Myth": Image and Reality in the Third Reich* (Oxford, 1987); see particularly chapter 9: "Hitler's Popular Image and the 'Jewish Question,'" 229ff.
10. H. and S. Obenaus, *"Schreiben, wie es wirklich war!" Aufzeichnungen Karl Duerkefaeldens aus den Jahren 1933–1945* (Hannover, 1985), 107ff.
11. Martin Broszat, "Zur Struktur der NS-Massenbewegung," *Vierteljahrshefte für Zeitgeschichte* 31 (1983): 74.
12. Broszat, "Zur Struktur," 76 (I am grateful to Professor Otto Dov Kulka for drawing my attention to this article by Martin Broszat.)
13. Letter of 17 August 1946, *Hannah Arendt—Karl Jaspers, Briefwechsel*, ed. Lotte Kohler and Hans Saner (Munich, 1985), 88–93.
14. Saul Friedländer, *Reflets du Nazisme* (Paris, 1982). The English translation is *Reflections of Nazism: An Essay on Kitsch and Death*, trans. Thomas Weyr (New York, 1984).
15. Werner Filmer and Heribert Schwan, eds., *Mensch der Krieg ist aus! Zeitzeugen erinnern sich* (Düsseldorf/Vienna, 1985).
16. Cf. Martin Broszat, "Der Despot von München: Gauleiter Adolf Wagner—eine Zentralfigur der bayerischen Geschichte," *Süddeutsche Zeitung*, 30–31 March 1985, weekend supplement. In this article, I attempted quite consciously to portray in a fairly plastic manner, and true to reality, the figure of this once so powerful *Gauleiter*, a man who in the standard works on Bavarian history is presented only in very phantomlike fashion by historians specializing in Bavaria.
17. The proceedings of the discussions can be found in the library of the *Wissenschaftskolleg* in Berlin.
18. Christian Meier, *40 Jahre nach Auschwitz: Deutsche Geschichtserinnerung heute* (Munich, 1987), 21.
19. Wolfgang Benz, "Warding Off the Past: A Problem Only for Historians and Moralists?" in this volume, p. 196.
20. Martin Broszat, "Wo sich die Geister scheiden: Die Beschwöring der Geschichte taugt nicht als nationaler Religionsersatz," *Historikerstreit*.
21. Hans Mommsen, "Such nach der 'verlorenen Geschichte'? Bemerkungen zum historischen Selbstverständis der Bundesrepublic," *Historikerstreit*.

7. Between Aporia and Apology: On the Limits of Historicizing National Socialism

Dan Diner

Describing National Socialism as "history" is possible if "history" refers merely to a complex of past events. But history in the true sense of the word is not just a cluster of bygone events, a narrative chronology. It also represents historicity, past events reworked and interpreted from a professionally distanced perspective. If National Socialism is history, it must be capable of being subjected to an approach that claims to be equally valid for all epochs.

Here, doubts are in order. Colloquial speech has assigned a special place to those twelve years, almost an absolute status; people speak of *the* past when they mean the National Socialist period. Absolutizing one particular point in time seems to have drained other periods and pasts of their meaning and even annulled them. The vehemence alone with which the notorious Historians' Debate has been conducted indicates once again that the Nazi period towers over all other epochs, that it occupies a special place in history and demands to be treated accordingly by historical research.

The historical profession has long directed its efforts *against* granting the National Socialist period a special status. Its general aim has been historicization of the Nazi era, its integration into the course of history, its relativization as history. But lurking behind the politically colored partisanship of the Historians' Debate lies a question that is excluded from the public debate and that especially concerns historians, although not historians alone: Can National Socialism truly become history?

Considering the events of postwar Germany, this seems doubtful. In no other European country does the interpretation of National Socialism play such an existential and politically important role as in the two German states. Both sides have justified their civil war–like opposition to each other with theories of history that relate directly to *the* past. For West Germans' understanding of their constitution, for example, the theory of totalitarianism has played a fundamental role, acting as a kind of supra-constitutional preamble. This theory views National Socialism as a variant of totalitarian rule, thereby focusing the comparison between Hitler and Stalin on their respective use of force. On the other hand, it would be no exaggeration to claim that East Germans justify the separate existence of the German Democratic Republic (GDR) through a different theory of fascism: the traditional Marxist interpretation of fascism as the organic union of capitalism and fascist rule. The GDR has divorced itself from German history and views itself as the geographic embodiment of an idealized Communist Party version of history. In spite of all their differences, the self-justifying credos of the two German states have one thing in common. Both of these underlying theories—the theory of totalitarianism, with its emphasis on coercive rule, and the theory of fascism, which proceeds from particular conditions of exploitation—ignore at least one event within National Socialism: the mass murder of millions, the killing for the sake of killing.

In Germany, *the* past—whether affirmed or denied—stands at the center of political symbolism. It is no coincidence that the solemnly staged historical turning point we know as "Bitburg" derives its deeper meaning from that past. This single act of symbolic politics combined an absolution of past sins with preparations for a new, active German political role in Europe—a policy that itself seems to require absolution. At the gravesides of Wehrmacht and SS soldiers, the Second World War was falsified into a regrettable, but in the final analysis normal, historical occurrence, analogous to World War I. What is more, "Bitburg" distorted the lines of conflict in World War II until the only apparent lesson of National Socialism became the need for the West to unite against totalitarianism. "Bitburg" was a kind of antitotalitarian reconciliation, and as such it *necessarily* took place without remembering the victims of mass murder—and hence at their expense.

At the same time, this festival of remembrance was aimed at the future. By inducing the Americans to swear symbolically to such an interpretation of the Second World War, those organizing Bitburg freed themselves in the long term from the obligations stemming from the phenomenon of "Auschwitz." After the West had jointly put such an interpretation of history in place, Germany would be free to turn toward a nationally oriented perspective, one no longer compromised by the monstrosity that was "Auschwitz." The solemnly celebrated reconciliation over the graves at Bitburg projected an optical illusion of Western unity while promoting just the opposite for the long term: a progressive shift toward the reconstruction of German "national identity" and its identity as the "center of Europe."

The turn toward German nationalism is very much a phenomenon that goes beyond party lines. Initially inspired in the late 1970s and early 1980s by the peace movement's critique of defense policies and strengthened by elements of the ecology movement oriented toward self-sufficiency, anti-Western resentments grew until they were once again appropriated by conservatives and the Right.[1] Open criticism of the superpowers' pragmatic desire for disarmament has enabled the movement to adopt views that would have been unthinkable a few years ago. Shifts on the issue of defense buttress the most diverse variants of nationalism in the process of defining the coordinates of explicitly German policies.

It is in this context, above all, that the Historians' Debate gains its contemporary significance: relativizing "Auschwitz" within history is a precondition for the growing nationalization of German consciousness and of future German policies. Nationalist consciousness is the sounding board that has been made to resonate politically by the current controversy over the interpretation of the past. The road to nationalism follows the signposts of a particular historical interpretation. Such a development is certainly not a product of chance, for the reconstruction of a particular self-image coincides with the return of the idea of Germany's position in *Mitteleuropa* (the center of Europe)—itself a corollary of Gorbachev's reform policies.

Whether coincidence or causality, the restoration of a positive national identity is a precondition for Germany's resumption of a dominant position in Europe. Nor are we speaking here of a complete, united Germany in the "center of Europe." The Federal Republic alone emits a gravitational pull which other states—especially in central and central-eastern Europe—will be unable to resist. Despite the emphatically proclaimed and celebrated supranational Western cultural community, historical consciousness in Europe has remained nationalistic. Moreover, it is becoming ever more so. Yet Germany's return to a positive "national identity" is blocked by an event which defies any integration: Auschwitz. It appears to have fallen to the historical profession to clear away this barrier to normalization, but the demand itself comes from the political sphere.

Alfred Dregger, parliamentary leader of the ruling Christian Democratic Party, has worked for many years for just such a normalization. His conviction, often repeated in the Bundestag and at commemorative events, is that German history must be removed from "Auschwitz." It often sounds like a threat when he complains that the "lack of a history" and the "disregard" for one's own nation worry him. He seeks the kind of elementary patriotism which, he claims, other peoples find self-evident but which the German people will not be able to survive without. He has denounced "the so-called overcoming of the past" (*Vergangenheitsbewältigung*) for rendering Germany incapable of facing the future. He himself has promised assistance in fighting this approach.

Recently Dregger has further sharpened his project of national reconstitution, pregnant with significance for the future, by daring to emphasize a view of the Second World War that is calculated to evoke empathy: since the soldiers at the front did not know what was taking place behind their backs, the argument goes, they share no responsibility for the extermination policies of the Nazis. Here the CDU's parliamentary leader expresses the deeply held wish of a dilettante historian that the professional historical community should proceed from the following paradigm: that the Wehrmacht acted to the best of its knowledge in good conscience and found itself faced with the tragic dilemma of either defending Germany, and with it Hitler, or allowing Hitler, and thus Germany as well, to go under.

A further fact is inextricably linked to this paradigm: the "defense of Germany" also allowed the crematoria to burn on. The machinery of mass murder could only continue to function unhindered as long as the front held. This very real overlapping of nationalism with National Socialism makes it hardly possible to dissociate the two retrospectively, and condemns any attempts at differentiation. Hence any demand to redeem nationalism retroactively in spite of National Socialism culminates, whether one likes it or not, in a relativization or minimization of mass murder. This is the price that must be paid for the reestablishment of nationalism in Germany—and this is also why its reestablishment is impossible.

The demands of Dregger, the politician, were nevertheless immediately taken up by historians. Andreas Hillgruber sought—and this is why his approach is problematic—to realize a nationalistic perspective capable of eliciting sympathetic identification. Such a perspective claims to be inimical to the Nazi regime; yet it still seeks to preserve national identification (and thus national continuity) in spite of National Socialism. Thus Hillgruber considers the defense of the German Reich, and its territorial integrity in the East during the final phase of the war, to have been justified. Moreover, Hillgruber evaluates the bitter defensive battle against the Soviet army on the Eastern front as a tragic historical dilemma even though he recognizes its connection to the machinery of death at Auschwitz. In this way he affirms the ready nationalism of his own subjective perspective on the era. The choice of such a perspective contains, whether explicitly or not, a clear historiographic judgment: for the sake of the nation, the historian takes sides in a "dilemma"—against the victims of National Socialism.

By proceeding from the experiences and subjective feelings of the greater part of the German populace to arrive at his paradigm of national identification, Hillgruber necessarily ignores the centrality of the phenomenon "Auschwitz" in his evaluation of National Socialism. Paradoxically, the conservative Hillgruber justifies his approach with what is usually considered a left-wing concern: the history of everyday life, or what might be called a locally oriented, close-up view of National Socialism. This might seem surprising; but when applied to Nazism, a close-up perspective oriented toward everyday experiences brings with it a depoliticizing, desubstantiating, structurally desubjectivizing effect. A closer examination of the special character of mass murder and its preconditions will make this clear.

The Holocaust was a collective, bureaucratically organized, and industrial action that was made possible by a social division of labor and the institutional smoke-screen generated by total political domination. Only thanks to this combination of factors did the regime find itself in a position to carry out mass murder without necessarily having to order the average person specifically to do so. This act of violence operated in a twilight zone that combined active participation with an effective subjective fiction of nonparticipation. To carry this point to its logical conclusion, I would argue that, by dissolving a process carried out mainly through a division of labor into a series of detailed, individually examined aspects, as historians do in a microscopic, close-up approach, one runs the risk of completely overlooking the defining feature of the regime: industrialized mass murder. Even attempts at a reconstruction of everyday life in the Third Reich that are inspired by an emancipatory consciousness can encounter this pitfall.

The history of everyday life, far removed as it is from actions of state and the central processes of the regime, is locally oriented and concerned with the individual feelings and experiences of contemporaries. As such, it brings to light an extremely banal and trivial reality. This will cause surprise among historians and a younger generation accustomed to the centrality of the phenomenon of Auschwitz; but an approach centered on everyday life in Germany under National Socialism reveals a picture of reality that corresponds to the lived experience of the overwhelming majority of the population: the normality of a "normal" German living a "normal" life.

What is more, thanks to its locally rooted, close-up perspective, such an approach will suggest to historians a periodization that does not correspond to the lines of demarcation we commonly associate with the history of Nazism— the years 1933 to 1945. Historical research has in fact revealed that those temporal markers, seemingly self-evident, are actually located elsewhere in the private memory of the population. Memories guided by lived experience will orient themselves according to dates that separate "good times" from "bad times."[2] And the "bad times" are not necessarily marked by the cutoff points indicated by the dates 1933, 1935, 1938, and 1941, dates decisive for the regime's victims. Rather, they are symbolically associated with more fluid lines of demarcation—the period from the beginning of the massive Allied air raids in 1942 to the onset of the postwar economic upturn following the currency reform of 1948, for example.

The everyday-life perspective, guided as it is by local experiences and feelings, yields a close-up view divorced from great events. In focussing on social context, it widens the temporal scope of the Nazi period (narrowly circumscribed in the general consciousness by the years 1933 and 1945) in both directions. Such an approach will in all likelihood result in a banal portrayal of National Socialist rule, especially when measured against the most significant and characteristic phenomena of the period. For histories of everyday life necessarily emphasize the long movements of "normal" social relations. But for those victims who were chosen for extermination, the Nazi period represents the exact opposite, an absolutely exceptional state of affairs, one distinguished from everyday normalcy and continuity precisely by its incisive and catastrophic character. To this extent, then, the reality of everyday life and that of existential exceptionalism can no longer be theoretically united within one history. The historiographic consequence is that two worlds exist side by side, and a truly synthesizing approach to history is no longer possible. The danger of simply reproducing the world which the Nazis created has thus moved a step closer.

Historians have often raised methodological concerns about the depoliticizing and trivializing consequences of a perspective focused on everyday life. They have done so especially in relation to the reconstruction of conditions under National Socialism. These concerns can in the end be traced back to a remark made by Norbert Elias, to the effect that, by definition, everyday life must stand in contrast to something specifically unusual.[3] Put another way, there can be no "everyday" except in contrast to "holiday." Applied to the everyday-life approach to Nazism, this insight necessitates that we ascertain the antithesis to daily "normalcy" under National Socialism. And that antithesis is mass murder, a phenomenon that cannot be understood through histories of everyday life.

The important thing, then, is to bring a "third dimension" of "simultaneous nonsimultaneity"[4] into play, once again via methodological criticism. Such a third dimension would be equally valid for both victims and perpetrators. So far, it has evaded the narrative techniques used in the reconstruction of everyday life. Above all, in carrying out such a reconstruction, one must be careful not to fall victim to the experiences of others. Experiences are subjective; they have their own social and psychological context; they make use of concepts whose appropriateness must be scrutinized. Since it is an inherent tendency of the everyday-life perspective to question long-established views of political events,[5] this tendency might be exaggerated to the point where "the superabundance of the normal, the banal, and the simple everyday would one day remove Hitler altogether from the social history of the Nazi period."[6] An absolutizing of the everyday-life perspective leads to an apologia for the Nazi regime—one that, depending on milieu and context, takes on a "right-wing" or "left-wing" cast.[7]

On the other hand, advocates of the everyday-life approach see in such a perspective the possibility of historicizing the National Socialist period, of removing it from mere moral judgments and rendering it accessible to an historical hermeneutic.[8] To realize this possibility, they argue, historians must emphasize more strongly the social changes that occurred under Nazi domination. These changes must be understood as instances—no matter how perverted—of a larger process of social modernization occurring throughout this century.[9]

Another argument for the everyday-life perspective credits that approach with dissolving the extremes in the perception of the Nazi period.[10] This development cannot and should not remain without consequences for the country's contemporary political culture. First and foremost, the depolarization attained by the close-up view opens up possibilities for overcoming the "problems of language and understanding" separating the generation that was born around 1945 and entered the university around 1968 from the generation of its parents, who either grew up or were active during the Third Reich.

A further claim is that the history of everyday life provides innovative perspectives which go beyond a purely moral way of regarding the Third Reich and thus make possible an historical understanding of that period.[11] This approach is therefore not just any thread within the fabric of methodological pluralism, but rather the very shuttle of historicization. It is concerned with a construction of memory which proceeds from the primacy of social continuity and from the continuous experiences of the German population, and is thus a perspective which has consciously decided to place the normalcy of those times in the foreground.

In order not to sidestep the particularity of the Nazi period, however, the close-up view of the history of everyday life needs to maintain a "distant view" of the central feature of National Socialism—beginning with industrialized mass murder, as it has been registered in the all-too-objectifiable experience of its victims. And it must do this without assuming only the perspective of the victim . In this way the pivotal point "Auschwitz" will have been added to the project of a historicization of Nazism. From this, the most extreme pole of National Socialist reality, the entire "normalcy" of those years will be opened up so that it might be better understood, or "understood" at all.

The concept of "understanding" has a double meaning, especially when applied to National Socialism. "Understanding" can denote a sympathetic identification with the actors in question—the process through which Hillgruber hopes to explain the situation of the German army and especially the German population in the East, those whom he has chosen as the grateful objects of his empathy. Ernst Nolte appears to go even farther here by trying out this approach on the process which led Hitler to decide on the extermination of the Jews. But "understanding" can mean more than simply an empathetic attitude toward a past situation. In relation to Auschwitz and the bureaucratically organized, industrialized mass murder carried out there, only the effort to make this phenomenon intellectually comprehensible can be termed "understanding." The attempt to "understand" Auschwitz would thus be a theoretical prerequisite for any project aimed at the historicization of National Socialism. Those who avoid that extreme situation, those who do not make the effort to "understand" Auschwitz, and to begin to approach the differentiatedness and complexity of National Socialist reality from this starting point, will only unconsciously reproduce in their reconstruction the same opposition that the Nazis themselves created. They will bring forth two histories of National Socialism—that of its perpetrators and that of its victims. Against this background, the title of Hillgruber's book, *Two Kinds of Downfall*, could be interpreted programatically: two perspectives on the Nazi period.

Understanding "Auschwitz"—understanding both in the sense of explaining through reconstruction and in the sense of comprehending intellectually—has been one of the principal aims of intellectual endeavor since 1945. The question of how Auschwitz could have been possible, which has taken on secular dimensions, has not yet received a satisfactory answer. On the contrary, the opposing positions seem to have become ever more entrenched as research has moved forward and as more layers of historical reality have been uncovered. An historiographic consensus is nowhere in sight.

So-called intentionalist approaches to interpretation claim to establish a direct causal connection between racist and anti-Semitic ideology, the explicit will to destroy, and the act of destruction itself. Yet they fail to explain the real and highly chaotic process by which ideology becomes policy—a process that passed through several stages of increasing radicalization and appears to have preserved a certain openness until 1941. The intentionalist approach, which causally links intention and act and thus gives short shrift to the decision-making process, has responded to its own inadequacies by creating a methodological "black box." Within this black box the intentional and unintentional, the latent and the virulent, are mixed and compressed in a manner that can scarcely be reconstructed and that defies intentionalist understanding. The end product of this mysterious mechanism of actualization is the Holocaust, an act whose sheer monstrosity and terror go far beyond the natural consequences of racial prejudice and anti-Semitism.

Historians who employ functionalist paradigms are better able to illuminate this black box. Like the everyday-life perspective, however, the functionalist approach leads to paradoxical results. The approach focuses on how an action carried out collectively and via a division of labor was originally conceived and implemented. It renders the horror of the event largely banal, for when an action is broken down into its constituent parts—social division of labor, institutional chaos, egotistical ignorance, and moral stupefaction—it necessarily loses its full significance. This historical approach does not ignore the circumstances that preceded and prepared the way for the Holocaust—whole ideologies or the explicit intentions of specific people or programs—in its overall evaluation. But these preconditions are so reduced in their significance compared to the mysterious contents of the black box that they no longer stand in any relevant relationship to the deed itself.

The functionalist approach can contribute much to an explanation, especially in terms of a description of the connection between ideological intentions, intermediate decisions, and an ever more radical internal dynamic. Yet it turns out to be not only ethically troublesome, but also highly unsatisfactory with respect to the overarching standards of "understanding," since in the end this approach desubjectivizes the overall event by dividing it into a variety of partial actions. However closely such a reconstruction approaches the phenomenon of mass murder itself, it misses its real significance. The approach shares a fate with the debates over whether the Holocaust should be regarded as a legally punishable act, an approach which is doomed to failure given the nature of the crime.

What is one to do, however, with an act that on the one hand clearly forced the experience of victimhood upon millions of actual individuals, yet on the other hand can only be attributed to abstractions such as the division of labor, rather than to specific personal subjects? The methodology of a close-up approach, whether functionalist or structuralist, is certainly appropriate in a formal sense. Yet in such an approach the banal elements of this monstrous crime against humanity gain the upper hand, and whether one likes it or not, a perspective reconstructed from the point of view of the victims becomes increasingly obscured.

The approach oriented toward the perspective of the victim in no way represents either a purely subjective or even a complementary way of viewing things. Rather, it is the more comprehensive perspective and the one more appropriate to the totality of the phenomenon, because it proceeds from the absolute extreme case. Only those who proceed from the extreme case can make sense of the simultaneity of what are on the one hand banal, unreal, yet actual normal conditions, and what is on the other hand their monstrous result. It is this simultaneity which the close-up view splits into the duality of everyday life and mass murder.

An approach that proceeds from the extreme case gives center stage to the element of meaninglessness and purposelessness represented by the destruction for the sake of destruction at Auschwitz. The break with civilization carried out in Auschwitz becomes the actual universal starting point from which to measure the world-historical meaning of National Socialism. Efforts at a historicization of this epoch should begin here if they wish to avoid the limitations of a particularist perspective. The National Socialist break with civilization, the practical negation of the principles of instrumental reason and self-preservation embodied in Auschwitz, paradoxically raises the *individual* and *particular* perspective of the victims chosen for annihilation to a *universal* standard. This is true because the very radical nature of the victims' experience coincides with a universal cognitive inability to imagine purposeless destruction—above all one's own destruction—in the context of instrumentally rational Western civilization. The person who gambles on the fact that the behavior of others is motivated by rational interests, or at least by the desire for self-preservation, and anticipates this in his or her own actions, is proven wrong by the senselessness of the extermination.

This is true especially for the lived experience of the victims. Activity that aimed at personal survival was nipped in the bud by the counterlogic constructed by the Nazis—as the Jews in the East discovered. Every rational assumption based on normal common sense was ultimately proven fatally wrong. The victims' intention to survive became an obliging instrument in the hands of the Nazis; every action, no matter how optimistically and rationally oriented toward survival, no matter how firmly based on all human and social laws of experience, led necessarily to destruction. Thus the fact of survival was due almost entirely to chance and not to any sort of rationality. This is the essence of "Auschwitz" that destroyed civilization; this is the pivotal point of extreme radicality from which thinking about mass extermination must begin.

If one starts from the *antirationality* of the Nazis and not, as is commonly but wrongly done, from their *irrationality*, then it is hardly surprising that efforts at historical reconstruction and understanding seem doomed to undermine themselves time and again—for example, by taking methodological refuge in the "normal" and socially contingent aspects of the Nazi period. Attempts to make the Holocaust comprehensible and universally comparable are not necessarily always motivated by nationalist pressures for absolution. It is a perfectly natural trait of human existence to avoid its own real negation, and it is vexing in a narcissistic way to be confronted with a phenomenon that defies the powers of human imagination and understanding. Such a negation is difficult to bear and to be asked to do so is perceived as an unreasonable demand.

It is therefore hardly surprising that a phenomenon of such dimensions has inspired a methodological revolt with a hidden agenda. We pursue understanding—even at the price of relativization and banalization. We push interpretive relationships until they exhaust themselves in rationalizations. Catchwords like "industrial society," "capitalism," or more recently "modernity" are poorly suited to explain the enigma of Auschwitz. Often enough, in the final analysis, they only serve to further an escape into historical trivialities. They do perhaps have a role to play when we evaluate the destructive and self-destructive *potential* of our civilization. They can still claim a certain validity when we speculate in general terms about future *probabilities*. But they are silent when that past *reality* is at issue—and for the historian past reality is the only legitimate object of research.

Auschwitz is a no-man's-land of understanding, a black box of explanation, a vacuum of extrahistorical significance which sucks in attempts at historiographic interpretation. Only via negation, only through the constant effort to understand the fruitlessness of understanding, can one properly grasp what sort of phenomenon might be at stake in this break with civilization. As the ultimate extreme case, and thus as an absolute standard of history, this event can hardly be historicized. Serious attempts at historicization have thus far run into insoluble historical and theoretical problems. Attempts at historicization of a different kind, those which relativize and flatten out this phenomenon, necessarily end in apologias. This is the lesson to be learned from the Historians' Debate.

Notes

1. Dan Diner, "Die 'nationale Frage' in der Friedensbewegung. Ursprünge und Tendenzen," in Reiner Steinweg, ed., *Die neue Friedensbewegung: Reihe Friedensanalyse* (Frankfurt, 1982), 83ff.
2. Ulrich Herbert, "Die guten und die schlechten Zeiten," in Lutz Niethammer, ed., *Die Jahre weiss man nicht, wo man die heute hinsetzen soll: Faschismuserfahrungen im Ruhrgebiet*, LUSIER (Bonn, 1986), 1:67–96.
3. Norbert Elias, "Zum Begriff des Alltags," in K. Hammerich/Klein, ed., *Materialien zur Soziologie des Alltags* (Opladen, 1978), 22–29.

4. Klaus Tenfelde in *Alltagsgeschichte der NS-Zeit: Neue Perspektive oder Triviali-sierung?* (Munich, 1984), 35.
5. Jürgen Kocka in ibid., 54.
6. Klaus Tenfelde in ibid., 33.
7. Heinrich A. Winkler in ibid., 31.
8. Martin Broszat in ibid., 20.
9. Hartmut Mehringer in ibid., 28.
10. Ibid., 27.
11. Ibid., 48.

8. Singularity and Its Relativization: Changing Views in German Historiography on National Socialism and the "Final Solution"

Otto Dov Kulka

I

One of the most remarkable developments in German historiography during the 1960s and 1970s appears to have been the gradually reached, overwhelming consensus on the central role of anti-Semitism in National Socialist ideology and politics. It was identified as the only constant element and as such as a key to the understanding of the inner contradictions of the Third Reich, of Hitler's unconventional war aims, and the singularity of the Holocaust.[1] During the last few years, however, radically different views have appeared in the works and polemics of several German historians.

In this essay I shall elaborate on several of the new tendencies to explain the nature of the Third Reich and its place in history. I shall examine the works of some of the most influential scholars and confront their central theses established in the 1960s and 1970s, which stressed the singularity of the Third Reich and the Holocaust in German and universal history, with the present tendency of what may be called "relativization" or "historicization" of National Socialism. It seems, however, that not only different methodological approaches but even divergent ethical attitudes led to some parallel conclusions in various spheres.

One of them, represented particularly by Ernst Nolte, uses the comparative perspective and identifies various genocidal phenomena in the twentieth century, both before and after the Holocaust. He claims there is a "causal nexus" between the "Asiatic" or "Judeo-Bolshevik" precedents of mass annihilation and the Nazi extermination of the Jews. In the light of other post-Holocaust genocidal occurrences in various parts of the world, all these phenomena are explained as a universal norm of our century. Nolte's theses imply not only the most far-reaching relativization of National Socialism and the Holocaust, but also the responsibility of the Jews themselves for their own mass annihilation: following their many "declarations of war" against Germany, the mass executions of millions of Jews are explained as preventive measures of the Third Reich taken during World War II.

In an entirely different approach advocated in a very impressive way by

Martin Broszat, the emphasis is shifted to internal German history and its social aspects. Under the term "historicization," he stresses the need to focus research on those developments in the Third Reich which seem relevant for the self-understanding of the Federal Republic as a democratic welfare society. The Third Reich is viewed in the perspective of the continuity of German history and thus, in a way, as a *Vorgeschichte* (prehistory) of the present German state. In this perspective, National Socialism appears as an expression of, or an answer to, the necessary structural changes in German society and its modernization. The preoccupation of historiography with the Jewish aspect and the problem of the world-historical uniqueness of the Third Reich is regarded as distorting historical reality and an obstacle to further research.

The third tendency stresses the overwhelming effect of the totalitarian structure of the Third Reich in which the impersonal bureaucratic machine of the German perpetrators and the Jewish leadership are both victims and at the same time "guilty." Here, too, the genocidal phenomenon appears as a possible recurrent pattern in the future practically everywhere in modern industrial society, including the State of Israel. It seems that the awareness of the relevance of the dominating power of an impersonal bureaucracy, as a threat to the individual in present-day German society, brought about the almost complete disregard of the ideological factor of National Socialism, including its anti-Semitism, which appears irrelevant for the self-understanding and historical consciousness of this society. These theories were brought forward particularly by Hans Mommsen, most recently in the context of his reevaluation of Hannah Arendt's views on the Holocaust.

Notwithstanding all these relativizing tendencies, other important German historians, most notably Eberhard Jäckel and the late Klaus Scholder, further developed and deepened the understanding of the essential role of anti-Semitism, the uniqueness of the Holocaust and its world-historical significance. Their approach, as well as my own, does not a priori exclude the comparative perspective. On the contrary, an examination of the different historical processes and a comparison of various genocidal phenomena with the Holocaust only accentuate the truly uncomparable singularity of the National Socialist attempt to exterminate the Jewish people, which implied the far-reaching intention to eliminate the universalist ideologies allegedly emanating from the Jewish spirit, in order to bring about a decisive turn in the course of world history. It is precisely the relevance of this meaning of German history during the Third Reich for the present German historical consciousness that is being emphasized, both for reasons of historical authenticity as well as on account of its ethical significance.[2]

II

I shall now touch on some crucial points in the development of German postwar historiography up to the 1980s. In the fifteen years that followed the fall of the Third Reich, during which the first comprehensive studies on

Nazi Germany, World War II and the destruction of European Jewry were published in non-German historiography, the history being written in Germany was characterized by almost total abstention from anything dealing with the years after 1933 and the subject of the Jews in particular. Besides the not very influential attempt of the old Meinecke to assess the meaning of the "German Catastrophe,"[3] the few initial studies on National Socialism deal with the circumstances and the "guilt" or responsibility for Hitler's rise to power, or seek to explain the processes of the decline and disintegration of the Weimar democracy.

The most comprehensive work to be mentioned here is Karl Dietrich Bracher's *Auflösung der Weimarer Republik* (1955), which briefly dwelt on the historical roots of National Socialist anti-Semitism. Toward the end of the 1950s, the comprehensive collective work of Bracher, Sauer, and Schulz, *Die nationalsozialistische Machtergreifung: Studien zur Errichtung des totalitären Herrschaftssystems in Deutschland 1933–1934*, was published. In this monumental volume, which signified a decisive scientific breakthrough in the treatment of the first formative stages of the Third Reich, a few pages of fundamental importance were devoted to the far-reaching role of National Socialist anti-Semitism, particularly in the section written by Bracher.

At the same time, an attempt to examine the nature of the National Socialist ideology and regime from another aspect was made by Martin Broszat. In his small and concise volume *Der Nationalsozialismus: Weltanschauung, Problematik und Wirklichkeit* (1960), he suggested that Hitler's anti-Semitism appeared to be the only constant element in the whole structure. Were the idea itself not absurd, in his view, it could have been regarded as a key to the contradictions and lack of consistency in all the other spheres, and even serve as a bridge between them. A year later, in his analysis of *Hitlers zweites Buch* in the *Vierteljahrshefte für Zeitgeschichte*, Broszat offers a view in this spirit, but without his previous reservations.

More or less at the same time, Ernst Nolte, in an article published in the *Historische Zeitschrift* in 1961, and particularly in his *Three Faces of Fascism* of 1965, further elaborated on the far-reaching significance of this centrality, presenting "Judaism" as a focal point and as a key to what may be called the bipolar unity of Hitler's anti-Christian and antidemocratic view: Judaism is the total enemy and destroyer of the natural state of society—its victory would result in an apocalyptic decline comparable to the destruction of the ancient Roman Empire by Jewish Christianity. In an overall view Nolte regards fascism, and National Socialism as its most radical form, as a twofold revolution whose universal message is the redemption of the world from the Judeo-Christian and Judeo-Marxist messianic creeds. I quote two of his main theses: (1) "Auschwitz was as firmly embedded in the principles of the National-Socialist race doctrine as the fruit in the seed. . . ."[4] (2) "for Hitler and Himmler as well as for posterity . . . this process [i.e., the extermination of Jews] differed essentially from all other extermination actions, both as to scope and to intention."[5]

One of the first to examine systematically the role played by Hitler's anti-Semitic ideas in shaping his conceptions in foreign policy was Andreas Hillgruber. In his monumental work *Hitlers Strategie: Politik und Kriegführung 1940–1941* (1965) and his concise study *Germany and the Two World Wars* (1967/1981), both of which are based on administrative, diplomatic, and military sources, predominance is given to the central and decisive role of the struggle with Judaism as a factor in Hitler's crucial decisions.

Similarly, Klaus Scholder convincingly elaborated on the centrality of anti-Semitism in the National Socialist attitude to Christianity and the envisaged final solution of the Church Question. I am referring here, *inter alia*, to his articles in *Das Parlament* (1971) and to the pertinent chapter in the first volume of his *Die Kirche und das Dritte Reich* (1977).

The most coherent and, to my mind, most convincing study of Hitler's ideological concepts undertaken in the sixties was Eberhard Jäckel's *Hitler's World View: A Blueprint for Power* (1969/1972). Jäckel examines the complex nature of Hitler's anti-Semitism as a central issue per se, as well as its role in shaping his concepts of domestic and foreign policy, and consequently its place in Hitler's overall concept of history leading from the apparently most ordinary to the unprecedentedly unique.

In the same year Bracher's authoritative volume *The German Dictatorship* presented a no less convincing analysis of the significance of anti-Semitism as a constitutive element in the singularity of National Socialist ideology and politics:

> The core, however, probably the only "genuine," fanatically held and realized conviction of his entire life, was already then anti-Semitism and race mania. An enormously oversimplified scheme of good and evil, transplanted to the biological and racial sphere, was made to serve as the masterkey to world history and world politics. . . .[6]

A different methodological approach, based almost exclusively on the research of the vast archival material produced by the Nazi bureaucracy dealing with the Jewish Question, was introduced by Hans Mommsen already in the early 1960s. In his "Nationalsozialistischer Polizeistaat und die Judenverfolgung (vor 1938)," published in the *Vierteljahrshefte für Zeitgeschichte* in 1962, Mommsen dwells on the fact that, contrary to the external monolithic image of the totalitarian regime, the inner contradictions characterize the dynamics of the radicalization leading toward the "Final Solution." Nevertheless, he concludes: "The persecution of the Jews can be considered a key to the analysis of the power structure of the Third Reich." Referring to Broszat's *Nationalsozialismus*, he states: "Racial anti-Semitism has to be considered a central part of the ideology of the regime . . ." (pp. 68–69).

In 1967, following Heinz Höhne's series in *Der Spiegel* on the history of the SS,[7] which included an extensive chapter on the SD and the "Final Solution," Mommsen raises the question of a possible reassessment of the Third Reich implied in the question mark of his article "Entteufelung des Dritten Reiches?"

The alleged ideological consistency turns out to be fictitious; under the empty formula of "National Socialist Weltanschauung" a latent struggle between heterogeneous ideological conceptions took place, which corresponded only with regard to the negative.

The dreadful crimes of the system did not originate in demonic, destructive drives; they grew out of a mixture of political delusions, perverted idealism, political inability, moral indifference and specified technical efficiency.

Does this mean a de-demonization [*Entteufelung*] of the Third Reich?[8]

No less complex are the views developed during the 1960s and 1970s in several works by Broszat, particularly *The Hitler State*, "Soziale Motivation und Führer-Bindung des Nationalsozialismus," and "Hitler and the Genesis of the 'Final Solution.'"[9] Although the predominance of the ideological background, stressed in his early works (1960–61), receded behind the thick walls of administrative and social structures, it nevertheless seems always present, if only in the form of "metaphorical" signposts which at the end mark the almost predestined road to the ultimate reality of the "Final Solution."[10] The conclusion that anti-Semitism constitutes "the very core" or "the dominant component" of National Socialism established itself in the last two decades even in the professional handbooks of German history.[11]

These results of West German historiography have been impressively summarized, though from a polemic position, in the East German historian Kurt Pätzold's study on the Holocaust:

In bourgeois historiography the approach depicting racism and anti-Semitism as the starting and the final point of every research of fascism prevailed. The whole fascist policy and World War II are supposed to be understood from the alleged central and highest aim of Hitler's fascism, that is the annihilation of the "Jews." All decisions and measures of the regime were apparently geared and subjected to this. Racism and anti-Semitism are purely and simply passed off as the nature and main characteristic of German fascism.[12]

However, in spite of this introductory statement, it seems that this noteworthy study—unique in the historiography of the German Democratic Republic—is closer to the views of West German authors than Pätzold himself admits, and apparently more so than any other publication in the socialist countries.

This leads to the ultimate question: What is the historical meaning of defining the centrality of anti-Semitism in National Socialist ideology and politics? Clearly, it is not that the Jews in their factual historical proportions gain such a central importance here, and perhaps even not the physical act of their mass extermination, which in many aspects might be compared with the liquidation of other population groups under the Third Reich, or elsewhere. On the factual level, the Jews were but a small minority among the Germans and other European peoples. The matter at issue is the significance attributed in the conceptual world of National Socialism to the ideo-historical concept of Judaism and its promoter—the Jew. It seems that only from this point of view is it possible to make an attempt at "explaining the inexplicable." In other words, this centrality is the only possible key to a historical understanding of the significance of the Holocaust and of the assault that the National Socialist "revolution" made on the very roots of Western civilization, its basic values and moral foundations. For on different levels of the ruling system in the Third Reich, the essence of the National Socialist counterrevolution was understood as a revolt against the all-embracing idea of the unity of the human race, which was fundamentally opposed to its own value system. In this context Judaism was conceived as the historical source and the continuous driving force of this idea, which was expanded in the course of world history through Christianity and later in the democratic and socialist systems.

Any attempt to explain the Holocaust without taking into account this substantial factor inevitably leads to explanations long refuted and proven indefensible concerning the causes of the "Final Solution," whether these define it as being based on allegedly economic reasons, or as a deceptive political manipulation of the masses, or an experiment in terror against one group as preparation for an imperialistic war of conquest and annihilation against other peoples or minorities, and even—more recently—as a more or less accidental by-product of the internally antagonistic "totalitarian anarchy."

III

As indicated in my introductory remarks, radical changes have been introduced or postulated by several German historians during the last few years. Some of these developments were highlighted in the course of the ongoing public dispute, initiated by the philosopher Jürgen Habermas.

The most conspicuous case seems to be that of Ernst Nolte. Diametrically opposed to his above-mentioned definitions of the singularity of the Holocaust which—and here I quote again from his *Three Faces of Fascism*— "distinguished itself . . . from all other mass annihilations," Nolte now regards this view as "a distortion and even falsification of the historical realities" of the present century. He points to the allegedly equal genocidal events outside German and European history, including the massacre of the Armenians, the mass annihilations in the Soviet Union, the "Holocaust on Water" in the aftermath of the Vietnam War, and the war in Afghanistan. Against his earlier emphasis on the inherent predetermination of Auschwitz in National Socialist ideology, he now claims that the Holocaust must be understood in its "causal nexus" to the precedents defined as an "Asiatic action" [*asiatische Tat*]. I am referring to his articles of 1985–86,[13] where the singularity of the "Final Solution" is relativized to the point that it becomes a quasi-"normal" phenomenon of world history in our century, and the responsibility for the Holocaust is virtually shifted to the entire world. But I am also referring to Nolte's article "Marxismus und Nationalsozialismus," published in the *Vierteljahrshefte für Zeitgeschichte* in 1983, which has been generally overlooked by his critics. There he speaks about the formation of racialist and genocidal ideas in Marx's theories and even denotes Marx's mentor Moses Hess, the father of the Zionist idea, as "the first National Socialist."[14]

Already in my letter to Nolte of July 18, 1986 (see Appendix), I dwelt upon the unacceptability of these general comparisons; I explained the incomparable uniqueness of the historical meaning of the National Socialist "Final Solution," although it is clear that each and every murder and brutality against whichever human being or group, as such, is in the strictly moral sense an equal crime. As to the comparison of Hess's profoundly humanistic use of the terms "nation" and "race" and his vision of a future universal harmony of races, with the National Socialist theory of race and its vision of an eternal war of annihilation between the races as the natural order, nothing can of course be more absurd. The monstrous distortion of presenting Marx as the predecessor of Hitler and his racialist ideas of mass annihilation needs no comment. What needs to be explained is Nolte's possible motivation in his search for the alleged antecedents of the "Final Solution."

The follow-up of Nolte's theory of the antecedents and the "causal nexus" leads paradoxically from these racial ancestors of the future victims of Auschwitz to the claim that Hitler's annihilation of the Jews was actually provoked through their own declarations of a war of annihilation against Germany. In this connection, Nolte refers not only to the much quoted proclamation of Chaim Weizmann of 1939, but also to a certain anti-German pamphlet published by unknown American-Jewish author, Theodore Kaufmann, in 1940.[15] Finally, in his article in *Die Zeit*, he takes out of context a satirical remark in a pacifist article by Kurt Tucholsky (also of Jewish origin) on the future gas war and the fate of the Germans, which Nolte's revisionist sources compare with Hitler's notorious proposal in *Mein Kampf* to annihilate thousands of Jews by gas as a preventive act of self-defense.[16]

In order to explain why the negative singularity of the Third Reich continues to exist in historiography, Nolte proposes the following intellectual exercise:

We need only imagine, for example, what would happen if the PLO were to actually succeed, assisted by its allies, in destroying the State of Israel. After that, the presentation of history in the books, lecture halls, and schoolrooms of Palestine would doubtless be fixated on only the negative traits of Israel: the victory over racist, oppressive, even fascist Zionism would then become the state-supporting historical myth. For decades, possibly a century, no one would dare to trace the moving origins of Zionism back to the spirit of resistance against European anti-Semitism.

Many of his critics pointed to the "bad taste" [*Geschmacklosigkeit*] in using this speculative example, but did not dwell sufficiently on its implications: namely, that we should understand that his own original concept of the centrality of anti-Semitism as a source of the singularity of the Third Reich, so convincingly advocated in the 1960s even against the prevailing views of former Allied historians like Bullock or Trevor-Roper, is presented now as historiography allegedly imposed by the victorious enemy, inspired by the former victims.

Hence the call for the revision of the historical picture of the Third Reich implies an ideological emancipatory appeal for a creation of a new authentic national-historical consciousness as a means to regain a sense of the lost national identity.

My analysis of Nolte's changing views to date was based on his abovementioned polemical articles published in 1985–86, which marked the initial stages of the Historians' Debate in the summer of 1986. As a matter of fact, my own critical involvement in this dispute started already with my letter to Nolte of November 24, 1985, which raised—among other points—a question my colleagues and I in Jerusalem were asking then: "Which one of the two Ernst Noltes should we regard as the authentic one?" In his reply, Nolte expressed his astonishment thath "this small article ["Between Myth and Revisionism"] was immediately noticed in Jerusalem." He nevertheless promised to deliver his final answer in a new comprehensive book—then in preparation—on the Soviet Union and Germany.[17] This work, *Der europäische Bürgerkrieg 1917–1945: Nationalsozialismus und Bolschewismus*, in the meantime has been published, and in the chapter "Genozide und 'Endlösung der Judenfrage'" his answer is clear-cut. Here he no longer talks about Auschwitz as inherent in National Socialist ideology "as the fruit in the seed," but about the "annihilation of the Jews as a punishment and preventive measure" [*Vernichtung der Juden als Strafe und Präventivmassnahme*].[18] Here Tucholsky's provocation of 1927 is complemented by the proclamation of the Soviet-Jewish writer Ilia Ehrenburg of 1942; and Weizmann's declaration of war in 1939, by "a far more passionate appeal of prominent Soviet Jews to Jews all over the world."[19] The mass shootings of between 1.3 and 2.2 million Jews (mostly women, children, and old people) by the *Einsatzgruppen* are "the most radical and sweeping example of a preventive struggle against an enemy."[20]

Discussing the mass annihilation of the Jews in the extermination camps, Nolte comments that the use of gas chambers "has been contested by a number of authors," and that "this literature has in no way originated exclusively with Germans or Neo-Fascists. . . ." After a review of the arguments of the "Holocaust-Denial" literature, Nolte closes with: "However, even if these arguments lead one to refrain from coming to a conclusion . . . the fact remains that several hundreds of thousands died . . . and the further fact that a conspicuously large proportion of these dead were Jews."[21] In the end Nolte returns to the question of original and copy:

The Final Solution . . . as a systematically complete annihilation of a world-nation is the precise mirror image of the systematically complete annihilation of a world-class through Bolshevism, and to that extent it is the biologistically remolded copy of the social original.[22]

When I first expressed my concern about Nolte's changed views as expressed in his articles, Nolte replied that it was merely a question of "a shift of emphasis."[23] In my answer of May 16, 1986, I claimed that it seemed more like "a shift of responsibility." In Nolte's new thesis of the mass murder of millions of Jews as a "preventive measure" following "Jewish provocation," the responsibility is shifted onto the victims themselves. The same is true for the relationship between the "original" of the Final Solution and its "copy." According to this "logic," the clear responsibility for the National Socialist copy lies with the originator, which is the "Jewish-Bolshevik" prototype.

Nolte's recently published *Der europäische Bürgerkrieg 1917–1945* reached me only after my present paper, as well as my article for the *Frankfurter Rundschau* (see note 16), was completed, but my criticism of Nolte could hardly find better justification than the few excerpts I have quoted here. It seems, however, that the significance of Nolte's attempt to reinterpret the historical meaning of National Socialism extends far beyond the dispute about his various specific arguments, and there remain some further questions to be clarified.

In his polemical book, *Das Vergehen der Vergangenheit*, he states that the Historians' Debate should have broken out as far back as twenty-five years ago, or possibly should have continued since then, for "everything which has provoked such excitement in the course of this dispute had already been spelled out in those books," including the thesis that the Gulag Archipelago was more original than Auschwitz, as well as the view that "*the simple scheme 'perpetrators—victims' reduces the complexities of history much too much [dass das simple 'Täter-Opfer-Schema' die Komplexität der Geschichte alzusehr reduziert]*."[24] If Nolte, after having presented his provocative theses about National Socialism and the annihilation of the Jews that are so clearly opposed to his initial positions, insists on the alleged unchanged coherence of his views, then I can think of two ways to resolve this "antinomy":

1. In Nolte's admitted "shift of emphasis," we are actually facing a total relativization of history, or rather of its basic criteria of value judgment. Nolte refers to this in his letter to me, dated October 22, 1986: "If I pursued my thinking from 1963 on, it was in a way along the line *that an overexaggerated right can equally be an evil, and that an overexaggerated (historical) evil can again, in some way, be right [dass ein überschiessendes Recht zugleich Unrecht sein kann und ein überschiessendes (historisches) Unrecht in gewisser Weise wieder ein Recht]*."[25] As I have already suggested in my letter to Nolte of July 18, 1986, regarding his new contribution to the *Historische Zeitschrift*, "Philosophische Geschichtsschreibung heute?" his "monocausal, retrospective explanations of universal history, which proceed from the contemporary situation of human society" appear as a classic example of "totalitarian thinking." Here the relativization is so far-reaching that in any changed historical situation it can easily apply the seemingly unchanged all-inclusive master concept. In this way, Nolte now wishes to ascribe to National Socialism—as an "overexaggerated evil"—a (historical) "right," and deny its victims not

only their right to life but also their place in history as victims of evil. The far-fetched consequences of this relativization, which is, in fact, a revaluation and reshaping of history, are evident in the legitimacy which Nolte accords to the argument of the radical right-wing literature, whose main subject and basic objective is the outright denial of the Holocaust.

2. Nolte's assertions, made in 1963, about the unique nature of "that crime, which is beyond comparison with anything the world has ever seen even including Stalin's reign of terror against his own people and his own party,"[26] must be seen as disguise for his true beliefs. After all, only few writings among those which he designates as "Victors' Historiography" have presented in such a convincing manner as he did that "negative uniqueness" of German history which he is now out to destroy.

Both of these possible explanations refute Nolte's claim to a genuine, unchanged continuity in his interpretation of National Socialism. To me, and probably to most of his critics among the historians, the importance of his earlier researches lies in their being the strongest refutation of his present views. His demand for a "retrospective and even retroactive Historians' Debate" over his works during the past twenty-five years is, at best, a form of apology for his writings of that earlier period. This apologetic tendency seems to be the real meaning of his present "*Aufforderung zur Wissenschaft*" (appeal to be scientific) which should see to it that the "negative vitality of the Third Reich does not petrify into a legend." In the final analysis, the revisionist tendency which is reflected in his totalitarian thinking not only relativizes the historical picture as such, but tends—in its "search for the whole"—toward a nihilistic approach to history and to the present alike.

The initial reactions of German historians to Nolte's plea for a revisionist approach to the history of the Third Reich seemed to be divided between two opposing camps. However, with the ongoing Historians' Debate, and particularly after the publication of Nolte's final theses in his voluminous *Europäischer Bürgerkrieg*, the voices of criticism became almost unanimous. In the words of Wolfgang Schieder, the Historians' Debate, as far as Nolte is concerned, became "a dispute between the historians and Ernst Nolte."[27]

One of Nolte's first and most decisive critics was Martin Broszat in his article "Wo sich die Geister Scheiden" (Where the spirits part ways) published in *Die Zeit* on October 3, 1986. He particularly pointed to Nolte's tendency of "relativizing the National Socialist genocide" and his dangerous experimentation with history, disregarding the elementary empirical principles. He saw the gravest danger, however, in the respectability and academic legitimacy given to the arguments of the right-wing revisionists' pamphlet literature, particularly to its theory on the "Jewish declaration of war against Germany," through the support of a leading German historian. His personal concern about the profoundly changed quality and attitudes in Nolte's recent publications as compared with his previous works is perhaps best expressed in his statement that "it might frighten particularly all those who, like myself, have been stimulated by Nolte's thinking." I admit that I myself fully identify with all those.

Nevertheless, in spite of the entirely different methodological approach and ethical attitude, the recent views of Broszat, also calling for a revision in German historical research on the Third Reich, depart from his own views which we have dealt with above. In his "Plea for the Historicization of National Socialism," he, too, states the following:

Historiography is still overwhelmingly dominated by the impact of the catastrophic end and end-situation [*des katastrophalen Endes und Endzustandes*]. It was also introduced *a posteriori* as a "red thread" to explain the motives, instruments and stages of National Socialism, its development and domination. . . . The morality of the victims of the National Socialist past has meanwhile been considerably exhausted and has lost its singularity through new world-historical violence and catastrophic experiences . . . [*die Moralität der Betroffenheit von der NS-Vergangenheit hat sich mittlerweile stark erschöpf und durch neue weltgeschichtliche Gewalt- und Katastrophenerfahrungen an Singularität eingebüsst* . . .].

Although in the sixties Broszat emphasized more than, and before any other Western or German historian, the central role of anti-Semitism as the only possible key to understand the unique nature and immanent "logic" of National Socialism, he now regards the formerly much admired founders of German postwar historiography—among them "those modern historians who were forced to emigrate after 1933 for racial or political reasons"—as the originators of the distorting interpretation of recent German history. In order to emancipate German historiography from these historical distortions, he now pleads for what he calls "historicization," or a shift of emphasis, to the more normal aspects of the Third Reich, which, in his opinion, are predominant in its social history. This approach enables a reintegration of the National Socialist period into the continuity of German history and particularly into the historical self-understanding of the Federal Republic.

One of Broszat's most poignant examples is his reference to a recent study of the development of the social policy of the National Socialist era. He points out that "the National Socialist social policy during World War II and the basic idea . . . which recurred later, made the legislation of social insurance passed by the Federal Republic in the 1950s into a significant achievement," and that "the DAF plan [of 1941–42] emerged almost simultaneously with the British Beveridge Plan, the ideological foundation of the welfare-state reform introduced by the British Labour Government after the war." This comparison serves to inspire the attempts at the historical self-understanding of the German Federal Republic, but the world-historical uniqueness of the Third Reich and even of its social policy lies precisely in the *duality* that alongside the German worker, hundreds of thousands of enslaved human beings "worked" in the National Socialist welfare-community, after members of their families had been murdered in the most gruesome way, and they themselves, after being worn out, were sent back to Auschwitz and annihilated in an industrially rational way. From this indispensable point of view the comparative perspective of allegedly parallel developments in Britain and Germany might easily conceal the abysmal difference between the two "historicized" examples.

Another similar example is Broszat's emphasis on the contribution of the *Führerprinzip* to the emergence of a new social elite by creating

thousandfold major and minor führer-positions . . . in which young and dynamic elements from the middle class . . . proved themselves in tough contests with other "Führers" and exercised their energy and capacity to improvise. . . . They were useful for almost everything, on all levels of society. . . .

This new type of entrepreneur later contributed decisively to the economic miracle of the Federal Republic. This, too, may be an important aspect in exploring the past for the possible "normal" elements in the *Vorgeschichte* of the Federal Republic, but for an understanding of the historical phenomenon of the Third Reich itself one has simultaneously to explore how the same "new social type of the National Socialist *Sonderführer*" made possible the creation and the terribly efficient functioning of the mass annihilation machinery and the gigantic slave industry of the Auschwitz complex.

In the same way one can relate to Broszat's high appreciation of the research which portrays the seemingly normal picture of the so-called National Socialist *Alltag* (everyday life) in small German communities, which perhaps more resembles than differs from the everyday life of those communities in the Federal Republic. Here whole communities are portrayed without, or only marginally, relating to their reaction to the disappearance and fate of their Jewish neighbors. But to understand the unique situation and character of this society of the Third Reich, one has to ask what kind of social ethics made them not react, or react as they did, to the deportations of the Jews from their midst and to the now convincingly proven, quite widespread knowledge about their mass extermination.[28]

In the overall view Broszat presents National Socialism as an answer to the much-needed structural changes and modernization of German society—or in his words: "As an answer to a number of social reforms neglected in the Weimar Republic . . . and a piece of belated social bourgeois revolution . . . [*Als eine Antwort auf manche in der Weimarer Republik unterbliebene gesellschaftliche Reform . . . und ein Stück nachgeholter sozialer bürgerlicher Revolution*]*". In this perspective the racialist aspect of this revolution and particularly the "Final Solution of the Jewish Question" seem to be regarded as somehow irrelevant. But here, too, the historian cannot ignore the unique duality characterizing this singular way [*Sonderweg*] of German history, and one is tempted to ask: Which needs of structural changes and social modernization of Germany were, or should have been, answered by Auschwitz? (Here, of course, as in the previous examples, Auschwitz figures symbolically, as representing an essential dimension of a whole structure, but also as a concrete reality demonstrated in its most "perfect" example.)

Although Broszat does not refer here explicitly to the origins of the theory on the modernizing effect of National Socialism on German society, he obviously reflects the original thesis of Ralf Dahrendorf in his already classic work of the 1960s, *Society and Democracy in Germany*. In this connection it is worthwhile to refer once again to Dahrendorf's presentation of the basic methodological and ethical questions, particularly "the first question" he raises again in the chapter "The Path to Dictatorship":

How was Auschwitz possible? Or, more precisely: How was an organized mass murder possible, in which thousands of "educated" Germans participated . . . ? The question how the National Socialist crimes were possible remains unanswered, unless our observations about humanitarianism and inhumanity in Germany are taken for an answer. Morally, the road to modernity could hardly assume more brutal and inhuman traits than it did in Germany.[29]

Taking into account this indispensable duality, presented by Dahrendorf as a precondition of research, the question is whether Broszat's one-dimensional comparative use of the terms "modernization" or "belated social bourgeois revolution," which point to phenomena or developments in other societies and periods, is more helpful than Nolte's comparative treatment of Marxism and National Socialism. Although I am convinced that the difference between the approaches of Nolte and Broszat is a substantial one, one cannot ignore here the potentially dangerous historical experimentation.

I believe that even if it seems more than self-evident, one always has to try to relate to the question of the world-historical significance of that duality of the Third Reich that transcends the boundaries of German history. As obvious as it may always appear, it seems necessary to return to the awareness of the fact that the existence of the present democratic welfare state of the German Federal Republic, and of the socialist German Democratic Republic, was made possible only because of the military defeat of National Socialist Germany, and that a possibly victorious Third Reich, with its inherent social "ethics," would have led to an entirely different reality of empire based on Social Darwinist biological selection and annihilation-politics, de-Christianized and definitely dehumanized, at least in regard to the non-German peoples of this empire.

There is no doubt that Broszat is conscious of all this, and there is no better way to learn about it than in his article. "On the Structure of the National Socialist Mass Movement."[30] The decisive question is, however, what is the new point of departure or the new historical *Fragestellung* (posing of a question) Broszat puts forward in his "Plea for a Historicization of National Socialism"? If he postulates the research of the Third Reich with the purpose of discovering the possibly relevant aspects of the *Vorgeschichte* of the Federal Republic in search of the lost German historical identity, this should be declared *expressis verbis*. This might, no doubt, be a legitimate approach to the study of the emergence of present-day German society. But this is not evident from the definition implied by the title he has chosen for his "Plea". This definition gives the clear impression that the "historicization" he proposes should be a new way to understand the essence and historical meaning of National Socialism as such. In other words, it may be understood as a call for a revision of the whole picture of the National Socialist past in German historiography, including (or perhaps excluding) its world-historical meaning.

Now I would like to present another approach: during the 1980s the most actively engaged German historian, with regard to the Third Reich and the Jewish Question, both in research and public discussion, has been Hans Mommsen. I am referring in particular to his contribution to the forthcoming volume on *The Historiography of the Holocaust Period*,[31] his two extensive studies: "The Realization of the Unthinkable: The 'Final Solution of the Jewish Question' in the Third Reich"[32] and his extensive introductory essay to the new German edition of Hannah Arendt's *Eichmann in Jerusalem* (1986), as well as to his numerous contributions to the Historians' Debate.[33]

As I have already noted, since the 1960s Mommsen too has contributed decisively to the theory of the centrality of the anti-Jewish policy in the National Socialist terror system and ideology, and the singularity of the "Final Solution." Moreover, his postulate of "de-demonization" of the Third Reich led, in the last two decades of research, to achievements without which our present understanding of important aspects of the Third Reich and the Holocaust would have been impossible. In his latest studies, however, some changes in his views, or emphasis, have appeared, which seem to raise new problems and questions. Consequently, this postulate, significant in its own right, could be misinterpreted so that it might also lead to a certain kind of relativization of National Socialism and the "Final Solution." This tendency of Mommsen, similar to that of Broszat, appears notwithstanding his being perhaps the most active and radical critic of Nolte and some other conservative German historians during the present Historians' Debate.

Mommsen was one of the first to use the phrase "A relativization of National Socialism" in his polemic against Nolte's claim that National Socialist genocidal anti-Semitism was merely a reaction to Bolshevism. I quote here from his two important articles mentioned above (see note 33):

For some time now things are being presented differently. Suddenly not only the "singularity" of National Socialism is being denied, but also its crimes. The debate revolves around the evaluation of the "Holocaust." Ernst Nolte pioneered this many years ago when he emphasized that the liquidation of millions of European Jews did not constitute a unique event in world history, but must be "relativized" in the perspective of universal history.[34]

Although Mommsen considers Nolte's approach, at least from a methodological point of view, as being in line with the progressive tendency of research, he sharply criticizes its specific implications with regard to the alleged role of Bolshevism:

> With the demand to place National Socialism within larger historical contexts, Ernst Nolte is in line with historians who have adopted a more pronounced progressive position. When he, at the same time, perceives genocide as a mere psychological counter-reaction to Lenin's "White Terror" which is described as an "Asiatic action," he moves, however, into a sphere in which all actions in any way directed against Bolshevism appear justified as such, and in which any concrete political responsibility disappears behind era-bound dispositions.[35]

Mommsen identifies this view as nothing but the long since outdated "theory of the totalitarian dictatorship" from the period of the Cold War.[36] Yet his own analysis of the totalitarian terror system of the Third Reich and the policy of the extermination of the Jews is heavily indebted to Hannah Arendt's *Origins of Totalitarianism*, written under the overwhelming impact of the last years of the Stalinist terror, and to her *Eichmann in Jerusalem*. Following Arendt's concept of the "banality of evil," which in his view covers not only the mental and psychological conditions under which the Holocaust was implemented, but the process itself, he first of all excludes any decisive role of Hitler's ideology. Mommsen claims that Hitler perceived the Jewish Question primarily in propagandistic terms and in a specific visionary context, while he did not show much interest, and certainly not much involvement, in the individual steps of the Nazi anti-Jewish policy.[37] From here he proceeds to an interpretation of the annihilation process itself which, under the circumstances, may be understood as a far-reaching relativization in two different spheres: (1) the genocide in Nazi Germany itself; and (2) the possibility of its recurrence in the future of other societies.

With regard to the Third Reich itself, he sees the overwhelming impact of the totalitarian terror system and its impersonal bureaucratic character as inevitably bringing about the dehumanization not only of the Jewish victims but also of the perpetrators. Following Arendt, Mommsen talks about an adjustment in the mentality of the persecutors and the persecuted, particularly their organizations, who all became victims and "guilty" alike.[38]

As to the other sphere of what may be understood as relativization of the National Socialist genocide, he foresees its potential recurrence in advanced industrial societies with their bureaucratic structures (cf. the closing passages in his "The Realization of the Unthinkable"). However, as the only concrete example of a people presently threatened by genocide, Mommsen singles out the "Palestinian Arabs," drawing, in a peculiar way, on Hannah Arendt's *Origins of Totalitarianism*, where, *in 1949*, she dealt with the problem of "displaced persons" in the wake of World Wars I and II.[39]

In view of the complexities and the dangers of possible misinterpretation of Mommsen's views elaborated particularly in his introductory essay to the new German edition of Arendt's *Eichmann in Jerusalem*, a more detailed critical analysis of this stimulating study is called for here.[40] The problematic issue actually already appears before Mommsen's introduction—in the editor's preface to the book. An excerpt, quoted from a letter by Karl Jaspers, introduces—on an apparently equal level—two central problems of Hannah Arendt's book: "The subject of the cooperation of the Jews with the Nazis is one. The theme of the Germans carries equal weight." The representative meaning of this presentation of the central problem of the whole book—as an attempt to interpret the historical process leading to the "Final Solution"—is unequivocally grounded by Mommsen on page ii: "It is obvious that she [Hannah Arendt] was concerned with an overall interpretation of the Holocaust." Thus, the choice of the quotation can be understood as a declared relativization of the Holocaust, similar, in a way, to the much disputed title selected for Andreas Hillgruber's *Zweierlei Untergang: Die Zerschlagung des Deutschen Reiches und das Ende des europäischen Judentums* (Two kinds of doom: The destruction of the German Reich and the end of European Jewry [Berlin, 1986]). It could be apprehended as comparing the situation and responsibility of the Jewish victims of the Nazi mass murder with those of the nation and state in whose name this mass murder was committed.

The problem becomes particularly grave in Mommsen's interpretation of Arendt's central thesis "that through indoctrination and terror the totalitarian rule virtually conditions all the groups of the population so that they are equally fit for the role of the perpetrators as well as for the role of the victims" (p. xvii). As he further elaborates, "the assimilation [*Angleichung*] of the mentality of the perpetrators and the victims, originally postulated by Arendt, has been confirmed through a series of studies." Of these studies Mommsen refers solely to Falk Pingel's book on the concentration camps (*Häftlinge unter SS-Herrschaft*), which is actually irrelevant to the issue dealt with here, namely, the problem of the Jewish organizations—the *Reichsvertretung* and *Reichsvereinigung* in Germany and the "Jewish Councils" in Eastern Europe. I think that for purely scientific reasons, as well as out of consideration for the audience of the younger German generation addressed by Mommsen at the end of his essay, at least a few of the most important works from the relevant comprehensive research literature published in the last decades should have been mentioned. This is all the more conspicuous when he comes to the other focal point of his essay—Arendt's theses and arguments pertaining to German resistance—which he treats quite differently, invoking detailed and up to date literature in his thorough critical examination of this issue.

Let me also mention in this connection that the subject of Jewish organizations and leadership under National Socialist rule, which Mommsen terms "taboo,"[41] has long ceased to be regarded as such. On the contrary, it has been the theme of open discussion and intense research activity by Jewish and non-Jewish scholars from Eastern and Western Europe and from America, as exemplified by the international symposium on the "Jewish Councils," held in Jerusalem in April 1977.[42]

I would like to add, however, that reference to the works mentioned here would place the blunt thesis of Hannah Arendt, so persuasively advocated by

Mommsen, in quite a different light. Rather than endorsing Arendt's assumption that under the totalitarian regime the mentality of the perpetrators and the victims became unavoidably assimilated, the findings of this literature demonstrate that, even under the extreme circumstances of the totalitarian terror-regime, human society, and in this case Jewish society, retained its own values and dignity. The *raison d'être* of the Jewish organizations under Nazi rule, in their self-understanding, was their effort to safeguard the material and spiritual existence of Jewish society, in all the stages of Nazi rule. Under the harshest conditions of the ghettos this became a desperate struggle to preserve the lives of the inmates and the human face of the community.

In the face of the possible danger of distortion or relativization of the historical picture, it might be useful here to return to Broszat's "Plea for a Historicization," particularly in regard to the social history of the Third Reich. If we apply his methodological observations to the research into the social history of the Jews under National Socialist rule, we should equally demand not to proceed here exclusively from the perspective of the "catastrophic end and end-situation," but to deal with all of its aspects throughout the National Socialist era and in the perspective of the continuity of Jewish history. In the light of my critical remarks on Broszat's article, it should, however, not have excluded the need to examine the various quasi-normal aspects of life from the perspective of the unique duality of the historical situation. This duality encompasses the continuity of internal Jewish life and activities in the face of the radically changing social and political status, the gradually emerging prospect of the end of Jewish existence in Germany, in German-occupied Europe, and ultimately the impending total physical destruction. This appears to me to be the necessary corrective of Mommsen's highly inadequate and even distorting treatment of Jewish communal life, organizations, and leadership in the Third Reich, which also implies a corrective of Broszat's stimulating methodological approach.

Let us now turn to another problematic issue in Mommsen's essay dealing with the prospective future genocide, relating to the possibly reverted roles of victims-perpetrators and deduced from the historical "Final Solution." On page xiii of the introductory essay to *Eichmann in Jerusalem*, Mommsen turns to Arendt's *Origins of Totalitarianism* in order to describe its preconditions [*die Vorbedingung der späteren Vernichtung*]: "the gradual outlawing of the expatriated and the stateless who lost not only their citizenship, but also their legal rights and their homeland." An examination of the pertinent passages (pp. 289–90 in *The Origins*) reveals that for Mommsen, as well as all other scholars of the Third Reich, including Hannah Arendt, the procedure described there must be regarded as an utterly indefensible explanation for the "Final Solution":

first to reduce the German Jews to a non-recognized minority in Germany, then to drive them as stateless people across the borders, and finally to gather them back from everywhere in order to ship them to extermination camps. . . .

The policy of emigration definitely had other purposes; the majority of Jews deported from Germany to the extermination camps never emigrated; the same is certainly true for the millions of Jews deported to the extermination camps from other countries, or those murdered without deportation. Hence Mommsen's attempt to find a parallel in the process of creating the phenomenon of "displaced persons" in the postwar period, "a modern fate which as such carried the danger of a new genocide" (introd. essay, p. xiii), is more than questionable. The most disconcerting fact is that from all the examples brought by Arendt of "refugees and stateless people . . . since the peace treaties of 1919 and 1920" and the post–World War II period, including the millions on the Indian subcontinent (*The Origins*, p. 290), Mommsen relates only to one case. In his formulation: "The expulsion of Palestinian Arabs appeared to her as a bad omen for a possible continuation of the cycle [of genocide]. . . ."[43] The comparison of Arendt's original text and Mommsen's paraphrase clearly indicates that she did not use the term "genocide," as claimed by Mommsen, and, obviously, did not relate here to this issue at all. She also did not repeat her reflections of 1949 in her book on Eichmann, even though, or perhaps precisely because, it deals with the "Final Solution" as its main topic. However, it becomes clear to all of Mommsen's readers that the foreseen potential genocide of the Palestinian Arabs would be perpetrated by the nation of the former victims of the National Socialist "Final Solution." The "evidence" for the juxtaposition of this nation with that of the perpetrators of the "Final Solution" must be understood as the ultimate relativization of the so far historically unique phenomenon of the Holocaust. This was certainly not Mommsen's intention and therefore one finds it hard to understand why he decided to create this construction, and paraphrase, in his own way, these rather problematic passages from *The Origins of Totalitarianism*.

Parenthetically, I wish to mention that a similar comparison of the National Socialist "Final Solution" with the potential mass murder in Palestine, made by Nolte in "Between Myth and Revisionism," was justifiably met by strong criticism and indignation. As we saw, Mommsen himself sharply criticized Nolte for the use of such a juxtaposition and the assumption of a "causal nexus," especially with regard to the "Judeo-Bolshevist" and National Socialist mass murders.

But here there is another point worth mentioning in comparing the essentially incomparable. Nolte's panopticum of genocidal phenomena throughout the world relativizes the Holocaust in the context of past and present events. Mommsen's totally different methdological approach and ethical point of departure make it possible to take the "Final Solution," hitherto regarded by him as a unique historical event, and relativize it as a part of the future perspective. He bases his view on the one hand on the assumption of the relevance of a situation in which modern industrial society is threatened by the all-embracing impersonal violence inherent in its bureaucratic structure, which he believes may be deduced from the nature of the Third Reich. On the other hand, he deduces the most far-reaching relativization, or transformation, of the mentality and historical position of the nation of the victims of that hitherto unparalleled genocide, from the hitherto too singular experience undergone by the nation of the perpetrators. I believe that such attempts to experiment with perceptions of the future may involve the danger that their real meaning and motivations may be misconstrued.

IV

In order to restore some balance to the historiographical picture, I have to mention at least some of the most important recent works of those German scholars who continued to explore or reestablish meaningful concepts of the historical singularity of National Socialism, in spite of, or along with, the present tendencies of relativization. One of them is the concise study by the late Kalus Scholder, "Judaism and Christianity in the Ideology and Politics of National Socialism."[44] Here, Scholder reexamines and further develops the basic concepts of the centrality of anti-Semitism and its far-reaching significance for the fate of the churches, elaborated in the monumental first volume of his history of the churches in the Third Reich.[45] In this context he also deals with the complexities and contradictions of long-term ideological goals and practical politics, and the close link between the "Jewish and the Christian Question" in the self-perception of the Christian population of Germany and its leadership under the Third Reich. I limit myself to a quote from his closing lines:

On July 11–12, 1941 in a lapidary phrase, Hitler declared: "The hardest blow that humanity has had to bear is Christianity; Bolshevism is the illegitimate son of Christianity; both were born of the Jews . . ." For Hitler the root of all evil was and remained Judaism. Because of this, the Jews were the first to feel his hate and his will to annihilate. As time went by, however, Christianity followed ever more closely behind, labeled as a Jewish invention.

The Jewish and Christian Questions in the Third Reich were thus much more closely linked than the Christian Churches were willing to acknowledge. Only Hitler's defeat in the war spared the Christians a violent realization of this fact.

The second work is the recently published book of Eberhard Jäckel, *Hitlers Herrschaft: Vollzug einer Weltanschauung*,[46] which reexamines and further develops his above-mentioned basic study, *Hitler's World View*. Here too, the basic ideological concepts, explored in the previous work, are examined in a detailed context of their political and administrative realization and social setting, thus reaching a rare synthesis of different methodological approaches. The use of comparative elements throughout the book, and the broad historical perspective of the last chapter, reestablish and reaccentuate the concept of singularity, in which the Jewish aspects dominate perhaps more than before.

In Jäckel's first contribution to the Historians' Debate in *Die Zeit* of September 12, 1986, he proposes a definition of this singularity which has meanwhile been adopted by the majority of German historians as an almost classical epitomization of their own credo:

This is not the first time I argue that the murder of Jews was unique because never before had a state, with the authority of its responsible leader, decided and announced its intention to liquidate as completely as possible a certain group of people, including the aged, women, children and babies, and to implement this decision by means of all the official instruments of power at its disposal.[47]

In his attempt to evaluate the results of the first year of the Historians' Debate, Jäckel arrives at the following conclusions:

This thorough and critical preoccupation with our history and in particular with the Hitler era is not detrimental but rather beneficial, it is no weakness but rather a strength. Precisely this benefit and this strength should be taken from us by all those who would have us believe that we should step out of the shadow of the Third Reich, that we have to relativize it, normalize, historicize. . . .[48]

To take upon oneself the responsibility . . . means to be honest and true, not to hush up anything, not to embellish, not to repress. Only when we take upon ourselves this responsibility can we walk upright. We then achieve freedom for ourselves and respect throughout the world.[49]

I wish to close with another, even more recent, critical evaluation of the Historians' Debate, which, in spite of the different methodological approach of its author—the outstanding German social historian Jürgen Kocka—arrives at similar conclusions:

there are certain attempts to achieve a greater acceptability of our past which cannot be permitted in professional terms. Distortions like Nolte's speculation on the anti-Bolshevik and defensive character of the Holocaust violate the standards of historical scholarship. Comparison must not be misused to relativize and trivialize the Nazi experience. . . . I would argue that a clear and lively recollection of the most disastrous period of our history does not paralyze us as a political society. It may well be the opposite. For many of us, a critical awareness of the Nazi period has been a major motivation for political, scholarly, and intellectual commitments and activities. . . . As Habermas and others have argued, one of the basic elements of the political culture of the Federal Republic of Germany (and also of the GDR) is stressing the difference between itself and the National Socialist past. In this respect, any relativization of the National Socialist past has the potential of undermining a certain element of the political culture of the Federal Republic.[50]

Appendix: From a Letter to Ernst Nolte, Jerusalem, July 18, 1986[51]

Let it be made quite clear that murder and brutality as such, against whichever human beings or groups, are, naturally, murder and brutality, and it is immaterial whether the Jews are the largest group exterminated by the National Socialists of not. The same applies to the atrocities and genocidal actions perpetrated by various other regimes against other population groups.

The uniqueness of the National Socialist mass murder of Jews must be understood in the world-historical sense attributed to it—as an attempt to bring about a change in the course of universal history and its goals. Thus,

National Socialist anti-Semitism must be regarded as an expression of perhaps the most dangerous crisis of Western civilization with the potentially gravest consequences for the history of mankind. . . .

If I come back, once again, to your explanation of the discrepancy in your studies of fascism, the Third Reich and the "Final Solution" as a "shift of emphasis," then the question inevitably arises about the motivation and driving forces of this changed perspective. I think they may be found in your description of the present situation of the Federal Republic, the self-understanding of its society and the need to find a new understanding of German history from this perspective. In this regard, I refer to your following statement [in the *Frankfurter Allgemeine Zeitung* of June 6, 1986]: "The more unequivocally the Federal Republic of German and Western society in general develop into welfare societies, the more alien becomes the picture of the Third Reich with its ideology . . ." The unique nature of the Third Reich and the "Final Solution," and the centrality of anti-Semitism inevitably appear here as something which on no account explains the normality of present-day society, nor has any meaningful connection with it. It is much easier, by contrast, to make an apparently possible comparison with the genocidal phenomenon in its different manifestations elsewhere, in our day. . . .

In one of my letters I asserted that the reexamination of your theses from the sixties does not proceed in a historiographic vacuum. I am thinking of parallel tendencies such as those in Martin Broszat's "Plea for a Historicization of National Socialism" or Hans Mommsen's *Adolf Hitler als Führer der Nation* (1984). Here, however, we are dealing, rather, with a "shift" in the emphasis on the "normal" aspects of domestic history than with a global perspective which you have outlined. . . .

Notes

This essay is based on two public lectures held at the meeting of the Historical Society of Israel (October 1986) and at the international conference on "Germany's Singularity? The *Sonderweg* Debate" at the Hebrew University of Jerusalem (March 1987). I wish to thank my friends and colleagues, in particular Saul Friedländer, Shmuel Ettinger, Israel Gutman, Jürgen Kocka, and Ian Kershaw, for their critical remarks and comments in the various stages of the preparation of this essay.

1. These observations were demonstrated in my study on the main trends and tendencies in German historiography on National Socialism and the "Final Solution." See "Die deutsche Geschichtsschreibung über den Nationalsozialismus und die Endlösung: Tendenzen und Entwicklungsphasen 1924–1984," *Historische Zeitschrift* 240 (1985): 599–640. A revised and extended English version appears in *The Historiography of the Holocaust Period*, Proceedings of the Fifth Yad Vashem International Historical Conference (Jerusalem, 1988).

2. My own views, which partially coincide with those of Jäckel and Scholder, are presented in the excerpts of my exchange of letters with Ernst Nolte at the end of this piece.

3. Friedrich Meinecke, *The German Catastrophe* (Cambridge, Mass., 1950).

4. Ernst Nolte, *Der Faschismus in Seiner Epoche* (Munich, 1963); English edition, *Three Faces of Fascism* (London, 1965), 359.

5. Ibid., 399.

6. Cologne, 1969; English edition, *The German Dictatorship* (London, 1970), 67.

7. Hienz Höhne, "Der Orden unter dem Totenkopf: Die Geschichte der SS", *Der Spiegel*, 1966–67; English version, *The Order of the Death's Head: The Story of Hitler's SS* (London, 1969).

8. "Ein Nachwort zur SS-Serie," *Der Spiegel* 11 (3 June 1967), 75–77.

9. Martin Broszat, *Der Staat Hitlers* (Munich, 1969); English edition, *The Hitler State: The Foundation and Development of the Internal Structure of the Third Reich* (London, 1981); idem, *Vierteljahrshefte für Zeitgeschichte* 18 (1970): 392–409; idem, *Vierteljahrshefte für Zeitgeschichte* 25 (1977): 73–125. An English version, entitled "Hitler and the Genesis of the 'Final Solution': An Assessment of David Irving's Thesis," was published in *Yad Vashem Studies* 13 (1979) and reprinted in H. W. Koch, ed., *Aspects of the Third Reich* (London, 1985).

10. For details, see my above-mentioned article in *Historische Zeitschrift* (note 1), p. 624, and esp. note 98.

11. We can find it in the assessments of Karl Dietrich Erdmann in Gebhardt's *Handbuch der deutschen Geschichte* (1976), or those of Theodor Schieder and Karl Erich Born in Schieder's *Handbuch der europäischen Geschichte* (1979), and similarly even in the paperback edition of *Pipers Weltgeschichte in Karten, Daten, Bildern* (1970), as well as in C. Zentner and F. Bedürftig's *Das grosse Lexikon des Dritten Reichs* (1985).

12. Kurt Patzold, "Von der Vertreibung zum Genozid: Zu den Ursachen und Bedingungen der antijüdischen Politik des faschistichen deutschen Imperialismus," in D. Eichholz and K. Grossweiler, eds., *Faschismus: Forschung, Positionen, Probleme, Polemik* (Berlin and Cologne, 1980), 181.

13. "Between Myth and Revisionism: The Third Reich in the Perspective of the 1980s," in H. W. Koch, ed., *Aspects of the Third Reich* (London, 1985), 17–38; "Vergangenheit, die nicht vergehen will," in *Frankfurter Allgemiene Zeitung*, 6 June 1986, also in *Historikerstreit;* "Die Sache auf den Kopf gestellt: Gegen den negativen Nationalismus in der Geschichtsschreibung," *Die Zeit*, 31 October 1986, also in *Historikerstreit*.

14. See particularly 392, 405, 412ff. An earlier version of these ideas appears in Nolte's *Deutschland und der Kalte Krieg* (Munich and Zurich, 1974), 136–37, 307, 331–32, 607.

15. Concerning this absurd allegation of Goebbels, following the German invasion of Russia and the beginning of the mass annihilation of the Jews, see Wolfgang Benz, "Judenvernichtung aus Notwehr? Die Legenden um Theodore N. Kaufmann," *Vierteljahrshefte für Zeitgeschichte* 29 (1981): 615–30.

16. On the origins of this distortion of Tucholsky's article against future wars in the so-called Holocaust-denial literature and Nolte's identification with the arguments of those authors, see my article in *Frankfurter Rundschau* of 5 November 1987, entitled "Der Umgang des Historikers Ernst Nolte mit Briefen aus Israel," part of which appears at the end of this essay.

17. Nolte, *Das Vergehen*, 125–26.

18. Ernst Nolte, *Der europäische Bürgerkrieg 1917–1945: Nationalsozialismus und Bolschewismus* (Frankfurt am Main and Berlin, 1987), 502.

19. Ibid., 509.
20. Ibid., 512–13.
21. Ibid., 513.
22. Ibid., 516–17.
23. Nolte, *Das Vergehen*, 125.
24. Ibid., 11–12.
25. Ibid., 136 (my emphasis).
26. Nolte, *Three Faces of Fascism*, 457; see also 425, 453.
27. *Frankfurter Rundschau*, 17 December 1987.
28. See O. D. Kulka and A. Rodrigue, "The German Population and the Jews in the Third Reich: Recent Publications and Trends in Research on German Society and the 'Jewish Question,'" *Yad Vashem Studies* 16 (1984): 421–35. See also Ian Kershaw's *The Hitler Myth: Image and Reality in the Third Reich* (Oxford, 1987), esp. chap. 9.
29. Ralf Dahrendorf, *Society and Democracy in Germany* (New York, 1967), 365, 394.
30. "Zur Struktur des NS-Massenbewegung," *Vierteljahrshefte für Zeitgeschichte* 31 (1983): 53–76. See, in particular, the closing part of this excellent study on pp. 74–76, where he concludes: "Apparently the NS leadership itself had its doubts whether the full knowledge of the crimes initiated by it would find popular support. However, these persecutions could not remain entirely concealed. The underlying inhuman conception, especially with regard to the fanatic hatred of the Jews, was also expressed publicly by the leadership on almost every occasion, and there certainly was a social sounding board [*Resonanzboden*] for those ideas. . . . The concept of a totally politicized and indoctrinated German society during the NS period is as wrong as is the concept suggested of late, associated with the term Hitlerism, that the German bourgeois society had been held at bay and controlled completely by the dictatorial NS regime. The truth is more disconcerting. It lies in between. Only in this way, it seems to me, can one understand the passive and apathetic attitude of the great majority of the German population during the last years of the war, when the integrative power of the regime had already vanished to a large extent. . . . Here apparently the awareness of a shared responsibility for and complicity in the excesses and crimes of the regime played a role as well [*Hier spielte offenbar auch das Bewusstsein herein, dass man mitverantwortlich hineinverwickelt gewesen war in die Exzesse und Verbrechen des Regimes*]."
31. See note 1.
32. Hans Mommsen, "Die Realisierung des Utopischen: Die Endlösung der Judenfrage im Dritten Reich," *Geschichte und Gesellschaft* 9 (1983): 381–420; English version, "The Realization of the Unthinkable," in Gerhard Hirschfeld, ed., *The Politics of Genocide* (London, 1986), 93–144.
33. The two most important ones—"Suche nach der 'verlorenen Geschichte'?" *Merkur,* September–October 1986, and "Neues Geschichtsbewusstsein und Relativierung des Nationalsozialismus," *Blätter für deutsche und internationale Politik,* October 1986—were published in *Historikerstreit.*
34. *Historikerstreit.*
35. "Neues Geschichtsbewusstsein" and "Suche nach der 'verlorenen Geschichte'?" in *Historikerstreit.*
36. *Historikerstreit.*
37. In addition to the above-mentioned recent articles, see also his *Adolf Hitler als*

"Führer" der Nation, Studienheft 11 in the series Nationalsozialismus in Unterricht, Fernstudium Geschichte (Tübingen, 1984).

38. In Hannah Arendt, *Eichmann in Jerusalem* (Munich, 1986), Introduction, xvii.

39. Ibid., xiii.

40. The following remarks are based on an exchange of letters with Mommsen. Although he regarded some of my conclusions as overinterpreted, he nevertheless did not refute any substantial part of my criticism.

41. Mommsen, Introduction to Arendt, *Eichmann in Jerusalem*, xvii.

42. Out of the numerous publications, I would like to mention at least the following: *Patterns of Jewish Leadership in Nazi Europe 1933–1945*, Proceedings of the Third Yad Vashem International Historical Conference (Jerusalem, 1979); Isaiah Trunk, *Judenrat: The Jewish Councils in Eastern Europe under Nazi Occupation* (New York, 1972); Israel Gutman, *The Jews of Warsaw, 1939–1942: Ghetto, Underground, Revolt* (Bloomington, 1982); O. D. Kulka, "The Reichsvereinigung and the Fate of the German Jews, 1938/1939–1943," in *Die Juden im nationalsozialistischen Deutschland, 1933–1945* (Tübingen, 1986), 353–63 (see also the references there to the Hebrew dissertation of Esriel Hildesheimer); on Western Europe, see Richard I. Cohen, *Burden of Conscience: French Jewish Leadership during the Holocaust* (Bloomington, 1987). Also relevant in some respects is the comprehensive volume *The Nazi Concentration Camps: Structure and Aims; The Image of the Prisoner; The Jews in the Camps*, Proceedings of the Fourth Yad Vashem International Historical Conference (Jerusalem, 1984); see also my article "Ghetto in an Annihilation Camp—Jewish Social History in the Holocaust Period and Its Ultimate Limits," ibid., 315–30.

43. "Like virtually all other events of our century, the solution of the Jewish question merely produced a new category of refugees, the Arabs, thereby increasing the number of the stateless and rightless by another 700,000 to 800,000 people. And what happened in Palestine within the smallest territory and in terms of hundreds of thousands of people was then repeated in India on a large scale involving many millions of people. Since the Peace Treaties of 1919 and 1920 the refugees and the stateless have attached themselves like a curse to all the newly established states on earth which were created in the image of the nation-state. For these new states this curse bears the germs of a deadly sickness. For the nation-state cannot exist once its principle of equality before the law has broken down" (Hannah Arendt, *The Origins of Totalitarianism* [New York, 1951], 290). In Mommsen's paraphrase, "She regarded statelessness as a modern fate, which as such entailed the danger of a renewed genocide [*Völkermord*]. The expulsion of Palestinian Arabs appeared to her to be a bad omen for the possibility of a continuing cycle. . ." (Introduction to Arendt, *Eichmann in Jerusalem*, xiii).

44. This appeared posthumously in the comprehensive volume *Judaism and Christianity under the Impact of National Socialism 1919–1945* (Jerusalem, 1987).

45. Klaus Scholder, *Die Kirchen und das Dritte Reich: Vorgeschichte und Zeit der Illusionen 1918–1934* (Frankfurt am Main, 1977); English edition, *The Churches and the Third Reich* (London, 1987).

46. Stuttgart, 1986.

47. *Historikerstreit*.

48. "Die Deutschen und ihre Geschichte," in Titus Hausermann, ed., *Die Bundesrepublik und die deutsche Geschichte* (Stuttgart, 1987), 19.

49. Ibid., 20.
50. Jürgen Kocka, "The Weight of the Past in Germany's Future," in *German Politics and Society* (Harvard University: The Center for European Studies, February 1988), 26–27.
51. The original German text of this letter is included in my *Frankfurter Rundschau* article (see note 16). For Nolte's preceding letter and his answer, see his *Das Vergehen*, 128–35.

Part Three

Appraisal

9. Reappraisal and Repression: The Third Reich in West German Historical Consciousness

H a n s   M o m m s e n

I

As the recent controversy over the place of the National Socialist past in German self-understanding has shown, the long repression of this uncomfortable legacy postponed but could never eliminate the need for certain fundamental historical debates. The Federal government's attempt to lead West Germany back onto the path of "normalcy" via Bitburg and the Bonn war memorial backfired. So, too, did its desire to cover questions of individual and collective responsibility for Nazi crimes with a blanket of universal reconciliation. What basic lessons for its internal politics and international role should the Federal Republic derive from the experiences of Nazism and World War II? This issue is now being raised more insistently than ever before. At the same time, the widespread consensus concerning the thoroughly reprehensible nature of the National Socialist regime is dissolving. What was earlier an academic dispute over methodology within the historical profession has now gained immediate political relevance.

The fact that the past has suddenly regained a place in public discussion is a result of a gradual shift in national values, encouraged by forces within the West German government and lately dubbed *die Wende* (the turning point). The recent controversy over the relationship of the Federal Republic to National Socialism has produced no new arguments or research results. The Berlin historian Ernst Nolte has been expounding his provocative views for years without either the press or the academic community making much of them. The essence of Nolte's position is that Hitler's murder of 5 million Jews must be seen as a reaction to a well-founded fear of Bolshevism. The essays of Andreas Hillgruber, collected in the book *Zweierlei Untergang*, were also published previously. Michael Stürmer's theory of Germany's "middle position" [*Mittellage*] in Europe already occupied an established place in discussions of the German question.

The immediate cause of the Historian's Debate was Jürgen Habermas's violent attack in the July 11, 1986 edition of *Die Zeit* on Nolte, Hillgruber, and Stürmer, as well as on Klaus Hildebrand, who had supported Nolte in a review in the *Historische Zeitschrift*. The sharpness of the confrontation, as well as the extent of the publicity surrounding it, can be attributed principally to the *Frankfurter Allgemeine Zeitung*'s partisanship for Nolte and its condemnation of left-wing intellectuals for supposedly attempting to use the Nazi past for their own political purposes. The paper accused the Left of seeking to torpedo the long overdue historical normalization being championed by the Federal government. Habermas has called this and similar attempts in the professional literature to relativize National Socialist crimes and to assign them a purely episodic character within German history "neorevisionism." But this neorevisionism has in turn served to underwrite a broader revival of nationalist values among conservative groups both inside and outside the government camp, a revival that has gained wider attention as "the new nationalism."

Although it is the historical and political assessment of the Holocaust that stands at the center of the Historians' Debate, the Holocaust itself has functioned largely as a symbol for the totality of National Socialist policies. Still, an emphasis on the Final Solution as the true mark of Nazi violence and inhumanity remains significant precisely because the Holocaust was long neglected by researchers in West Germany. This new emphasis can perhaps be explained by the fact that with the changing of the generational guard in the Federal Republic, a preoccupation with the responsibility for the Nazi seizure of power has faded, while at the same time, consciousness of the long-term consequences of the National Socialist terror system and of the Second World War has increased. The real issue, however, remains the relative weight of the Nazi period within the broader continuity of both German and European history. The passage of time and the ensuing evolution of historical perspective have lent this problem a new dimension.

II

Over the past forty years, a number of identifiable concerns have inspired research on contemporary history. In response to Allied accusations of war guilt, Germans in the immediate postwar period did their best to highlight the terrorist nature of the Nazi dictatorship and the role of German resistance to Hitler's regime. Researchers accentuated the effect of the SS state, and the opposition to Hitler—a movement now christened "the other Germany"—came to stand for the nation as a whole. From this perspective, both the internal politics of the regime and the persecution of the Jews were pushed into the background. At first, an intellectual-history approach, linking National Socialism to the exaggerated nationalism of the imperial period, predominated. Slowly, however, the theory of totalitarian dictatorship established itself as *the* valid explanatory model. In this model, Nazi ideology was depicted primarily as a conscious instrument of manipulation.

Despite many variations in detail, theories of totalitarianism all assumed that the structure of the National Socialist system of domination was fundamentally monolithic, thus echoing the regime's own propagandistic self-interpretation. Later research, based primarily on documents impounded by the Allies and released after 1961, lent only partial support to the assumptions of the totalitarian model. This research revealed political fragmentation and instability in the institutions that the Nazis created as well as those they had inherited. In so doing, it contradicted the image of a totalitarian system organized down to the last detail in the service of power considerations. Yet the totalitarian image could still be maintained by interpreting the antagonisms within the regime as an attempt on Hitler's part to buttress his own unrestricted veto power through a strategy of divide-and-rule. Related to this was the tendency in the literature to regard Hitler, despite his obvious personal weaknesses, as the ultimate author of National Socialist policies and to emphasize the internal logic of his actions when seen in the light of his programmatic writings. Often this view went so far as to attribute to Hitler a coherent, ideologically motivated plan which he set about realizing in a methodical and gradual fashion.

The Hitler-centered interpretation of Nazism is so attractive as an explanatory model because it seems to lend consistency to a series of confusing and often contradictory actions. However, just because no one mounted effective opposition to Hitler, the symbol and embodiment of the Nazi regime, we should not necessarily conclude that he himself planned all Nazi politics and systematically put them into effect. It is only in the last decade that researchers have freed themselves from a preoccupation with Hitler as the sole center of decision-making. They have now discovered those areas of politics determined by the autonomous decisions of other leaders, areas where Hitler often exercised his (by no means systematic) influence only through haphazard intervention. The regime has begun to reveal itself as a political system that had a certain degree of openness, albeit within fixed ideological parameters.

Tim Mason has called the debate among historians over the personality and role of Hitler a clash between intentionalists and structuralists. The best way to decide scientifically between these two positions is to determine which explanatory model provides the best answers to specific important questions. Yet rather that resolve the intentionalist/structuralist controversy in a purely professional manner, historians in the Federal Republic have pursued it at a high emotional pitch. Perhaps this intensity can be explained in social-psychological terms: after the consolidation of power, Hitler became the very incarnation of German national identity, so it is logical that after 1945 he should become the central focus of blame for the German catastrophe. By personifying the events of National Socialism in the figure of Hitler and presenting the average German as the victim of a subtle mixture of propaganda, cynically exploited patriotism, and terroristic repression, historians could at least partially justify the conduct of the German people as a whole.

This perspective went hand in hand with the attempt to emphasize the break marked by January 30, 1933, and to excise the period between 1933 and 1945 from the continuity of German history. Accordingly, many historians sought to depict the foreign and domestic policies of the Nazis as a revolutionary break with all that had gone before them. This position found its culmination in Karl Dietrich Bracher's theory of the psuedo-legal totalitarian revolution, a revolution that distinguished itself from its bourgeois antecedents by its unscrupulous manipulation of power. In implicitly equating 1933 with the October Revolution, Bracher overlooked fundamental differences between the Bolsheviks' seizure of power and the transfer of power to the Nazis. This recasting of the formation of Hitler's "cabinet of national concentration," his coalition with the bourgeois parties in 1933, reflected a desire to impose a retrospective quarantine on those twelve years of Nazi rule—a period which, as Eberhard Jackel recently put it, led out of German history and into a previously unimagined abyss.[1]

For these reasons the National Socialist period was assigned a place of historical "singularity" that was justified on the one hand by the destructive role of Hitler and on the other by the sheer magnitude of Nazi crimes, unparalleled even by those of other fascist or authoritarian systems. This emphasis on the singularity of Nazism was directed especially at those historians who had taken up Ernst Nolte's theory of comparative fascism but had replaced its phenomenological-ideological perspective with a Marxist one. While explanatory models based on economistic or agency theories have encountered widespread resistance, structuralist approaches that stress similarities in the styles and institutions of fascist politics have allowed a more nuanced picture of the NSDAP and its internal dynamics. The historiographic adherents of "Hitlerism" (Hans Buchheim's term) have criticized the comparative perspective for minimizing the horror of National Socialism. The real motive, however, behind the "Hitlerists'" rejection of any comparisons between Nazism and other fascist movements or regimes is that such an approach undercuts their own desire to equate National Socialism with communism.

Stressing the uniqueness of Nazism also served to negate the efforts of other researchers to uncover the historical roots of the movement and to identify the links between National Socialism and various bourgeois nationalist, neoconservative, and populist (*völkisch*) movements. These researchers naturally emphasized the strains of anticommunism, antisocialism, antiliberalism, and antiparliamentarianism shared among a broad range of bourgeois groups in the period after World War I. Their opponents, the Hitlerists, have tried to discredit the claims of continuity between Nazism and various strains of bourgeois nationalism (claims admittedly often exaggerated) by focusing attention on the field of electoral analysis. They have sought to prove that the NSDAP attracted a considerable number of members and sympathizers from the proletariat and that an exchange of voters took place between the KPD (Communist Party of Germany) and the Nazis, especially after January 30, 1933. Linked to this claim is the argument that the parties of the republican center in the Weimar Republic were in fact strangled by extremists from both

Right and Left. This claim is based on various episodes of cooperation between Nazis and communists, normally the bitterest of enemies.

This argument, still a favorite in the popular media, corresponds to the denunciation of the Nazis during Weimar as "brown Bolsheviks." It has received only weak support from serious historical scholarship, although anti-Bolshevism certainly played an important role in the success of National Socialist propaganda. The equation between Nazis and communists obscures the crucial role of the conservative elite in the events of 1933. Because of their opposition both to the "Marxist" SPD (the Social Democratic Party) and to the parliamentary system in general, the conservatives allowed Hitler's entry into the Cabinet—though they would have preferred a more purely authoritarian rule. In the wake of recent scholarly reevaluation of Heinrich Brüning's government, the literature now reflects a broad consensus concerning the strong continuity, both in personnel and in policies, between the earlier presidential cabinets and the "cabinet of national concentration." Nor does anyone dispute the fact that there was no significant purge of higher government functionaries (except for the generally applauded removal of Jews) after 1933, and that the regime owed its relative stability principally to the support it received from the army, the civil service, and the staff of the Foreign Office.

Meanwhile, there was a major convergence of political goals among the traditional elites and the inner circle of Nazi leaders after the Nazi seizure of power, even though each group differed in its choice of preferred methods and its degree of willingness to court risk. Ironically, it is foreign policy research, once seen as the field *par excellence* for the systematic realization of Hitler's world vision, that now takes a non-Hitlerist approach, emphasizing strong historical continuities reaching back to the imperial period. This work has forced the intentionalists, who had previously concentrated mainly on domestic policies, to attempt to define those elements of the Nazi system that would most clearly distinguish it from its imperial predecessor. The elements they propose include the typically fascist reversal of the relationship between ends and means; the Nazis' desire to present the highly organized fascist party as a "movement"; and their avoidance of a specific program in favor of a purely propagandistic mobilization. This reversal of methodological positions, exemplified by the intentionalists' use of arguments drawn from the literature on comparative fascism, underscores the fact that the latest controversy over historical continuity has produced no new insights and has become largely counterproductive.

III

When viewed against this historiographic background, the "change of paradigm" now advocated by a prominent group of West German historians seems rather paradoxical. Klaus Hildebrand, who, like all intentionalists, has previously always insisted on the uniqueness of the Nazi regime, now joins Ernst Nolte in promoting a relativizing, world-historical perspective on this phenomenon. They no longer view National Socialism as an unfortunate accident coming at the end of the Weimar Republic, but rather as a complicated tangle of world-historical circumstances of tragic proportions. Stalin's dictum, "The Hitlers come and go, but the German people remain," has been taken up by conservatives in order to alleviate the traumatic psychological tensions which the Nazi experience has produced between the generations. Former United States ambassador Richard Burt also contributed to the "national rediscovery" sought by conservatives with his supportive comments.

In the case of Ernst Nolte, a relativist perspective leads directly to the anti-Bolshevism that has always been the hallmark of his approach to the past. It has motivated him to trace the development since the Industrial Revolution of what he calls an ideological "postulate of extermination" and its instantiation by the Bolsheviks, a phenomenon unparalleled in history. For Nolte, the Holocaust is, in the final analysis, nothing more than a reaction to the class destruction committed by the Bolsheviks, crimes with which Hitler became obsessed.

Nolte's superficial approach which associates things that do not belong together, substitutes tenuous analogies for causal arguments, and—thanks to his taste for exaggeration—produces a long outdated interpretation of the Third Reich as the result of a single factor. His claims are regarded in professional circles as a stimulating challenge at best, hardly as a convincing contribution to an understanding of the crisis of twentieth-century capitalist society in Europe. The fact that Nolte has found eloquent supporters both inside and outside the historical profession has little to do with the normal process of research and much to do with the political implications of the relativization of the Holocaust that he has insistently championed for so long.

Nolte argues that Hitler's "destruction of the Jews" was not in its essence genocide, but rather "the most radical and at the same time most desperate form of anti-Marxism." He attempts in this way to provide a psychological explanation for the translation of the "extermination postulate" into actual, biological reality. Such an enterprise provokes immediate objections. For Nolte, "anti-Marxism" always carries positive, freedom-preserving connotations; hence, in his view, Hitler merely fell victim to an unfortunate perceptual error while pursuing comprehensible aims. As far as their content is concerned, it is in fact not inaccurate to identify anti-Bolshevism with racial anti-Semitism, and Hitler was not alone in equating them. He merely radicalized the existing anti-Semitism of the early postwar years.

In Nolte's historical sketches, the Third Reich appears as an unfortunate response to the threat posed to German society by Bolshevism. According to him, this threat, although certainly exaggerated even with regard to the revolutionary period 1917–21, called forth a psychologically justified anxiety embodied most extremely and most tragically in the person of Hitler. The fundamentally apologetic character of Nolte's argument shines through most clearly when he concedes Hitler's right to deport, though not to exterminate, the Jews in response to the supposed "declaration of war" issued by the World Jewish Congress; or when he claims that the activities of the SS *Einsatzgruppen* can be justified, at least subjectively, as operations aimed against partisans fighting the German army.

IV

Ernst Nolte is not the real problem, however. As a nonconformist, in some respects path-breaking, thinker, he obviously runs the risk of being identified with the ever more confident neofascist movement in the Federal Republic. More important is the fact that the new message of the Bolsheviks' responsibility for National Socialism has been eagerly taken up by groups that have for years lamented the absence of a healthy German national consciousness. They see the lack of nationalist sentiment as a regrettable weakness that may even pose a threat to the very survival of the German people, and they hope to respond by undoing the postwar reorientation of values and by fostering an aggressive national consciousness—one unashamed of the German performance during the Second World War. Ideas that just a few years ago still defined only a marginal neoconservative position have now entered the political mainstream, thanks to the support provided by prominent CDU/CSU spokesmen. Whether the younger generation in the Federal Republic will be receptive to such views remains in doubt.

Historical writing has functioned above all as an indicator of the changed state of political consciousness regarding this reorientation of values. The fact that the fortieth anniversary of the German capitulation set off a lively public debate was due at least superficially to the failed spectacle of Bitburg, itself a reaction to the Allies' D-Day Celebrations. The claim made at Bitburg that all republican forces in the FRG share a common anticommunist goal provoked a broad, totally unexpected historical-political response from the West German Left. As this response indicated, a reevaluation of the Federal Republic's relationship to National Socialism was long overdue. The Left's response was also a reaction to the quiet rejection of the antifascist consensus previously shared by all of West Germany's democratic parties. This rejection stemmed from the influence of German nationalist and revisionist groups in the government coalition, and had already been prepared by the far-right and neoconservative press.

The West German parliamentary system, which can no longer simply hearken back to the achievements of the democratic reconstruction period and has tended to distance itself from the electorate's primary political interests, is currently experiencing a growing crisis of legitimacy. As a result, the temptation to buttress a crumbling political consensus through recourse to a "national" view of the past has gained in strength. Questions of historical interpretation have become, as they were in the Weimar period, a battlefield for largely ossified political parties. In this situation, the totalitarian model of National Socialism, already increasingly undermined by the latest historical research, proved unable to stand up to accusations leveled from the Left that not enough was being done in either the political or the judicial sphere to confront the Nazi past. The peace movement has drawn analogies between certain structures in the Federal Republic and the Third Reich by reviving the notion of a "right to resistance" common in the 1950s. The violent and exaggerated criticisms provoked by this analogy demonstrated that such comparisons are extremely uncomfortable. At the same time, however, the government parties alluded freely to political conditions during the 1930s in order to denounce the Left.

What had until then been a fairly homogeneous picture of Weimar and the Third Reich thus began to fragment along party lines. Characteristic of this process was the tendency of historians closely associated with the government to depict the destruction of the bourgeoisie and the removal from power of the traditional upper classes as a central aim of the Nazis. In so doing, they recapitulated older conservative interpretations of National Socialism as the product of "mass democracy" and the unavoidable reaction to the threat of a left-wing dictatorship. Meanwhile, these same historians claimed that excessive wage demands made by the working class were primarily responsible for the collapse of Weimar. On the other side, historians who sympathized with the left republican positions of the 1920s and 1930s blamed heavy industry for destroying the sociopolitical compromise of the Republic's early years and thus bringing about the progressive breakdown of the parliamentary system. The decisive change in the almost canonical "totalitarian" view of the Third Reich occurred during the 1970s, when it became increasingly impossible to uphold the view that a small clique of fanatical Nazis were alone responsible for the criminal policies of the regime. Such a claim was no longer plausible given the evidence of broad involvement by higher army officers, diplomats, and industrialists in the plunder of Eastern Europe, the exploitation of prisoners-of-war and forced laborers, and the extermination of the Jews.

Evidence for the political polarization of attitudes toward the Nazi past can be found in a speech delivered by Alfred Dregger, parliamentary leader of the CDU/CSU, on November 11, 1986, to mark West Germany's Memorial Day [*Volkstrauertag*]. In his address Dregger insisted that most German soldiers—and implicitly most of the general public as well—were ignorant of Nazi crimes. The only people in the know, according to Dregger, were "political functionaries," "a few higher army officers," and those in the support services behind the front lines, who were involved in activities that "violated every tradition of military honor." Dregger failed to mention that the war in the East, which aimed at the utter subjugation of the enemy, had from the beginning renounced all "military honor." Instead, he complained that the Allies had directed their demand for unconditional surrender at Germany as a whole rather than just at Hitler—thus echoing arguments previously formulated by Hillgruber. He described the dilemma imposed on the German soldiers, who indirectly facilitated Nazi crimes by defending their homeland. Dregger did not seem to realize that this bitter choice (defending the nation versus helping to end Nazi crimes) was a foreseeable consequence of policies that the military leadership, at least initially, unanimously approved. He preferred to regard the Third Reich as a system of domination forced on Germany by Hitler and a small band of criminals.

Similarly, the word "seduction" [*Verführung*] appears in the plans for a Museum of German History in Berlin, again implying that the Third Reich was the result not of misguided long-term policies, but of deceptive propaganda. Nor can the cooperation of the army, bureaucracy, and industry in carrying out the regime's criminal domestic and foreign policy goals be made to disappear simply by invocations of the "dictated peace" [*Diktatfrieden*] of Versailles, or the misdeeds of other nations. Such attempts to rewrite the past understandably fulfill the need for self-justification felt by many older Germans, who would like to free themselves from the guilt heaped upon them from both inside and outside the country. These attitudes indicate that the past has been confronted on a moral, but not on a political or analytical, level; the result is a sense of painful surprise but not of accountability. One need not be an apologist to acknowledge that collaborators in German-occupied territories and ethnic minorities in the Soviet Union shared responsibility for Nazi crimes. But to claim that "the Germans are obsessed with guilt," or that Allied efforts at reeducation undermined national values, merely diverts attention from the Nazi destruction of traditional values—a process whose ultimate results were the complete corruption and then the disintegration of the very fabric of German society.

The representatives of the Right, including professional historians like Michael Stürmer, share the mistaken impression that their opponents seek to sustain collective feelings of guilt. This impression must be corrected. By reacting to National Socialism only with shock and moralizing self-criticism, as has so often been the case in the Federal Republic, Germans have managed to avoid the sensitive question of how the general public and the elite functionaries were responsible for the Holocaust. The failure of the overwhelming majority of the German people to protest the abuse and deportation of the Jews can be only partially explained by their fear of the state's power. The point of studying the Third Reich cannot be simply to produce shock and sadness; rather, it must lead to guidelines for action aimed at preventing a recurrence of the constellation of circumstances that permitted the Holocaust. The task is to uncover the mechanisms that explain the growing moral indifference, especially among the upper classes, during the aftermath of World War I, and to identify the complex conditions under which genocide and a war of racial destruction could be conceived and carried out.

V

When Martin Broszat called for a "historicization" of National Socialism, he sought to distance himself from contingent interpretations of the regime, such as the one that attributes the escalation of violence and terror solely to the conscious calculations of Hitler. Such interpretations over-look the conditions in which even people who did not belong to the hard core of the NSDAP and who were not greatly motivated by ideological concerns nonetheless participated (directly or indirectly) in the killing machine. His-toricization means taking seriously the diversity, the relative openness, and the contradictory character of the Nazi system rather than simply rejecting it out of hand. It means analyzing both the destructive elements of the system and the features that appeared promising in the eyes of many contemporaries. Historicization will thereby allow us to explain how someone like Adolf Hitler, whose pathological refusal to face reality is uncontested, could come to enjoy such great (through never unlimited) popularity and, thanks to the systematic propagation of the Führer myth, could continue until well into the spring of 1945 to act as a symbol of national integration above and apart from the conflicts of state and party.

What is vexing is the understanding of the term "historicization" that takes it to mean merely relativization—that is, the acceptance of the Third Reich as historically inevitable, and the use of events and personalities from that pe-riod simply as metaphors. When this occurs, as with Helmut Kohl's com-parison of Gorbachev to Goebbels, it indicates that the deep challenge that Nazism continues to pose for a society committed to individual freedom and the preservation of human dignity has not been understood and remains un-met. This applies equally to the particular way of settling accounts with the past that has recently found its way into the legislation of the Federal Republic.[2] The fact that all manner of political claims have been and will be committed in no way alters the specific constellation of circumstances under which they occurred in Germany. The thinking of the regime's satraps, like Himmler and Goebbels, as well as of Hitler's conservative Cabinet colleagues, shows that they consciously sought the elimination (if only temporary and partial) of otherwise uncontested normative guidelines, and that they ac-cepted a state of emergency as the normal condition for state action. The pretexts they used, such as the "threat" to national security, were clearly contrived and transparent. To the extent that psychotic compulsions drove the regime's henchmen to carry out their work, these were derived from self-created anxieties that had long been politically instrumentalized. A par-ticular example is their hybrid anti-Bolshevism already formed by 1917, which bore no relation to the real threat posed to Germany by Lenin's pro-gram of world revolution.

Ernst Nolte therefore makes a fatal misrepresentation when he blames the anti-Bolshevism and racial anti-Semitism consciously fomented by the Pan-German Association and the right wing of the Conservative Party (DNVP) entirely on the Bolsheviks and their program of class murder, as if the hatred vented during the Russian Civil War had nothing to do with the tsarist autoc-racy and its methods of repression. Even more troublesome is the way in which Nolte identifies Hitler personally as a final cause. Some of Nolte's crit-ics, including Eberhard Jäckel, have not taken sufficient notice of this. Nolte does not see that the road to the Final Solution was paved with a complex interaction of ideological motives and technocratic incentives. It can only be explained in close connection with the internal and external developments of the regime, a process in which Hitler's fanatical anti-Semitism was only one, and possibly not even the most important, factor.

One could simply disregard such prejudiced and intellectually esoteric explanations if it were not for the fact that they tend to cloud the lessons drawn by the overwhelming majority of Germans from the National Socialist experience. These lessons have taught a sober skepticism vis-à-vis nationalist slogans and the setting up of ideological enemies. Memories of the wartime air-raids and mass destruction have made the country unsympathetic to strategies of mass political mobilization and the use of military force. Germany today is ahead of its neighbors in its wariness of patriotic appeals and violent solutions to domestic conflicts. It is an illusion to believe that the moderation or absence or nationalism among the Germans makes them pathologically susceptible to antidemocratic slogans. Those who continually warn of the "German neurosis" completely overlook the fact that for the younger generation neither the Bismarckian nation-state nor the conflict of national loyalties under the Nazi regime retain any great importance.

The Historians' Debate is in many respects simply a proxy war fought along the fault lines of West German politics between adherents of authoritarian democracy and reformist republicanism. Behind it lies the problem of the unresolved political identity of the generation socialized under the Third Reich. When Alfred Dregger in his Memorial Day address uses a political slogan right out of the 1930s and ascribes the collapse of Weimar to "the Versailles *Diktat*," one is reminded of the 1928 election, when the DNVP made prominent use of Grand Admiral Tirpitz in its campaign even though less than a third of the electorate could remember his role during the prewar period. The plans for a "House of History" in Bonn and a "German Historical Museum" in Berlin also raise the suspicion that their primary purpose is self-justification for the in-between generation raised under the Third Reich, rather than education about the German past for the younger generation. Michael Stürmer revealed the political intentions behind these museum projects when he stated that the future belongs to those who control the past and that the Germans must be made more "predictable" in both domestic and foreign affairs with the help of a balanced picture of the past. Yet the desire to use history to such manipulative ends is hardly compatible with the political maturity Germans have acquired through the bitter and sobering recognition of their complicity in the crimes of the Third Reich.

At the same time, the debate unleashed by the Historians' Debate concerning the historical place of the Nazi period is more than a mere episode. It should mark the end of efforts to counter neo- or postfascist interpretations with legal sanctions or to render them socially taboo. For it will not be possible to prevent neofascist publications from drawing their own conclusions from the neorevisionist relativization of the Holocaust or from Hillgruber's question about whether the attempt on Hitler's life of July 20, 1944 can still be seen as justified in light of the atrocities committed by the Red Army against the German people in 1944. There will be open disagreement over whether the overthrow of the regime and an end to the killings at Auschwitz deserved to take priority over the stabilization of Germany's eastern frontier.

Acknowledging that German soldiers were motivated by a desire to protect their homeland from Soviet invasion does not change the fact that their efforts objectively helped to prolong the Nazi rule of crime and destruction. If contemporary history has taught the German people anything, it is the ability to recognize this contradiction and to draw conclusions from it for their future political behavior. Margret Boveri has analyzed this state of affairs under the concept of "betrayal in the twentieth century," and in so doing has made it clear why it is psychologically impossible for Germans to use a broken and morally perverted tradition of the nation-state in order to find themselves. No exhortations of the "new nationalism," no matter what terminology it employs, can avoid this fact. Thus, neither a "reconstruction of the European center [*europäische Mitte*]" nor an exonerating theory of "Germany's middle position [*deutsche Mittelage*]" is necessary.

Notes

1. Eberhard Jäckel, *Hitlers Herrschaft: Vollzug einer Weltanschauung* (Stuttgart, 1986), 146.
2. Mommsen is referring to the so-called Auschwitz Law of 1985 that forbids insults to the victims of the National Socialist or other dictatorships. See the piece by Wolfgang Benz in this volume, p. 196, for details—ED.

10. Explaining the "German Catastrophe": The Use and Abuse of Historical Explanations

Hagen Schulze

I

Are National Socialism, Hitler, and Auschwitz part of German history? The question is not as absurd as it first appears. It lurks in the background of the current debate initiated by Jürgen Habermas, and upon examination it displays a number of surprising facets. Habermas himself answers the question with notable ambivalence. On the one hand, Auschwitz is for him the key to the modern Federal Republic as a Western democratic, constitutional state. He sees a direct historical, political, and moral link between the crimes of Hitler's regime and the virtues of its free, democratic successor. Yet on the other hand, he argues that the historian cannot turn to a time before Auschwitz for an understanding of current German identity. The utter singularity of German fascism prohibits relating it to broader historical continuities, lest the uniqueness of Hitler's state be relativized and its decisive importance for West German constitutionalist patriotism be diluted.

Habermas seems unconcerned by the fact that his postulate is troublesome in light of his own political and pedagogical intentions. Whoever absolutizes a historical event as he does also in effect removes it from the course of history. One is reminded here of quite different interpretations of the Third Reich, by historians such as Friedrich Meinecke, Michael Freund, and Gerhard Ritter, that were in vogue for a time after World War II but now seem long outmoded: the view of Hitler's regime as a result of demonic forces, as a terrible deviation from the basically rational, progressive march of history.

One can object to Habermas's arguments that anything so emphatically singular must be not only unhistorical, but irrelevant to contemporary politics. It is inexplicable, because any event must be embedded in its historical context if it is to be adequately understood. The singular teaches us nothing about the future, for by definition it can never be repeated. The pressing need for an explanation and the crucial political necessity of avoiding similar occurrences in the future therefore demand a resolute historicization of National Socialism and its crimes. We must inquire into the continuities of

German history that made Hitler possible, and we must determine which tools of the historian's craft will allow us to uncover these continuties.

II

January 30, 1933: under this date in the diary of an otherwise unknown schoolteacher from Hamburg stands the following entry:

Hitler is chancellor! And what a cabinet! One we wouldn't have dared to imagine in July. Hitler, Hugenberg, Seldte, Papen!! Much of my German hope is pinned on each one. National Socialist dynamism, Conservative judgment, the unpolitical Stahlheim, and Papen, whom we have never forgotten. It is unimaginably wonderful . . . Hindenburg has really done it![1]

What President von Hindenburg had done to prompt the rejoicing of millions of German citizens had a long prehistory that need not be recounted here. It was the history of a democracy born of defeat and revolution, the history of a nation repeatedly humiliated by an armistice, a peace treaty, demands for reparations, and persistent foreign policy discrimination. It was the history of a chronically ill economy battered by inflation and depression; the history of a republic without republicans; of powerful organized interests that did everything possible to shake the foundations of the system; of democratic parties that proved incapable of following parliamentary democracy's categorical imperative of compromise between opposing groups and so, ultimately, threw in the towel. It was the history of a civil war, a latent crisis always in the background of the Weimar state; of the ultimately fruitless attempts by bureaucratic authorities schooled in the spirit of enlightened absolutism to govern the ungovernable with the help of emergency decrees. It was the history, finally, of people: politicized soldiers, East Elbian Junkers, Social Democrats, prelates, conservatives, reactionaries, and revolutionaries. At the center of this ever-more unmanageable field of actors stood a president full of good will, a royal Prussian field marshal elected by the majority of the German people as an ersatz kaiser and who had sworn an oath on the constitution and would now seek to uphold it as though it were the Prussian field service regulations; a president under the hermetic influence of irresponsible agrarian and conservative forces. He was also an old man who suffered from memory lapses after five in the afternoon. This pitiable figure had been trying since the beginning of the year to find his way out of the disaster, a way out of the carousel of chancellors, emergency decrees, and parliamentary dissolutions. And so on January 30, 1933, after lengthy and honorable resistance, he appointed as chancellor the leader of the largest parliamentary party, because this was now the one person who could promise him a majority in the Reichstag and thereby bring an end to the reign of emergency decrees.

Let there be no illusions: the majority of the people welcomed the naming of the new cabinet. Their hopes for a fresh start far outweighed their doubts. The fact that Chancellor Hitler and the two other National Socialist ministers were surrounded by a cabinet of conservative political hue reassured many because it appeared to guarantee that this strange new element in German politics would be controlled and domesticated by proven, conservative, predictable forces. Only a few realized that things would turn out quite differently. In addition to the traditional political parties and their rapidly dwindling band of followers, these included isolated individuals like Hindenburg's former chief of staff General Ludendorff, once Hitler's ally. On February 1, 1933, he wrote to his former superior, President Hindenburg:

By naming Hitler chancellor you have turned our holy German fatherland over to one of the greatest demagogues of all time. I solemnly prophesy that this wretched man will plunge our country into the abyss and bring untold misery upon our nation. Future generations will curse you in your grave for this action.[2]

Like the German people as a whole, the teacher quoted earlier was to see herself deceived. The diary was found near her body in the ruins of her bombed-out house. The title of a book written in 1945 by Friedrich Meinecke, *The German Catastrophe*, conveys something of the shock that affected a whole generation. Proximity to the events, combined with a collective sense of guilt, led to simple formulas: what they had experienced was unique. The search for exoneration and apologia also played a role, and attempts at explanation made in the immediate aftermath of the war relied heavily on the concept of fate. Hitler was viewed as an emanation of satanic forces, the Third Reich as an exception to history, the catastrophe as destiny.

That was one explanatory model; but its obvious sterility rendered it increasingly obsolete, and today it no longer plays any role. The same cannot be said for another explanation, one that arose even earlier and—in many guises and with many variants and qualifications—still holds center stage today. Countering the thesis of total discontinuity, this is the theory of total continuity. According to this theory, the National Socialist dictatorship was the necessary final stage of the misguided trajectory of German history, the German *Sonderweg* of development. In this view, ever since the unification (and possibly before) there has been something peculiar about the German people and their history that sets them fundamentally apart from the general path of European development and accounts for both the greatness and the horror of the German past.

The theory of a German *Sonderweg* exists in two mutually exclusive versions, representing two sides of the same idea. The positive version came first, asserting a Prussian mission in Germany and a German mission in the world. This version was based on a metaphysical elevation of the Prussian-German state, vaunted for its superior moral qualities and usually contrasted polemically to the Western democracies. Such a view can be traced back to Hegel and to the historiographical tradition of one branch of German historicism. It finds its most famous expression in the prophecies handed down from the podium of Heinrich von Treitschke. The theory survived World War I unscathed, and it largely determined the self-understanding of the Germans up until the collapse in 1945. Certain new versions of this idea are now once again apparent on the German intellectual landscape.

A "black legend" succeeded this "golden legend," and it is with this second version that we must concern ourselves. It stems from many sources. The French historian Edmond Vermeil, for example, goes all the way back to the Italian expeditions of the Hohenstauffen emperors to explain the German idea of a national mission. Another author claims that the battle of the Teutoburg Forest was responsible for the fact that Germany did not become romanized and so remained wedded to barbarism for all time. The British historian A. J. P. Taylor harks back to Luther in search of that mixture of inwardness and deference toward authority characteristic of the Germans right down until the present; while others among his colleagues sense in Prussian militarism since the Great Elector the source of all evil. The continuity is clear: wherever one begins, according to this theory, there is a German predilection for authoritarianism. As a result, Germans had the misfortune of not undergoing a bourgeois revolution and thus drifted farther and farther away from the normal Western path toward freedom and equality, plunged Europe into war, and finally fell victim to National Socialism.

The idea for this theory can be traced back to the English tradition of Whig historiography, which tends to use British constitutional development as the standard against which the evolution of other countries is measured. The theory was further elaborated by historians at Oxford during World War I as a means of legitimizing the Allied role in the war. It found its way into the interpretations of a generation of young, nonconformist German historians between the wars, such as Alfred Vagts and Eckard Kehr, who sharply opposed those established historians still under the influence of nationalist myths. The way was thus clear after World War II for a devastating and thorough critique, one admirably fashioned by Hans-Ulrich Wehler as a direct challenge to the historical profession:

> Over and over . . . the question will be raised concerning the special burdens of German history, the serious obstacles placed in the way of the growth of a society of mature, responsible citizens (or which it placed in its own way), the resolute and all-too-successful resistance first to a liberal, then to a democratic society—a resistance with fatal consequences. . . . Without a critical analysis of this historical burden . . . the path which led to the catastrophe of German fascism cannot be illuminated.[3]

In what follows, I will raise the question of those continuities that led to Hitler's chancellorship on January 30, 1933. In so doing, I will discuss both matters that are evident and ones that are more doubtful. I will close with some remarks on the dubious character of my own initial question. I ask in advance for your indulgence if in so doing I am unable entirely to avoid expositions of a theoretical nature.

III

In discussing historical continuities, we are immediately faced with a serious problem: in history, clearly, everything is connected in some way with everything else. We must therefore be selective. But selectivity refers not only to our choice of which aspects of the question we should consider (a choice one must make in examining every historical question) but also to the logic of the explanation we select. Apart from the problems which arise in connection with any scientific explanation, and which for lack of space I cannot discuss here, there is the problem of specificity. There must be a standard that will guarantee that the continuities we pursue actually stand in a causal relationship to the event, so that we can eliminate irrelevant connections, like the Italian expeditions of the medieval emperors mentioned above. In other words, we must dispense with links that are merely associative, limiting ourselves to those that are demonstrably causal. It therefore follows that we can only admit those continuities that do not lead to different results in parallel cases. In the case at hand, then, we must exclude all aspects of German history that are echoed in more general European developments, since fascist revolutions did not occur in the neighboring countries of Western Europe.

By this logic, several explanatory models often proposed in relation to our question simply do not work. The modern state's monopoly on internal and external violence, for example, is a universal phenomenon in Europe, as is the increasing bureaucratization of states and parties. What Max Weber called "the Western process of rationalization" applies to the whole Atlantic world; and this includes the emergence of a more scientific and less mystical view of the world. The same holds true of the industrial revolution and all that went with it and resulted from it. Patterns of social stratification in Germany do not differ significantly from those of its neighbors. Germany's industrial and economic system in the twentieth century functions largely like those of France and the United States; the intertwining of state and economy, "organized capitalism," "state interventionism," and "the military industrial complex"—all these phenomena can be found throughout the contemporary Western world. Yet unlike Germany, most capitalist states did not turn fascist. And of those states that did, Italy had only just begun her industrialization, and Croatia and Romania had barely left the agrarian stage of development.

Just as the concept "capitalism" contributes little to our investigation, so the same can be said for other pan-European movements like social Darwinism, anti-Semitism, imperialism, and de-Christianization. All of these are necessary components of any explanation for the success of National Socialism, but by themselves they do not suffice. The same is true of the theory of "authoritarian personality," favored by the Frankfurt School and very popular after 1945. This theory purports to describe a peculiarly German trait primarily apparent in the tradition of German education and childrearing. Yet a glance at the similar educational system in France raises doubts about the value of this social-psychological explanation.

We reach more secure ground when we investigate long-standing features of German history and approach the year 1933 with them in mind. The French historian Fernand Braudel, in his magnificent theory of historical time, distinguishes among short-term historical events, the longer range of social and economic conjunctions, and the still longer time frame of largely unchanging structures. Braudel regards the continuity of geography as the firmest structure of them all, as the *longue durée* par excellence. He suggests that all of history be related to such layers of unchanging structures in order "to rethink it anew, beginning from the infrastructure."[4]

The significance of geography is certainly not something peculiar to Germany. It is equally great, for example, in the cases of Poland, Hungary, Austria, or Switzerland. In all of these countries, characteristic developments and dilemmas in the course of their national histories have arisen specifically as the results of the countries' geographic positions. These developments and dilemmas, albeit in combination with the individual historical conditions of each country and thus in the most diverse forms, have all stemmed from a characteristic framework for domestic and foreign policy of a kind not found, for example, in island states. What is special about the German case, among other things, is the peculiar tension between its national history and the history of the Holy Roman Empire: the transnational *raison d'être* of the Empire was at odds with the requirements of a modern, centralized, linguistically and territorially homogeneous state. The result was the early emancipation of the Empire's different regions and territories, which in turn led to the Reformation and Counter-Reformation and the division of the Reich along religious lines, whereas in almost all other European countries the same conflict was fought out and resolved in favor of one side or the other. Also important was the amorphous geographical form of a country without a natural center or natural borders, with its axes of transportation transected by rivers and mountains. And, finally, one must keep in mind the divergent patterns of law, culture, and land ownership that existed in Germany, a consequence of the earlier location of the lines of demarcation between Germans, Romans, and Slavs.

The decisive factor in the German case, however, was that this manifold splintering of central Europe had a wider Europan function, for it was only in this way that a balance of power on the continent could be preserved. A glance at the map shows why: whichever country controlled the center of Europe, whether a great power from the periphery or a "native" central European state, would only need to ally itself with one other power in order to dominate the continent jointly. As Ludwig Dehio wrote: "Germany, formless by nature, lay at the intersection of the force lines generated by continental great power politics, and its disorganization was for three centuries closely linked to the organization of the state system."[5]

For this reason, other European countries regarded the extensive legal autonomy of the more than three hundred German territorial states and imperial cities as a guarantee of European freedom, of the balance of power, and of the survival of the state system. The German "liberties" were consequently assured in an international agreement, the Treaty of Westphalia, in 1648; and thereafter, the constitution of the Empire became a part of international law, a matter of concern for all European powers.

This system was gradually undermined, first by the rise of Prussia in the eighteenth century and later by the development of a German national state in the nineteenth century. The dictates of geographic position now meant that because of their open borders, Prussia and its successor, the German Empire, felt themselves at the mercy of external pressures. There are only two ways out of such a situation. One is to open oneself to the political influences of neighboring powers and allow them a role in domestic politics, as Poland did. This reassures other nations; but the consequences for Poland's own history are well known. The other alternative is to organize and arm oneself in order to wage war along all the far-flung borders and against foreign alliances.

The outcome of this latter option was a state with an exceptionally effective administration and a greater role for its military than in any other European country. Hence the image of Prussia familiar since the time of Frederick William I: an image of military-bureaucratic excess, of military domination even of civilian life; an image of that exertion, seriousness, and a lack of urbanity, joie de vivre, and civil courage which makes the Germans so unpopular among their neighbors. This whole constitutional and political culture, whose influence extended into the twentieth century, was in fact the result of a powerful effort to prevent the Prussian state, in its exposed central European position, from sinking back into insignificance before its time—the fate of many other rising powers in similar circumstances. The Prussian experience thus represents a permanent struggle against the logic of geography and balance-of-power politics.

The internal character of Prussia and later Germany was therefore always closely related to external conditions. The attempt in 1848 to found a liberal Great Germany on the principles of popular sovereignty and the rights of man failed first and foremost because the three great powers, fearing this radical change in the map of Europe, threatened to intervene. The next impetus toward German unification, this time supported by Prussian arms and conceived of as a confederation of princes, succeeded only because Europe was suffering the effects of the Crimean War, because England and Russia had drifted far apart, and because France was defeated. It is clear that the German Empire had to be on its best behavior if it wanted to remain a permanent part of Europe. Bismarck's assurances that the Empire was now satisfied were not enough. The new state had to make credible its ability to dampen and control its impulse toward expansion beyond the borders of the Reich and to tame the unruly forces within it. Such forces included above all a growing movement of bourgeois-liberal nationalism, whose adherents saw the smaller Empire of 1871 as merely the down payment toward the utopian realization of a national state embracing all Germans. They also included economic interests that pushed forcefully beyond the borders of the old Customs Union and now called for colonies and spheres of influence. And not least, they included the Fourth Estate, with its ever more vocal threats of social revolution. It is not for nothing that German Social Democracy was considered the pacesetter of the Socialist International.

This, then, was the dialectic of domestic and foreign policy that necessarily dominated Germany: as the Empire rapidly became more liberal and democratic, newly freed dynamic political and social forces ran up against the limits placed on Germany's existence by the European balance of power. John Robert Seeley's claim that the internal freedom of a state stands in inverse relation to the external pressure on its borders has never found more accurate confirmation than in the case of Germany in its central European location. Although it was thoroughly caught up in the rapid economic and social changes of the nineteenth century, the German Empire remained a state with traditional, preindustrial structures of power and domination. It was thus logical that Bismarck pursued a policy of social and legal repression at home while at the same time he sought equilibrium and the avoidance of war in the international arena: Germany's neighbors would tolerate it only as long as it kept the lid firmly closed on its seething internal tensions. It was the inability of Bismarck's successors to maintain this delicate balance of domestic and foreign policy compensations against the pressures of industrial interests and mass-based nationalism that eventually led both to a European war and to Germany's defeat.

This, then, is the thread of continuity leading to the events of 1933 (a thread which, incidentally, was broken by the defeat of 1945 and the division of Germany, since the two German states no longer find themselves in the center of Europe, but instead on the periphery of two great power blocs). In our view, geographic position was a basic factor that created inescapable political constraints. These had important consequences for Germany's internal constitution, encouraging the German tendency toward authoritarian rule and the survival of old power elites—among them the conservative agrarian groups who isolated and influenced President von Hindenburg during the post–1930 crisis more effectively than they had been able to do earlier with Wilhelm II. The same constraints also promoted a form of bourgeois-liberal parliamentarism, its supporters characterized by a low level of self-esteem and inclined, when faced with difficult situations, to abdicate in favor of the supposedly higher wisdom of bureaucrats and authoritarian rulers.

On another level, these currents within the state in the broadest sense resulted in a whole complex package of collective attitudes, ideologies, and mentalities that we normally group together under the somewhat vague concept "political culture." These included a hypersensitive, even neurotic attitude toward the concept of the national state, an ideal to which reality could never attain and which was simultaneously utopian and maximalistic. With this attitude, Germans were doomed to be perpetually frustrated and disappointed, from the 1849 failure of the dream of a Greater German Unification to the Versailles Treaty. German political culture also included a positive attitude toward military norms and modes of behavior that extended far into civilian life. A belief in established authority was also apparent, along with the social-psychological sense of insecurity called forth by the "contemporaneity of the noncontemporaneous"—that is, the furious social and economic transformation of Germany beginning in the mid-nineteenth century within the context of unchanging inherited political structures. This insecurity expressed itself as an inner resistance to the modern, technological society to which Germans would nonetheless still have liked to belong. Antiparliamentary and antiliberal residues were part of this culture, along with an intense longing for internal uniformity and political harmony which, in turn, went hand in hand with a fundamental discomfort vis-à-vis class differences and social diversity.

Hence, there is no German *Sonderweg*, for crucial structures like the economy, class stratification, the degree of social conflict, and the oft-mentioned "union of the elites" against liberal social reforms did not, in fact, differ that markedly from the European mainstream. On the eve of the First World War, liberal-parliamentary states were scarce throughout Europe. What was unique to Germany is better described, in the words of Karl Dietrich Bracher, as a "special consciousness" (*Sonderbewusstsein*). It was this "special consciousness" that was rendered virulent by the great crisis beginning in 1929/30. No one succeeded better than Hitler in bringing together the specifically German frustrations, hopes, and fears, packaging them, and making the popular masses conscious of them in order then to present himself as the figure who would realize and complete that great current in German history.

IV

So much for the continuity of German history which, even when related principally to geography, is much too complicated a phenomenon to be adequately discussed here. Germany's special religious problems must also be considered, along with the particular pattern of the nation's industrialization. Nevertheless, such a model of German historical continuity, no matter how attractive and complete it may appear, is of only limited value to us. This is true for several reasons.

First, there is a theoretical problem: long-term processes, structures, and continuities are only real in a very restricted sense. I would not go as far as Thomas Nipperdey, who calls such connections a priori "constructs."[6] There are physical continuities, like geography, climate, and biological and anthropological constants. But we have great difficulty proving any kind of derivation. This is the case because the claims of historical research cannot be checked by means of laboratory experiments and also because the great wealth of factors that come into play make it impossible to establish causality in history with any certainty. Although I have linked a variety of relationships to the problem of Germany's position in the middle of Europe, I have not proved a necessary causality. When it comes to complex statements of this type, we historians find ourselves in the embarrassing predicament of having to operate by appealing to plausibility and probability—appeals that become more uncertain with every degree separating the related levels of reality. Deriving the organization and constitutional form of the state from a nation's geopolitical position is already problematic, and the problems multiply in the case of similar attempts to explain patterns of mentality and political culture. Any theory of continuity, whether materially grounded or otherwise, must face such fundamental objections.

To this problem must be added the fact that in constructing continuities we are, strictly speaking, proceeding in an ahistorical fashion. We identify a particular line of development in light of an event that stands at the end of it—in this case, from the perspective of the events of 1933. Yet we would not find 1848, for example, on this line of development. If we wanted to explain the revolution of that year using hypotheses of continuity, we would need to seek other threads. Moreover, perspectives change over the course of history. The contemporaries of the unification in 1871 saw themselves as standing in quite different lines of long-term historical development and even Hitler himself had very precise ideas about his place in the continuity of German history, although they deviate significantly from our own. At heart, we pursue teleologies. In order to uncover structural relationships, we act as if history advanced directly and inexorably toward certain events and outcomes. The border that separates history from the philosophy of history, and hence from metaphysics, thus becomes very narrow.

We should therefore be very careful not to rest our interpretations of historical events too heavily on theses of continuity. Large structures form what is merely a broad framework within which certain developments are more likely than others. Short-term influences, in turn, possess their own explanatory value: in this case the defeat of 1918, the Versailles Treaty, the 1923 inflation, the Depression, and the rise of the United States and the Soviet Union as world powers with an influence on European and German politics, to name just a few. To these must be added contingencies and chance simultaneities, which begin to have an effect only when combined—the domestic recession in Germany combined with a world economic crisis, for example, and both occurring in conjunction with the weakness of the parliamentary forces upholding the Republic. Finally, one must take into account how much freedom of action key individuals in decisive positions actually had. Without Hindenburg's grudging willingness to appoint Hitler chancellor, the National Socialist leader would not have come to power, at any rate not along the same path.

None of these arguments precludes looking at the long term, at large structures, or at relationships between historical periods. The *longue durée* proves its own worth by making clear broader frameworks which would otherwise remain blurred in investigations of particular events. It is only within such frameworks that the unity of history takes shape out of many particular narratives. Yet the broader our investigation becomes, the more it necessarily removes itself from the phenomena themselves—from historical sources, the only "facts" to which our discipline can appeal and which are indissolubly linked to phenomena as we understand them.

Keeping these objections in mind, we can draw the following conclusions: the events of the years after 1930 occurred within the context of a powerful, widely drawn line of historical continuity which made possible a particular spirit of the times. This *Zeitgeist* in turn expressly favored a constitutional change toward an authoritarian state. Nevertheless, it is clear that the Weimar Republic did not have to fail in the way it actually did. Hitler could have been avoided in many ways; alternatives existed right up through the last days of the so-called seizure of power. Not even the strongest continuities or the most compelling structural determinants can eliminate those decisive moments when individuals in positions of responsibility, faced with an uncertain future, choose between alternatives and thereby make historical decisions. No matter how attractive thinking in terms of continuities may be, we should still recognize the final responsibility of those who act: both in order to avoid an historically grounded fatalism and also so that we may demonstrate and insist on the potential culpability of politicians—and we are all politicians—as the ethical-moral basis for our own behavior.

Notes

1. Cited in Werner Jochmann, *Nationalsozialismus und Revolution. Ursprung und Geschichte der NSDAP in Hamburg 1922–1933* (Frankfurt, 1963), 421.
2. Cited in *Ursachen und Folgen*, 7:766.
3. Hans-Ulrich Wehler, *Das deutsche Kaiserreich 1871–1918*, 4th ed. (Göttingen, 1980), 11–12.
4. Fernand Braudel, "Geschichte und Sozialwissenschaften—die 'longue durée'"; German edition in Claudia Honegger, ed., *Schrift und Materie der Geschichte* (Frankfurt, 1977), 58.
5. Ludwig Dehio, *Gleichgewicht oder Hegemonie? Betrachtungen über ein Grundproblem der neueren Staatengeschichte* (Krefeld, 1948), 189.
6. Thomas Nipperdey, "1933 und die Kontinuität der deutschen Geschichte," *Historische Zeitschrift*, 227 (1978): 102–3.

11. Warding Off the Past: Is This a Problem Only for Historians and Moralists?

Wolfgang Benz

It is generally agreed that as a subject for scientific investigation, National Socialism falls principally within the professional bailiwick of the discipline of history. Yet perhaps the time has now come to question this. After four decades of historical research, the outline and structure of National Socialist rule have been laid bare, and the details of the events and facts have been illuminated to a greater extent than for any other period in German history. The dramatis personae and program of the regime have been described; and the total picture of state and society as well as the character of the Nazi period have been elucidated. We are now enlightened about almost every aspect that can be grasped using the methods of the historian. The field of research focussing on current history is doubtless one of the most successful of scholarly disciplines (as far as success can be measured), if science is conceptualized as an enterprise founded on clarifying events and assuring their objective basis in reality, marshalling proof for every sort of hypothesis and attempting to arrive at knowledge—all this for the sake of the topic at hand.[1]

Yet historians also enjoy especial success whenever the results of their research and their interpretations are in harmony with the longings, dreams, and yearning for deliverance of the rulers and society of their times. Prime examples of this are the historians Heinrich von Sybel, Gustav Droysen, and Heinrich von Treitschke. Riding on a wave of public approval, they articulated the aspirations of the bourgeoisie for a small-German national state under Prussian leadership. What served to give this generation of nineteenth-century historians legitimation was the fact that—supported by the authority of science and embellished with titles of privy councillor and other high-sounding appelations—they also propagated the ideology of national unity as publicists and politicians. This brought them fame and influence, and functioned to create a bond of identity between academic scholarship and public aspirations. Society was proud of its historians, and vice versa.

This was certainly an enviable solution. Thus, the suspicion might arise that historians in the second half of the twentieth century, or at least a portion of them, disadvantaged as a consequence of the unpropitiousness of their "late birth" and the exceptional unpleasantness of their subject matter, were indeed suffering as a result. Such a suspicion would, in any event, help to explain several especially original theses which have been applauded by interested politicians and have caused considerable dismay among the ranks of the knowledgeable. Universities are crowded, competition is fierce and—this probably is the most decisive factor—treatment of National Socialism has passed from a positivistic phase into one that is historicist in orientation. The generation of historians which took up the study of National Socialism immediately after 1945 enjoyed a double advantage. As they dug and sifted through veritable mountains of source materials, the historical researchers at that early hour were able to offer an interested public more and more new details and many an item that was sensational. At that time, a broad consensus prevailed in the moral judgments on the object of research.[2]

This probably also induced numerous historians to preach from the scholarly pulpit. Moralizing didacticism was sometimes mistaken for the obligation to enlighten, yet a weariness with "mastering the past" also emerged as a result of other reasons as well. Moreover, the other, chiefly commercial branch of the interest in the Nazi period began to wither, because now the only way left to cause a sensation was by the use of questionably venturesome means, as was painfully noted in the case of Hitler's alleged *Diaries*.

The "Historians' Debate" is hardly the suitable forum for providing relief for the sensation-seekers. However, it does signal that the treatment of National Socialism in the future will be marked by a new historicism. In the future, the focus will no longer be on the creation of consensus via disgust for a criminal regime and the numerous entanglements of contemporaries implicated in it (yes, and of later generations as well). Rather, emphasis will be on viewing and placing the National Socialist era within the continuity of German history as a whole. Increasingly, what will also be in demand is an evaluation and interpretation of the phenomenon aimed at underscoring in particular the positive aspects of that past era—this in order to faciliate a positive identification with the past in toto and, in so doing, to create for the society of the prosperous successor state of the German Reich a historical meaning endowed with a perspective for the future. "No people can live with a criminalized past"—this was the dictum of that "historian" Franz Josef Strauss who, on the occasion of a drinking party in honor of the 130th anniversary of the Association of Catholic German Student Societies, also admonished us not to forget the "right of the Germans to normality."[3] In contrast and with antithetical motivation, the philosopher Jürgen Habermas has termed the most recent attempts to escape the dilemma between "creation of meaning" versus scholarship in dealing with National Socialism as an effort to achieve "a kind of indemnification," a compensation for damages and loss.[4]

What Habermas is referring to is the attempt to remove the supposedly obstructive debris of history blocking the path of the self-confidence of the

Germans, their civic joy and their need for international recognition and popularity. However, such an enterprise cannot be carried out solely within the confines of the historian's workshop. It is no accident that the confrontation is taking place in the public media, though naturally the requisite academic attitude is duly maintained. The dispute about the singularity and comparability of National Socialist rule and its impact makes it clear, above all else, what deficiencies and shortcomings are still present in thinking about National Socialism, and just how limited the possibilities for historical analysis and interpretation actually are. The psychological dimension of National Socialist rule and its associated society is still largely unexplored and "unmastered". Even twenty years after the Mitscherlichs' *The Inability to Mourn*, a political psychoanalysis which conceptualizes attempts to deal with the National Socialist past as a group process and offers explanatory models remains in its infancy.[5] However, it is asking far too much of historians, philosophers, jurists, and social scientists to expect that they should be the sole interpreters of the Hitlerian state and society. Although they did their best, they naturally were unable to satisfy the desire on the part of citizens in postwar society to be released from the shadows of the past. Yet neither are the methods and possibilities of depth psychology directly applicable, presupposing that one indeed wishes to make use of them to overcome the trauma of National Socialism. Since Auschwitz, one premise of classical psychoanalysis is no longer valid: namely, that reality is surpassed by fantasy. According to Freudian method, therapy consists of a confrontation with the unconscious, with those instinctual wishes secretly lived out in fantasy, in an effort to render such wishes conscious; its objective is to prevent a recurrence of the identical material. Not to remember, not to discuss—this is what generates the compulsion for repetition. Yet what if the most horrible instinctual desires have indeed already been lived out to frightening excess? National Socialism also remains a challenge for this field, from theoretical social psychology all the way to psychotherapeutic practice.

Research findings are ineffective against the array of emotional and psychological defense mechanisms which have been built up in order to avoid dealing with the most recent past. These mechanisms function all the more smoothly, the longer they are operative. It does not matter whether what is involved is the exact number of the victims murdered by the regime in the concentration and extermination camps, the question of who bears ultimate guilt for the Second World War, the destruction of the economy and finances of the German Reich, or the causes and consequences of Nazi rule. This is because human consciousness is constituted in such a manner that undesirable and unpleasant elements can be split off from reality, and simply not perceived; the way people deal with the National Socialist period—in the memory of contemporaries to the events as well as in the reflection of those born later—offers a wealth of illustrative material in support of this observation.[6]

A characteristic example of this defiant revolt against reality is a letter written by a father to a teacher of religion at a high school. In his letter, the father explains why he refused to permit his son to take part in a school excursion to the former concentration camp Dachau. He writes that he volunteered for the military at the age of eighteen to serve his fatherland in 1939; naturally, his five cousins were also soldiers, and they did not return from the front. The writer goes on to say that he feels an obligation to these cousins, and to many other friends killed in battle. The man (a doctor and professor of medicine) continues his argument as follows: the Dachau concentration camp was handed over to American soldiers by its guards during the final few days of the war. These guards were then stripped of their weapons, beaten, and summarily put to death, without any trial. This father, protesting against a visit to the Dachau camp memorial, wrote that he also was well aware of a salient fact: that the gas chamber in Dachau had only been built later on by the American army, just like the crematorium, which had not been planned and constructed until after the camp had been under the control of the American military government for a considerable period of time. Moreover, the father concluded, the Institute for Contemporary History in Munich had itself confirmed that no gassings had taken place there—indeed, not only in Dachau, but in none of the concentration camps located within the former territory of the Reich.[7]

This man had obviously prepared himself very thoroughly before writing the letter, and had collected other data in addition to what he knew from personal experience: "The Bavarian Ministry of Finances, Dept. of Construction, provided the funding for this American venture in Dachau," he wrote, and the proof offered by the medical professor is that "one of my friends was in charge of this sector at that time." He then went on to the climax of his argument:

So how should a sixteen-year-old deal with such matters? Those sections of the camp constructed by the occupying power are presented to him as though they were an essential element of the National Socialist period. And you yourself, as a teacher, are not allowed to discuss this with him, since the federal government, in its new legislation on the "Auschwitz lie," has turned any discussion of this topic into a dangerous activity; in fact, it has rendered such a discussion impossible. All that is left to us now is to retain as much distance as we can from these matters.

The arguments mustered by this father are all familiar recurrent themes in the right-wing radical denial of reality, and were refuted long ago. As the example shows, such arguments are not only employed by adherents of the extreme right, but rather are useful for a general strategy of defense against dealing with the unpleasant past, since the underlying intention is to deny the entire historical reality by the seeming refutation of certain select details. The notion that the U.S. Army, with a cold smile, executed the guards of the camp, whom the enraged doctor pictures as elderly heads of families "who were only fit for service on the home front," has possibly served to assuage the sense of suffering and guilt of many individuals, because this story is bandied about repeatedly. The fact of the matter is that the overwhelming majority of camp guards fled before the arrival of the U.S. Army. It is also a fact that American troops were fired at from the watchtowers, and that the riflemen paid for this with their lives. The thesis that the Nazi regime allowed its concentration camps to be guarded by harmless old men who were only fit for limited duty is more than grotesque.[8]

Yet what would be changed if the assertions actually were true? The frequently cited "finding of the Institute for Contemporary History" that no gassings took place "in any concentration camp located on the former territory of the Reich" is mentioned by this father, so concerned about the critical abilities of his sixteen-year-old son, for a very specific purpose: he wants to suggest—and to underscore by the citation of expert opinion—that *no one whatsoever* was murdered in German concentration camps by gassing. The expert opinion referred to consists of a reader's letter written in 1960 to a weekly newspaper by an associate of the Institute (today its director). The letter's intention was to point out that the extermination camps, in which millions were murdered in the gas chambers, were not located on the territory of the German Reich within the 1937 boundaries, and that the quasi-industrialized killing took place outside the old borders of the Reich: in Auschwitz (which, by the way, formally was in fact even a part of the German Reich at the time, since this corner of Poland had been annexed and incorporated into Upper Silesia), Chelmno, Belzec, Sobibor, Treblinka, Maidanek, and Stutthof near Danzig.[9]

This geographical elucidation, of course, changes nothing in regard to the murder of millions or the responsibility for the crimes perpetrated. For the sake of completeness, by the way, it should be recalled that gas was used to murder people in camps within the *Altreich* territory as well, namely in Sachsenhausen and in the women's concentration camp Ravensbrück, though not on such a massive scale. The same holds true for the Mauthausen camp near Linz in Upper Austria. Moreover, of greater service to the cause of truth than the captious citation of marginal details would be to recall the more than 70,000 victims of the euthanasia program, the systematic annihilation in 1940/1941 of "life unworthy of life." This was carried out in six institutions, and under medical supervision; five of these were located within the territory of the old Reich, and the sixth was in Hartheim near Linz in Upper Austria.[10]

The fairy tale about the later construction of the gas chamber and crematorium in Dachau—which is supposedly substantiated by absurd "proofs" (not only were the conditions and installations which the American troops found upon entering Dachau documented by the U.S. Army, including a film made on May 3, 1945, but the reports on these conditions and installations had a powerful impact on the public in the Allied nations)—had one purpose: to negate the *entire* event, the *entire* system by means of the denial of a detail. The fallacious reasoning involved goes as follows: if the gas chamber in

Dachau (which existed, but was not operational, as is specifically pointed out in the Dachau memorial museum) was built only after the collapse of Nazi rule, then that rule, that system was not as bad as it is depicted to be.

There is little point in pursuing the arguments of this professor of medicine as expanded in additional correspondence with his son's high school and the Bavarian Ministry for Education and Religion, since he has a sole interest: to confound and create confusion by stringing together the familiar themes of refusal and denial. He garnishes these by such "important" biographical details as an alleged meeting between the eight-year-old boy and Konrad Adenauer in his parents' home—a fact which naturally has nothing to do with the matter at hand, but which is intended to establish the authority of the writer, or at least impress the reader. The letters are of little interest as documents reflecting the overbearing self-assertiveness of German-nationalist Philistinism, since the writer celebrates only the familiar rites by his references—in all the false eloquence of the educated middle-classes—to the duke of Alba, Catherine of Medici, the Inquisition and related misdeeds of the Catholic Church, such as the extermination of the Albigensians or the persecution of other heretics. Nevertheless, he did find a publisher willing to bring out a paperback edition of the letters. Since there was far too little text to warrant a small book, the publisher had to supplement the letters by other items: several more pamphlets, a presentation of figures entitled "Balance-Sheet of Horror" on the total losses incurred in World War II (first published in 1956 in the *Cannstatter Zeitung*), as well as a few texts devoid of any clear connection with the topic at hand.[11]

The publisher's blurb states: "With legal acuity, a debate is conducted here on the so-called and often-cited 'Auschwitz Law,' a discussion impressive by dint of the thoroughness of its critical relevance to the time." This "polemical pamphlet on Dachau and the 'Auschwitz Law'" was embellished with the title *Anti-Germanism*, and this term is the only truly noteworthy element in the entire story. In a gesture of defiance, a new catchword is juxtaposed here to real and existent anti-Semitism. This catchword, over and beyond its function to relieve and exonerate, expresses the sense of weakness of identity and the uncertainty which have been articulated alternately since the second *Kaiserreich* either in a plaintive feeling of being at a disadvantage or in an aggressive nationalism. From concern over having too little importance on the oceans of the world and too small a part to play in colonial expansion, people worked themselves up into a martial attitude which inspired fear amongst all nations. After the defeat in World War I (which had not, after all, simply been the unjust fate of an "innocent" German fatherland), the sense of self-pity of those harboring nationalist sentiments was aggravated into hatred for the Republic and for democracy; it sought refuge in irrational rage directed at Jews, other minorities, and outsiders. The Versailles Treaty, certainty no masterpiece of diplomacy and the art of pacification, acted as a stimulant at that time for the disappointed patriots. It served as a motive for joining

Hitler's movement, because that movement advocated the revision of the Versailles accords. Down to the present day, in fact—and in recent years even more frequently—that treaty has been trotted out as an alibi whenever the Nazi period threatens to stand in the way of a new and positive national feeling.

Whoever is willing to accept the defeat in the First World War as sufficient justification for unleashing the Second World War, considers the formula "Anti-Germanism" adequately justified if there is the mere mention of the horrors of the Nazi period. The infantile defense mechanism does not come into being via the crime, but rather the memory of it. The "Auschwitz Law" repeatedly cited by the father of that high school pupil in order to justify his arguments against any involvement with the National Socialist past—because that "law" supposedly prevents discussion, compels belief in an officially sanctioned version, and turns children into accusers—is a figment of the imagination. What is referred to is the "Twenty-first Amendment Law to the Penal Code" of June 13, 1985. The law states that (a) those persecuted by "National Socialist—or other regimes of violence or dictatorship" cannot be insulted with impunity because of this persecution and that (b) the memory of those who lost their lives "as victims of the National Socialist—or another regime of violence or dictatorship" cannot be defamed with impunity. What other person would find it necessary to rebel against just such an instrument of law—passed by the German Bundestag and signed by president Weizsäcker, chancellor Kohl, and minister of justice Engelhard [12]—than one who harbors the wish to insult and defame those persecuted by National Socialism?

Another example can serve to demonstrate that the aggressive patriotism which, for purposes of self-justification, must perforce declare the reality of Auschwitz to be a lie, corresponds in various aspects to the egocentric narrow-mindedness of the complacent Philistine: an individual who remains unfeeling and unmoved in the face of the suffering of others, even when he fully perceives the most horrifying facts of the situation. A teacher from the district Celle—or, more precisely, from Bergen, the town near which, in addition to an army training base, one of the most terrible concentration camps in the Third Reich was located—reported in August 1947 about his experiences:

The concentration camp in Belsen has now been leveled. The ruins of a crematorium stood there for a long time. Large gardens have been planted, and a memorial monument was erected by two firms in Bergen. It consists of a base with a sandstone pillar, supporting a plate on which there is a large sphere. The inscription is in English on one side and in Yiddish on the other, and is dedicated to those Jews who died there. I was able to decipher one word: "nazimurderer." The monument was built by the firm Borchert from Bergen using a crew of twelve men. It is three meters in height, and a Jewish committee initiated the project. I helped construct the monument. Our foreman used to say: "The work is not what is being paid for, it's your time!" We received a daily ration of one can of meat, one can of milk, one jar of jam, something to smoke, and one loaf of bread. We used to prolong the work, drag it out. We'd lie down behind our windscreen, make a fire and do nothing. My job was to accompany the driver in a truck. We said to ourselves: "look, someone has to build it, so it's also a chance to earn some nice things for ourselves!" When the monument was finished, the ground was supposed to be levelled and covered over with sand. We said that was not our job. The Jew asked: "OK, what do you guys want on top of the daily ration?" So for this one-hour job, we got an additional can of meat, another loaf of bread, a bar of chocolate and a can of milk, a jar of jam, some cigarettes and other stuff. We loaded sand onto the truck, spread it in a thin layer over the ground near the monument, and finished up earning this extra stuff mighty fast. Now an even larger monument is being planned.[13]

The concentration camp Bergen–Belsen was liberated on April 15, 1945 by British troops. The sanitary conditions in the overcrowded camp and the quality of the food there were even worse than in other concentration camps. This led to large numbers of deaths, and that continued even after the camp was liberated in the spring of 1945. Approximately 14,000 additional former inmates died between April and June 1945.[14] Yet the teacher from Bergen had other worries. When he referred to those "bitter years," he was only alluding to his own situation, since he temporarily had not been allowed to practice his profession. While his denazification was being processed, he gave private math lessons in a camp where young Jews were living; they were between the ages of nineteen and twenty-one, and were waiting for an opportunity to emigrate after having been liberated as concentration camp inmates. The teacher would drive on out there to give private lessons for a fee of thirty marks, plus coffee and cigarettes. He wrote about his pupils as follows:

These boys were all alone. Their parents had died in the camps. Eisenberg always had a lot of bread. He had the ration cards of all his relatives who had been killed. He had four cards. So he could bargain when things were distributed, and used to get four to five extra loaves of bread. The young guy Grock hadn't lost any relatives in the camps, and so he didn't have much to bargain with. Eisenberg was smart and hard-working. Grock didn't look or behave Jewish; what was important for him was that I was satisfied with my fee. Eisenberg, on the other hand, counted every nickel and dime.

Yet the teacher had praise solely for the attitude displayed by Grock, and he did so in words that he reiterates for the record in all innocence: "Look, you're no Jew, at least not as far as your character is concerned!"[15]

Not far away, in Wietze, the electrician H. and his wife were living. They had to vacate their house on April 13, 1945 for the British troops, but were allowed to keep their store. The experience of the war concentrated itself in the minds of these decent and respectable people in their concern about the condition of their home and the maintenance of decorum:

So they were living in a pretty rotten way upstairs in our nice little place. Our piano was brand new, and they made a lot of rings on it with their hot glasses of tea. They marched into the house at 6:30. Right away there was a radio blaring and music from a record player, as if there were a circus here. The windows were wide open and the

curtains were blowing out onto the street. I stood downstairs and watched the spectacle, and then I said to our young girl from the office: "Anneliese, go on up and close
the curtains again!" I thought they wouldn't do anything to such a cute young kid.
And they didn't. During their victory celebration, the beer ran down through the ceiling into the store downstairs, and the lights under the ceiling were dancing back and
forth. They would usually sit on the window ledge. A Jew, about nineteen or twenty,
was a very arrogant guy, he'd been born in Vienna. Whenever he wanted to talk to me,
I'd just walk away and leave him standing there.[16]

An offended sense of orderliness in their dealings with liberated former
concentration camp inmates and Allied troops not only dominated the memories of these people, as manifested in the early postwar period. Four decades
later, the provincial politicians were still arguing along the same line of anx-
ious and assiduous compulsive cleanliness. In June 1987, there was some discussion in the small community of Ottobrunn near Munich about erecting a
war monument. The mayor of the town responded in extremely negative
fashion to a query from the town council as to whether it would be possible,
together with the planned monument, to put up a memorial plaque commem-
orating the external camp of the concentration camp at Dachau which was
located during the war in Ottobrunn. The mayor argued that Ottobrunn did
not even exist at that time as an independent township. But above all, he contended, the town should be spared the label of "concentration camp town";
just think of the "terrible reputation" that Dachau has all over the world.[17] A
few years previously, the members of the town council in Hersbruck, an old
town near Nuremberg in northern Bavaria, took offence at a pamphlet by a
high school senior who had done a local history project and wished to publish
his findings under the title: "The Concentration Camp Hersbruck: The History of an External Camp in Flossenbürg." The objection was raised against
the title that it would cast a false light on Hersbruck, would falsify the actual
facts and damage the town's name. The term "secondary branch camp" or
"external station" was, it was contended, the accurate designation.[18]

This indeed sounds more innocuous when you read it. Similar examples
can be cited from all over West Germany. Near Landsberg in Upper Bavaria,
there were eleven camps in which inmates worked as forced laborers for the
armaments industry of the Third Reich; approximately 8,000 people died
there, but there are local politicians who deny the very existence of these concentration camps and would prefer to see the more friendly term "work
camp" used. In addition, they argue that Landsberg has such an illustrious
past, so why should this small dark stain be given such particular emphasis?[19]

Yet it would appear that the provincial spirit is blowing strongest at the
current moment in Dachau, where local town politicians have been mounting
a harshly worded attack on a projected International Encounter Center for
Youth. The Center is planned as a "place of learning" and a forum for discussion located in close proximity to the concentration camp memorial museum,
and it is supported by the churches and by members of the Bundestag from
the major parties. The local politicians who are opposed to it contend that

there is a "moral right to resist" such a "place for the 'mastering' of the past," and that people should "oppose it down to the last drop of blood."[20] In May 1987, an article in the *Dachauer Nachrichten* stated that the 1,200-year-old market town of Dachau should take pains to "set an example against all those cantankerous leftists and self-appointed 'masterers of the past,' whose goal is to make Dachau the center of Nazi history—the sole center."[21]

The reactions mentioned are typical of the mechanisms of irrational defense against a past perceived to be burdensome. One can put together an entire catalogue of defensive reactions and then check the correctness of the list on a daily basis at one's place of work, in the media, down at the local tavern, and in the city councils and state senates. This catalogue of German primal anxieties is where the strategy to eliminate problems by "forgetting," by not mentioning them belongs, an attempt which is easy to account for in psychological terms. The fear to remember is apparently rationalized by that pivotal precept: "Don't foul your own nest." Yet individuals so concerned about this kind of cleanliness fail to note that fallacy in their thinking: namely, that the befouled nest will not be cleaned up by passing lightly over the dirt with silence.

This banal confusing of "collective guilt" on the one hand, and joint historical responsibility on the other, leads to a further reaction, one of the most troublesome and dangerous ploys: namely, the game of figures, the weighing up of numbers and loss on both sides of the ledger. The crimes of the Nazi regime cannot be blotted out either by the Allied destruction of Dresden or the millions of Germans who were harassed and expelled from their homeland in territories east of the Oder-Neisse line, from Czechoslovakia, Hungary, Romania, and elsewhere after the end of the war. The fact that 3.3 million Soviet prisoners of war died in German camps[22] can be neither undone nor excused by presenting proofs of German suffering (suffering which, of course, no one denies).

Minimizing the seriousness of reality—its trivialization—also serves as a defense against the oppressive sense of guilt and suffering. An example of this is the suspicion, functioning as a source of personal assuagement, that the concentration camps were "correctional institutions" (admittedly strict, but nonetheless only correctional in purpose), where chiefly criminal elements were incarcerated for a well-deserved stay. It is not very far from espousal of such an argument to an attitude of general distrust directed toward all former concentration camp inmates and victims of the Nazi regime. Among the most wretched and contemptible legacies left by the Third Reich is the circumstance that those who were persecuted by the regime—people active in the resistance, as well as those who were forced to emigrate because they were unwilling to conform to the dictates of the system (and subsequently became victims, were they unable to flee in time)—are by no means generally held nowadays in high esteem. The scale of bourgeois prejudice and bias against the resistance fighters and émigrés ranges from the accusation that they behaved as though they had no fatherland, to their wholesale disparagement as "communists" (often meant more as a moral condemnation than a political one), to the charge that by dint of their resistance or exile they were traitors to Germany. At some time or other, almost everyone has experienced the conformists' distrust—not just Willy Brandt, who was attacked for having worn a Norwegian uniform (years after the controversial career of the former Nazi jurist Hans Globke had reached its postwar acme in Bonn); or the Social Democrat Herbert Wehner, who was once prevented from giving a speech at a memorial service for the victims of the July 20 conspiracy against Hitler, since he had not been a solid conservative, but rather a left-wing, communist opponent of National Socialism.

The collective process of defense, of warding off, not only involves such patterns of behavior or a certain specifically German form of sniveling self-pity, fixated on one's own suffering, and employing catchphrases such as: Dresden, the Allied bombing-raids in general, the loss of the German territories in the East, the occupation by the Allies, and finally the division of Germany. No: this self-pity is supplemented in the case of many Germans, who love to present themselves as being ever so cosmopolitan and internationally minded with another part of their consciousness, by a peculiar kind of provinciality. They would prefer to treat the National Socialist past as a German family matter (or, if need be, as a family quarrel). But as little as possible of this should be allowed to leak out beyond the borders: only the "good German" should be presented abroad. Misunderstandings are preprogrammed by such an approach, since National Socialism still remains one of the most intriguing of German topics for people abroad. This is always abundantly evident whenever right-wing extremists in Germany make the news, no matter how few and ridiculous they may be. If, in their provincial self-restraint, citizens of the Federal Republic do not wish to broach these matters, then they should not be surprised when doubts are expressed as to the stability of West German democracy, even if there is not the slightest reason for any such dubiosity. At such times, the handful of right-wing extremists and neo-Nazis no longer seem quite so ridiculous and inconsequential in the eyes of foreign observers. The world has not forgotten that National Socialism was a bit more than just a chapter in German history.

Uncertainty in dealing with National Socialism manifests itself in a quite different, indeed contrary manner: in a kind of excessive verbal zeal, the inflationary use of expressions of wholesale condemnation serving to characterize the Hitlerian state, or to articulate feelings of disgust and outrage. However, talk about the "regime of injustice," "contemptuous of human life," to mention but two such common attributions, merely arouses a sense of boredom—or serves even to strengthen the mechanism of warding off, of psychological defense, since one senses an underlying intention here to moralize and sermonize, devoid of any objective content.

How then can one offer a cogent explanation for this canon of behavioral modes that function to ward off the Nazi past? Using the means available to the historian, it is nonetheless possible to make a number of points and observations.

1. The rule of National Socialism was founded upon the ecstatic support of the majority of those ruled. This was at least the case as far as the "good" years are concerned: those years of economic and political success (largely in foreign policy) enjoyed by the Third Reich—chiefly the period between the Nazi seizure of power and its implementation in 1933/1934 and the summer of 1940, when France had been defeated and Hitler accepted accolades as the "greatest field commander of all times." A broad consensus in support of the goals of the regime prevailed during this period. Many who were not National Socialists in an ideological sense or by dint of membership in, or even sympathy with, Hitler's movement, felt that their deepest political yearnings and desires had been understood; they felt they had been delivered from the national disgrace of the Versailles peace accords, whose revision was a policy issue for the Hitler government. They felt freed from the bickering and squabbling of the *Systemzeit*, as the period of the Weimar Republic had been dubbed. They now saw that an end had been put to the humiliations of the German Reich—disarmament and Allied control, occupation of the Rhineland, the struggle in the Ruhr, pressure to repay reparations. In part, they also found themselves on the same side as the regime over against those who had been the losers after the seizure of power: namely, the communists, the "seditious intellectuals," the Jewish minority.

2. During the course of the war, and in the face of the military catastrophe which began to emerge clearly after Stalingrad in early 1943, the ecstasy of the populace (which the regime went about "staging" on a permanent basis, and kept operative by perfect self-portrayal and perfect management of public life) was supplanted by a defiant patriotism: uninterested in causes, concerned only about the threat to the fatherland, which had to be unconditionally defended, even if there was an evil regime in power. In addition, the terror apparatus of the regime, which had been built up and tested during the consolidation phase, had by then become so perfected that it was possible to remain in power almost effortlessly, even without acclamation. To a certain extent, consensus and enthusiastic assent had been superseded by a fear of the means of coercion. Added to this, however, was anxiety about a conceivable defeat by communist Russia. Presumably, this apprehensiveness even constituted the most powerful motive for lending support to the regime and continuing to survive and endure: namely the primal anxiety, stirred up with a vengeance by Goebbels's propaganda machine, in the face of a potential defeat at the hands of the culturally inferior East. One shuddered to think of a Red Army, a successor to the Huns and Tatars, raging out of control on German soil. So people drew closer together and closed ranks.

3. After the war and the collapse of Nazi rule, all the variant forms of erstwhile assent to the regime—ecstatic support, toleration for patriotic reasons, or a lack of opposition due to fear—required their justification. This neces-

sity to justify oneself was joined by a sense of shame, both about what had transpired and about the fact that, even if they had not applauded and sanctioned these things, people had at least accepted them in acquiescent silence. Any available argument to justify this stance was welcome, such as reference to the outrages perpetrated by the victors during the war, Allied war crimes, their management of the war, and the policy of needless terror against the civilian population of large German cities from the air. Another argument suggested itself more readily, and was more logical, namely, the claim to having been ignorant and unaware of the atrocities committed by the Nazi regime (or their extent) against political opponents in the concentration camps, dissidents and minorities, and against individuals and property in the occupied territories: atrocities perpetrated against the victims of National Socialist racial ideology, the millions of murdered Jews, Gypsies, and Slavs. Those completely devoid of any imagination convince themselves, in any event, that war is war, and that seems adequate to explain everything as far as they are concerned.

4. The horror, shame, and remorse—or, at the very least, the condemnation of the Nazi regime, its functionaries, and the crimes committed or ordered by it—were all overshadowed in the course of the first postwar decade by efforts at reconstruction and overcoming the destitution and misery, and were finally absorbed into an attitude of warding off, of defense. The argument was often voiced that the unfortunate past had been dealt with sufficiently, and besides, people had learnt a great deal from it. Further remembrance was now viewed as a burdensome stirring up of old memories; in any case, many had preferred silence to any kind of reflection.

5. Another factor was that work on remembrance, memory work, had also been institutionalized: in research, teaching, and political education. On the one hand, this provided the comforting feeling that certain institutions were officially engaged in the "mastering of the past," and had been appointed to the task. On the other hand, such relegation of "working-through" the National Socialist past to others engendered uncertainty and new pain. The modus of clarification offered to the populace was spurned, since it did not provide the individual with any possibility for identification. This was sensed by the Americans as early as 1945, when they marched the German civilian population, which had not been involved in the atrocities, past the mountains of corpses in order to demonstrate visibly to them the horrors of the Nazi regime. The film *Todesmühlen* (Mills of death), assembled by the U.S. Army from authentic materials and released for showing in German motion picture theaters in 1946, also failed to fulfill its educational purpose precisely for this reason, and in the end had a counterproductive effect.[23]

In addition, there was the fact that condemnation of National Socialism constituted a key element in the program of "reeducation" of the Germans instituted by the occupying powers. The pride of the German *Kulturnation* recoiled from this program of "reeducation," and a substantial portion of the effort to work through the past, to confront it, simply fell victim to dogged

Allied insistence that the Germans had to engage in a process of reflection about Hitler.

6. The attitude of defensiveness, of warding off the past, finally shifted to an attitude of defiance and self-pity. The widespread opinion was as follows: people had expiated, paid for it, provided restitution and compensation; despite all that, "the Germans" were being asked to continue, perhaps for all eternity, to wear the hair shirt of the penitent. The thesis of collective guilt was being sustained without any end in sight, and the need for revenge on the part of former enemies and victims remained limitless.

7. The demand now heard is that a new consciousness must put an end to all that. The good days of the German past should now be highlighted in order to build national identity and foster a crucially needed sense of self-confidence. The time has come, the argument goes, finally to step out from under the shadow of Hitler.

Yet to leave the orb of the twelve years of National Socialism is impossible as long as crimes go unexpiated and victims have still not received compensation; and that impossibility is not only due to ethical reasons. As a political demand, the call for an end to involvement with this unpleasant subject is highly effective as a publicity ploy, so that such a postulate will doubtless be raised in public ever more vocally as time passes. As a research topic, the Nazi period is not likely to lose any of its inherent fascination, even if scholars develop new questions and approaches, and choose to regard the Third Reich as a period in history like other periods. This is legitimate in scientific research if it serves to promote knowledge and truth. It becomes a dangerous undertaking when political interest is decked out with quasi-scientific questions and then utilized merely in order to divert attention, to balance off one set of figures against another, to relativize past events or trivialize their importance.

However, National Socialism will also remain a ubiquitous psychological problem within German society after Hitler for many years to come.[24] Those born to a later generation know no "grace," and even enjoy no special advantage. No one can evade working through the confrontation with the generation of the fathers and go unscathed. The "inability to mourn" is what renders the legacy so disastrous: that hopeless attempt on the part of at least an entire generation to isolate National Socialism as a political, historical, and legal phenomenon, and to split off the social-psychological dimension of the topic.

Yet one need not go so far as to define Hitlerian National Socialism as the incarnation of all that is disagreeable and appalling in the German character:

What repeatedly proved to be the downfall of the German people: that lack of moderation in the use of force, that intolerability in happiness and contemptibility in defeat, that lack of dignity and bearing, that cowardly brutality, which never has the courage to accept responsibility for the atrocities it commits, that sentimentality, desirous of blotting out the traces of its blood-intoxication by means of false feelings, that bestial lack of restraint vis-à-vis the weak, that whimpering servility vis-à-vis the strong, that mendacity rooted in the depths of the spirit, which has no notion whatsoever of what truth is, honesty, moral bravery—all this returns once more in heightened form, extending all the way to perversity.

This highly condemnatory judgment was written by Ernst Niekisch, who spent eight years in prison as an opponent of the National Socialists.[25] He was a resolute enemy of National Socialism, from both an extreme left and an extreme nationalist position. An attempt has been made to define the direction of his thought as "National Bolshevism," because it was as far removed from Marxist internationalism as it was from Stresemann's rational-republican leanings toward the West; in its vehement rejection of the Versailles Treaty, it had shared certain points in common even with the Strasser wing of the National Socialist Party. Ernst Niekisch, sentenced by the People's Court in 1937 to life in prison, did not write those words quoted above after the catastrophe, but rather during its midst, in 1935 and 1936. At that time, the intoxicated support of an overwhelming number of Germans for the Hitlerian state was still on the rise.

Of no less consequence for consciousness than such gleeful support was the psychological corruption of those who conformed to the regime, although they rejected it, suffering a significant loss of self-esteem as a result. Bruno Bettelheim has given a vivid description of this process—the loss of self-esteem and inner autonomy—using the example of the Nazi salute:

This salute was deliberately introduced so that whenever people encountered each other—at public and private meeting places such as in restaurants, railroad cars, offices, or factories, and on the street—it would be easy to recognize anyone who hung on to the old "democratic" forms of greeting his friends. To Hitler's followers, giving the salute many times each day was an expression of self-assertion, of power. Each time a loyal subject performed it, his ego was boosted.

For an opponent of the regime, it worked exactly the opposite way. Every time he had to greet somebody in public he had an experience that shook his ego and weakened his integration. Had it been only his superego that objected to the salute, it would have been easier; but the salute demand split the opponent's ego right down the middle.[26]

However, this split in consciousness, whose impact extended beyond the downfall of the Nazi regime, offers only one approach toward explaining the difficulties inherent in the process of breaking free from National Socialism—both individually and collectively. A further obstacle lies in the suppressed feelings of guilt, in the process which the Mitscherlichs have called "de-realization of reality":

Germans have paid not ungenerous compensation to those remaining European Jews whom they persecuted but did not manage to kill. Yet Germans still have no emotional perception of the *real* people whom they were ready to sacrifice to their dream of being a master-race. As people, these have remained part of the de-realized reality.[27]

The situation is by no means what the propagandists of a "new trend" in dealing with National Socialism would like to have us believe: namely that a large proportion of the Germans, in penitential hair shirts, are now engaged in an unceasing litany of self-accusation. On the contrary: the difficulties are due to the fact that the feelings of guilt and shame are not being articulated, and that there is a refusal to engage in work on memory. The reactions to the unparalleled and courageous attempt by Niklas Frank to engage in memory work in public, merciless toward both his own person and his father, Hitler's infamous governor-general in occupied Poland, are a lesson in themselves. Sample reactions were published in the weekly *Stern*, which also carried the series by the son. Some considered it to be nothing but "fouling of one's own nest," others felt the confrontation with his father was obscene, and a few suggested unabashedly that the writer be hanged.[28]

Thus, an open candid approch to National Socialism, and its treatment—solely for purposes of scholarly interest—as one era of German history among others, does not yet appear to be such an easy and ready option. An interval of only forty or fifty years is still not enough to render the Nazi period something historical.

Notes

1. On the current state of historiography dealing with the Nazi period, see B. Faulenbach, "NS-Interpretationen und Zeitklima: Zum Wandel in der Aufarbeitung der jüngsten Vergangenheit," *Aus Politik und Zeitgeschichte* B 22/87 (30 May 1987): 19–30.

2. Cf. the paradigmatic article by Helmut Krausnick, "Unser Weg in die Katastrophe von 1945: Rechenschaft und Besinnung heute," *Aus Politik und Zeitgeschichte*, B 19 (9 May 1962): 229–40 (the text was given as a lecture at the Conference of the Protestant Church, Berlin, July 1961); see Bundeszentrale für politische Bildung, ed., *Rückschau nach 30 Jahren: Hitlers Machtergreifung in der Sicht deutscher und ausländischer Historiker* (Bonn, 1963).

3. *Süddeutsche Zeitung* (22 June 1987).

4. J. Habermas, "Eine Art Schadensabwicklung: Die apologetischen Tendenzen in der deutschen Zeitgeschichtsschreibung" *Die Zeit*, 11 July 1986; in English translation, *New German Critique* 44 (Spring/Summer 1988) and *Historikerstrait*.

5. Significantly, the dispute among psychoanalysts began with the debate about the role of the field and the history of psychoanalysis under National Socialism. See L. Rosenkötter, "Schatten der Zeitgeschichte auf psychoanalytischen Behandlungen," *Psyche* 33 (1979): 1024–38; E. Brainin and I. J. Kaminer, "Psychoanalyse und Nationalsozialismus," *Psyche* 36 (1982): 989–1012; G. C. Cocks. "Psychoanalyse, Psychotherapie und Nationalsozialismus," *Psyche* 37 (1983): 1057–106.

6. S. Speier, "Der ges(ch)ichtslose Psychoanalytiker—die ges(ch)ichtslose Psychoanalyse," *Psyche* 41 (1987): 481–91.

7. On the facts, cf. E. Kogon, H. Langbein and A. Rückerl, eds. *Nationalsozialistische Massentötungen durch Giftgas: Eine Dokumentation* (Frankfurt, 1983).

8. Cf. B. Distel, "Der 29. April 1945: Die Befreiung des Konzentrationslagers

Dachau," *Dachauer Hefte* 1 (1985): 3–11; H. Weiss, "Dachau und die internationale Öffentlichkeit: Reaktionen auf die Befreiung des Lagers," ibid., 12–38.

9. Reader's letter by M. Broszat in *Die Zeit,* 19 August 1960. It is stated there, in conclusion to remarks on the elucidation that the *mass extermination* of the Jews was carried out in Auschwitz-Birkenau, Sobibor, Treblinka, Chelmno, and Belzec: "This necessary distinction certainly does not change one iota in respect to the criminal nature of the concentration camps. Yet it may help to eliminate the unfortunate confusion which arises because certain impervious individuals make use of isolated and correct arguments that have been polemically quoted out of context"; cf. Kogon et al., *Nationalsozialistische Massentötungen durch Giftgas.*

10. E. Klee, *"Euthanasie" im NS-Staat: Die "Vernichtung lebensunwerten Lebens"* (Frankfurt, 1983).

11. G. Sudholt, ed., *Antigermanismus: Eine Streitschrift zu Dachau und zum "Auschwitz-Gesetz"* (Berg, 1986).

12. "21. Strafrechtsänderungsgesetz vom 13.6. 1985," *Bundesgesetzblatt* I (1985): 965–66.

13. The text (dated 4 August 1947) is taken from a series of similar first-hand reports from the Celle district contained in the Central State Archives in Hannover. A volume containing selected materials is now in preparation: R. Schulze, ed., *Unruhige Zeiten: Erlebnisberichte aus dem Landkreis Celle 1945–1949* (Munich, in press).

14. Cf. E. Kolb, "Bergen-Belsen," in *Studien zur Geschichte der Konzentrationslager* (Stuttgart, 1970), 130–53, here p. 151.

15. Ibid., note 13.

16. "Elektromeister H. und seine Frau erzählen am 28. November 1945: Erlebnisbericht aus Wietzel," ibid., note 13.

17. *Süddeutsche Zeitung* (2 June 1987), 15.

18. *Fränkische Landeszeitung* (19 September 1983).

19. *Süddeutsche Zeitung* (13 July 1984); cf. *Landsberger Tagblatt* (16 February 1984).

20. *Süddeutsche Zeitung* (14/15 March 1987; 19 March 1987), as well as a statement by the Promoting Association, *Internationale Jugendbegegnungsstätte* Dachau e.V.

21. *Dachauer Nachrichten* (21 May 1987).

22. C. Streit, *Keine Kameraden: Die Wehrmacht und die sowjetischen Kriegsgefangenen 1941–1945* (Stuttgart, 1978).

23. B. S. Chamberlin, "Todesmühlen: Ein früher Versuch zur Massen 'Umerziehung' im besetzten Deutschland 1945–1946," *Vierteljahrshefte für Zeitgeschichte* 29 (1981): 420–36.

24. Cf. in particular I. Grubrich-Simitis, "Vom Konkretismus zur Metaphorik: Gedanken zur psychoanalytischen Arbeit mit Nachkommen der Holocaust-Generation—anläßlich einer Neuerscheinung," *Psyche* 38 (1984): 1–28; K. Grünberg, "Folgen nationalsozialistischer Verfolgung bei jüdischen Nachkommen Überlebender in der Bundersrepublik Deutschland," *Psyche* 41 (1987): 492–507; see also D. von Westernhagen, "Die Kinder der Täter," *Die Zeit,* 4 April 1986; P. Sichrovsky, *Schuldig geboren: Kinder aus Nazifamilien* (Cologne, 1987); H. Epstein, *Children of the Holocaust* (New York, 1979).

25. The book, whose manuscript served as evidence for the prosecution against the author, could, of course, only be published after 1945: E. Niekisch, *Das Reich der niederen Dämonen* (Hamburg, 1953), 270.

26. B. Bettelheim, "Remarks on the Psychological Appeal of Totalitarianism," in *Surviving and Other Essays*, ed. B. Bettelheim (New York, 1979), 318.

27. A Mitscherlich and M. Mitscherlich, *The Inabilty to Mourn* (New York, 1975), 65.

28. N. Frank, "Mein Vater, der Nazi-Mörder," *Stern*, 21 May 1987. The readers' letters published in the 10 June 1987 issue are highly instructive.

12.   Unburdening the German Past?
A Preliminary Assessment

H a n s - U l r i c h   W e h l e r

Looking back at the controversial themes and aspects of the Historians' Debate, we can now draw up an interim balance sheet on the controversy and its results. Like an accountant, we will use a "double-entry" method.

The first assessment is altogether negative. The widely publicized political and academic offensive led by Nolte, Hillgruber, Stürmer, and their allies has caused a great deal of harm. Their common aim, pursued for different reasons and motivated by various interests, was to bring about a revision of a well-founded view of the past. In so doing, they merely confirmed diehards in their old prejudices. They brazenly violated indispensable standards of historical practice and epistemological reflection. By attacking elements of a self-critical West German consensus well worth defending, they hardly won friends for the revisionism they claim to find more convincing. On the contrary, they undermined history's reputation in academic circles as a rigorously reflective and empirical science and damaged as well the political reputation of the Federal Republic abroad. The first phase of the Historians' Debate has shown just how much china can be smashed in a very short time if one puts one's mind to it.

However, there is also a positive side to this controversy that will have much greater consequences. The political criticism directed at the new currents of nationalist, apologist revisionism was powerfully convincing. The academic objections leveled against Nolte's notion of "Asiatic" deeds committed with the help of a "rat cage," against calls to identify with the wrong side, against the hunt for a new national identity gilded with neoconservative ideology, soon proved themselves superior. The debate revealed the vigilence of critical public opinion. It demonstrated the willingness of numerous historians to engage in public debate.

The Historians' Debate has thus far ended with the victory of critical reason and professionalism over the imputations of a new revisionism. In short, in the terms of a cost-benefit analysis or a comparison of debits and credits, the positive effects of the controversy have far outweighed the negative.

This in itself is an important result. It is also significant because the Historians' Debate continues today. The constantly growing numbers of articles, documentary collections, and books confirm this judgment. The future task is thus to protect the advantage currently enjoyed by scientific reasoning and political criticism. When Hillgruber's forthcoming "extended account" appears, describing the collapse of the Eastern front in 1944/45 as "the most burdensome result of the war," or after Nolte's soon-to-be-published history of the "European civil war" between Reds and Browns has come out, then their previous critics (and many new ones, I hope,) will face a new test. The following prognosis is quite likely to come true: the ranks of those who will immediately and carefully examine these new books both here and abroad will not be limited to professional historians. Rather, they will also include many members of a politically sensitized public who will attentively assess the cogency of the arguments presented and their political thrust.

If one looks a bit more closely at the Historians' Debate, examining the controversial theses, motives, and goals of those historians who have been criticized, it becomes very clear that this debate is first and foremost a public political controversy, not merely an academic discussion among specialists. Nolte and Hillgruber now complain mightily about this, yet it was they who deliberately sought wider publicity in the beginning. To this day, anyone can take part in this controversy. Participation has not become the privilege of experts, as Nolte and Hillgruber would now prefer.

In the course of this public discussion, the effort to shore up the Federal Republic's weakened basis of legitimacy (a legitimacy that was shaken by social, economic, political, and cultural crises beginning in the early 1970s) through a "regeneration of a national historical consciousness" that is spared attentive self-criticism and instead outfits itself with a clear set of enemies, has failed.[1] This political purpose, never openly admitted except by Stürmer, was served by attempts to unburden German history of its worst aspects, especially of the Nazi period's ruins and barricades that now block the way back to an older German past. Such efforts are, at the same time, symptoms of a minor "cultural revolution" from the Right. Within the context of the Historians' Debate, neoconservatives have tenaciously pressed for cultural hegemony in the realm of political ideas. They hope to disseminate their fashionable vocabulary ("identity," "inheritance," "identification with the German past," etc.) more widely, and to establish their interpretation of German history more firmly. Their goal is the power to define key concepts, to set the interpretive tone when judgment is passed on the fundamental character of the recent German past and when plans are drawn up for a better German future.

Despite the controversy's basic character as a "public conflict of opinion," academic factors and hypotheses have also played a significant role, although often in a transparently instrumental form.[2] The result has been a melange of political, scientific, and pseudo-scientific motives, intentions, and arguments. The reflections and theses put forth with claims to scientific validity have been and must be examined just as carefully as the political intentions of their authors. However much the Historians' Debate may be a public debate, the hypotheses and (real or supposed) research results which it has spawned must nevertheless be subjected to careful scrutiny.

One consequence of the nature of the controversy has been that historians have had a certain professional advantage, or at least they have been provoked into taking a clear stand. This also means that they have been called on to clarify controversial historical issues. It is difficult to understand why so many historians of Eastern Europe who are experts on many of the key problems in the debate have failed to come forward. And it remains a peculiar and regrettable aspect of the Historians' Debate that competent political scientists, political sociologists, and other social scientists—with the exception of Habermas, Sontheimer, and Euchner—as well as constitutional theorists, political philosophers, etc., stayed on the sidelines as interested but mute observers. Will this curious apolitical abstinence continue in the future? At this point it is hard to avoid the conclusion that the controversy has virtually been delegated to liberal journalists and a group of historians of the contemporary period.

All this did not prevent a commentator from the *Frankfurter Allgemeine Zeitung* from making the remarkable assertion that the dispute really hinged on "a confrontation" between Nolte and other historians on one side and "a few social scientists" on the other. In the nomenclature of the *FAZ*, historians had previously been either "historians" or "scholars of the humanities" [*Geisteswissenschaftler*]. Now critical historians like Jäckel, Broszat, Kocka, Meier, Winkler, and the Mommsens were suddenly transformed into mere "social scientists." The derogatory tone of this term was combined with the following charge, no more insightful than it is respectful: that "Habermas and his helpers" had dared in their "lordly discourse" to bestow criticism rather than applause. Despite the enviable accuracy of this professional judgment, not to be confused with a nasty scolding, many in Frankfurt and elsewhere will still be amazed at what a large staff of highly paid servants a professor of philosophy is able to maintain even today. More surprising is the increasing number of new "domestics" from abroad—from Europe, America, and Israel—who constantly offer their services.[3]

But let us leave these journalistic polemics and return to the Historians' Debate itself. The much-discussed amalgamation of politics and scholarship was apparent in the contributions of all those historians who came under critical attack—not least in those cases where the historians had energetically disavowed such a fusion. One of the central theses put forth by Ernst Nolte, for example, was the dubious claim that the supposedly unparalleled "Asiatic" killings the Bolsheviks, inspired by the Marxist theory of extermination, unleashed in the bourgeoisie a panic-stricken anxiety. This anxiety then came to engulf Hitler himself, the National Socialist "movement," and those who voted for it. Driven by existential fear, according to Nolte, Germany attempted to imitate and outdo this "model" with ever more radical policies of its own.

It has not yet been possible to lend this thesis even remote plausibility as an explanation for the Nazis' extermination policies. The key example of the "rat cage" has turned out to be entirely unconvincing. For Nolte's claims to be persuasive, the massive source material documenting Hitler's contempt for Jewish Bolshevism and for the internally decaying Soviet system, as well as his open admiration for Stalin's brutality, would first have to be called into question by new empirically grounded argumentation. Until that happens, the sources will retain their "veto power" over all speculation.

Unless that occurs, one critical conclusion will remain defensible. Nolte's thesis concerning the fatal consequences of the Bolsheviks' anxiety-producing class warfare is directed above all against a well-grounded interpretation: that Hitler and National Socialism were products of German and Austrian history. Only after factors rooted in that past have been assessed should the broader European context be considered. Nolte has sought to undermine this hard-won insight by displacing the "primary historical guilt" onto Marx, the Russian Revolution, and the extermination policy of the Bolsheviks. I shall emphasize below the main points of the opposing view—a view that is better grounded empirically and more convincing in its interpretive approach than Nolte's theory:

—Hitler and countless other National Socialists had internalized a fanatical anti-Marxism long before the First World War; that is, before the Russian Revolution, the civil war, and class warfare in the new Soviet Union could confirm and strengthen their hatred of the "Reds."

—Social Darwinism in its vulgar (racist) form was one of the strongest forces driving the highly ideological "worldview" of Hitler and many other Nazis well before 1917. Contemporary developments thereafter only served as confirmation to these confused minds.

—The poisonous morass of German and Austrian anti-Semitism was the source of the crazed ideas associated with the Nazi hatred of the Jews. The new racist, political anti-Semitism that flourished in the late 1870s quickly led to the explicit idea of extermination. For example, in its Hamburg resolutions of September 1899, the German Social Reform Party claimed publicly and without any embarrassment that "in the course of the twentieth century, the Jewish question must be solved . . . once and for all by the complete separation and (if necessary for defensive purposes) the definitive extermination of the Jewish people."[4] What was new in the 1930s was "only" that Hitler and his cohorts took this program literally—and brought with them the will to carry out the deed itself.

—The Nazis effortlessly adopted the widespread, fully developed antidemocratic, antiliberal, and antiparliamentary political ideology that had already been fully developed by the German Right before 1917/18.

—The Nazis were able to exploit the deeply corrosive anticapitalist resentments of the Protestant, provincial bourgeoisie and of peasant society. They were also able to counter the difficult conflicts of a modern class society with the hypertrophied idealization of an oft-invoked *Volksgemeinschaft* [national community].

—National Socialism benefited from long-term conditions in Germany: the antagonisms of Germany's social structure, an authoritarian mentality, the peculiarities of Prussian militarism, the Protestant subservience to the state, the national susceptibility to charismatic leaders, a particular kind of political philosophy, etc. Hitler's regime also profited from more recent conditions that stemmed from the experiences of the period 1914–33. Among these were "the experience of war," "the nation in arms," the "total war" of 1916–18, the beginning of the defeat, the renunciation of all war aims, the stab-in-the-back myth, the "disgraceful peace" at Versailles, the war reparations and postwar hyperinflation, and the destructive force of the Depression. These events belong to a long list of favorable factors with fatal consequences.

Above all, the traditions and burdens of Germany's past influenced the course of National Socialism. Only after these have been identified should historians proceed to analyze the influence of the wider European and world-historical context. The undeniable fear, at the time, of a two-pronged attack from the Left—by the German Communist Party from within and by the increasingly powerful Soviet Union from outside—belongs in this wider context. Although those two forces never actually intended to cooperate in a Communist revolution, the very real fear of such a possibility was extravagantly played up in the years between 1917–20 and 1933. Nolte is merely the latest in a long line of doomsayers who would turn this hoary revolution-myth into a real and deadly danger.

Hitler supposedly believed in the reality of this danger. Moreover, his dread of being overwhelmed by the "Asiatic" Bolsheviks was allegedly the prime motivating force behind his policies and personality. Nolte restated his axiom—one which perhaps reflects the naiveté of an historian who has devoted his life's work to the power of ideologies—in a blunter, more pointed form then ever before in the fall of 1987: "To view Hitler as a German politician rather than as the anti-Lenin," he reproved hundreds of knowledgeable historians, "strikes me as proof of a regrettable myopia and narrowness." Starting from this premise, and falling under the sway of the very fears and phobias that he himself has played up, Nolte once again defiantly insisted: "If Hitler was a person fundamentally driven by fears—by among others a fear of the 'rat cage'"—and if this renders "his motivations more understandable," then the war against the Soviet Union was not only "the greatest war ever of destruction and enslavement," but also "in spite of this, objectively speaking [!], a preemptive war."[5]

While Nolte may like to describe his motive as the purely scientific interest of (as he likes to put it) a solitary thinker in search of a supposedly more complex, more accurate understanding of the years between 1917 and 1945, a number of political implications are clearly present. The basic tendency of Nolte's reinterpretation is to unburden German history by relativizing the Holocaust. Nolte claims the Nazi mass murder was modeled on and insti- gated by the excesses of the Russian Revolution, the Stalinist regime, and the Gulag; that it countered this "Asiatic" danger by imitating and surpassing it.[6] This new localization of "absolute evil" in Nolte's political theology leads away from Hitler, National Socialism, and German history. It shifts the real origins of fascist barbarism onto the Marxist postulate—and the Bolshevik practice—of extermination. Once again the classic mechanism of locating the source of evil outside one's own history is at work. The German war of de- struction certainly remains inhuman. But because its roots supposedly lie in Marxist theory and Bolshevik class warfare, the German perpetrator is now seen to be reacting in defensive, understandable panic to the "original" inhu- manity of the East. From there, it is only one more step to the astounding conclusion that Hitler's invasion of the Soviet Union in June 1941 and the war of conquest and extermination that followed were "objectively speaking"— one can hardly believe one's eyes—"a preemptive war."

Whoever thinks, in spite of this, that it is an exaggeration to claim that Nolte's theses tend toward exculpation should take notice of Nolte's own, hardly unpolitical, view as he expressed it in an interview with *Die Welt* in September 1987: Germans were "once the master race [*Herrenvolk*], now they are the guilty race [*Sündervolk*]. The one is merely an inversion of the other." So it's off to the Promised Land, where no one "will demand of the Germans as Germans that they declare themselves guilty."[7] If there were any need for further proof that Ernst Nolte's "pure science" is chock-full of po- litical implications—and all historical writing possesses a political dimension, either implicit or explicit—then Nolte's vehement rejection of the concept *Sündervolk* should suffice. But can even the shadowy concept of Hitler's Greater Germany, panic-stricken and quaking at the threat of "Asiatic" deeds and hence imitating the work of extermination with inexorable consistency and industrial methods, redeem the *Sündervolk?* Nolte will have to prove this precisely and with professional historical methods.

An even closer connection between academic and political interests is ap- parent in Andreas Hillgruber's *Zweierlei Untergang* where the plight of the German army on the Eastern front and the civilian population of eastern Ger- many is treated without any countervailing consideration for the fate of the Jewish and Slavic "subhumans," the members of the German opposition, and incarcerated groups, or indeed for the Europeans subject to German occupa- tion, and the German people themselves, all caught up in a senselessly pro- longed "total war." Such a position unavoidably carries immensely oppres- sive political implications. His laments over the destruction of the "European center," Germany's intermediary position between East and West, and her loss of great power status is shot through with countless political value judg- ments. His guiding perspective (later admitted openly), according to which the loss of the eastern provinces and the expulsion of the German population westward represented "probably the most burdensome consequence of the war," is in itself a matter for political discussion.

Such political implications can only lead us down the wrong path—not to mention into a scientific dead-end. In all likelihood it was Hillgruber's aversion to methodological and theoretical reflection that was largely responsible for this wrong turn, though this supposition cannot be proven in any strict sense. Be that as it may, the political effect of *Zweierlei Untergang* has been downright fatal. It has led to the return of an unreflecting nationalism, in which sympathetic identification with the German army on the Eastern front and with the German civilian population has become dogma. Such a worldview has led an otherwise extremely knowledgeable historian to extrude and exclude the victims of National Socialism from his narrative, an omission that would once have been unimaginable but that we now see in black and white. The consequences of a naive attempt to identify with the subjects of historical writing could hardly be demonstrated more drastically.

In placing a good part of the responsibility for the amputation of the eastern provinces and for the division of Germany (and thus for the destruction of the "European center") onto the Allies and their evil war aims, Hillgruber repeats in a certain sense Nolte's far more disturbing attempt to shift blame eastward, this time with regard to the West. No impartial reader could in all seriousness call this an apolitical argument. And Hillgruber's politically disastrous and scientifically unproductive fixation on "the war's most burdensome consequence" leads one to anticipate with fear and dismay his forthcoming "more detailed treatment," inspired as it will be by such crass misinterpretations and politically disastrous judgments.

Lastly, Michael Stürmer has put forth two of his pet themes in a way that, up until now, has been anything but scientifically convincing. He has not yet formulated the problem of national identity in such a way that the process of identity formation and the nature of national identity could be examined in a scientifically productive manner with promise of new insights. Endlessly reiterated, formulaic invocations of identity cannot mask this striking deficiency.

The same holds true of the fad for geopolitics, which has led to the new doctrine of Germany's central position in Europe [*Mittellage*], a doctrine supposedly derived from an intimate knowledge of historical processes. As long as the influence of geographic factors on politics and society, on the economy and culture, cannot be determined in the precise, nuanced, and relativizing manner of the best French studies, the unrestrained pathos of the "logic of power geography" will continue to nourish well-founded doubts about such "geographism." The goals sought by the champions of this approach are clear. They would like to encourage a shift away from the liberal-democratic interpretation of German history that has established itself since the 1960s. In other words, a critical, pluralistic paradigm is to be replaced by the primacy of one-sided, homemade dogmas whose claims to get to the heart of "Germany's destiny" are as naive as they are arrogant.

At least Stürmer, unlike the others, has never made a secret of his political intentions. But his attempts at a neoconservative "formation of identity" [*Identitätsstiftung*] have led him to formulate an ideal so repulsive that it will be met by sharp criticism in the future. When, for example, Stürmer complains that people "do not walk with their heads held high" because of "an excess of contemporary history on the German side," or when he demands a purified national consciousness appropriate to the new conservative turn [*Wende*], that kind of "new German identity" deserves to be decisively and immediately opposed. Eberhard Jäckel is correct in claiming that Stürmer's efforts to reach a consensus on a view of history ("an entirely inappropriate object of agreement," according to Jäckel) could easily end in an "episode of old-fashioned tutoring."[8]

In the political discussion as well, the rhetoric of the *Mittellage* has displaced a more nuanced analysis. Since Stürmer gives explicit precedence to the rigid conditions of "power geography" over all other "continuities" in German history, this newly dressed-up old doctrine amounts to a call to replace complex analysis with a few handy rules of thumb. If Bonn's actual policies were ever to follow these rules, consequences would inevitably result.

Here and now, however, our task is to point out the important developments clarified by the first phase of the Historians' Debate.

It was Nolte, Hillgruber, and Stürmer, not their critics, who called into question a politically and scientifically well-grounded consensus. These historians have attempted to relativize the uniqueness of Nazi crimes by recourse to a Marxist "postulate of extermination" or to the actual extermination committed by the Bolsheviks, or by presenting German fascism as a reaction to the models provided by previous atrocities. In doing so, they have no more right to reject questions about their own political motives than those who seek to boil down all essential differences among fascist regimes into a pseudo-world-historical "Age of the Tyrants."

These historians see a glaring Marxist-Bolshevik threat (which, according to the insightful historian, also produced Germany's "radical fascism") as *the* problem of the twentieth century. In promoting their views, they not only revive an old bogeyman, but also lend ideological ballast to the difficulties preventing a sober assessment of present and future developments in Soviet domestic policy and in international relations. Such an assessment is already difficult enough to make.

These same historians, by speaking in favor of a neoconservative change of identity, undermine the existing, resilient loyalty toward the Federal Republic more quickly than one might think. This loyalty to the liberal democratic polity is at the same time critical of nationalism. The FRG's citizens have no need for such a change of identity.

These historians' unreflective nationalism leads them to seek identification with the army fighting in the East or with the civilian population in the eastern provinces, rather than adopting as their standard the quickest possible liberation of all who suffered under the fascist tyranny and the quickest possible end to "total war." They formulate trite reproaches concerning England's war aims, the destruction of the European center, and Germany's loss of great power status. Finally, they place all of this in the "right" perspective with extremely irritating remarks about the "most burdensome result of the war." In so doing, they undermine the oft-invoked "bonds with the West" far more effectively than do the Greens with their facile insistence on pulling out of the Western alliance.

If it is true that these distressing, even threatening developments have in the meantime been brought to a halt by reinforced defenses; if the promoters of such ideas are now under pressure to justify themselves; and if, after their hasty advance into the public sphere, they find this painful; then we have liberal public opinion and those historians who defended the Federal Republic's critical self-understanding in the Historians' Debate to thank. It is this successful defense that justifies a positive assessment of the debate so far. Because this victory was won by the vigilance and critical judgment of liberal public opinion and committed historians, it is really liberal political culture that has here proved its mettle—a political culture whose demise has often been foretold, but which showed its strength in the defense against revisionism.

All of this justifies the hope that the superior arguments of those in the Historians' Debate who fought against revisionism will retain the upper hand in the future as well. Vigilance and decisive intervention remain indispensable, for, despite recent victory, the temptation to promote once more a nationalist and apologist "unburdening" of German history will long remain with us.

Notes

1. H. Mommsen, "Das Dritte Reich," in *Niemandsland* 1: (1987) 17; see also H. Grebing (ibid., 12), who speaks of a "de-tabooization of interpretations of German history which otherwise clearly stand outside democratic consensus."

2. Jäckel in *Frankfurter Rundschau*, 6 June 1987. On what follows: a preliminary critique of the reticence of sociologists to become involved is in T. Herz, "Nur ein Historikerstreit? Die Soziologen und der Nationalsozialismus," *Kölner Zeitschrift für Soziologie* 39 (1987): 560–70. As far as I can tell, silence reigns in the other disciplines.

3. K. Adam, "Subjektiv: Abermals: "Nolte und die DFG," *FAZ*, 5 June 1987; See his earlier article, "Erpresst?" in *FAZ*, 13 May 1987.

4. W. Mommsen, ed., *Deutsche Parteiprogramme* (Munich, 1960), 84.

5. E. Nolte, *Das Vergehen der Vergangenheit: Antwort an meine Kritiker im sogenannten Historikerstreit* (Berlin, 1987), 18, 80, 109, 134. ("Anti-Lenin"—a concept which, if I remember correctly, was already used by Ernst Niekisch—also appears in Nolte, "Die Ausschau nach dem Ganzen," *FAZ*, 18 July 1987). The title of the new book is E. Nolte, *Der europäische Bürgerkrieg 1917–1945: Nationalsozialismus und Bolschewismus* (Berlin, 1987).

6. See on this point G. Peschken ("Wort zum Sonntag," in *Niemandsland* 1 (1987): 52–53: Nolte's "tact is truly unique." The Germans kill 20 million Russians in the Second World War, and now Nolte says to them, "It's all your own fault!" And what's more, he pins the extermination of the Jews on them as well. In addition, Nolte's notion of the "Asiatic" horrors contains the implication that they are the norm there, but the exception by us. "That used to be called self-righteousness."

7. Nolte in *Die Welt,* 21 September 1987.

8. Stürmer, "Was Geschichte wiegt," in *FAZ,* 26 November 1986, and in *Historikerstreit;* see also idem, "Lernen aus der Geschichte," in *FAZ,* 2 April 1987; Jäckel in *Frankfurther Rundschau,* 6 June 1987.

13. The *Historikerstreit* and Social History

Mary Nolan

At first glance, the *Historikerstreit* seems to have little connection to the history of the working class and of everyday life under German fascism. The current controversy about the meaning of National Socialism and the methods appropriate to studying it focuses on macropolitics and international comparative analysis. The social history of workers and peasants, women and youth, leisure and popular culture concentrates on the microanalysis of issues and actors marginal to politics as traditionally conceived. The *Historikerstreit* has debated the uniqueness and moral meaning of the Holocaust, while *Alltagsgeschichte*, or the history of everyday life, as much social history from below is called, has all but ignored that issue. Participants in the *Historikerstreit* seek consciously to shape national political identity among contemporary Germans, while social historians have attempted to reconstruct the much more local identities of Germans in the 1930s and 1940s.

With the important exception of Martin Broszat, students of the working class and of everyday life did not immediately leap into the fray against the conservative reinterpretation of Nazism. Rather, the principal critics of Ernst Nolte, Michael Stürmer, Andreas Hillgruber, and Klaus Hildebrandt have been—in addition obviously to the philosopher Jürgen Habermas—such figures as Hans Mommsen, Hans-Ulrich Wehler, and Jürgen Kocka, i.e., historians who have pioneered the structuralist, as opposed to the intentionalist, analysis of the Nazi state and its policies or have developed that variety of German social history known as *Gesellschaftsgeschichte* or the structural history of society.[1] The 1960s generation of new social historians, such as Alf Lüdtke, Detlev Peukert, and Lutz Niethammer, have not featured prominently in the highly politicized *Historikerstreit*.[2] And this despite the fact that *Alltagsgeschichte* has been done primarily by the Left, as part of its political project.

First impressions notwithstanding, the *Historikerstreit* and social history intersect in complex and significant ways on both the political and intellectual levels. To begin with, the *Historikerstreit* would not have taken the form it has without the innovative work of social historians. As we will see, the Right has rethought its analysis of National Socialism in part by borrowing, altering, and often gravely distorting the concepts, methods, and conclusions of social history. The Right's discourse is filled with pleas to normalize the study of Nazism, to empathize with the little man, and to recognize that many aspects of the Third Reich, including its most horrendous acts, were not unique. Ironically, it was Broszat who first argued explicitly for an "historicization" of National Socialism.[3] It was *Alltagsgeschichte* which first emphasized the normality of much of life in Nazi Germany. It was history from below which first sought to reconstruct nonelite groups' perceptions of fascism.

If *Alltagsgeschichte* has shaped the arguments of the Right, the Right, in turn, has exposed the ambiguities, lacunae, and limits of the social history of National Socialism as it has been written. The *Historikerstreit* has raised difficult questions about whose identity should be studied, through which methods and for which pruposes. It has challenged social historians to speak less glibly about the "normality" of everyday life in Nazi Germany, to inquire about the penetration of politics into everyday life. It has pointed out the need to investigate the links between normality and the regime's successes and, more importantly, between everyday life and terror. The centrality of the Holocaust to the *Historikerstreit* serves as a deserved reprimand to Left historians who have ignored anti-Semitism, racism, and the Final Solution. In short, the Right has challenged social historians to connect everyday life and high politics, and to rethink each in light of the other. At stake is the issue of whether history from below can remain critical and radical, whether it can avoid inadvertently serving conservative and apologetic ends.

The *Historikerstreit* is much more than an academic exercise. It is part of a larger controversy about the political uses of history and the relationship between historical consciousness and identity. Pitting conservative politicians and historians against their Social Democratic and left-wing counterparts, this conflict concretizes many of the issues debated more abstractly in the *Historikerstreit:* Is Germany a land without history? Who, if anyone, should write its "official" history? Should Germany have a national historical museum and would it promote a critical engagement with historical issues? What sort of national identity is possible and desirable for Germans after fascism?

I

Before discussing the multiple ways in which the *Historikerstreit* and social history intersect and conservative and social historians conflict and challenge one another, it is essential to introduce the historiography and historians who are at the core of my concern. There are three principal approaches taken to social history in Germany: structural or process history, working-class history not focused on the organized labor movement, and *Alltagsge-*

schichte or the history of everyday life. The latter two approaches share many questions, concepts, and methods and their practitioners are sympathetic to one another. Not so the first approach.

Gesellschaftsgeschichte, as practiced by Kocka, Wehler, and the members of the Bielefeld school, is quite distinct from and generally hostile to social history from below.[4] German social structural history has been strongly influenced by American social science and by a theoretical mixture of Weber, Marx, and modernization theory. It focuses on impersonal structures and processes, such as industrialization, and not individual experiences and perceptions. It claims for itself a commitment to theory and a conceptual clarity lacking in other approaches.[5] Structural history analyzes high politics in light of long-term structural developments—or, as in the case of Germany, its misdevelopment or "special path."[6] In studying Nazism, its principal concern has been with the pre-Nazi and precapitalist roots of German fascism, not with the contradictions of Weimar capitalism or the Third Reich itself. This school has neither paid particular attention to working-class history nor striven to reconstruct—from below—the experiences and attitudes of workers or women or any of the groups forgotten by traditional history. Although Kocka and especially Wehler have participated actively in the rebuttal of the positions espoused by Nolte, Hillgruber, and others, *Gesellschaftsgeschichte* has not been at issue. Substantively, conceptually, and methodologically it has contributed least to the *Historikerstreit* and been least affected by it. Thus, my focus will be on those who have written either studies of the working-class or of everyday life in the Third Reich.

Prior to the 1970s, the working class was not the subject of historical investigation by scholars of Nazi Germany. Whether the regime was viewed as a totalitarian system that effectively "coordinated" all groups and organizations or a more complex dictatorship of party, army, bureaucracy, and big business, as Franz Neumann posited, it was assumed that the working class and workers' movement had effectively ceased to exist.[7] In the wake of the fascism debate which began in the late 1960s, however, historians reexamined the relationship of economics and politics and the complex manifestations of class and class conflict in Nazi Germany.[8]

The pioneering studies were done by Timothy Mason, in numerous works in both German and English.[9] Relying heavily on Gestapo records and other government documents, Mason reconstructed not the admittedly tragic and ineffectual formal resistance of the Social Democratic and Communist parties, but rather the history of workers' opposition which occurred outside of formal parties and unions and in unorganized, untraditional, if one will, immature, forms. He insisted, contrary to earlier studies, that the working class had neither been crushed nor fully coopted. Rather, class continued to exist, even if its forms of expression altered, and workers were not integrated into the *Volksgemeinschaft.* Absenteeism, slowdowns, job changes, these were not merely expressions of a desire for economic betterment but represented opposition to the Nazi state and ideology. And that opposition, Mason argued, influenced state social policy, encouraging concessions to a recalcitrant working class. It limited efforts at total economic mobilization for war, discouraged the regime from conscripting women for industrial work, and even influenced the timing of the outbreak of World War II.[10]

Mason has subsequently modified his initial claims about the pervasiveness of worker opposition and developed a more nuanced and ambivalent assessment of popular opinion. Opposition, he admits, was seldom thoroughgoing. The same worker who illegally changed jobs, wrote antiregime graffiti, or engaged in slowdowns on the shop floor might remain uncritical of Hitler, go on an occasional Strength through Joy trip, or send his sons to Hitler Youth meetings out of fear. Terror, cooption, and partial endorsement of some regime policies thus shaped attitudes along with, and often in contradiction to, opposition to the attack on traditional working-class rights and institutions and the workers' material position.[11]

This line of analysis has been continued above all by Peukert, whose work has moved from analyzing the failures of formal political resistance by the KPD to studies of less formal manifestations of discontent—youth gangs, grumbling, and jazz dancing, for example. He strongly argues that such oppositional behavior coexisted with partial endorsement of the regime and allegiance to the myth of a benevolent Hitler. Moreover, although it created problems for the regime, it also reflected and reenforced atomization and the erosion of traditional working-class solidarities and cultures.[12] Others have explored the working class from different perspectives. Tilla Siegel has used her detailed exploration of Nazi wage policy to examine how wage systems and redefinitions of skill led to a partial restructuring of the working class. Hasso Spode has attempted to untangle the myth and reality of the Labor Front's leisure organization, Strength through Joy. Annemarie Tröger has explored the ideology which justified women's waged work, although on distinctly inferior terms, while Carola Sachse has reconstructed company social policy toward women workers.[13] Finally, the two major regional studies of society under fascism, the Essen oral history project on the Ruhr and the Institut für Zeitgeschichte's Bavarian project, contain much on the working-class experience. In their methodology, conception, and scope, however, they belong more to *Alltagsgeschichte*.

Alltagsgeschichte, though closely related to working-class history, has a somewhat different intellectual and political origin. The studies of the working class which emerged from the vigorous and innovative left debates about fascism in the 1960s sought to link working-class experience and high politics. They focused almost exclusively on the factory and on male workers. *Alltagsgeschichte*, as methodology, was influenced by English social history and cultural anthropology and initially analyzed primarily pre- and early industrial periods and problems.

The impetus for its application to the Nazi era was twofold. According to Broszat, who directed the multivolume *Bayern in der NS-Zeit*, an investigation of the everyday experiences of a variety of social groups was necessary for two related reasons. First, *Alltagsgeschichte* would counter the prevailing popular view that Nazism was an effective totalitarian dictatorship which imposed itself in a uniform and uncompromising manner on all groups. Second, *Alltagsgeschichte* would end the monumentalization of the concept of resistance (*Widerstand*) which had focused exclusively on those whose politically principled resistance led to martyrdom, such as the KPD or the men of the July 20, 1944 plot to assassinate Hitler.[14] Conceptually and empirically it would lead to a more nuanced and accurate view of the regime, society, and the possibilities of opposition. In their introduction to a collection of essays on the 1930s entitled *Die Reihen fast geschlossen*, Peukert and Reulecke give an account of the origins of *Alltagsgeschichte* that is as much political as historiographical. The effort to reconstruct the history of everyday life under fascism emerged in the wake of popular discussions of the TV film *Holocaust*, when it was shown in Germany in 1979. To quote Peukert and Reulecke:

> Looking back, people's own everyday experience seemed to have been so different that they could not find themselves in the picture which historians painted, because in their own remembrance the everyday situation of their life history was often viewed positively. Even those who strove for a critical coming to terms [*Bewältigung*] with their experience of repression, of yielding to the temptations of the regime and of involvement with its criminal inhumanity, [even they] often remained at a loss about how to build a bridge from their own experience to the contemporary historical-critical state of knowledge.[15]

Alltagsgeschichte encompasses a diversity of themes and groups. The three volumes of the Bavarian project devoted to "authority and society in conflict," for example, include studies of workers, peasants, and nobles, women war workers, village elites, and youth protesters. The theater and the architectural profession are investigated as well as the more predictable subjects of big business and the judiciary. And anti-Semitism and concentration cramps, themes ignored by working-class history, are given their due. The Ruhr oral history project focuses more narrowly on blue- and white-collar workers, but follows them out of the factory into the neighborhood and home, explores their experiences in war as well as peace, and contrasts the histories of women and men.[16]

Whatever its specific themes, sources and methods, *Alltagsgeschichte* has dedicated itself to uncovering subjective experience, to reconstructing everyday life, to recapturing the normality of many aspects of a world whose extreme abnormality had been extensively analyzed. According to Alf Lüdtke:

> *Alltagsgeschichte* concentrates on the forms and meanings of social practice. In question are the ways of perceiving and acting through which people experience and "appropriate" the conditions of their life/survival. [The aim] is to show how societal demands and inducements are perceived, worked through, as interests or needs but also as anxieties or hopes.[17]

In the words of Broszat, *Alltagsgeschichte* shows the reciprocal influence of society and politics. It suggests that concepts which have been considered diametrically opposed, such as totalitarian dictatorship and modernization, are interdependent. By reconstructing subjective experience and the fine-grained details of lived social conditions, *Alltagsgeschichte* challenges neat stereotypes about collaboration and resistance, bad Nazis and good antifascists.[18]

Alltagsgeschichte represents a clear rejection of *Gesellschaftsgeschichte* in the mode of Wehler and Kocka. To begin with, *Alltagsgeschichte* is practiced as much outside the academy as within. The movement for *Alltagsgeschichte*— and movement is the appropriate term—is supported not only by younger academics such as Lüdtke and Niethammer, but by many who are marginal to or completely outside of the university establishment, such as the growing History Workshop movement, high school students doing projects for the yearly national history competitions, and members of Germany's diverse left and alternative scenes. By embracing history from below in the mode of E. P. Thompson, Herbert Gutman, and the British History Workshop movement, *Alltagsgeschichte* adopts a local rather than national focus and concentrates on culture more than class. Eschewing grand theory and relying little if at all on quantification, *Alltagsgeschichte* requires, according to Broszat, the use of imagination and intuition.[19]

The response from the practitioners of *Gesellschaftsgeschichte* has been predictably hostile. According to Kocka, *Alltagsgeschichte* represents "neo-historicism" and "a loss of intellectuality in historical science." With its alleged "flight from the rigor of concepts" and its "skepticism of theory," it embodies the prevalent "fin-de-siècle mood."[20] These comments seem both exaggerated and off the mark. They neither acknowledge the enormous contribution *Alltagsgeschichte* has made to our understanding of German fascism nor do they suggest the vulnerabilities which the *Historikerstreit* has revealed.

Recent histories of the working class and everyday life have changed our understanding of German fascism in several crucial ways:
1. The view of Nazism "from below" strongly supports those who argue that Germany was not a totalitarian, centralized dictatorship. Rather, rule was polycratic; *Gleichschaltung,* or coordination, affected different groups and institutions unequally; and both terror and benefits were dispersed differentially.
2. The *Volksgemeinschaft* was hardly as homogenous and united as the Nazis claimed. There was much disaffection, grumbling, and even oppositional behavior. The Bavarian project has used the term *Resistenz* for such "effective warding off, limiting, damming up of the NS rule or its claims, regardless of its motives, reasons or strengths."[21] *Resistenz* covers a multiple of behaviors and attitudes that lie between fundamental political and ideological opposition on the one hand and enthusiastic endorsement of the regime on the other.[22]
3. *Resistenz* was much more pervasive than organized, political opposition. Although it rarely led to the latter, it was, many argue, more effective.
4. There were seldom clear lines between supporters and resisters (in the sense of *Resistenz*). Only victims could be definitively identified. In most in-

dividuals and groups, conformity and nonconformity coexisted. People actively opposed some aspects of the regime, intellectually and emotionally rejected others, but endorsed still a third group—either from cooptation, belief, or terror and the threat of it. They criticized individual policies and personalities but seldom Hitler himself.

5. Much of everyday life in the Third Reich was "normal." This "normality" is reflected in people's perceptions and memories. But it is also evident in the continuities that existed in the realm of everyday life—in work, wages, sociability, family, and consumption. Everyday life and concerns in the Third Reich were not of an entirely different order than those in Weimar or the Federal Republic.

6. Finally, in terms of methodology, the history of National Socialism must be integrated into that of twentieth-century Germany. Not only must continuities be investigated but the full range of historical methods must be applied to issues directly related to fascism as well as to those more autonomous from it. The aim of this kind of historicization or normalization, according to Broszat, must be not just a history of the dictatorship, but a history of the Nazi era. The aim is not apology, but "authenticity and concreteness for the moral element in history as well." [23]

II

The work of *Alltagsgeschichte* has met with a mixed reception from the newly resurgent Right within the historical profession. These diplomatic and political historians have seconded the call for the historicization or normalization of National Socialism and adopted the themes of continuity and normality—albeit with a quite different meaning and intent. They have become concerned with reconstructing the experiences of nonelite groups—although not to uncover *Resistenz*.[24] Their (mis)appropriation of the concepts, methods, and conclusions of social history has presented serious challenges to liberal and left students of the working class and everyday life. Nowhere is this clearer than in the conflicts about the relationship between historical understanding and political identity. These conflicts have been political: Who, if anyone, should write Germany's "official" history? Should there be a national historical museum? What sort of contemporary national/political identity can and should be fostered by historians? But they have also been historiographical and methodological: Should history and historians search for and reconstruct identity, and if so, whose? Can a concern for identity as easily serve conservative purposes as critical and emancipatory ones? Let us explore the political controversy first.

Issues of identity—national and political identity—have been very much in the forefront of public life in Germany in the 1980s. First there was Bitburg, the most visible effort to rewrite the history of World War II, to recategorize perpetrators and victims. Then came the sustained controversy about the proposed Museum of German History in Berlin and the House of

History of the Federal Republic in Bonn. Finally, there is the *Historikerstreit*. The centrality of issues of identity account for the passion invested in these controversies and for the fracturing of fronts that has characterized them.[25]

Each of these controversies, which were initiated by actions from the Right, reflect the growing desire of conservative politicians, such as Helmut Kohl and Franz Josef Strauss, and conservative historians, such as Stürmer, for a "usable past." All seek a new, proud, "normal" national identity, even if, as Anson Rabinbach has made clear, they disagree about the form it should take.[26] In part, the Right is seeking to counteract the historical interpretations and grass-roots initiatives of the Left. Of greater importance, it is striving to emancipate nationalism from its discrediting by fascism and its entanglement with the dead issue of German reunification. A reinterpretation of history, above all of the Third Reich, is integral to this construction of a conservative national identity.[27]

Stürmer, who is both a prominent historian and a close adviser of Kohl, has been the most vociferous advocate of the need for a new national and nationalistic history. Germany, Stürmer claims, is a "country without history," a land where "a loss of orientation" (*Orientierungsverlust*) and "the search for identity" are integrally related. This potential link between past and future means, he noted in one of his most often quoted statements, that "he who fills the memory, defines the concepts and interprets the past, wins the future."[28] In equally melodramatic fashion, the conservative historian Hagen Schulze has argued that

the flight from history has come to an end. The attempt of postwar West German society simply to cast off the burden of the past in order to live with the perfect future has failed. A nation can confuse itself with a society aiming at the highest possible gross national product for only so long. . . . The more uncertain the present, the darker the future, the greater the need for historical orientation. . . . For individuals just as for peoples, there can be no future without history; and what is not worked through in the memory will reemerge as neurosis or hysteria.[29]

Stürmer and his colleagues are well aware that Germany is not a "country without history" if by that is meant a country with no interest in history or few practitioners of it, inside and outside the academy. Just the opposite. In the last decade, Germany has experienced a perhaps unparalleled effervescence of interest in history, in its own most recent and troubled history. If the German fascination with *Heimat* suggests that some such interest is romantic, not to say reactionary, much else testifies to a popular historical consciousness and culture that seems enviable from the perspective of Reagan's America. Thousands of high school students enter the yearly history competitions, doing projects on such themes as "Everyday Life in the Third Reich." The extensive grass-roots history workshop movement has encouraged all sorts of local and oral history endeavors. Like its counterparts in other countries, it has taken history out of the academy and taught nonhistorians how to investigate their own history. Local museums are thriving, and historical books and television programs are enormously popular. The problem for the Right is that all too much of this historical interest and analysis is sponsored by the Left and tainted by its concerns and categories. It is unsuited to inculcate a positive and proud identity and to encourage the varied political projects of a Kohl, a Stürmer, or a Hillgruber.

Having lost ground in the history war at the grass-roots level, the Right took the initiative on the national front, around Bitburg, and preceding and following that, around the proposed national historical museums. The Kohl government, advised and supported by Stürmer, Hillgruber, and like-minded historians, began planning two historical museums in the early 1980s. Insisting that every nation had a national historical museum, they argued that it was only fitting for Germany to follow suit. (In fact, aside from the German Democratic Republic's Museum of German History, only Israel and Mexico have such national historical monuments.) For several years, politicians and historians debated whether the proposed institutions should be forums with changing exhibitions or museums with permanent collections, whether they should collect original items or emphasize interpretive exhibits employing modern media. At issue was whether the museums should provoke a critical confrontation with the past or promote national identity.[30]

In 1987, the Kohl government decided to locate the Museum of German History near the old Reichstag building and the Wall in Berlin. It would cover the full sweep of German history until 1945 in a series of largely permanent exhibits. The House of History in Bonn would be devoted solely to the Federal Republic, thereby supporting the *Stunde Null* hypothesis of a sharp break between the Federal Republic and the previous period.

For leftists and liberals, the issues of identity and history have proven complex. All would agree with Broszat's protests against the misuse of history as a substitute religion which seeks to instill a special national consciousness.[31] None favored a traditional museum, geared to arousing patriotic emotion. But there is division about the sort of identity that does or should exist. Habermas endorses a posttraditional identity, a "constitutional patriotism" that represents both a clear departure from previous political and cultural nationalism and an unequivocal acknowledgment of the Federal Republic's acceptance of Western values.[32] In his recent contribution to the debate, Wehler insists th . a rational, critical, liberal democratic identity not only can but already does prevail.[33] For both, as for Broszat, history can foster precisely this kind of consciousness. The practitioners of *Alltagsgeschichte* are equally concerned with identity, but of a more parochial sort. The argument is that local and oppositional identities did and perhaps still can serve as alternatives to a national/nationalistic consciousness.

These divisions were reflected in responses to the museum controversy. Historians such as Kocka tried to criticize and shape the museum projects from within, ultimately losing to the determined political will of Kohl. The proponents of *Alltagsgeschichte* were divided between radical proposals for structuring the proposed institutions and a total rejection of the very idea of a national museum. In a collection of essays entitled *Die Nation als Ausstellungs-stück* (The nation as an exhibition piece), the history workshop movement laid out the inevitably conservative implications of a museum covering hundreds of years of history via permanent exhibits, focusing on the nation and high culture. Even if the museum included changing exhibits on particular themes, few visitors could absorb such a vast narrative, and fewer still could develop critical perspectives on it. The Third Reich need not be ignored nor its crimes denied. Those troublesome twelve years would be effectively submerged, their importance minimized, their meaning normalized, in a vast panorama of cultural development and varied political regimes. Moreover, consolidating historical treasures in a national museum would rob local and regional museums of their valuable materials and deflate the grass-roots support that had bolstered them—undoubtedly a happy by-product of a national museum in the eyes of the Right.[34]

Although the intellectual and political arguments of the history workshop movement are compelling, their practical effects were virtually nil, as neither the historical establishment nor any political party except the Greens joined that protest.[35]

III

It was in this charged political environment of Bitburg, the museum controversy, and the conservative *Wende* that the *Historikerstreit* erupted. And the problem of historical consciousness, identity, and politics took on added dimensions. For all concerned with issues of identity, defining the past is integral to defining the present. A Habermas or a Wehler, as much as *Alltagsgeschichte* and the new conservatism, seek to instrumentalize history in the interests of identity creation. But whereas the Right wants a uniform and emotionally felt national identity, Habermas, Wehler, and Broszat strive for a calm and reasoned acceptance of constitutional democracy, built on a critical understanding of Germany's recent past. And left social history attempts to recapture the identities of small groups—work gangs, neighborhoods, youth groups—which were, and might again be, autonomous and oppositional.

While the intentions of *Alltagsgeschichte* are diametrically opposed to those of the Right, the former may harbor strongly conservative implications and be readily used by conservatives. In a recent essay Michael Schneider, a working-class historian connected with the Social Democratic Friedrich Ebert Foundation, expressed unease about the new social history. Its concern with unraveling the intellectual and emotional logic of the behavior of individuals and small groups, with recapturing its meaning to them in a very small-scale context, seemed to have the same depoliticizing effects as the Right's search for identity via history. Reconstructing the self-understanding of individuals and groups becomes all, while the political and organizational context in which the full meaning of identity is played out is ignored.[36]

Certainly, such worries are intensified when we look at Hillgruber's *Zweier-*

lei Untergang (Two Kinds of Collapse). In his impassioned essay on what he sees as the tragic and historically fateful destruction of the German Reich, Hillgruber—far from denouncing history from below, as the Right used to do—seems to embrace it. There is, he insists, only one possible perspective from which to view events on the Eastern front in 1944 and 1945. An identification with Hitler is impossible, but so also is one with the "coming victors," who could only be seen as liberators by concentration camp inmates. (That some of these inmates were Germans seems not to have occurred to Hillgruber.) The historian, he argues,

must identify with the concrete fate of the German population in the east and with the desperate and costly struggle of the German eastern army and of the German navy in the Baltic area, who sought to protect the population of the German East from the Red Army's orgy of revenge, from mass rape, arbitrary murder and indiscriminate deportation. . . .[37]

Hillgruber does not, in fact, employ the methodologies of social history. Although he claims to view events from the perspective of local mayors, army and SS officers, and foot soldiers, he cites no memoirs, oral history interviews, or local studies. This notwithstanding, Hillgruber's very claim, coupled with Schneider's unease, suggest the dangers of uncritically writing a history of subjective experience, of focusing on identity and meaning to the exclusion of all else. The problem is threefold.

First, a focus on identity and meaning can lead to one-sidedness, a one-sidedness in which both alternative perspectives and appropriate contexts are missing. That is most evident in Hillgruber, who insists on identifying the Germans solely with the defenders of the Third Reich—even the conservative resistance is dismissed as detrimental to the national interest—and who glosses over the fact that defense of the Eastern front meant continued murder in the camps. But left history can succumb to similar one-sidedness. In unraveling layer upon layer of subjective meaning, it is easy to forget that actions and attitudes operate in a world beyond the immediate environment of individuals and small groups, beyond the local and ostensibly unpolitical level on which *Alltagsgeschichte* focuses. Actions and attitudes have consequences not necessarily intended or desired. The often remembered stances of *"Durchkommen"* or *"Bleib-übrig,"* the discovered "many small forms of civil courage," may have dramatically different meanings when viewed from the local and the national perspective, from that of the actor and that of the system's victims.[38] It is precisely the tension, the gap between intention and results, between remembered or claimed meanings and actual consequences which needs examination. And, quite obviously, multiple perspectives need to be incorporated.

Second, the methods used to recreate meaning, to recapture subjective experience, can have a strongly conservative bias. Oral history is frequently used. While oral history can empower, and both leftists and feminists have tried to use it in this way, it can also omit, obfuscate, rationalize, and justify. It can reproduce the initial popular reaction to Nazism that emerged after 1945—a claim to have known nothing, an insistence on remembering only the good times, what was normal. People plead ignorance about the terror, persecution, and genocide that went on—allegedly behind their backs and without their knowledge. As Adelheid von Saldern has insisted, historians cannot be content with memories of only the good side of the Third Reich. They need to capture the double character of normality and terror.[39] They need to interrogate their informants, compare their memories with our knowledge of what was both happening and knowable at the time. They must examine how memory is structured and legitimated by the culture and political system.

This is admittedly extremely difficult, but by no means impossible, as the essays of Lutz Niethammer and Ulrich Herbert show. Niethammer analyzed ten war memoirs of Ruhr workers, seeking to determine what was remembered and forgotten, what had been worked through and what could not be. The attempt was less to obtain insight into the war experience than into the memory of it which shaped individual and collective consciousness in the postwar period. Herbert investigated why and how Ruhr workers so frequently and unexpectedly discussed the slave laborers who had been forcibly brought into Germany during World War II. He contrasted individuals' memories of how foreign workers lived, of how individuals helped them, and of how foreigners, the victims, ostensibly became plunderers and criminals at the war's end, with information from many other sources. Of equal importance, he assessed Germans' fascination with this theme, arguing that the presence of foreigners, living in virtual apartheid, altered the class structure and workers' consciousness of it, not only during the war but afterwards. In perverse ways, slave labor redefined notions of above and below and challenged the seeming permanence of the social order.[40]

The *thick description* favored by many historians of everyday life is no less problematic. This borrowing from anthropology does enable one to recreate experience in all its complexity and detail, but it can also produce a static, synchronic picture. The problem is not that this approach lacks theory, although, to borrow Geertz's formulation, theory does hover low over data and interpretation.[41] Nor does it flee from concepts, as Kocka charges, even if its concepts are not those of modernization theory, Marxism, or Weberian sociology. Certainly, thick description should not be accused of telling us more and more about less and less and thereby trivializing the study of Nazism.[42]

The problem is that this approach can become more and more distant from the larger context which in part shaped the world thickly described and in part determined the very meanings of actions there to the actors themselves. Lüdtke has found *Eigensinn*—the self-constructed meaning, the self-controlled space of workers—in the 1890s, the 1920s, and the 1930s. But it certainly did not have the same implications for the stability and functioning of the state, for example, under these three different regimes. Nor was the relationship of *Eigensinn* to the formation of workers' communities, solidarities, and collective responses the same before and after 1933. Lüdtke himself has recently suggested the need to explore such shifting meanings in his perceptive discussion of the idea of "deutsche Qualitätsarbeit" (German quality work.) Both before and after 1933, *deutsche Qualitätsarbeit* expressed workers' pride in their accomplishments, as well as a rejection of shoddy mass-produced goods. The Nazis' constant insistence on, and praise of, *deutsche Qualitätsarbeit* in their rearmament campaigns harnessed this concept, which was prevalent among skilled workers and had been endorsed by the workers' movement, for ends of which workers did not necessarily approve. The idea of quality work not only benefited rearmament and the war economy but helped create a broad consensus among Nazi party bosses, managers, army officers, and workers.[43]

The third problem of identity raised by the *Historikerstreit* again emerges most clearly in the work of Hillgruber. Here, the question is not of one-sidedness but of how to deal with the history of individuals and groups with whose actions we are distinctly unsympathetic. There has been a tendency by oral historians—most of whom are leftist or feminist or both—to asume that recreating the history, the consciousness, the cultural logic of groups would help empower them. And there has been a rather complacent assumption that this was our method, our movement, to be used for our purposes. As in so much else, the Right has imitated the Left. How then, should we respond?

Is it for the best that the views of ex-front soldiers, SS men, and Nazi party officials be aired in scholarly forums? After all, such ideas are hardly new, as they have been the stuff of *Stammtisch* discussions in local pubs for decades. I am of two minds about this. The espousal of such views by right-wing scholars certainly shows an interesting circularity of cultures, with popular culture shaping high culture rather than the reverse. Hillgruber's images of heroic German soldiers valiantly guarding the territory of the fatherland and the virtue of its women against the invading communist barbarians, intent upon rape and pillage, are the theme of innumerable *Landserhefte* or journals of the common foot soldier. In the *Landserhefte,* as in Hillgruber, the defenders of the Eastern front were premature anticommunists, whose actions must now be commemorated. This genre, published serially and in novel form, has sold millions and millions of copies in West Germany since the late 1940s.[44]

But if conservatives alone write this history, the results are hardly unbiased. Hillgruber's portrayal goes against recent scholarship on the Eastern front, which, among other things, shows the army's deep complicity in the Holocaust and its brutal mistreatment of Soviet prisoners of war.[45] The effort to fabricate a new, politically more respectable and useful history of the Eastern front is part of the larger project of rewriting the history of World War II in a way markedly different from that of the victors. Bitburg and the museums are integral to this project as well.

There are no easy solutions to writing the history of, let us say, the common soldier on the Eastern front, but in the face of a resurgent Right, left social historians must undertake such projects. I would suggest that Claudia Koonz's *Mothers in the Fatherland* is a model of how to proceed. Although her major interest is in Nazi women, she presents the multiple perspectives of Nazi and non-Nazi, Aryan and Jew, Catholic and Protestant. She allows Nazis and their sympathizers and supporters to speak, to recreate the world as they saw it, to explain its meaning for them. But she interrogates those voices, memories, and silences with context and consequences. Her concern is with a group, women, ostensibly totally excluded from the political sphere and by and large proud to be so marginalized. She deftly shows how deeply their attitudes and actions were shaped by politics and how they, in turn, were implicated in not only day-to-day political affairs but repression, terror, and genocide.[46]

IV

The challenge which right-wing historians present to social history does not end with the complex of issues surrounding the relationship of history and identity. The call for historicizing National Socialism has come under intense scrutiny in light of its adoption by Nolte, Hillgruber, and their colleagues. While some historians of everyday life, such as Ian Kershaw, have minimized the problems inherent in, and the potential for misuse of, concepts like historicization and normality, others, such as Saul Friedländer, seem all but ready to dismiss them entirely.[47] For their part, German practitioners of *Alltagsgeschichte* have begun vigorously debating these issues. The very titles of the collections in which these debates are contained, *Ist der Nationalsozialismus Geschichte?* (Is National Socialism History?) and *Normalität oder Normalisierung?* (Normality or Normalization?), reflect the uncertainty which social historians feel in the face of the newly revealed ambiguities and vulnerabilities in their approach.[48]

Wherein then lies the challenge from the Right? Not from the kind of historicizing and relativizing in which Ernst Nolte has engaged with so much publicity. Nolte and his expanded totalitarianism arguments not only posit structural and functional parallels between Nazi Germany and Soviet Russia but also consider Russia both model and cause for the worst aspects of Nazi Germany, above all the Holocaust.[49] His unsubstantiated claims and outrageous hypotheses have justifiably provoked political indignation. But they are intellectually irrelevant. Much more serious is the Right's reassessment of the place of Nazism in German and twentieth-century history.

Until recently, the Right had insisted that National Socialism bore no relationship to the German regimes and societies which preceded and followed it. 1933 and 1945 marked sharp breaks, and the only relevant comparisons were between Nazi Germany and Soviet Russia, for both were totalitarian. It was the Left that sought continuities and compared Nazi Germany to other fascist and nonfascist capitalist states. It was progressives who historicized and relativized. Now, in the words of Hans Mommsen, "instead of excluding the Third Reich from historical continuity, conservative representatives of the profession tend toward historical relativization."[50] In part, relativization is achieved by comparing Nazism not only with Soviet Russia but also with other authoritarian regimes in the Middle East, Africa, and Asia, such as those of Ataturk, Idi Amin, and Pol Pot. The unifying thread that ostensibly makes comparison relevant is the twentieth century's propensity to mass extermination, a propensity rooted, according to some, in the project of modernity begun by the Enlightenment, or, according to others, in a fateful marriage between some unchanging human condition and modern technology.[51] Such comparisons enable the Right simultaneously to acknowledge the Holocaust while denying its uniqueness and avoiding blame. Embedded in the context of twentieth-century genocide, the Final Solution and the state and society responsible for it seem neither unique nor singularly evil.

The defenders of both Nolte's extreme causal argument about the relationship of the Gulag and the Holocaust and of the more pervasive stress on comparative mass murder claim the high ground of intellectual pluralism and methodological innovation by insisting, in Hillgruber's words, that there must not be any *Frageverbot* or prohibition of questioning. Despite the blatant opportunism and insincerity in this claim, the reversal on the Right has to be taken seriously.[52] It challenges all left historians to clarify which comparisons are historically legitimate, morally justified, and intellectually fruitful and which are not.

V

The Right's effort to historicize and relativize National Socialism has not been limited to new international comparisons. Equally integral to this project has been the stress on normality within the Third Reich and the acknowledgment of continuities which extend both backward and forward from it. This has raised the troubling issue of the relationship between the "normalization" of National Socialism which the Right advocates and the "normality" on which *Alltagsgeschichte* insists. It suggests the ambiguities and limitations of social history's treatment of everyday life.

One of the most significant contributions of *Alltagsgeschichte* has been to discover the normality of much of the Third Reich, the ongoing everydayness of everyday life. Using memoirs, Gestapo papers, the reports compiled by the SPD in exile, and above all oral history, historians have recreated the daily world of the factory and work group, of the neighborhood and family. To be sure, the impact of fascism is noted, the destruction of preexisting organizations, the impact of new welfare policies, the tendency toward a privatization of politics and a politicization of the private, in Lüdtke's words.[53] The emphasis, however, is on people's memories of the marginality of politics traditionally understood, on how the rhythms of life were determined by the ups and downs of the economy, the vicissitudes of personal life, not—at least until the wartime bombings—by the regime and its policies.[54] To be sure, normality did not mean substantively the same thing to different groups, and normality is always a relative concept. Nonetheless, the term does convey the sense of many contemporaries and historians that much of life went on as before, uninfluenced by Nazi ideology or policy.

The emphasis on an unpolitical normality is reenforced by the manner in which oppositional behavior has been treated. "The many small forms of civil courage" with which historians of everyday life have been so concerned are attributed less to political beliefs than to the pursuit of interest, the strength of local communities, and the defense of cultural autonomy. Politics seem as irrelevant to *Resistenz* as to daily life. And when the state does impinge, it is often as modernizer, intentionally or not. Here it is not politics but impersonal, suprapolitical economic and social forces that are primarily at work.[55]

The emphasis on normality does capture part of the reality of the Third Reich, a part that is essential to understanding why people failed to resist, or accommodated themselves or gave active support. But focusing exclusively on normality is both intellectually misleading and politically risky. The Right seeks to integrate the history of the Third Reich into German history and identity, to domesticate it, by stressing continuity and normality. This has led the editors of the history workshop collection *Normality or Normalization?* to pose the difficult question:

If one believes in the normality described in reports of everyday life in National Socialism, is it still possible to oppose Franz Josef Strauss and others' claim, the "claim to normality," i.e., the demand for a "normalization" of history, including the "Third Reich?"[56]

In light of this dilemma, social historians are reassessing and refining the concept of normality. Some are calling into question people's memories of "the normal." According to von Saldern, the memories of contemporaries strongly tend to separate the *Normenstaat* from the *Maßnahmenstaat*, to use the terms of Ernst Fraenkel. She pleads for an historical analysis which captures the double character of Nazi Germany as both a normal, legal, bureaucratic state and an exceptional state. The historian can thereby expose the "false character of the ostensibly normal."[57] Lüdtke and Peukert, acknowledging that such a separation does occur in memory, are now concerned to explain why that is so. Lüdtke insists that *Alltagsgeschichte* can explain under what conditions "such a 'separation' was formative for memory and orientation" for "the many."[58] Detlev Peukert attributes the split character of German memory not only to the desire to repress terror and genocide but also to the fact that

the memory of an unpolitical "normality" in the 1930s could have taken hold of the collective memory also because a certain structural parallelism existed between the "normality" of the first German economic miracle in the 1930s and the economic miracle society of the 1950s.[59]

Historians need to look not only at how memory constructed the normality of everyday life but also at "the formation of everydayness" (*Alltäglichkeit*), to quote Klaus Tenfelde.[60] Everyday life is neither a timeless given nor solely the creation of the nonelite classes and groups who feature so prominently in it. It is also a product of structural conditions and political influences. For the Third Reich one needs to explore concretely what might be meant by Lüdtke's suggestive phrase, "the politicization of the private." People may have marginalized politics in their memories, but what did they read in the press or hear on the radios which appeared in more and more homes? How many avoided participation in all Nazi activities, be it only a national holiday here or a charity drive there? How were the most basic patterns of sociability and solidarity transformed by the regime's practices? How were the meanings of common concepts, *deutsche Qualitätsarbeit* for example, altered in a new context? How were the categories for understanding certain groups, such as Jews, homosexuals, and the mentally ill, fundamentally redefined? And what is the full import of a politicization of everyday life in a society in which politics traditionally conceived has ceased to exist? If *Alltagsgeschichte* has shown that many remained immune to the regime's ideological appeals and even opposed some policies, it has not paid sufficient attention to how people's lives and consciousness were subtly transformed. And those transformations altered the possibilities of resistance and of alternative politics, both during the Third Reich and later.[61] The aim should not be somehow to embed everyday life in politics, as Kocka and Winkler insist, for such a formulation implies an everyday life without politics. Rather the possibilities and limitations of politics traditionally conceived needs to be rethought in terms of an everyday life which is itself politicized.[62]

Alltagsgeschichte has been accused not only of failing to expose "the false character of the ostensibly normal," in von Saldern's words, but also of failing to link the "banality of the unreally constructed real normal conditions" and their "monstrous outcome," to quote Dan Diner's charge.[63] Despite all acknowledgment that there were few pure opponents, there is little effort on the part of social history to link victims with resister/supporters, for want of a better term. Opposition and acquiesence are portrayed as going on at the local level—in the factory, the youth gang, the neighborhood. Anti-Semitism, terror, euthanasia, deportation and genocide go on too—but out there, where "the system" is.[64] Daily life, palpable, immediate, complex, and contradictory on the one side; the system, abstract, depersonalized, ruthless, and directed on the other. This view is comforting but hardly historically adequate.[65]

Everyday life needs to be linked both to the regime's successes and to its crimes. As Heide Gerstenberger correctly notes, social historians, in their concern to discover *Resistenz*, have interpreted withdrawal, silence, retreat into the home only under this rubric. Yet indifference, silence, and withdrawal can as easily be treated as factors stabilizing the Nazi regime. Moreover, a focus on resistance and cultural autonomy has led social historians to ignore the contribution of individuals to the creation of "the social practice of public discourse." The creation of fascist forms of discourse and the social practices that led to their dominance is interpreted—as people retrospectively interpreted it—as something imposed from outside and above. Gerstenberger does not advocate the dominance of the system over everyday life, but rather argues that popular participation, from whatever motives, was essential to the creation of fascist forms and content in public discourse.[66]

Recent works on doctors, medicine, and forced sterilization in the Third Reich have suggested how everyday professional life intersects with both the regime's success and its crimes. They indicate just how elastic the concept of the normal could be. The medical profession shared the Nazis' commitment to eugenics, or racial hygiene as Germans preferred to call it, and many doctors shared their anti-Semitism as well. Far from being coerced into supporting compulsory sterilization or euthanasia, doctors willingly participated in such programs, indeed, helped design them.[67] They saw such programs as a logical extension of previous eugenic theories and as a part of their normal medical practice. Even in the camps, some doctors conceived of genocide as medicalized killing to cure the *Volk*. Others tried to deny responsibility for murder by convincing themselves that despite their role in selections and experiments, they remained professional healers, doing what they could under extreme circumstances.[68]

Peukert's solution to the problem of exposing the links between normality and terror is to explore what he calls "the hidden everyday history of racism." Between the horrifying fact of the Holocaust and the everyday normality of National Socialism, there was, he insists,

a fatal continuum of discrimination, selection and rejection/elimination [*Ausmerze*], whose monstrous consequences perhaps remained hidden from most contemporaries in their totality but whose inhumane [*menschenverachtender*] daily racism was not only constantly and everywhere present but until today has not been critically worked through.[69]

In her discussion of the popular treatment of people without work and homes, Gerstenberger gives an example of such racism and suggests the kind of investigation which would elicit its formation. Whereas such people had previously been labelled *Landstreicher,* a popular and rather picaresque term, they came to be known in working-class communities in the 1930s as *Nichtseßhafte*. Those who adopted the social scientific/legal term also absorbed the attitude that people without homes and jobs suffered from character faults. The homeless became part of that key Nazi category, the asocial. Ultimately they, like others labeled asocials and racially inferior, came to be considered "lives not worthy of life." Research has traced this kind of subtle fascization of worker colonies in ways that challenge facile claims about cultural autonomy and suggest the full implications of the complex mixture of support and resistance that characterized most people's behavior. To explore the transformation of public discourse and social practice in this way, to make clear its relationship to Nazi persecution and extermination policies, means, as Gerstenberger notes, "to contest the political innocence of everyday life."[70]

VII

Nowhere do the problems of *Alltagsgeschichte*—its narrow focus on subjective experience, its lack of context, its overemphasis on normality and *Resistenz*, its failure to link victims and nonvictims, and its inattention to racism—become clearer than in relationship to the Holocaust. And the *Historikerstreit* makes these problems particularly evident, for it has accorded centrality to the Holocaust. The Holocaust has been the great unexplored topic in left analyses of Nazism from the fascism debate of the 1960s through the social history of the present. Anti-Semitism, racism, and genocide are not categories which can be inserted comfortably into debates about the relationship of fascism and capitalism, with their concern with class struggles, the relationship of the state and big business, and the organization of the economy for war. Nor do they fit neatly into discussions of *Resistenz* and cultural autonomy, for these stress indifference to the regime's ideological appeals and immersion in an intensely local and unpolitical everyday life.

Recently, social historians have turned their attention to the Holocaust. The resulting interpretations are innovative, important—and very troubling. To begin with, the Left has rightly remined us that if Jews were the most numerous victims, they were far from the only ones. Gypsies and Poles, political prisoners and asocials, criminals and homosexuals were all incarcerated and exterminated. In seeking to recover the history of these other victims, however, social historians run the risk of downplaying the centrality of the Jews in Nazi genocide.

Those who do pay attention to Jews minimize anti-Semitism. The works of Ian Kershaw and Sarah Gordon illustrate one way this has been done. In his study of popular opinion and political dissent in Bavaria, Kershaw argues that *Alltagsgeschichte* reveals little virulent anti-Semitism. For Kershaw, "The road to Auschwitz was built by hate [the hate of a few] but paved with indifference [the indifference of the many]." [71] Gordon goes beyond indifference to argue for active opposition to anti-Semitism, basing her case on the number of Germans charged by the Gestapo with either friendship or sexual relations with Jews. [72]

Leaving aside the conservative political uses to which such arguments can and have been put, what are their intellectual merits? To begin with, the significance of ostensibly mild anti-Semitism may look much different depending on the context in which it is viewed. Does the silence on Jewish policy, for example, look less like indifference when contrasted to the outcry against euthanasia? And we simply do not know how mild anti-Semitism and indifference fit into the construction of fascist public discourse, which Gerstenberger wants to explore or into the history of everyday racism, which Peukert proposes to investigate.

Of greater importance, the regime did not need militant, virulent anti-Semitism; it only needed passive acceptance of its policies. The recent work of Robert Gellately suggests that it got that and more. Investigating Gestapo files similar to those Gordon used, he discovered that many cases resulted from charges leveled by neighbors, coworkers or friends for a variety of motives. Far from providing firm evidence of opposition to the regime's racial policies, many such cases were totally unfounded and never resulted in convictions. His conclusion, sharply at odds with those of Kershaw and Gordon, is that

for nearly every incident of mild, verbal non-compliance, there seems to have been a denouncer willing to inform. If the cases contain indications that some people expressed solidarity with the Jews, they contain much evidence of accommodation and collaboration.[73]

Recent studies of social rationalization and eugenics also downplay anti-Semitism—not by denying its prevalence but by subsuming it under broader rubrics. The work of Götz Aly and Susanne Heim, for example, argues that the Holocaust was seen as a form of economic and social rationalization, as a model of development endorsed by economists, population planners, and other social scientists. Jews, who represented the economically retrograde manufacturing and trade sector in Central and Eastern Europe, fell victim to this modernizing campaign, not because they were Jews, but because they were socially and economically backward.[74] This analysis of the vision of those seeking to create a new economic order in Eastern Europe does shed light on the participation of key groups in the Holocaust. By avoiding all talk of racism, however, the social rationalization argument avoids the difficult issues of popular consciousness and the broad appeal of nationalism, anti-Semitism, and racism. It presents a simplistic and distorted stereotype of the Jew as backward, rather than the much more complex and contradictory image of the Jew as both backward and modern, powerless and powerful, which had long pervaded German anti-Semitism. Finally, this argument assumes that anti-Semitism was functional for rationalization, when it may well have been the reverse. The new emphasis on eugenics subsumes anti-Semitism in the same way. Jews become simply one among many inferior categories defined by racial hygiene, one among many groups deemed to be "lives unworthy of life." Certainly an analysis of eugenics can help us understand how mass murder became medicalized and legitimized, how science served destruction. It helps us understand the active participation of professionals. But it alone cannot explain why the Jews were singled out.[75]

Instead of exploring the interaction of eugenics and anti-Semitism or rationalization and anti-Semitism, these new approaches seek to substitute the former for the latter. The danger is a Final Solution with no anti-Semitism; a Holocaust that is not unique. Complicity is minimized in those approaches that argue for indifference or even opposition to the regime's racial policies, whereas it is ascribed only to a relatively small group of professionals in those stressing social rationalization. Both ignore the pervasiveness of complicity, in however differential a form. An examination of the appeal of eugenics, if not pursued at the expense of anti-Semitism, offers one way of studying involvement and responsibility. The work of Koonz, which shows how the maintenance of normality in everyday life, a role in which women were especially prominent, facilitated the Holocaust, suggests another. Such analyses, do not necessarily represent a return to crude theories of collective guilt. Rather, they offer a way to link normality and terror, supporter/resister and victim, everyday life and Auschwitz.

Notes

I would like to thank Renata Bridenthal, Marion Kaplan, Claudia Koonz, and Anson Rabinach for their comments on an earlier draft of this essay.

 1. Intentionalist arguments posit a powerful and centralized dictatorship and explain developments in the Third Reich largely in terms of Hitler's ideological intentions. Structuralists see Hitler as weaker and power as polycentric. They explain the cumulative radicalization of Nazism as the result of the complex interaction of different power centers, goals and regime needs. For an overview, see Ian Kershaw, *The Nazi Dictatorship* (Baltimore, 1985), 61–81.
 2. Jürgen Kocka, "Geschichtswerkstätten und Historikerstreit," *Die Tageszeitung*, 26 January 1988.
 3. Martin Broszat, "Plea for the Historicization of National Socialism," in this volume, p. 77.
 4. See Hans-Ulrich Wehler, *The German Empire* (Leamington Spa, 1985), for a classic example of this school. See also Robert Moeller, "The Kaiserreich Recast? Continuity and Change in Modern German Historiography," *Journal of Social History* 17 (1984): 655–83.
 5. See Jürgen Kocka, "Klassen oder Kultur?" *Merkur* 36 (October 1982): 955–65, and "Zurück zur Erzählung? Plädoyer für historische Argumentation," *Geschichte und Gesellschaft* 10 (1984): 395–408.
 6. For the controversies surrounding the idea of Germany's *Sonderweg*, see David Blackbourn and Geoff Eley, *The Peculiarities of German History* (Oxford, 1984) and Richard Evans, "The Myth of Germany's Missing Revolution," *New Left Review* 149 (1985): 67–94.
 7. Franz Neumann, *Behemoth* (New York, 1966) and Mary Nolan, "Class Struggles in the Third Reich," *Radical History Review* 4, nos. 2–3 (Spring–Summer 1977): 138–59.
 8. See, for example, Tim Mason, "The Primacy of Politics: Politics and Economics in National Socialist Germany," in S. J. Woolf, ed., *The Nature of Fascism* (New York, 1969), 165–95, and Nicos Poulantzas, *Fascism and Dictatorship* (London, 1974).
 9. Timothy Mason, *Sozialpolitik im Dritten Reich* (Opladen, 1977); "Women in Nazi Germany," *History Workshop Journal* 1 (Spring 1976): 54–113 and 2 (Autumn 1976): 5–32; "The Workers' Opposition in Nazi Germany," *History Workshop Journal* 11 (Spring 1981): 120–37.
10. Mason's work has been subject to three kinds of criticism. Some, such as John Gillingham, argue that protest was not all that extensive and did not interfere with rearmament and war production. "The Ruhr Miners and Hitler's War,"

Journal of Social History 15, no. 4 (1982). Others, such as David Abraham, insist that Mason exaggerates the importance of such "subpolitical" manifestations of discontent. "Nazism and the Working Class," *Radical History Review* 18 (Fall 1978): 161–65. Finally, most diplomatic historians dispute Mason's claim that working-class behavior and the regime's assessment of it influenced the timing of the outbreak of World War II.

11. Tim Mason, "Die Bändigung der Arbeiterklasse im nationalsozialistischen Deutschland," in *Angst, Belohnung, Zucht und Ordnung*, ed. Carola Sachse, Tilla Siegel, Hasso Spöde and Wolfgang Spöhn (Opladen, 1982), 11–53.

12. Detlev Peukert, *Die KPD im Widerstand: Verfolgung und Untergrund Arbeit am Rhein und Ruhr, 1933–1945* (Wuppertal, 1980); *Die Edelweiss Piraten: Protestbewegungen jugendlicher Arbeiter im Dritten Reich*, ed. Detlev Peukert (Cologne, 1980). For the most complete summary of his views, see *Inside Nazi Germany: Conformity, Opposition and Racism in Everyday Life* (New Haven, 1987).

13. Tilla Siegel, "Lohnpolitik im nationalsozialistischen Deutschland," in Sachse et al., 54–199; Hasso Spode, "Arbeiterurlaub im Dritten Reich," in ibid., 275–328; Annemarie Tröger, "The Creation of a Female Assembly-Line Proletariat," in Renate Bridenthal, Atina Grossmann and Marion Kaplan, eds., *When Biology Becomes Destiny: Women in Weimar and Nazi Germany* (New York, 1984), 237–70; Carola Sachse, *Betriebliche Sozialpolitik als Familienpolitik in der Weimarer Republik und im Nationalsozialismus* (Hamburg, 1987), 113–92, and the case study on Seimens, 200–239.

14. See the introduction to *Soziale Lage und politisches Verhalten der Bevölkerung im Spiegel vertraulicher Berichte*, ed. Martin Broszat, Elke Frölich, and Falk Wiesmann, *Bayern in der NS-Zeit* (Munich/Vienna, 1972), 1: 11–12; the introduction to vol. 2, *Herrshaft und Gesellschaft im Konflikt*, ed. Martin Broszat and Elke Frölich (Munich/Vienna, 1979), xvii–xviii; and vol. 4, *Herrschaft und Gesellschaft im Konflikt*, ed. Martin Broszat, Elke Frölich, and Anton Grossmann (Munich/Vienna, 1981), "Eine Zwischenbilanz des Forschungsprojekts 'Widerstand und Verfolgung in Bayern 1933–1945,'" 691–709.

15. *Die Reihen fast geschlossen: Beiträge zur Geschichte des Alltags unterm Nationalsozialismus*, ed. Detlev Peukert and Jürgen Reulecke (Wuppertal, 1981), 13. See also Alf Lüdtke, "'Formierung der Maseen' oder Mitmachen und Hinnehmen? 'Alltagsgeschichte' und Faschismusanalyse," *Normalität oder Normalisierung? Geschichtswerkstätten und Faschismusanalyse*, ed. Heide Gerstenberger and Dorothea Schmidt (Münster, 1987), 19.

16. "*Die Jahre weiss man nicht wo man die heute hinsetzen soll*," ed. Lutz Niethammer, vol. 1 of *Faschismus Erfahrungen im Ruhrgebiet. Lebensgeschichte und Sozialkultur im Ruhrgebiet 1930 bis 1960* (Berlin/Bonn, 1983).

17. Alf Lüdtke, "Mythen Erfahrungen," *Kommune* 6, no. 3 (1988): 64.

18. Martin Broszat, untitled lecture, *Alltagsgeschichte der NS-Zeit: Neue Perspektive oder Trivialisierung? Kolloquien des Instituts für Zeitgeschichte* (Munich, 1984), 17–20.

19. Broszat, lecture, *Alltagsgeschichte der NS-Zeit*, 18.

20. The charges, all of which were made by Jürgen Kocka, come from, in order, his comment in *Alltagsgeschichte der NS-Zeit* 52; "Klassen oder Kultur?" 965; and "Zurück zur Erzählung?" 403–4.

21. Martin Broszat, "Resistanz und Widerstand, Eine Zwischenbilanz des Forschungsprojekts 'Widerstand und Verfolgung in Bayern 1933–1945,'" in *Nach*

Hitler: Der schwierige Umgang mit unserer Geschichte: Beiträge von Martin Broszat, ed. Hermann Graml and Klaus-Dietmar Henke (Munich, 1987), 75–76.

22. Hartmut Mehring, comment, in *Alltagsgeschichte der NS-Zeit* 25.

23. Broszat, "Plea."

24. For the major statements of Ernst Nolte, Michael Stürmer, Klaus Hildebrandt, and Joachim Fest on these themes see *Historikerstreit.*

25. Geoffrey Eley, "Nazism, Politics, and Public Memory: Thoughts on the West German Historikerstreit, 1986–1987," *Past and Present* 121 (November 1988).

26. Anson Rabinbach, "German Historians Debate the Nazi Past: A Dress Rehearsal for a New German Nationalism?" *Dissent* (Spring 1988): 192–200.

27. For a discussion of the Right's new-found concern with history, see Hans Mommsen, "Such nach der 'verlorenen Geschichte'? Bermerkungen zum historischen Selbstverständnis der Bundesrepublik," *Historikerstreit.*

28. Michael Stürmer, "Geschichte in geschichtslosem Land," *Historikerstreit.*

29. Cited in Manfred Asendorf, "Wie man dem Geschichtsbewusstsein der Bundesbürger auf die Sprünge helfen will," in *Wider die Entsorgung der Deutschen Geschichte: Streitschrift gegen die geplanten historischen Museen in Berlin (W) und Bonn,* ed. Die Grünen im Bundestag (1986), 23.

30. *Geschichte und Gesellschaft* contains useful contributions from various stages of the debate. See Jürgen Kocka, "Die deutsche Geschichte solls ins Museum," 11 (1985): 59–66; Hartmut Boockmann, "Zwischen Lehrbuch und Panoptikum: Polemische Bemerkungen zu historischen Museen und Ausstellungen," 11 (1985): 67–79; Gottfried Korff, "Forum statt Museum," 11 (1985): 244–51; Wolfgang Ruppert, "Zwei neue Museen für deutsche Geschichte?" 12 (1986): 81–92.

31. Martin Broszat, "Wo sich die Geister scheiden," *Historikerstreit.*

32. Jürgen Habermas, "Eine Art Schadensabwicklung," *Historikerstreit.*

33. Hans-Ulrich Wehler, *Entsorgung der deutschen Vergangenheit? Eine polemischer Essay zum "Historikerstreit"* (Munich, 1988).

34. *Die Nation als Ausstellungsstück,* ed. Geschichtswerkstatt Berlin (Hamburg, 1987).

35. *Wider die Entsorgung der deutschen Geschichte.*

36. Michael Schneider, "In Search of a 'New' Historical Subject: The End of Working-Class Culture, the Labor Movement, and the Proletariat," *International Labor and Working Class History* 32 (Fall 1987): 52–53. Schneider's solution, a return to the old labor history, is too simple, but his critique is nonetheless still valid.

37. Andreas Hillgruber, "Der Zusammenbruch im Osten 1944/45 als Problem der deutschen Nationalgeschichte und der europäischen Geschichte," in *Zweierlei Untergang: Die Zerschlagung des Deutschen Reiches und das Ende des europäischen Judentums* (Berlin, 1986), 24–25.

38. *Durchkommen* and *Bleib-übrig* (survival) as well as *Eigensinn* are categories used by Lüdtke, "Mythen," 64. The civil courage quote is from Broszat, "Resistenz," 70–71.

39. Adelheid von Saldern, "Hillgrubers 'Zweierlei Untergang'—der Untergang historischer Erfahrungsanalyse?" in *Normalität oder Normalisierung?* 166–67.

40. Lutz Niethammer, "Heimat und Front: Versuch, zehn Kriegserinnerungen aus der Arbeiterklasse des Ruhrgebietes zu verstehen," and Ulrich Herbert, "Apartheid nebenan: Erinnerungen an die Fremdarbeiter im Ruhrgebiet," *"Die Jahre,"* 163–232 and 233–67.

41. Clifford Geertz, "Thick Description: Toward an Interpretation of Culture," *The Interpretation of Cultures* (New York, 1973), 25.

42. See *Alltagsgeschichte der NS-Zeit* for the most thorough debate about this change.

43. Lüdtke, "Mythen," 65–66.

44. George L. Mosse, "Two World Wars and the Myth of the War Experience," *Journal of Contemporary History* 21 (1986): 498–99. Hillgruber is not alone in seeing the Nazis as premature anticommunists. This was a central theme of Bitburg and the writings of historians like Joachim Fest about it. See Eley, "Nazism."

45. See *The Policies of Genocide: Jews and Soviet Prisoners of War in Nazi Germany*, ed. Gerhard Hirschfeld (Boston, 1986).

46. Claudia Koonz, *Mothers in the Fatherland* (New York, 1987).

47. Ian Kershaw, "Nazism and German Society: The Problem of 'Historicization,'" chap. 8 of his *The Nazi Dictatorship*, 2d. ed. (London, 1989).

48. *Normalität oder Normalisierung?* and *Ist der Nationalsozialismus Geschichte? Zu Historisierung und Historikerstreit*, ed. Dan Diner (Frankfurt am Main, 1987).

49. For a summary of his many presentations of these views, see Ernst Nolte, "Zwischen Geschichtslegende und Revisionismus?" and "Vergangenheit, die nicht vergehen will," in *Historikerstreit*.

50. Mommsen, "Suche," 870.

51. In addition to Nolte, Joachim Fest has defended such comparisons. See "Die geschuldete Erinnerung," in *Historikerstreit*. For an attack on this, see Jürgen Kocka, "Hitler sollte nicht durch Stalin und Pol Pot verdrängt werden," in *Historikerstreit*, and Hans Mommsen, "Neues Geschichtsbewusstsein und Relativierung des Nationalsozialismus," in ibid.

52. See the interview with Hillgruber, "Für die Forschung gibt es kein Frageverbot," *Historikerstreit*.

53. Lüdtke, "'Formierung der Massen,'" 27.

54. See, for example, Ulrich Herbert, "'Die guten und die schlechten Zeiten': Überlegungen zur diachronen Analyse lebensgeschichtlicher Interviews," "*Die Jahre*" 67–97.

55. David Schoenbaum's *Hitler's Social Revolution* (New York, 1967) is a classic example of this argument.

56. Heide Gerstenberger and Dorothea Schmidt, introduction, *Normalität oder Normalisierung?* 10.

57. Von Saldern, *Untergang*, 166–67.

58. Lüdtke, "'Formierung der Massen,'" 33, n. 13.

59. Detlev Peukert, "Alltag und Barbarei: Zur Normalität des Dritten Reiches," *Ist der Nationalsozialismus Geschichte?* 55.

60. Klaus Tenfelde, comment in *Alltagsgeschichte der NS Zeit*, 37.

61. See Peukert's suggestive discussion of this in *Inside Nazi Germany*, 236–42.

62. Kocka, "Geschichtswerkstätten und Historikerstreit"; Heinrich August Winkler, *Alltagsgeschichte der NS-Zeit*, 29–32. For a critique of embedding *Alltag* in politics, see Axel Kuhn, *Alltagsgeschichte der NS-Zeit*, 53–54.

63. Cited in Lüdtke, "'Formierung der Massen,'" 33, n. 13.

64. Heide Gerstenberger, "Alltagsforschung und Faschismustheorie," *Normalität oder Normalisierung?* 41–42.

65. See, for example, Frances Henry, *Victims and Neighbors: A Small Town in Nazi Germany Remembered* (South Hadley, 1984).

66. Gerstenberger, 40–43.

67. Gisela Bok, *Zwangssterilisation im Nationalsozialismus* (Opladen, 1986); Robert J. Lifton, *The Nazi Doctors* (New York, 1986); Robert N. Proctor, *Racial Hygiene: Medicine Under the Nazis* (Cambridge, Mass., 1988).

68. See Lifton, part 3 on the psychology of genocide, for extensive discussion of the arguments Nazi doctors used and the identities they developed.

69. Peukert, "Alltag und Barbarei," 57.

70. Gerstenberger, 44.

71. Ian Kershaw, *Popular Opinion and Political Dissent in the Third Reich: Bavaria 1933–1945* (Oxford, 1984), 277.

72. Sarah Gordon, *Hitler, Germans, and the "Jewish Question"* (Princeton, 1984), 165–316 passim.

73. Robert Gellately, "Enforcing Racial Policy in Nazi Germany," paper presented at the conference Re-Evaluating the "Third Reich": Interpretation and Debates, University of Pennsylvania, April 8–10, 1988, 27. See also his "The Gestapo and German Society: Political Denunciation in the Gestapo Case Files," forthcoming, *Journal of Modern History*.

74. Susanne Heim and Götz Aly, "Die Ökonomie der Endlösung, Menschenvernichtung und wirtschaftliche Neuordnung," *Sozialpolitik und Judenvernichtung: Gibt es eine Ökonomie der Endlösung*, ed. Aly, Heim, Miroslav Kárny, Petra Kirchberger, Alfred Konieczny (Berlin, 1983), 11–90.

75. Detlev Peukert, "The Genesis of the 'Final Solution' from the Spirit of Science," Conference on Re-Evaluating the "Third Reich": Interpretation and Debates, University of Pennsylvania, April 8–10, 1988.

Part Four

Ramifications: Germans, Jews, and the Left

14. Negative Symbiosis: Germans and Jews After Auschwitz

Dan Diner

Gerschom Scholem has correctly rejected as false the portrayal of German-Jewish relations before the Nazi Regime as a "symbiosis." The image of a German-Jewish symbiosis is a distortion because it suggests that the limited, idealized period between the emancipation of the Jews and National Socialist barbarism, which lasted only two generations, was the rule rather than the exception. This image of German-Jewish symbiosis becomes especially misleading when, in the wake of Auschwitz, it is stylized as a deplorable loss. Such heightened reverence toward the intellectual patchwork that was German-Jewish creativity disrupts our view—already clouded enough—of the monstrosity of the greatest crime in human history.

After Auschwitz it is actually possible—what a sad irony—to speak of a "German-Jewish symbiosis," albeit a negative one. For both Jews and Germans, whether they like it or not, the aftermath of mass murder has been the starting point for self-understanding—a kind of communality of opposites. Once again, Germans and Jews have been brought together. For generations to come, this negative symbiosis, created by the Nazis, will color the relationship between the two groups. The facile and optimistic hopes that distance from Auschwitz would soften the memory of its horror, would weaken the impressions of that nightmarish break with civilization, have proven to be unfounded. The memory of Auschwitz, the living presence of what is euphemistically termed a "past" event, has gained ever greater weight within contemporary consciousness.

Thus it appears that Auschwitz, that "past" event, may make its most lasting impact on consciousness in the future. With increased distance, the view of this incomprehensible occurrence has become sharper; its outlines have emerged more distinctly in the aftermath of the disorienting shock that this break with civilization had upon the West. The effect of Auschwitz now goes beyond the creation of a common identity among its victims and survivors. The mind demands a rational response even to irrational events, to the actualization of senselessness.

To live in the shadow of Auschwitz? Not a very pleasant prospect, at least not for the communities of the perpetrators and the victims. The two groups necessarily live in different, even opposite, ways with the memory of what occurred, or try to avoid its memory altogether. Thus Jewish victims perceive German attempts to forget as plots against the collective memory. And such attempts can, in the face of continuous Jewish reminders of that horror, turn into blind rage—anti-Semitism as a result of Auschwitz? The failure to overcome the past because the monstrosity of the crime makes overcoming impossible, intense efforts that prove to be at best hopeless attempts to free oneself from the burden of the past—these are the fruits of a culture deeply marked by guilt over Auschwitz and constantly in search of relief. Yet these understandable attempts at avoidance are in vain. The omnipresence of the event leads those who seek to flee it Sisyphus-like back to memories saturated with Auschwitz. For Jews, the memory of Auschwitz produces a horror vacui of boundless helplessness—an incomprehensible emptiness best kept plugged with other memories and distractions if life is to go on.

Above and beyond the extermination of the Jews, Auschwitz was a practical refutation of Western civilization. An unfathomable act of purposeless destruction for destruction's sake repulses a consciousness steeped in the logic of instrumental rationality. An understanding formed by secular patterns of thought cannot integrate such an action—at least not without splitting apart. This impossibility makes the victims' failure to act in the face of the gas ovens understandable: the power of imagination needed for action is impossible in the case of the unimaginable.

In an article written many years ago, the Dutch historian Louis de Jong aptly described the conceptual trap represented by Auschwitz: understanding Auschwitz in the face of Auschwitz is comparable to staring with open eyes directly into the sun. The victims, individuals equipped with defensive mechanisms which protect them and permit them to survive and live on, must evade this dread-inspiring reality. "It may sound paradoxical, but it is a fact that can be explained both historically and psychologically: the Nazi death camps only became a psychic reality for most people . . . when, and precisely because, they no longer existed."[1] This accords with the recent and paradoxical discovery: coming to terms intellectually as well as emotionally with Auschwitz requires temporal distance. This coming to terms leads, for both Jews and Germans, to those necessarily opposing perceptions and patterns of reaction which have had such an enduring impact on the contemporary consciousness—above all of those born after 1945.

In a letter to Karl Jaspers in 1946, on the occasion of the Nuremberg Trials, Hannah Arendt addressed the basic idea of a "negative symbiosis" of Germans and Jews after Auschwitz. She also touched on the problem of a guilt that would be commensurate with the crimes committed, yet could not be traced back to particular individuals. Describing the basis for an expanding, free-floating collective guilt that would affect above all the younger generation, she wrote:

These crimes cannot be dealt with in the normal legal manner, and it is precisely that which makes them so monstrous. There are no fitting punishments for such crimes. To hang Göring is necessary, but it is by no means enough. Such a guilt, in contrast to all criminal guilt, goes well beyond, in fact shatters, any legal order. This is the reason why the Nazis at Nuremberg are so pleased: because of course they know this. And the innocence of the victims is equally inhuman. Human beings cannot be as innocent as those people were as they stood together before the gas ovens. . . . One can do nothing either personally or politically about a guilt that lies beyond crime and an innocence that lies beyond good or virtue. . . . For the Germans are burdened with thousands or tens of thousands or hundreds of thousands who can no longer be properly punished within a system of law; and we Jews are burdened with millions of innocents, because of whom each Jew today looks like innocence personified.[2]

The abstractness of the extermination, that is, the functional participation of German society as a whole in industrial mass murder organized through a division of labor, renders everyone, with the exception of active resistance fighters, a part of the killing process. The younger generation's feelings of guilt confirm this. Even though the actual criminals and those directly responsible have been punished, a critical mass of guilt remains which cannot be attributed to any particular person. This is a result of the abstract, depersonalized, and collective division of labor through which the extermination of the Jews was carried out. Attempts to reconstruct the genesis of Auschwitz historically also run up against the phenomenon of the Holocaust's abstractness. Can the extermination of the Jews be traced back to a clear intention, to a criminal aim present from the very beginning? Or was this an autonomous, functional process, rooted in a blind self-radicalization of the system, in which the atomized individuals who were part of an industrial division of labor became the unconscious executors of the Holocaust?

The crime is, in fact, too monstrous to be reduced to intention alone. Moreover, the reactions of the victims and witnesses alike are incomprehensible if one attributes the act only to a clear design that was present from the start. The road to Auschwitz was not straight; in retrospect, other possible routes can be constructed, at least hypothetically. In West Germany, however, the theory of an overpowering totalitarian system, of a directionless autonomous process ending in Auschwitz, encourages an exculpating approach that sees no actors, although the event took place.

However the debate among the historians develops—and the latest publications lead one to fear the worst—the abstract sense of responsibility that afflicts society as a whole culminates in a conceptualization that both refers to the deep collective cause of the Holocaust and is also helpful in characterizing the guilty feelings of the younger generation: Auschwitz has taken place. It has happened—*it* [*id*] in an emphatically psychoanalytic sense. Auschwitz is thus part of the unconscious in a double sense: as something unconscious that was *realized* in a collective act, and as a continuing, collective sense of guilt caused by the act.

It is possible to react in various ways to a sense of collective guilt. It may manifest itself as an archaic feeling of immanent punishment if there is no expiation for the horror of the Holocaust, an occurrence which was not part of the war, but was carried out in its shadow. Through identification with parents or grandparents—bound together through an intergenerational psychic wound—the fear of anticipated revenge, of anticipated expiation (in a word, a punishment anxiety) is passed on. In moments of real or imagined political crisis, the repressed or denied punishment anxiety over Auschwitz can burst forth in a productive manner—unless it is condemned to silence by a complicitous pact between the generations, in which case it may later lead to demands for exoneration from guilt.

An episode recounted by a psychoanalyst illustrates well the persistence of punishment anxieties induced by Auschwitz, of a refusal to give oneself over to the horror of the past, and of the complicity between the generations. The analyst discusses the problem of real and imagined anxiety induced by the threat of nuclear war, but unconsciously rejects the patient's offer, embedded in the exchange, to take up the subject of the past.

The analyst reports that a twenty-eight-year-old patient had the following anxiety dream at the beginning of his therapy:

> It was just before or just after a nuclear attack. I was in a bunker, but decided to go out, even though I was not sure whether everything outside was radioactive and I would be done for. I walked through empty streets and finally came to a warehouse with a ramp where trucks could be loaded. I saw that bars of gold were stored inside the warehouse and there was even a sign indicating that gold was the main business of the place. I experienced a feeling of fascination and attraction. Yet in the same moment I realized I shouldn't be there, because it was a restricted area.[3]

Although the analyst prominently cites this dream right at the beginning of his report, he does not explore it any further. On the contrary, towards the end of his article he makes clear that he considers the anxiety to have been real:

> The therapy of the patient whose dream was cited earlier underwent a remarkable change soon after that dream. This was the case even though, or, I would prefer to claim, precisely because I took his anxiety fantasies about the military and ecological situation in our world seriously.[4]

The analyst does not relate the stark images of a fenced-in camp, a ramp, and gold, or the patient's ambivalent feelings, back to Auschwitz or the presence of the past in even a tentative manner. The defensive hermeneutic is airtight.

The existence of an uncomprehended past in the present is not without its consequences. It can, for example, lead to a ritualized self-stylization as a victim, such as wearing a yellow star as a sign of political protest. This is presumably not just an instance of tasteless, false identification with the real victims of National Socialism. Rather, the past appears here as a subterranean fear, stemming from inherited feelings of guilt and anxiety which have been symbolically reversed and magically invoked. One presents oneself as a supposed victim in order to shake off the burden of guilt transmitted by one's parents. In so doing, however, the possibility of bringing this guilt to consciousness and dealing with it is lost.

In their book *The Inability to Mourn*, the Mitscherlichs have shown that, while history does not always repeat itself, the compulsion to repeat it is always realized in some way. No political event provides a better illustration of this claim than the German reaction to the Israeli invasion of Lebanon in 1982. It is important to remember, in this context, that Israel always possesses a double meaning in the Christian West: first as a reality (an aspect not to be discussed here) and second as a metaphor. It is a metaphor which stands in close relation to the Western image of the Jew and thus belongs to the historical context of anti-Semitism. If that is so, then it should be impossible in West Germany to judge Israel simply as the Israeli state, since the German consciousness in relation to the Jews has been darkened by a myth, in the face of which every attempt at enlightenment must look like magic. When Israel's behavior was characterized as "genocide," as a Holocaust, one could not help but feel that it was not the horrors of war, the helplessness of the Palestinians, or the suffering of the Lebanese victims that was really at issue here. Rather, it was as if the Jews were being spontaneously encouraged actually to commit genocide, so that the German sense of guilt could be excised through expiation and the fearful punishment anxiety finally lifted.

The Right has attempted to gain political capital from such reactions by ascribing them solely to the Left. But punishment anxiety, combined with fantasies of Jewish power connected with the state of Israel, are universally shared in Germany. In light of the reactions in 1982, the view that the pro-Israeli enthusiasm of 1967 in West German public opinion can be explained by an identification with the military successes of these "Prussians of the Middle East" must be revised. If it is true that guilty feelings toward the Jews are universal in Germany, then the noisy manifestations of joy at the victories won by the former victims were actually expressions of relief that the awaited punishment had been meted out to others, to the Arabs, and that expiation— albeit via the wrong people—had finally occurred.

The threatening presence of Jews in the German collective consciousness after Auschwitz has brought forth strange means of dealing with the past, such as the phenomenon of "covering memories" (*Deckerinnerung*). This term refers to a certain way of living with the past, one characterized by a new historical assiduity that brings one closer to the events of 1933–45, yet at the same time leaves out the source of one's own unease. Other victims of National Socialism are thus thrust into the foreground in order to avoid confronting the particularity of the extermination of the Jews, an act which is still felt to be exceptional. Let there be no misunderstanding: no hierarchy of victims is being advocated here. The point is not to rate Jewish victims higher than other groups that were also singled out by the Nazis for ethnic or biological reasons. The sacrifice of those exterminated because of anti-Semitism is no different in quality from that of those victims killed for reasons of so-called racial or social hygiene. It is only within the collective memory that a hierarchy of victims is first established. This may be a consequence of the fact that the fantasies linked to the different victims of Nazism touch various levels of historical memory. Thus anti-Judaism and anti-Semitism go far back into Western history and are, indeed, part of the founding myth of Christian civilization. Antagonism toward the Jews is older than racism. On the other hand, racism rests on deeper strata of the unconscious, evokes richer myths than either eugenics or so-called social hygiene. There thus exists an historically differentiated stratification of memories that pertain to the victims. This differential hierarchy of victims within the collective unconscious means that Auschwitz will be associated with the Nazis' principal victims for as long as historical memory lasts.

The guilt, the guilty conscience tied to Auschwitz and the Jews leaves the impression that the Christian reproach against the Jews for the crucifixion of Christ has been reversed. The supposed guilt of the Jews for killing God has now, through Auschwitz, been thrown back on Christianity itself. If one proceeds from the collective feelings of the younger generation, then Auschwitz appears to have been the true crucifixion. In light of this deep-seated emotional disposition, all attempts to normalize life after, and in spite of, Auschwitz, that is, to emerge from the shadow of this monstrous occurrence, are doomed to failure. More than this, it is to be feared that those who remind us of the gravity of Auschwitz will be blamed for this remembrance and in such a way as if the mythical murder of God were at stake.

Negative symbiosis as a result of Auschwitz also means that Jewish encounters with this event are also accompanied by "covering memories"—although, of course, for opposite reasons. In addition to the incomprehensibility, abstractness, and monstrosity of industrially organized mass murder, whose secular meaning becomes understandable even to the victims only with greater distance, there are also other reasons for the tenacity of "covering memories," reasons that are directly related to the extermination itself. The victims cannot bear the fact that at Auschwitz something senseless and purposeless occurred. To be sure, the genesis of the Holocaust is unimaginable without a historically latent anti-Semitisim. But while traditional anti-Semitism was a requirement of the Shoah, the Holocaust did not of necessity flow from such anti-Semitism. Integrating industrial mass murder into the confines of an exclusively Jewish view of history removes it from its universal context and transfigures the Holocaust into a meaningful national martyrdom.

A further element in a misleading Jewish perception of the Shoah is shame: shame at the supposed failure to resist; shame at the fact that the Jews allowed themselves to be led away "like lambs to the slaughter." This is not the place to rehearse the historical and sociological conditions that might have made resistance possible. Suffice it to say that "the Jews" as a coherent national group or a cohesive collectivity did not exist in Europe. The Nazis, especially in Germany, first had to define Jews in order to treat them accordingly. What level of social and political density would have been necessary within an atomized population, one which had been brought together in the first place only by the Nazis, in order to have made military resistance even thinkable? For such is the notion of resistance seemingly contained in the implicit reproach; the image of lambs being led away to the slaughter.

If Auschwitz is already difficult enough, even with the benefit of hindsight, for survivors and the younger generation to understand as methodical, but not preplanned, industrial mass murder, how impossible it must have been for the victims, living in the shadow of war and blinded by historical experience, to comprehend what was happening around them. On the contrary, the fact that military resistance occurred at all is what truly requires an explanation, not the understandable mass passivity in the face of such terror. Paradoxically, resistance occurred in those places where people, interpreting their experiences on the basis of tradition, believed they were defending themselves against a pogrom, or where, for political or other reasons, a degree of social cohesion existed that made possible the level of organization necessary for military action.

It may be difficult to accept such an interpretation. But in light of human experience and conceptual capacity formed by Western rationality, the victims could not react in any other way. The hopelessness of their situation alone left them no other choice. The question that Jews ask themselves time and again, why there was no resistance—that shame-filled reproach, that as victims they acted dishonorably—is based on an insistent refusal to understand Auschwitz. This lasting ignorance leads one to suppose that, because of its secular monstrosity, this occurrence should not be understood.

A Jewish barrier to understanding Auschwitz is also created by attempting to derive an exclusively particularist interpretation from it. As mentioned above, as an expression of anti-Semitism the mass extermination would be comprehensible only in a narrowly Jewish view of history; understanding the Holocaust only as a giant pogrom would confirm the correctness and necessity of the classic reaction to European persecution of the Jews—a withdrawal from the world of the non-Jews. The Zionist answer to the anti-Semitism of persecution may on the whole be a perfectly consistent one. Yet such an answer is necessarily wrong and fruitless when the classic anti-Semitism of persecution becomes an anti-Semitism of extermination.

This was novel: the Nazis sought to deprive the Jews of life wherever they could get hold of them, even in Palestine. Historically speaking, of course, it is pointless to speculate about what might have happened if Montgomery had not stopped Rommel at El Alamein. But one thing is certain: the nagging feeling (a constant reminder of Auschwitz) that one survived because of pure chance, rather than because of Zionism, must be so unbearable that it is masked by a "historiosophic" construction of reality: Israel as a reaction, an answer to the Holocaust that is once again integrated into a view of history shaped by traditional anti-Semitism. Because of the proto-Zionist conscious-ness of Jews after 1945, Israel has become a constituent part of the "covering memory," part of that plug of memory, of that psychic crutch, that is sup-posed to, and in the last analysis really does, give life after Auschwitz a mean-ing and a purpose. For the conflict in and over Palestine, the link between Nazi mass murder and traditional anti-Semitism is of course disastrous. On the one hand, the uniqueness of the Shoah is inadmissably extended; on the other hand, the confrontation between Jews and Arabs which is at the heart of this conflict is falsely turned into one between Jews and non-Jews—a re-versal of the anti-Semitic world view. In this way, both the causes of the con-flict and the possibilities of its solution are ignored. In such an interpretation, the confrontation between Jews and Arabs fits into the hopeless and apoc-alyptic opposition between Jews and non-Jews.

And what of Jews in Germany? For them, more than for anyone else, Israel represents a psychic support, a substitute identity, because they must explain over and again, both to themselves and to Jews elsewhere, why they, by living in the hangman's house, have helped give the impression that after Auschwitz normality has returned to German-Jewish relations—a normality that implies that nothing happened. This certainly corresponds to the interests of the West German state's representatives. The presence of Jews here was of great importance for the moral rehabilitation of the Germans; the existence of Jew-ish communities in the Federal Republic bolstered its international legit-imacy. The current and increasingly marked reidentification of Germans with Germany continues to depend on the presence of Jews as a support for this German desire for normality.

The presence of Jews in Germany after the war was not the result of a re-turn; it was not a pitiful effort to reestablish contact with a past that was gone forever. The majority of Jews living here are, rather, displaced persons who have stayed behind, remnants of that stream of hundreds of thousands who came here in the wake of the Allied armies as they waited to immigrate to other countries. They saw their presence here as hardly more than tempo-rary; in their view, they were not living in Germany, which in fact no longer existed as a political entity, but rather in zones of occupation under the pro-tection of the Allies. As the flotsam and jetsam of history, they had been washed ashore in Germany and yet were at the same time not really there. Moreover, the Jews here are mainly of eastern European origin, above all from Poland. As paradoxical as it may seem in light of the mass extermina-tions, their rejection of their native country may have been even stronger than their feelings toward Germany and the Germans. Polish anti-Semitism was an everyday affair, an element of the nation's culture, an experience that had been psychologically integrated over the centuries and was therefore tangible. Industrial mass murder, Auschwitz, was abstract, and everyday feelings are hard to mobilize against an abstraction. This may serve as the seemingly par-adoxical explanation for the fact that non-German Jews apparently can live more easily in Germany than even in countries where they have experienced traditional and thus more "imaginable" anti-Semitism.

Nevertheless, these Jews became ever more conscious of their presence in the land of the Germans as the Federal Republic gained its sovereignty and life there was normalized. The fact that they had landed in Germany during the late 1940s or early 1950s without really meaning to do so became increasingly irrelevant. The more German Germany became, and becomes, the more strongly the Jews will run up against that history that, in so terrible a manner, both binds them to and separates them from the Germans.

What keeps the Jews in Germany today? Prosperity alone is not a sufficient explanation. Worldy considerations may have been important for many, but the real reasons probably lie deeper. It sounds overdrawn, even presumptuous: Jews in Germany, disparaged and ostracized by Jews in the rest of the world for their presence in that country, seem to stay there because by maintaining the closest possible proximity to the scene of the crime and to the collectivity of the perpetrators, they maintain the strongest ties to the past. It is as if in Germany they could make good the eternal loss, fill the void created by Auschwitz. There the memory is strongest, there their constant presence challenges the collectivity of the perpetrators to remember their deeds—as if in Germany, with the help of the Germans, that which was lost could be found again.

Such a linkage renders the negative symbiosis, the relationship between Germans and Jews after Auschwitz, even more difficult and conflict-ridden as the distance from the events themselves increases. This is true especially as the passive normality that has been characteristic of Germany since 1945 is transformed into an active normalization of the Germans as Germans, a change that is taking place because of a desire for reconciliation with the generation of the parents, a phenomenon which is being expressed in German political culture as the demand for a positive national identity.

German national identity after Auschwitz? One suspects that the desire to make this a reality will run up against the absolute barrier of Auschwitz, with the result that the significance of Auschwitz—not only as the mass murder of Jews, but also as a break with civilization itself—will be pushed aside, or sidestepped through a process of historicization. The tendencies pointing in such a direction are evident. It may be that after forty years—the span of a biblical generation—the collective stays are loosening, that the rigidity of the older generation, which has until now passed along its reserved emotions in eloquent silence, is now dissolving in the children, thereby making it possible to live out the desire for reconciliation with the past.

As a result, new light is being shed on the much-lamented inability to mourn. What sort of mourning was meant here? Mourning for the victims of Nazism, empathy with the Jews? This sort of identification led in the 1960s to a break with the stubbornly silent older generation. The rift was as deep as an abyss; a call for reconciliation had the effect of an invitation to treason. The pent-up fury of the older generation at the student protest movement, which began with the memory of Auschwitz, testified to a conflict of generations that was provoked by the attempt to mourn the victims.

Or was the lament over the inability to mourn instead directed at the loss of one's own relations? Did the mourning perhaps concern those who belonged to the collectivity of the perpetrators and had been lost? Both forms of mourning were, perhaps should have been, meant. But this is hardly possible. This contradiction encapsulates the dilemma of younger Germans: empathy with the victims seems to block the path to reconciliation with their parents; and reconciliation with their parents gives the impression of a betrayal of that empathy with the victims. Today, the balance of feelings is tilting toward normality, toward reconciliation with oneself and the nation's past. The examples are legion—to say nothing of the attack on memory festively carried out at Bitburg. The powerful of this world seem to be growing tired of admonitions and reminders of the past, of Auschwitz. Furthermore, such reminders have a disruptive effect on the future of the Atlantic alliance. The United States brought power and morality to Europe in 1944; only the power remains. In recompense for stationing the intermediate range missiles, it was agreed to foreswear reminders of the past, and thus also of the symbol of that morality, represented by the Jews.

Jürgen Habermas has spoken of an "unburdening of the past" (*Entsorgung der Vergangenheit*). Against the background of the nuclear present the implication is that Auschwitz represents something like a radioactive mass, whose half-life is obviously unknown. The attempt simply to dispose of is is unlikely to prove successful. If the drive for "unburdening" the feelings turns out to be insatiable, then history with its ever admonishing Jews may not repeat itself, but that ritualized compulsion to repeat will dominate the political culture of the Federal Republic.

And the Jews? Can they stand silently by and allow Auschwitz to be declared part of the distant past in Germany, can they agree that living memory be historicized in order to be free of it? Jews in Germany can legitimate themselves in their own minds only so long as they understand themselves as guardians of memory in this country. They cannot avoid this task without risking the loss of their honor. Max Horkheimer noted such a consequence in his *Notizen* already in the mid-1960s, as many were ahistorically invoking works he had written *before* the Holocaust:

"We Jewish intellectuals who have escaped a martyr's death under Hitler, we have only one task. That is to help ensure that those horrors never return and are never forgotten. We must unite with those who died in unspeakable anguish. Our thought, our work, belongs to them. The accident of our escape should not weaken our unity with them, but strengthen it. Whatever we experience must stand under the sign of that horror that was meant for us as well as for them. Their death is the truth of our life. We are here to express their despair and their longing."[5]

Notes

1. Louis de Jong, "Die Niederlande und Auschwitz," in *Vierteljahrshefte für Zeitgeschichte* (1969): 16.
2. Hannah Arendt and Karl Jaspers, *Briefwechsel 1926–1969*, ed. Lotte Köhler and Hans Janer (Munich, 1985), 90.
3. Hans Dieckmann, "Angstträume und Wirklichkeit. Reaktionen unseres Unbewussten auf Atomkrieg und ökologische Krise," in Klaus Horn and Eva Senghaas-Knobloch, eds., *Friedensbewegung: Persönliches und Politisches* (Frankfurt, 1983), 62.
4. Ibid., 69.
5. Max Horkheimer, *Notizen 1950–1969 und Dämmerung*, ed., Werner Brede and Alfred Schmidt (Franfurt, 1974), 273.

15. Coping with the Past: The West German Labor Movement and the Left

Andrei S. Markovits

The Bitburg incident, the controversy surrounding Rainer Werner Fassbinder's *Garbage, the City and Death,* the award of the Goethe Prize to Ernst Jünger, the impassioned debates concerning the construction of a House of History in Bonn and a German Historical Museum in Berlin, and most certainly the still-continuing *Historikerstreit*—consuming some of the leading German historians and historians of Germany with a passion rarely seen in academic circles—these events are merely among the most visible manifestations that the past and its *Aufarbeitung* are far from "normalized" in today's Federal Republic.[1] Once again Germany and the Germans seem to disquiet if not downright haunt the politically attentive public in the United States and Europe. While the substance and form of the controversial issues and, above all, the geopolitical context of their articulation, differ markedly from the late 1920s and early 1930s, *les incertitudes allemandes,* as the French so characteristically put it, still pertain in the view of many observers both within and outside Germany. It is only against the backdrop of the still un-solved "German question"—of which a perhaps permanently inadequate *Aufarbeitung* of the past forms an integral part—that these events have at-tained such central importance in the public debate concerning contemporary Germany reality and political identity.[2] With the lulling days of the famous "economic miracle" relegated to memory in an increasingly competitive and uncertain world market which has caused similar dislocations and structural problems in the German economy as elsewhere in the advanced industrial world, the specter of Germany's past lends many of these issues a particular urgency well beyond their apparent meaning. Given Germany's past, 2.5 mil-lion unemployed in today's Federal Republic mean something more foreboding and troublesome to the world than do even more scandalous conditions in Great Britain, France and virtually all of Western Europe with the notable exception of such small countries as Austria, Sweden, and Switzerland. In Germany's case, the perennial question, "Isn't Bonn still basically Weimar, especially when the chips are down?" never lurks far from the surface.[3] No other European country bears a similar burden, thus making "Germany" in general and the Federal Republic in particular unique.

It is therefore not by chance that the debates concerning the substance of these issues are inextricably linked to a related matter, namely whether these events were unique and *sui generis* or in fact comparable to occurrences that happened at different times and in other places. While once again reemerging with a vengeance, especially in the Historians' Debate, the uniqueness versus relativism controversy has been present in most of the scholarship dealing with the recent German past. After all, much of the disagreement between the "structuralists" (sometimes also known as "functionalists", though neither should be confused with the sociological school of "structural functionalism") and the "intentionalists" focused on the latter arguing that it was Hitler's unique intentions which were mainly responsible for the horrors of the Third Reich and the former contending that they emerged out of a constellation of bureaucratic politics quite comparable to that of other advanced industrial states.

It seems to me that uniqueness, too, is relational, hence subject to an inherent relativism. This is the very foundation of the comparative method in history and the social sciences, even—some would say especially—when a single case is used to explain a certain phenomenon.[4] It is only in this context that the many singularities—or exceptionalisms —make any sense, be they American (as in "American exceptionalism," i.e., the absence of a large, mass-based labor party in the United States making it "unique" among advanced industrial countries); French (as in "French exceptionalism," i.e., France being "unique" among Western liberal democracies by virtue of its retarded economic development); or German (as in the "German *Sonderweg*," i.e., Germany's "unique" political creation between 1933 and 1945 as a consequence of the country's "unique" political and economic developments during the nineteenth century). In all of these cases, uniqueness can only be a valuable analytic category if it is implicitly comparative, which, in turn, makes it relational and relative.

The uniqueness of German fascism was the Holocaust, i.e. the systematic attempt to use every available means on the part of the state apparatus totally to annihilate an entire people defined by racial criteria, regardless of where its members might reside in the world.[5] But one can only understand this uniquely destructive dimension in National Socialism if one compares it to other fascisms (say Italian, Spanish, Japanese, or Romanian), other tyrannies (say Stalin's Soviet Union or Kim Il Sung's North Korea) and other regimes engaged in mass murder (say once again Stalin's Soviet Union and Pol Pot's Cambodia). It is, after all, this particular uniqueness—mostly referred to as the "Holocaust"—which sets the National Socialist agenda apart from other horrors of history. "Coping with the past"—what I have preferred to call *Aufarbeitung* (instead of *Bewältigung*) *der Vergangenheit*—refers first and foremost to the Holocaust. No one feels this more deeply and instinctively than the Germans. The fact that little had been done about this in terms of concrete, tangible and lasting *Aufarbeitung* over the past forty-two years attests first and foremost to the enormity of the crime, its equally enormous legacy and the political constellations in the domestic and international realms which partly impeded, partly neglected and partly even failed to recognize the necessity and validity of a thorough "coping with the past."

It will be the task of this essay to discuss briefly whether, if and how the German labor movement—as represented by the Social Democratic Party (SPD) and the German Trade Union Federation (DGB)—and the Left, widely construed, have coped with this unique event in recent German history. The results, I am afraid to say, will not prove encouraging.

1945/49–1967: Amnesia, Displacement, Reorientation, and Reorganization

Let me start with a general *caveat* regarding any discussion of "coping with the past." We always assert—far from incorrectly I would argue—that the rapid onslaught of the Cold War and the ensuing "Economic Miracle" (*Wirtschaftswunder*) somehow replaced any possible *Aufarbeitung* with a *Verdrängung* (repression) of the past. While this "crowding out"—sort of a Gresham's Law of memory management—undoubtedly occurred, it would be helpful to contemplate a counterfactual: what indeed would have happened had there been an earnest "coping with the past" immediately following the war? Could this realistically have happened given the enormity of the crime? Moreover, who is to say that this *Aufarbeitung* would have occurred in the "good" sense, i.e., filled the Germans with that remorse and comprehensive reeducation which were to make the past the centerpiece of an ongoing and active process of self-evaluation in the public and private spheres? Could this really have occurred in a devastated country, populated by hungry and destitute people, confused about their fate, hateful of their predicament and resenting their occupation?

Each of the actors had to proceed gingerly immediately following the end of World War II. Their balancing act had to lead them along a path which obviously avoided the mistakes committed during the Weimar period (ones that had helped bring about National Socialism's eventual triumph over the frail republic) while at the same time it established a definite continuity for the purposes of legitimation with the pre-Nazi past. In a certain sense, this was easier for the Left than for the Right in the late 1940s, since there could be little argument that the Left, too, had been victimized and brutalized by the Nazis' horror regime. This relative "ease" led to an amnesia on the Left's part vis-à-vis the Holocaust. Since the world was fully aware of the fact that the Left had nothing to do with these atrocities, the Left hence was spared the difficult task of addressing this issue with the determination and rigor necessitated by the enormity of the events.

Instead, the Left remained completely preoccupied with its own Weimar trauma, i.e., the irreconcilable split and internecine conflict between communists and Social Democrats. A thorough perusal of the literature on this period indicates that this question, more than any other, captured the Left's attention. Somehow, strategies had to be devised, lest the dreadful Weimar past repeat itself, once again leading to democracy's demise on German soil. As will be indicated later, this strategy was blessed with remarkable success in the world of industrial relations.

A number of other urgent topics prevented the Left from addressing the Holocaust at the time. Foremost among them was, of course, the whole complex of a unified Germany as opposed to a divided one with each part to develop into a loyal satrap of its respective occupier. This unification versus division debate—though ultimately not decided by the German Left and at the time still exacting a rare intracamp unity in favor of a unified Germany—ironically once again later led to yet another rematch between the Social Democrats and the Communist Party (now called the SED in East Germany) on a different playing field of politics.

The Left's amnesia regarding the Holocaust also resulted from the theoretical legacy of its rather crude, mechanical, and economistic interpretation of Marx and Marxism.[6] Seeing the "Jewish question," like any other ethnic politics, as an epiphenomenon to capitalism, the German Left hardly needed another theoretical explanation for what happened at Auschwitz. With National Socialism subsumed under fascism, which in turn continues to be seen by the Left merely as a particularly heinous political expression of a crisis-ridden and moribund capitalism, there was little room for an analysis of the Holocaust as an event *sui generis* in the larger context of an advanced capitalist environment.

Developed to its fullest as a state ideology, this interpretation of history became the cornerstone of the German Democratic Republic and remains essential to its self-legitimation to this day.[7] Initially deriving its legitimacy from a complete break with the past, the German Democratic Republic had to be less concerned with establishing continuity than its western neighbor, whose *raison d'être* and very identity evolved via its claim to be the sole legitimate representative of all Germans, which of course meant being willy nilly the official successor to the Third Reich. In the East, the solution was simple. The Holocaust, having been an epiphenomenon of capitalism, had little relevance to a new socialist Germany. The extermination of six million Jews was interpreted as completely ancillary and incidental to the fascist politics of a capitalist economy. As such, the Holocaust in the German Democratic Republic remains to this day subsumed under one of many crimes perpetrated by the capitalist Nazis.[8]

The Left's increasingly beleaguered position in the West led to an even greater clinging to its old ways. The sanctity of the working class, for example, represented just such an issue. Suspending all debate on the topic, the Left rejected any notion of collective guilt in dealing with the Holocaust because this would have automatically included the working class as well, which—being by definition anticapitalist, hence antifascist—was not only an empirically erroneous but, more importantly, theoretically untenable position.

The Left's amnesia concerning the Holocaust led to an eventual monopolization of the "Jewish question" by the conservative forces around the Federal Republic's first chancellor, Konrad Adenauer. It was this political camp which successfully filled this important arena left virtually untouched by the West German Left. The conservative camp recognized that for the Federal Republic to develop its core identity as the sole legitimate representative of all Germans, the country had to assume some responsibility for the Third Reich. Yet, the Federal Republic at the same time had to distance itself from the atrocities commited by the Nazi regime. This was not only essential to gain reentry into the family of nations but also to reestablish self-esteem among a morally battered citizenry. This was in good part achieved by the instrumentalization of the "Jewish question" and the Holocaust.[9]

Concretely, this meant that the conservative forces envisioned the Federal Republic's main mode of distancing itself from the Nazi past by casting this episode as a unique and aberrant period of brutal anti-Semitism. Once the Federal Republic and its governing elites could establish themselves as bonafide philo-Semites, so the calculation, the most heinous ties to the Nazi past would automatically be severed while the more "innocuous" ones could continue more or less unbated. Thus, just as the German Democratic Republic and most of the West German Left, "instrumentalized" the Holocaust by simplifying it for their own purposes of legitimation, so, too, did the Federal Republic led by its conservative state builders. To the latter, the Holocaust was a singular political construct of evil men. Almost never did the official ideology of the West German state analyze the Holocaust in the larger context of German history, European anti-Semitism, imperialism, fascism, racism, or capitalism. Indeed, just as the German Democratic Republic used the Holocaust to break with capitalism, so the Federal Republic employed it to legitimate the "reconstruction" of capitalism on its territory. By dividing the Germans into "good" and "bad"—not like in the German Democratic Republic along "capitalist" and "proletarian," but rather along "Nazi" and "non-Nazi" lines—the Federal Republic could once again claim respect from Germany and Germans if it could only emphasize the "good" and at least contain, if not extirpate, the "bad."

Thus developed the myth of the "good" Wehrmacht and the "bad" SS; the "good" putschists of July 20, 1944 and the "bad" henchmen of the Gestapo. This, of course, is not to argue that the Gestapo and the SS were not indeed "worse" than the armed forces and the aristocratic resistance fighters who only wanted to do away with Hitler by the time the war was lost and return to a pre-1918 Germany without a republic and dominated by Junkers and industrialists. Rather, it is to point to the very limited, hence flawed, analysis by the hegemonic Right and its conservative allies of the complexities of the Nazi terror regime which in the first half of the 1950s may have helped the legitimation process of this new republic but certainly failed to construct a basis for its citizens to understand, and ultimately cope with, their recent past and the larger issue of the German-Jewish relationship in the twentieth century.

The full unfolding of the Cold War not only stopped even the most meager attempts at "denazification" and "reeducation" which the Allies had introduced soon after the war, but it introduced a new and very welcome bogeyman (*Feindbild*) which by the early 1950s had become part and parcel of mainstream political culture in the Federal Republic, completely eclipsing even the faint remnants of a dominant preoccupation with National Socialism. Anticommunism became the order of the day, and—as can be well imagined—this made the already beleaguered life of the West German Left hardly conducive to any renewed offensives concerning their own and the Germans' relationship to the Holocaust. Pushed into the defensive, the Left simply embraced with added vigor a major mechanism of displacement which had developed into one of the mainstays of the Federal Republic's foreign policy and self-legitimation at this time continuing uninterruptedly to the present: the special relationship to the State of Israel.

Nowhere has this been more manifest and more openly sought than on the part of the German Left. Especially its two institutional representatives, the SPD and the trade union organization (the DGB), have been in the vanguard (no Leninist pun intended!) of fostering this special relationship as an act of reconciliation between Germans and Jews and as the most important ingredient in the Germans' coping with their past. It is crucial to remember that it was the West German Left which actively initiated personal contacts between Germans and Jews as of 1952 via the first meetings between members of the SPD and the Israeli Labor Party (Mapai) and also some unionists belonging to the DGB and the Israeli Trade Union Federation (Histadrut).[10] In addition to the establishment of close ties between the two countries' labor movements, which have lasted to this day, and the inauguration of German-Israeli links in the societal realm preceding those on the state level by over ten years, the organized Left's engagement on behalf of Israel also had major implications in domestic politics. Had it not been for the SPD's unequivocal engagement on behalf of reparation payments to the Jews and Israel, and its completely unified bloc vote in the Bundestag on behalf of these measures, the 1953 reparation law would have never been created.

While it is true that Konrad Adenauer's personal shame and genuinely felt disgust at the Nazi atrocities represented one of the major reasons behind the Federal Republic's reparation to the Jews and Israel, these sentiments were hardly shared by all Bundestag delegates of Adenauer's party, the Christian Democratic Union (CDU), and its Bavarian affiliate, the Christian Social Union (CSU). Indeed, the political Right and conservative forces in West Germany were very much against any restitution to the Jews and Israel, since they viewed this act on the part of the state as clearly being tantamount to admitting unilateral guilt, something this political camp in the Federal Republic has steadfastly refused to do until today. In addition to the obvious issues of guilt and the generally low popularity of this measure in a period when the Federal Republic was still far from being economically prosperous, many representatives of the conservative parties expressed a pro-Arab sentiment, duly reflecting a tacit but widespread consensus among the West German business community at the time.

The displacement via Israel of coping with the past also assumed center stage for West Germany's leftist intellectuals. Often located to the left of the SPD and the trade unions, these intellectuals embraced Israel by the mid-1950s as an example of a socialist society *with* democratic politics. More important than the actual reality of Israel was, however, the fact that these leftist intellectuals used the concept of Israel as a mechanism to deal with their own immense guilt and that of their silent countrymen. These Germans belonged to a younger generation that had only passively experienced National Socialism, and Israel provided for them a positive identification with Jews. This was a German generation that basically had never encountered Jews in its daily experience and somehow wanted to atone for the crimes of its elders. Tacit philo-Semitism in West Germany was transformed into something active by a vocal minority of radical intellectuals.

Leftist students went to Israel to work on kibbutzim, to get to know the country and basically to repent for their parents' sins. They formed friendship societies with Israeli students and established Israel clubs at West German universities. Above all, they protested West German complacency about the many high-ranking ex-Nazis in important official positions in both the public and private sectors. Led by the Sozialistischer Deutscher Studentenbund (SDS) which was the SPD's official student affiliate until it was expelled in 1961 for not supporting the party's rightward turn at Godesberg, many West German leftists at numerous universities protested the presence of West German engineers in Egypt's missile industry and rejoiced in the death sentence meted out against Eichmann by an Israeli court. To these young leftists, Israel represented a marked contrast to what they perceived as a politically dull West Germany, dominated by a preoccupation with material acquisitions and fearful of any radical challenges to the increasingly comfortable status quo. Then, in 1965, Israel and the Federal Republic opened a new era in German-Jewish relations by officially recognizing each other and opening diplomatic relations. Two years later came the Six Day War. As discussed below, it was to represent yet another major turning point in the complex relationship between Germans and Jews, mainly altering the leftist intellectuals' perception of Israel, the Jewish question and their relation to both.

Perhaps the most successful and lasting legacy of reorientation and reorganization on the part of the West German working class (as a direct response to the National Socialist experience) has to be the formation of a unitary trade union structure (*Einheitsgewerkschaft*) and the industrial union (*Industriegewerkschaft*).[11] Traumatized by the constant internecine battles between communist and Social Democratic workers on the shop floors of the Weimar Republic, Germany's union leaders were determined never to let a similar experience weaken, even paralyze, the working class. A number of models were conceived in the various exiles, Hitler's concentration camps, in the resistance or wherever Germany's labor leaders found themselves during the Nazi regime. However, all of them had two things in common: the complete obliteration of industrial representation along party lines; and the abolition of multiunionism in one plant, firm or company. Thus, from the very beginning of the postwar period, the union movement established itself as unitary—that is, encompassing all organized workers regardless of party affiliation—representing an organization which was nominally independent of all political parties yet not neutral of politics. Furthermore, again countering the Weimar experience, the unions alleviated interunion competition at the workplace and among workers of differing skills by decreeing that only one union could exist in one industry and, above all, in one plant. These two organizational innovations, the *Einheitsgewerkschaft* and *Industriegewerkschaft,* have remained the most uncontested foundations of the postwar West German union structure. Attacks upon these concepts in subsequent years in the form of creating splits along political lines have always been met with unmitigated opposition from all quarters of the labor movement, legitimating their actions in light of labor's fatal mistakes during Weimar which led to its repression by the Nazis.

It would not be far-fetched to view the SPD's Godesberg revision as part of a reorientation in the wake of the Nazi trauma. The party emerged immediately after the end of the war with basically the same outlook on politics that it had developed by the early 1900s and that it maintained, alas, with so much rigidity until the bitter end in the spring of 1933. With the possible exception of its anticommunism which—given the developments regarding the German Democratic Republic—became even less compromising during the 1950s, the party's analysis of capitalism and its political strategies therein differed little in Bonn from those pursued in Weimar. Yet there was a constant awareness in the decade after 1945 that the SPD's old ways, its strategic and intellectual stagnation were at least woefully inadequate against, if not complicitous in, National Socialism's rapid triumph. Ultimately, the party could only learn one of two lessons in the wake of the Nazi legacy: it could decide to move to the left, practice for once in reality what it continued to preach in print for decades and become a genuine counterforce to the capitalist reconstruction which defined the Federal Republic from the very day of its inception. Conversely, it, too, could identify with this new and seemingly successful order, and remain content with assuming the role of a loyal opposition to the powers that be. Traumatized by communism, the SPD coped with the past by fully embracing the second option which, after all, rendered the party some benefits in bringing it to state power between 1966 and 1982. Godesberg would not have happened without Social Democracy's traumas in the fall of Weimar, the Nazi experience and communism's victory in the eastern part of Germany. Haunted by the specter of totalitarianism, the SPD developed by the end of the 1950s into the staunchest advocate of the liberal democratic order.

One should, of course, never minimize this position. It was by virtue of this posture that the party took up the battle with vigor and conviction against the growing forces on the Right which wanted to close the past by having the statutes of limitation on Nazi war crimes expire. Repeatedly as of the early 1960s—in 1960, 1965, 1969 and 1979 to be exact—the SPD mustered all its parliamentary powers to argue on a number of levels the uniqueness of the Nazi crimes and the Germans' obligation to themselves and the Nazis' victims never to forget this period by facilely letting Nazi crimes expire like any other.[12] The SPD's valiant efforts were not only crowned with the tangible success of never having Nazi war crimes expire, but also with a moral triumph vis-à-vis the rest of the world which witnessed Social Democratic empathy at its best.

The Post-1967 Period: Major Shifts, Though No Solutions

Following the Israeli "Blitzkrieg" led by the "desert fox" Dayan in "Rommel-like" fashion, there occurred a nearly 180-degree turn in the way West Germans related to Israel and the Jews. Suddenly the political Right, whose moderate faction had previously maintained a silent philo-Semitism and whose more radical wing still came out with anti-Israeli statements bordering on anti-Semitism, rejoiced at Israel's "superman-like" victory over the "lazy" and "cowardly" Arabs. Led by the influential Springer press, which enjoys near-monopoly status among daily newspapers in large areas of the Federal Republic, the panegyrics regarding Israel's accomplishments often reached orgiastic dimensions.

One could not help but feel a certain relief among West German conservatives regarding their bottled-up guilt with respect to the Jews: Finally they had proved to be men; they had showed the world that they are fighters just like we were; they had stopped being helpless victims; their victory promised to free us from our guilt. Israel became the unquestioned darling of West Germany's conservative circles. Few tried to hide their vicarious pleasure with the Israeli victory, and many went so far as to bestow the ultimate compliment on Jews: they planned, thought, and acted just the way Germans did in the good old days.

The Left, suffering from a view of Jews and Israel just as simplistic as the Right, reacted as unidimensionally to the Six Day War as did its political foes. The student Left, now completely caught up in the turmoil of the New Left in such key university cities as Berlin and Frankfurt, abruptly reversed its position. From being Israel's most outspoken supporter in the Federal Republic, it became the harshest critic of the Jewish state. Suddenly the Jews ceased to be victims. Rather they basked in the glory of victory, praised by the much-hated Springer press, which on the same page it extolled Israeli accomplishments also called for brutal repression of the West German student movement by the police.

An Israeli victory, achieved with such precision and efficiency, and applauded by a reactionary West German establishment and the United States (which was, in the meantime, busy dropping napalm on Vietnamese villages) could not at this time be anything but highly suspect in the eyes of a young German leftist. What happened to the Jews? Suddenly they exhibited traits previously associated only with militaristic and repressive regimes, above all the Nazis. Maybe the Israelis were in fact the new "Nazis" and their victims, i.e., the Palestinians, the new "Jews." Zionism, being a "fascist" political formation, equalled National Socialism. Thus was the previously simplistic philo-Semitism of the student Left transformed in a matter of months into a rabid anti-philo-Semitism which expressed itself not only in anti-Zionist sentiments but often bordered on the old anti-Semitic clichés of the traditional Right. By the end of the 1960s, positions in the Federal Republic regarding Israel and the Jews had been reversed. Now it was the conservatives who approved of virtually anything Israel did, while the radical Left not only opposed Israel's actions but also questioned the legitimacy of its existence.

Whatever this reversal meant for internal West German politics, it clearly attested to only one thing: the citizens of the Federal Republic, be they on the left or right, had failed to cope with their own past. Their relationship to Israel simply mirrored the one-dimensionality with which the Germans had tried to overcome their own historical encounters with the Jews.

The Left's post-1967 views and attitudes have more or less remained intact to this day. To the vast majority of Social Democrats and trade unionists, the friendship with Israel—if not with its rightist governments which led the country for much of the time since 1977—continues to assume as great an importance as it did prior to June 1967. Institutional ties have not abated and personal contacts between the two countries' labor movements are as intensive as ever. Whereas the SPD's criticism of Israel has intensified over the last twenty years, the party has never questioned the fundamental necessity and legitimacy of a Jewish state, and has always been careful to include explicit rebuttals of Palestinian radicalism and rejectionism. Unlike the radical Left, the moderates gathered in the organized labor movement and the SPD carefully point out that comprehending the development and necessity of Zionism hardly means condoning everything the Israeli government does, just as understanding Palestinian aspirations does not *ipso facto* amount to approval of the most hateful, anti-Israeli elements within the Palestinian national movement.

The legacy of 1968 spawned a new era in European politics. So-called "new social movements" arose everywhere, clustered around "new" issues such as feminism, peace, ecology, and nuclear energy to mention but the most internationally common. While it would be nothing short of irresponsible to make sweeping generalizations about such a complex phenomenon comprising such a motley group of participants and a multitude of political ideas and strategies, it would certainly not be incorrect to see the new social movements as direct challengers of the old political and social order which has usually placed them in direct competition with each country's traditional Left. The very fact that none of this has occurred with greater vigor, success, and significance than in the Federal Republic of Germany attests in and of itself to the complex issue of coping with Germany's uniquely burdened past. One simply cannot understand the staying power of the New Left and its legacy in the form of a highly politicized subculture, leaving few, if any, of West Germany's traditional private and public institutions untouched, without putting these developments into the context of some sort of response by the postwar generation to the troubled past of their elders. It was this milieu which created the Green Party, arguably among Europe's most interesting, innovative, and exciting political actors since 1945.

While it is true that many among the Greens and their sympathizers see themselves as "neither left nor right but ahead," thus consciously defying conventional political categorizations, it would not be wrong to consider the Green Party on virtually any dimension as being objectively on the Left of the West German political spectrum. (The SPD, I am certain, would sadly corroborate this assessment.) Hence, a few words on the Greens' coping with the past, especially in connection with the Holocaust and German-Jewish relations, seem appropriate in concluding this essay.

On the positive side, their record during their brief tenure is quite remarkable. The Greens have thus far been the only party in the history of the West German Bundestag to dismiss one of its representatives merely for having been a member of the NSDAP.[13] Never before was membership in the Nazi party sufficient reason for dismissal from the Bundestag on either side of the parliamentary aisle. Furthermore, it was only the Greens who unanimously and unequivocally opposed the Bitburg spectacle in the Bundestag. Moreover, it was only this party which deemed it important to commemorate the fortieth anniversary of the end of the Second World War with a trip to Auschwitz. Lastly, mention should also be made of the Greens' vehement opposition to the construction of either of the two museums which they view as an unnecessary exercise in excessive nationalism.

And yet, the Greens, too, have continued wearing some of the blinders regarding the Holocaust which their elders could never shed. Moreover, they maintained a number of distortions which the New Left bequeathed them in the wake of the events of the late 1960s and all throughout the decade of the 1970s. I would like to mention only some of the tasteless behavior during their visit to Israel, their demonstrations against Shimon Peres in Berlin, their complete failure and disconcern to mobilize protest activities in support of foreign Jewish groups during the Bitburg incident and some of the terrible analogies reached by Green sympathizers during Israel's invasion of Lebanon.[14] Much of this is understandable since to the Greens the Holocaust remains as much of an epiphenomenon as it always was in the history of the German Left—East or West, Old or New. Epiphenomena by their very nature require first and foremost explanation and understanding in terms of the phenomena which created them. As such, they are always subordinate events—

"sideshows" as one scholar called them in this context [15]—which remain subsumed by the "real thing." To the Greens—very much in the tradition of the German Left—fascism remains the "real thing." As long as the Greens continue to speak about German "fascism" as opposed to National Socialism, and as long as they view anti-Semitism as ancillary to fascism rather than as an integral part of National Socialism, they will always see Auschwitz as an epiphenomenon to fascist domination rather than as one of the driving forces of National Socialism. Yet until they understand Auschwitz, they will fail to comprehend Israel, Zionism, and the tormented relationship between Germans and Jews.

The Greens have been viciously maligned by conservatives in West Germany and the rest of the advanced industrial world for coming dangerously close to the Nazis and their precursors by virtue of their (the Greens' and Nazis') mutually shared romanticism, love of nature, and suspicion of modernity. This is not the place to refute this accusation which is mainly intended to discredit an unpleasant newcomer rather than to make an analytically sound analogy. Suffice it to say that the differences between Greens and Nazis—even in these areas of potential commonality—are far more pronounced than any similarities. Yet, by not being sufficiently aware of the continued uniqueness of Germany's burdened history in the eyes of her neighbors (both east and west) as well as those of the victims (such as the Jews, for example), some of the Greens' statements and policies have led to costly misunderstandings and undue anguish, and have at best only furthered the cause of those elements in the Federal Republic whom the Greens have rightly tried to confront precisely because of their eagerness to silence the past once and for all. One cannot avoid the impression that the Greens have on occasion unleashed a force which they not only fail to control but which ultimately works to the benefit of their political enemies. However, the very fact that they remain insensitive to this development attests to their incomplete coping with the German past. Whether they, or anyone else for that matter, will ever master this complex burden only time will tell.

Notes

1. Following Lily Gardner Feldman's pioneering distinction between *Vergangenheitsbewältigung* and *Vergangenheitsaufarbeitung*, I, too, would like to use the latter term, since I am of the opinion that a past—be it individual or collective—can never be *bewältigt*. In that sense, I find the English "coping with the past," which is the best approximation to *aufarbeitung*, much more useful than the often heard "coming to terms with the past," which clearly is closer to *Bewältigung*.
2. The "German question" haunts Europe again. Be it the French who are suddenly terrified by a pacifist, neutralist Germany led by politicized hippies, or the Eastern Europeans for whom the concept of *Mitteleuropa* has once again attained spe-

cial significance in this *glasnost*-dominated world, Germany's search for its identity is anxiously observed by all its neighbors, immediate or otherwise.

3. It is precisely because of the special role of unemployment in German history combined with its renewed persistence in the social fabric of the Federal Republic that it has been West German sociology in particular which has contributed some of the most innovative scholarship on (un)employment, work, and leisure. For an excellent review of this literature, see Hans-Peter Müller, "Wertwandel und Arbeitsmarktkrise: Zehn Thesen zur Diskussion um die 'Krise der Arbeitsgesellschaft,'" *Kölner Zeitschrift für Soziologie und Sozialpsychologie* 2 (1987).

4. For an excellent presentation of the inherently comparative nature of the well-designed case study, see Arend Lijphart "Comparative Politics and the Comparative Method," *American Political Science Review* 65 (September 1971): 682–93.

5. I mean to say here that *all* Jews, regardless how far they resided from Germany, were seen as deadly and dangerous enemies of the German people who had to be liquidated. In the history of enmity—and the policies informed by it—geographic distance and physical proximity usually correlate inversely with the intensity of antipathy and the readiness to act upon it. Thus, the further away an enemy, the less hatred one developed for it, at least in the pre-TV era of international communication. This did not pertain to the Nazi view of Jews. Geographic distance and physical proximity were irrelevant in the Nazis' pursuit of the Jews and their ultimate destruction.

6. This economistic interpretation of Marx and Marxism had gotten the German Left into deep trouble on a number of occasions, not least of which was the complete misreading of Hitler and the Nazis in the early 1930s. In that context, this misreading is particularly sad and incomprehensible.

7. For an excellent analysis of this phenomenon, see Matthew A. Siena, *Nazism— The View from East Germany: SED Antifascist Policy, 1949–1985* (unpublished senior thesis, Princeton University, 1986).

8. This emerges quite clearly in the German Democratic Republic's notion of reparation and restitution to the Jews. All Jews in the GDR receive higher pensions from the government than their non-Jewish compatriots. However, they obtain these pensions not as Jews but as "anti-fascists" or "victims of fascism." In addition to pensions, Jews in the German Democratic Republic have also been entitled to other special benefits such as apartments and easier access to certain educational facilities. These privileges, too, have been given to them as "anti-fascists" rather than as Jews.

9. On this concept of "instrumentalization," see the innovative article by Moishe Postone, "Anti-Semitism and National Socialism: Notes on the German Reaction to 'Holocaust,'" *New German Critique* (Winter 1980), esp. p. 98.

10. On this, see Lily Gardner Feldman, *The Special Relationship between West Germany and Israel* (Boston, 1984), 220, 224–25.

11. See Andrei S. Markovits, *The Politics of the Western German Trade Unions: Strategies of Class and Interest Representation in Growth and Crisis* (Cambridge, 1986), 61–83.

12. For an excellent treatment of the whole expiration-of-the-statute-of-limitation controversy, see Richard Hamilton Kreindler, *Die Verjährungsdebatten: Die Parlamentarischen Dimensionen der "Vergangenheitsbewältigung" in der Bundersrepublik*

Deutschland, 1960–1979 (unpublished master's thesis, Ludwig-Maximilians-Universität, Munich, 1982).

13. I am referring here to the Werner Vogel incident. To their dismay and shock, the Greens discovered in the spring of 1983 that the oldest member of their just-elected Bundestag delegation was a convinced member of the NSDAP during the Third Reich. They immediately forced him to resign from his parliamentary seat and from the party, even though this man would have automatically become the Bundestag's *Alterspräsident* by virtue of having been the most senior member of the legislature, certainly no mean loss for a brand-new party constituted mainly of young people.

14. My sample here is based on an array of readers' mail published in the alternative daily *Taz*. While I have no official corroboration of these readers' political affiliations, it seems quite safe to assume that most of them belong to West Germany's "greening" subculture and thus are quite close to the Green Party, at least in spirit and culture, if not in their actual voting.

15. For the most pronounced interpretation of the Holocaust as a "sideshow," see Rainer C. Baum, *The Holocaust and the German Elite: Genocide and National Suicide in Germany, 1871–1945* (Totowa, 1981).

Part Five

Closure?

16. German Identity and Historical Comparison: After the *Historikerstreit*

J ü r g e n   K o c k a

At the heart of the Historians' Debate, which began in the summer of 1986 and ended at the turn of the year 1987/88, stood a central question: What is the place of National Socialism in German history, and (by corollary) what is its meaning for the identity of the Federal Republic?[1] All the themes of the debate, no matter how different in other ways, were related to this question, and it was this problem that lent the controversy its sharpness and earned it such notoriety.

At issue were several points. First was the question of how to compare National Socialism and Nazi mass murder to other events. Second was the quite different question of the extent to which Nazi genocide could be interpreted as an understandable reaction to the Bolshevik mass extermination during the civil war and Stalinist periods. A subsidiary concern was the controversy over the extent to which Germany's geographic position in the center of Europe could explain its singular history. The thorny problem of "historicizing" National Socialism was also on the agenda, although the participants interpreted this extremely ambiguous concept in very different ways: should one understand those horrible events from the perspective of those who lived through them (and if so, then the further question arises, From the view of *which* contemporaries?), or should one adopt the consciously "distancing" perspective of the historian? Moreover, what is the relationship between understanding, analysis, and judgment? Finally, a broader, more general issue turned up in practically all the subsidiary discussions: the problem of collective identity, and the kind of contribution that historical memory, or the historical profession, can make to that identity.

No attempt will be made here to provide an overall assessment of the Historians' Debate. Instead, one of the main problems raised by the debate will be explored: the issue of cross-national comparison. In this context I will argue that a long and fruitful, though recently neglected, approach to German history from a comparative perspective, the *Sonderweg*, or "special path" theory, should be readopted, abeit in modified form.

Historical Comparisons: How and Why?

The most provocative and untenable hypothesis proferred during the Historians' Debate was Nolte's claim that there was a causal connection between the "Asiatic class murder" committed by the Bolsheviks and the National Socialist mass murder that followed it. He interpreted the Holocaust as an understandable, in a sense preemptive—and therefore reasonable—reaction to the Bolshevik mass murders. Scarcely a single historian has defended Nolte's hypothesis.[2]

The demand advanced by Fest, Nolte, and others (one they never carried out) that National Socialism and the Holocaust be *compared* with other twentieth-century cases of dictatorship and mass murder, provided a better basis for further discussion, even if Nolte's intention thereby was to call into question the uniqueness of Nazi crimes. Comparison is an indispensable methodological tool for the historian, in certain respects the (imperfect) functional equivalent of the scientist's experiment. In order to explain something, one must compare.[3] Even if comparison were, in fact, to relativize the significance of the events being compared—and this view seems to be widespread[4]—this would in no way call into question either the methodological value of the comparison or its scientific legitimacy. (Incidentally, "uniqueness" does not strike me as an especially useful category either methodologically, politically, or pedagogically. If one declares National Socialism to have been absolutely unique and exempts it from comparative analysis, one implies that something similar could never happen again. In so doing, does one not obscure precisely the lessons that could otherwise be learned from this bygone catastrophe?)

Admittedly, a few qualifications and additions must be added to this plea for the fundamental validity and necessity of a comparative approach. A comparative interpretation of National Socialism is hardly new; it does not have to be built up from scratch. Concepts like "totalitarianism" and "fascism" have long been used to gain a comparative perspective on National Socialism—as opposed to the view of Nazism as "Hitlerism," which tends to emphasize the uniqueness of the phenomenon.[5] At the same time, it must also be admitted that neither concept truly does justice to the phenomenon of the Holocaust itself.[6]

National Socialism and Stalinism

Historical comparisons look not only at the ways in which phenomena are similar, but also at those respects in which they differ. In comparing mass murder under the Nazis and under Stalin, as was proposed in the Historians' Debate, one is first struck by the almost incomprehensible scale of the death, terror, and suffering, the violations of human rights and human dignity that occurred in both cases. It must be added, however, that research into the Soviet case is much less advanced than the German since the subject was long suppressed and rendered taboo in both Soviet public discussion and Soviet historical writing. The number of those who perished on the Soviet side is still unclear and in dispute. One must distinguish among the victims of the civil war following the Revolution, those of the so-called Kulak persecutions in 1929–33, and those of the later "purges" of 1936–38. One must also distinguish between those who starved during the great famines (an outcome for which the government bore partial responsibility) and those who were victims of direct state persecution. In any event, millions were killed in the Soviet Union (not counting those who died during the war) and millions more survived only after the most extreme exploitation in the labor camps and penal colonies.[7] It is to be hoped that reforms in the Soviet Union will allow the historical truth to come to light, especially since its suppression over the past several decades has hardly been a source of intellectual, moral, and political strength for the Soviet Union.[8]

With an opening of the archives, comparisons between Stalin's and Hitler's atrocities could be more securely grounded. But what would be the point of such comparisons? In order to compare in a systematic manner, one must first determine what questions the comparison is aimed at answering. The purpose of such a comparison cannot be to excuse or exonerate one side by comparing it to the other. Why should a better insight into the motives, extent, mechanisms, and consequences of the Bolshevik terror diminish the guilt and complicity of the Germans vis-à-vis the Nazi crimes or even lighten the burden of their memory? This would not be possible even if historical research had the means of measuring the kind of guilt in question here and of assessing its magnitude in comparative perspective. The historian's tools are not well suited to such a task.

A precise comparison between the National Socialist and Stalinist terrors could allow us to recognize better the peculiarities of each and thus the differences between them: the difference between a bureaucratic, emotionless, nearly perfect, and ultimately incomprehensible system of mass murder in the concentration camps of Hitler's highly organized Reich, on the one hand, and the brutal mixture of civil war atrocities, mass "liquidations," deportations, slave labor, starvation, and internal struggles ("purges") in Stalin's backward empire, on the other. The mass exterminations under Stalin's rule were the secondary effects—often thoughtlessly borne though perhaps also secretly welcomed or cynically planned—of policies motivated primarily by economic concerns (forced labor, accelerated industrialization, the development of Siberia and other regions, shortages) and power-political considerations (the protection of positions of power under real or supposed threat, the elimination of real, potential, or suspected opposition). On the other hand, the systematic genocide practiced on Jews, Gypsies, and other persecuted groups in Hitler's Germany was consciously willed, planned, and carried out as such. The racist "logic" of the Nazi extermination apparatus seems more hopeless, inexorable, irrational, and incomprehensible when compared with the horrors of the Stalinist system of persecution, which was oriented toward class conflict and forced economic development.[9]

Finally, leaving aside the differences between the German and Soviet cases sketched out above, one could undertake a comparison of National Socialism and Stalinism in order to determine the conditions and causes that facilitated or encouraged state-sponsored murder in the first half of the twentieth century. The answer to this question would point to factors long identified in the literature on totalitarianism: the preliminary neutralization of practically all democratic, legal, and constitutional principles; the creation of a one-party system with a monocratic leadership; the institutionalization of a state ideology with strong chiliastic tendencies; processes of mass mobilization with a tendency to develop their own dynamic, and so forth.[10] One would also be able to point to the fact that both countries had made tremendous efforts to survive the First World War, but that both had nonetheless suffered catastrophic defeats. A certain distance to Western culture and its institutions was common to both countries, although to quite different degrees.

Nevertheless, the quite divergent social-historical positions of the two totalitarian systems place narrow constraints on further questions and suppositions of this sort. By 1933, Germany had attained a much higher level of modernization than the Soviet Union at the time of its birth or at any point during the 1920s or 1930s. The Stalinist terror had a role to play as a phase of developmental dictatorship; quite the opposite was true of the Holocaust. The Nazi genocide took place in a country which had fully participated in the great developments of European history, from the medieval separation of spiritual from temporal power, through humanism and the Reformation, to the Enlightenment and the rise of science in the nineteenth century. Germany had also reached a high socioeconomic level, as measured by the standards of the interwar years. Russia, by contrast, had been affected only tangentially by these European developments, most often experiencing them as imports, and the Soviet Union was almost a Third World country when compared to Central and Western Europe. It is therefore unlikely that comparisons between Nazism and Stalinism will lead to a fundamental and comprehensive explanation of the twentieth century's totalitarian reign of terror. The comparative enterprise would founder helplessly if the persecutions of Pol Pot in Cambodia and Idi Amin in Uganda were also included, as has been suggested.

In any case, the question of the preconditions for totalitarian dictatorship, with its mass exterminations, is more far-reaching than this. It would be necessary to bring into the comparison countries that are similar to either Germany or the Soviet Union, but that differed from them on the crucial point: that in spite of similar preconditions and challenges they did not become fascist or Stalinist. Looking at things from this angle, the comparison between Germany and the Soviet Union seems of little value. Comparisons between Germany and other Western countries promise greater results. Such comparisons have enjoyed a long and fruitful tradition under the ambiguous notion of a German *Sonderweg*. But the Historians' Debate pushed aside this "Western orientation" of comparative German history in favor of a curious

"Eastern orientation" that has so far yielded little new information. It may therefore be worthwhile to return to the *Sonderweg* debate, which now appears in a new light thanks to the research and discussions of the past few years.[11]

Germany and the West: The Theory of a Sonderweg

In the late nineteenth and early twentieth centuries, many people were convinced of the existence of a special "German path" of development which set the Reich apart—in accordance with its particular geographic position and historical tradition—in a positive way from France and England. They regarded the nonparliamentary character of the German "constitutional monarchy" as an advantage. Many were proud of the strong government that stood above the parties, the respected and efficient German bureaucracy, and the long tradition of reforms from above which distinguished Germany from the Western principles of revolution, laissez-faire, and party government. German "culture" seemed superior to Western "civilization"—an ideology that culminated in the "ideas of 1914."[12] After the First World War, some scholars, like Otto Hintze and Ernst Troeltsch, began to relativize this positive variant of the *Sonderweg* thesis. After the Second World War it had ceased to be convincing at all. Since then, the idea of a positive German *Sonderweg* has played little role in comparative interpretations of German history.

After 1945, a liberal-democratic, critical version of the *Sonderweg* thesis emerged. Its progenitors included Friedrich Engels and Max Weber. Émigrés and other critics of National Socialism also played an important part in its formulation. The essence of this critical variant of the *Sonderweg* thesis was its attempt to explain why Germany, in contrast to other highly developed and comparable countries of Northern and Western Europe, turned to fascism or totalitarianism during the crisis of the interwar period. Identifying the causes of National Socialism became the central issue of historical interpretation. The new *Sonderweg* thesis embodied Germans' attempt to explain "the German catastrophe" from a comparative perspective and to acknowledge it as an oppressive, yet undeniable, part of their historical heritage, while at the same time distancing themselves from it.[13]

The great importance of short-term factors in the collapse of the Weimar Republic and the rise of National Socialism were, of course, not overlooked from this perspective. Who could possibly have disregarded the consequences of Germany's humiliating defeat in World War I? It was also generally recognized that the difficulties of international economic relations between the wars and the Depression intensified the problems of the first German republic and ultimately contributed to Hitler's rise.

Yet, at the same time, researchers looked back to the eighteenth and nineteenth centuries to uncover the deeper roots of the Third Reich. Through comparisons with England, France, the United States, or simply "the West," they attempted to identify the peculiarities of German history, those structures and processes, experiences and turning points, which, while they may not have led directly to National Socialism, nevertheless hindered the long-term development of liberal democracy in Germany and eventually facilitated the triumph of fascism. Many authors made various contributions to the elaboration of this argument, usually without actually using the word *Sonderweg*.

Helmuth Plessner, for example, spoke of the "belated nation" [*die verspätete Nation*], the delayed creation of a nation-state "from above." Other historians have argued that nationalism played an especially aggressive, precociously right-wing destructive role during the Second Empire. Ernst Fraenkel, the young Karl Dietrich Bracher, Gerhard A. Ritter, M. Rainer Lepsius, and others identified powerful long-term weaknesses in the Empire's system of government: the blocked development of parliamentarianism, the severely fragmented system of parties that resembled self-contained blocs, and other factors that later burdened Weimar and contributed to its breakdown. Leonard Krieger, Fritz Stern, George Mosse, and Kurt Sontheimer emphasized the illiberal, antipluralistic elements in German political culture upon which National Socialist ideas could later build.

Hans Rosenberg and others argued that preindustrial elites, especially the east Elbian landowners (the Junkers), upper-level civil servants, and the officer corps retained great power and influence well into the twentieth century. In the long term, they represented an obstacle to democratization and parliamentarianism. As Heinrich August Winkler has shown, their effort is visible in the pernicious role played by agrarian interests in the collapse of the Weimar Republic. The unification of Germany by means of "blood and iron" under Prussian hegemony expanded the political influence and social weight of the officer corps with its status-oriented claims to exclusivity and autonomy. Along with the old elites, many traditional and preindustrial norms, ways of thinking, and modes of life also survived. These included the authoritarian outlook and antiproletarian claims of the petty bourgeoisie as well as militaristic elements of middle-class political culture, such as the institution of the "reserve officer." The liberal Max Weber criticized the "feudalization" of the upper bourgeoisie, which seemed to accept both the disproportional representation of the nobility in politics as well as aristocratic norms and practices instead of striving for power on its own terms or cultivating a distinctly middle-class culture. Lacking the experience of a successful revolution from below, schooled in a long tradition of bureaucratically led reforms from above, and challenged by a growing workers' movement, the German bourgeoisie appeared relatively weak and—compared with the West—almost "unbourgeois."

According to the extremely influential interpretation put forth by Hans-Ulrich Wehler, the Second Empire juxtaposed highly successful capitalist industrialization and socio-economic modernization, on the one hand, with preindustrial institutions, power relations, and ways of life on the other. It was thus a system with little stability, whose internal tensions necessitated oppression and manipulation at home and a relatively aggressive foreign policy abroad. In this context, Germany bore special responsibility for the outbreak of the First World War, as Fritz Fischer and his students have emphasized.[14]

Adherents of this interpretative approach naturally understood that the defeat in World War I and the 1918/19 revolution represented a deep break with the past and changed the inherited constellation of power in Germany. The traditional authoritarian state, the civil service, and the army lost much of their former legitimacy, the old elites were partially replaced, and a parliamentary democracy was erected. The labor movement was one of the winners in this process. The Social Democrats may have split, but they also gained power. The development of the welfare state made rapid progress. Yet in spite of all this, according to the *Sonderweg* thesis, many of the old problems remained and contributed to the special weaknesses of Weimar democracy. As a result, the Republic collapsed in the face of the Depression, whereas the more stable democracies of Western and Northern Europe survived.

As is well known, there is much to be said for this argument. Because parliamentarization had been hindered for so long, the new system—born of defeat—was not powerful enough to defuse the deep social tensions that emerged in the wake of war and economic turbulence. The core elements of the Wilhelmian party system were still in place after the revolution; the parties had not learned in time how to act in a parliamentary manner, how to accept the compromises necessary in a democracy. Traditional attitudes and elitist expectations remained characteristic among large segments of the upper class— among the Junkers, the upper bureaucracy, the officer corps, the judiciary, and portions of the bourgeoisie—and these traditional, predemocratic, and in part pre-modern attitudes and claims increasingly conflicted with the realities of Weimar.

All of this explains why a substantial portion of the upper class was hostile to the new democratic republic and helped bring it down. Segments of the petty bourgeoisie also continued to direct their usual demands at the state. These demands turned into protests against the new political system once the republic showed itself incapable of protecting the lower middle classes against the challenges of modernization. Despite Berlin and the flourishing of modernism in Weimar, the illiberal elements of German political culture survived and gained in strength. In complicated and circuitous ways, it was the Nazis who benefited from this trend.

From this perspective, then, it was not only economic crisis, explosive class antagonisms, and the destabilizing consequences of modernization that brought on the crisis of Weimar. These "modern" factors were certainly important, but they were, after all, present also in other countries. In Germany, however, such factors were intensified by premodern structures and traditions which, though under attack, continued to make their presence felt. This was the legacy of the *Sonderweg*.[15]

Criticism and Anticriticism

The multifaceted interpretation sketched out above (dubbed the "*Sonderweg* thesis" more often by its critics than by its supporters) has never enjoyed universal support. In recent years it has come under increasing fire. The chief objections can be briefly summarized as follows:

1. To view German history only in relation to 1933 (or 1933–45) is a one-sided approach. As National Socialism recedes ever further into the past, it becomes less and less reasonable to interpret German history of the nineteenth and twentieth centuries principally in terms of Weimar's collapse and the triumph of Nazism. German history before 1933 is more than just a prelude to 1933. It is also part of the prehistory of 1988, for example; and moreover it is an epoch in its own right.[16]

2. According to another objection, the notion of a German *Sonderweg* presupposes that a "normal" path of development existed, from which Germany deviated. If "normal" is taken to mean "average," "probable," or "most frequent," then it would be difficult to show that the French, English, or American patterns of development represented "normality"—completely leaving aside the fact that they are ill-suited to be lumped together in a single "Western" model.

If "normal" is meant in the sense of "norm," then the difficulties multiply. For if "the West" is taken as a normative standard from which Germany deviated to its own detriment, then this implies a subjective value judgment—and with it the danger of an idealization of "the West."[17] This objection has gained in resonance as doubts increasingly arise concerning the Western model of modernization.

3. Recent empirical studies seem to show that the causal significance of premodern attitudes, structures, and elites for the crisis of the Weimar Republic has perhaps been exaggerated. Instead, greater emphasis is placed on the consequences of defeat and inflation, the world economic crisis, and the supposedly precipitous construction of a welfare state. Other authors have taken up an older line of argument and stressed that rapid modernization itself led to social and cultural *anomie* and tensions, which in turn intensified the Weimar crisis and destabilized the system. The failure of Weimar was thus the result of the "contradictions of classic modernism."[18]

4. Recent interpretations of the Wilhelmian Empire have strongly emphasized its modernity: its achievements in the areas of education, science, and architecture, its allegedly well-developed bourgeois character—in civil law, the press, the theater, and other areas of culture. In addition, a comparative approach appears to show that those characteristics long interpreted as the peculiar weaknesses of the German bourgeoisie—the influence of the aristocracy on the upper bourgeoisie, for example—were in fact phenomena shared across all European nations.[19]

In light of these and other criticisms, the Sonderweg thesis must be rethought, made more precise, and partially modified.[20]

There are certainly many problems and topics in German history worth investigating. Different people pose different questions to the past and such queries change over time. But as the Historians' Debate has shown once again, the question of the place of National Socialism within German and world history remains central even today. The reason for this is that the otherwise brief Nazi period carries exceptional moral, political, and anthropological weight and has had profound effects on German, European, and world history. As long as this remains true, there is little danger that interpretations focusing on 1933 will become outdated or fail to address contemporary concerns.

The concept of a German *Sonderweg* makes sense only in the context of an inquiry into the causes, history, and significance of National Socialism. A *Sonderweg* concept is presumably pointless and misleading in the case of comparisons related to other topics and derived from other questions—for example, the causes and effects of industrialization during the nineteenth century in a range of countries.[21] In a certain sense, of course, every country—and every locality—has its own *Sonderweg*. But this insight is banal and no great thesis can be derived from it. It must also be admitted that the peculiarities of German development look quite different when seen from the perspective of East-Central or Eastern Europe rather than from the West.

Given these undeniable facts, historians should reserve the hypothesis of a German *Sonderweg* (although not necessarily the ambiguous term itself) for the comparative discussion of a fundamental and, as yet, not fully clarified problem: Why was the liberal-democratic rule of law in Germany perverted into a fascist or totalitarian system, whereas nothing of the sort occurred in those nations to which Germans like to compare themselves (and to which they should be compared), and this even though those countries were also faced with similar conditions and challenges?

Admittedly, the choice of this comparative perspective contains a normative component. But faced with the alternative "fascism versus the democratic rule of law," the performance of these Western (and Northern) nations was simply better, and their development more fortunate, than was the case in our own homeland. For this reason, the Western path of development, which from this point of view is quite uniform, can serve as an historical (and not merely abstract) model. It is, of course, not possible to prove conclusively that Germany should be compared to France, England, the Scandinavian countries, or North America; but there are good reasons for this juxtaposition if one seeks an explanation for the "German catastrophe" and its significance using the comparative method. For Germany was linked to these other Western countries not only by similar levels of economic development and modernization, but also through shared traditions of the Enlightenment, human and civil rights, and the constitutional state. Yet it was Germany that turned fascist and totalitarian while these other Western nations did not. Why? That is the essence of the question concerning the *Sonderweg*.

With whom should one compare oneself? This is a crucial question not only in private and public life, but in historical research as well. The decision taken influences the results of the comparison and necessarily contains normative implications.

What is one to make, then, of the empirical objections to the *Sonderweg* thesis? First of all, no serious historian would argue that the peculiarities of German history led directly and of necessity to 1933. Without question, there were many additional causal factors—from the consequences of defeat to the personality of Adolf Hitler—and it might still have been possible to prevent the Nazi victory as late as the end of 1932. Nevertheless, the structures and processes identified in the *Sonderweg* literature intensified the difficulties of the Weimar Republic and facilitated the rise of the Nazis. Recent research has added new elements to the overall picture and shifted emphases, yet the broad outlines of interpretation have not been revised. The rejection of the Weimar Republic by broad sectors of the upper class, antidemocratic nationalism, the difficulties of the parliamentary system, the power of large landowners and the officer corps, illiberal elements of the political culture, the weakness of the democratic and republic camp: such factors help explain the collapse of the Republic and are themselves the products of preceding processes and structures identified by the *Sonderweg* thesis. References to the "contradictions of classic modernism" fit well into the contemporary atmosphere skeptical of modernization, but other countries were also modern—and yet they escaped Germany's fate.[22]

In addition, much has changed over the past few years in the interpretation of the Wilhelmine Empire and, with it, a central element of the inherited *Sonderweg* thesis. The "feudalization of the upper bourgeoisie" turns out to have been much less advanced than had long been thought, and at any rate the close connections between upper bourgeoisie and aristocracy was a phenomenon common throughout Europe. The German middle class was indeed relatively weak in an economic and political sense when compared to its counterparts in the West, but in Germany as a kind of compensation, a precocious and strong bourgeoisie of culture and learning [*Bildungsbürgertum*] emerged. The continuing power of liberalism on the local level also made up to some degree for its weakness on the national level.

Other examples could also be mentioned, but on the whole the latest comparative research on the bourgeoisie has substantiated the essence of the *Sonderweg* thesis: there were peculiarities in the relationship between aristocracy and bourgeoisie which confirm the weaknesses of the German middle classes. The fairly marked differentiation of the bourgeoisie in Germany was a function of its relatively weak powers of attraction and integration. The many "unbourgeois" characteristics of middle-class society during the Wilhelmine Empire can be accounted for in this way. The bureaucratic tinge to German bourgeois culture also highlights one of its most painful limits.[23]

Comparative research over the past several years has repeatedly confirmed this peculiarity—among others—of German development: the importance and continuity of a bureaucratic tradition. German development distinguished itself from that in both East and West by the presence of a precocious, efficient, respected, and influential professional civil service and a long tradition of successful reforms from above. A strong, authoritarian state emerged which achieved much and became the object of widespread, and not unjustified, admiration. But the price paid for this, in a certain sense, was the specific weakness of bourgeois-liberal virtues.

The bureaucratic tradition influenced many different spheres of life: the formation of classes and status groups, the educational system, the structure and mentality of the bourgeoisie, the labor movement and the party system, the organization of large-scale industry, even the social theories of Max Weber. It facilitated the early development of a welfare state, but also helped to block the parliamentarization of the Empire and its member states up to 1918. The various social groups looked to the state for initiatives, and when these state-oriented expectations were disappointed they were easily transformed into protests directed at the existing system. The bureaucratic and authoritarian character of deeply rooted ideas, modes of behavior, and attitudes certainly helps to explain why there was so little resistance during the 1930s and 1940s to atrocities committed by the state.[24]

Much remains open and in dispute. The state of research remains in flux and the questions guiding it change. But when, as in the case of the Historians' Debate, the place of National Socialism in German history, the nature of German identity, and the role of comparison are at stake, then the line of interpretation identified with the idea of a *Sonderweg* still offers the best hope for further progress. The *Sonderweg* thesis also helps explain developments since 1945 and allows the present to be situated in its historical context. Those peculiarities of German history which facilitated the rise of National Socialism appear to have been decisively weakened by its victory and rapid subsequent defeat. The break after 1945 and the furiously paced modernization that followed seem to have brought the *Sonderweg* to an end.[25] The catastrophic manner in which this happened has left indelible traces. This is what the Historians' Debate was all about. Yet out of the catastrophe came an unexpected chance for a new beginning, one that has not entirely been wasted. This break with tradition stands at the center of our tradition.

Notes

1. Interest in this issue declined sharply after the beginning of 1987 when it became clear that Nolte's voluminous book *Der europäische Bürgerkrieg 1917–1945: Nationalsozialismus und Bolschewismus* (Berlin, 1987) was unable to substantiate empirically the author's prior sweeping claims. At the same time, Hans-Ulrich Wehler's very combative work *Entsorgung der deutschen Vergangenheit? Ein polemischer Essay zum "Historikerstreit"* (Munich, 1988) summarized, sharpened, and

added to the arguments of the critics of Nolte, Stürmer, Hillgruber, et al. and documented the whole controversy in an exhaustive manner. No public response was forthcoming from those attacked, and on both sides the feeling spread that all the arguments were now on the table and there was little to be gained by repetition.

2. Klaus Hildebrand did offer unqualified praise for Nolte in an article in *Historische Zeitschrift* 242 (1986): 466.

3. See H.-J. Puhle, "Theorien in der Praxis des vergleichenen Historikers," in J. Kocka and T. Nipperdey, eds., *Theorie und Erzählung in der Geschichte* (Munich, 1979), 119–36.

4. See Albert Soboul's curious fear of the generalizing concept of an "Atlantic Revolution" (R. R. Palmer), intended for comparative purposes, which includes the French Revolution but allows it "to be submerged in an indeterminant international ferment." In this way the French Revolution is "degraded in an unfortunate manner" and robbed of its national significance, special depth, and dramatic intensity and influence. Cited from B. W. Bouvier, *Französische Revolution und deutsche Arbeiterbewegung: Die Rezeption des revolutionären Frankreich in der deutschen sozialistischen Arbeiterbewegung von den 1830er Jahren bis 1905* (Bonn, 1982), 20.

5. See *Totalitarismus und Faschismus: Eine wissenschaftliche und politische Begriffskontroverse* (Munich, 1980). While the concept of totalitarianism helps bring the undeniable similarities between Hitler's Germany and Stalin's Soviet Union into sharper focus, the "fascism" approach illuminates parallels among fascist movements and systems, such as those between Germany and Italy. Both approaches are open to political manipulation, but are in principle useful. Just as one must be wary of the usual disparagement aimed at the concept of fascism, it would also be wrong to turn "totalitarian" comparisons of Nazism and Stalinism into a taboo.

6. See Martin Broszat and Saul Friedländer, "A Controversy about the Historicization of National Socialism," in this volume, p. 102. Also R. Hillberg and A. Sollner, "Das Schweigen zum Sprechen bringen: Über Kontinuität und Diskontinuität in der Holocaustforschung," *Merkur* 42 (1988): 535–51.

7. By way of introduction, see G. Schramm, ed., *Von den autokratischen Reformen zum Sowjetstaat (1856–1945)* (*Handbuch der Geschichte Russlands*, vol. 3, Stuttgart, 1983), 579ff., 639–49, 836–51; P. Scheibert, *Lenin an der Macht: Das russische Volk in der Revolution 1918–1922* (Weinheim, 1984), 91ff; R. Conquest, *The Great Terror: Stalin's Purges of the Thirties* (New York, 1968); idem, *Harvest of Sorrow: Soviet Collectivization and the Terror-Famine* (London, 1986). According to Conquest, the famine in the Ukraine (1932–33) was the result of an intentional policy of repression and extermination by Stalin, and hence of genocide practiced upon the Ukrainians, one that cost six to seven million lives (even more if one includes all those killed since the beginning of the persecution of the "kulaks" in 1929 and those who never returned from the labor camps). Conquest's interpretation and numbers are very much in dispute. See the following, which also contains references to other relevant works: St. Merl, "'Ausrottung' der Bourgeoisie und der Kulaken in Sowjetrussland? Anmerkungen zu einem fragwürdigen Vergleich mit Hilters Judenvernichtung," *Geschichte und Gesellschaft* 13 (1987): 368–81; idem, "Wieviele Opfer forderte die 'Liquidierung der Kulaken als Klasse?'" ibid., 14 (1988): 534–40.

8. There is something to be learned from this case for the evaluation of the quite different German situation: in the Federal Republic, after the German defeat and

the removal of those directly responsible, a full and complete disclosure of Nazi crimes took place. The continuing consciousness of these crimes in the minds of the population has, it is sometimes claimed, made it more difficult for West Germans to walk with their heads high and has weakened their capacity for collective action. A comparison with the Soviet system suggests that this assertion is false.

9. See Raul Hilberg, *The Destruction of the European Jews* (New York, 1961); M. Gilbert, *The Holocaust* (New York, 1985); E. Jäckel, "Die elende Praxis der Untersteller," in *Historikerstreit*; Maier, *Vierzig Jahre nach Auschwitz: Deutsche Geschichtserinnerungen heute* (Munich, 1987).

10. See Hannah Arendt, *The Origins of Totalitarianism* (New York, 1951); K. D. Bracher, *Zeitgeschichtliche Kontroverse: Um Faschismus, Totalitarismus, Demokratie* (Munich, 1976); B. Siedel and S. Jenkner, eds., *Wege der Totalitarismus-Forschung* (Darmstadt, 1974).

11. What follows draws upon J. Kocka, "German History before Hitler: The Debate about the German 'Sonderweg,'" *Journal of Contemporary History* 23 (1988): 3–16 (further references can be found there); idem, "Der 'deutsche Sonderweg' in der Diskussion," *German Studies Review* 5 (1982): 365–79; H. Grebing, *Der "deutsche Sonderweg" in Europa 1806–1945: Eine Kritik* (Stuttgart, 1986); B. Faulenbach, "Eine Variante europäischer Normalität? Zur neuesten Diskussion über den 'deutschen Weg' im 19. und 20. Jahrhundert," in *Tel Aviver Jahrbuch für deutsche Geschichte* 16 (1987), 285–309; E. Aschheim, "Nazism, Normalcy and the German 'Sonderweg,'" *Studies in Contemporary Jewry* 4 (1988): 276–92.

12. See B. Faulenbach, *Die Ideologie des deutschen Weges: Die deutsche Geschichte in der Historiographie zwischen Kaiserreich und Nationalsozialismus* (Munich, 1980).

13. Friedrich Meinecke, *The German Catastrophe* (Cambridge, Mass., 1950).

14. See H. Plessner, *Die verspätete Nation: Über die politische Verführbarkeit bürgerlichen Geistes* (Stuttgart, 1959); E. Fraenkel, *Deutschland und die westlichen Demokratien* (Stuttgart, 1964); K. D. Bracher, *Die Auflösung der Weimarer Republik* (Villingen, 1955); G. A. Ritter, *Deutscher und britischer Parlamentarismus: Ein verfassungsgeschichtlicher Vergleich* (Tübingen, 1962); M. R. Lepsius, "Parteiensystem und Sozialstruktur: Zum Problem der Demokratisierung der deutschen Gesellschaft," in W. Abel et al., eds., *Wirtschaft, Geschichte, Wirtschaftsgeschichte: Festschrift für Friedrich Lütge zum 65. Geburtstag* (Stuttgart, 1966), 371–93; L. Krieger, *The German Idea of Freedom* (Boston, 1957); F. Stern, *The Politics of Cultural Despair: A Study in the Rise of the Germanic Ideology* (Berkeley, 1961); G. L. Mosse, *The Crisis of German Ideology: Intellectual Origins of the Third Reich* (New York, 1964); K. Sontheimer, *Antidemokratisches Denken in der Weimarer Republik* (Munich, 1962); H. Rosenberg, *Bureaucracy, Aristocracy and Autocracy: The Prussian Experience 1616–1815* (Cambridge, Mass., 1958); idem, "Die Pseudodemokratisierung der Rittergutsbesitzerklasse (1958)," in idem, *Machteliten und Wirtschaftskonjunkturen* (Göttingen, 1978), 83–101; H. A. Winkler, "Die 'neue Linke' und der Faschismus: Zur Kritik neomarxistischer Theorien über den Nationalsozialismus," in idem, *Revolution, Staat, Faschismus* (Göttingen, 1978), 65–117; H.-U. Wehler, *The German Empire, 1871–1918* (Leamington Spa, 1985); F. Fischer, *From Kaiserreich to Third Reich: Elements of Continuity in German History, 1871–1945* (London, 1986).

15. See J. Kocka, "Ursachen des Nationalsozialismus," in *Aus Politik und Zeitgeschichte* B 25/80 (1980): 3–15; H. A. Winkler, "Unternehmerverbände zwischen Ständeideologie und Nationalsozialismus," in idem, *Liberalismus und Antiliberal-*

292   *Jürgen Kocka*

ismus: Studien zur politischen Sozialgeschichte des 19. und 20. Jahrhunderts (Göttingen, 1979), 175–94; H. Möller, "Parlamentarismus-Diskussion in der Weimarer Republik: Die Frage des 'besonderen' Weges zum parlamentarischen Regierungssystem," in M. Funke et al., eds., *Demokratie und Diktatur: Geist und Gestalt politischer Herrschaft in Deutschland und Europa* (Düsseldorf, 1987), 140–57.

16. T. Nipperdey, "1933 und die Kontinuität der deutschen Geschichte," in *Historische Zeitschrift* 227 (1978): 86–111.

17. See D. Blackbourn and G. Eley, *The Peculiarities of German History: Bourgeois Society and Politics in Nineteenth Century Germany* (Oxford, 1984).

18. Thus D. J. H. Peukert, *Die Weimarer Republik: Krisenjahre der Klassischen Moderne* (Frankfurt, 1987); in a similar vein: M. Stürmer, *Deutsche Fragen oder die Suche nach der Staatsräson: Historisch-politische Kolumnen* (Munich, 1988), 70: "Hitler's rise came out of the crises and catastrophes of a secularized civilization lurching from revolution to revolution and characterized by disorientation and a fruitless search for security." See also J. Kocka, "German History before Hitler," 27, nn. 9–13, where the titles of books by J. W. Falter, E. Lederer, M. R. Lepsius, K. Borchardt, G. D. Feldman, and G. L. Mosse are listed.

19. See above all Blackbourn and Eley, *Peculiarities;* R. Evans, ed., *Society and Politics in Wilhelmine Germany* (London, 1978); M. Stürmer, *Das ruhelose Reich: Deutschland 1866–1918* (Berlin, 1983). This new line of interpretation is already present in H.-U. Wehler, "Wie bürgerlich war das Deutsche Kaiserreich?" in J. Kocka, ed., *Bürger und Bürgerlichkeit im 19. Jahrhundert* (Göttingen, 1987), 243–80. On the "feudalization" thesis, see H. Kaelble, "Wie feudal waren die deutschen Unternehmer im Kaiserreich?" in R. Tilly, ed., *Beiträge zur quantitativen vergleichenden Unternehmensgeschichte* (Stuttgart, 1985), 148–71.

20. I will refrain from discussing here a new version of the *Sonderweg* thesis which stresses Germany's geographic position in the center of Europe (Hagen Schulze, Michael Stürmer, and Klaus Hildebrand). On this subject, see J. Kocka, "Germany Before Hitler," 9–10, and n. 16. See also the further development of this new version of the thesis by Hagen Schulze, "Explaining the German Catastrophe: The Use and Abuse of Historical Explanations," in this volume, p. 185.

21. See the criticism, perfectly justified in this sense, of the *Sonderweg* thesis in H. Kaelble, "Der Mythos von der rapiden Industrialisierung in Deutschland," in *Geschichte und Gesellschaft* 9 (1983): 106–18; W. Fischer, "Wirtschafts- und sozialgeschichtliche Anmerkungen zum 'deutschen Sonderweg,'" in *Tel Aviver Jahrbuch für Deutsche Geschichte* 16 (1987): 96–116.

22. See M. Prinz, "Wohlfahrtsstaat, Modernisierung und Nationalsozialismus: Thesen zu ihrem Verhaltnis," in H.-U. Otto and H. Sünker, eds. *Soziale Arbeit und Faschismus* (Frankfurt, 1988). For a good overview, see E. Kolb, *Die Wiemarer Republik* (Munich, 1984); G. D. Feldman, "The Weimar Republic: A Problem of Modernization," in *Archiv für Sozialgeschichte* 26 (1986): 1–26.

23. This is the conclusion of a research group at the Zentrum für interdisziplinäre Forschung at Bielefeld University, documented in J. Kocka, ed., *Bürgertum im 19. Jahrhundert: Deutschland im europäischen Vergleich*, 3 vols. (Munich, 1988).

24. See Kocka, *Bürgertum*, in this connection as well; in general, see J. Kocka, "Capitalism and Bureaucracy in German Industrialization before 1914," in *Economic History Review*, 2d ser. 33 (1981): 453–68; see also H. Gerstenberger, "Alltagsforschung und Faschismustheorie," in J. Kocka and D. Schmidt, eds., *Nor-*

malität oder Normalisierung? Geschichtswerkstätten und Faschismusanalyse (Munich, 1987), 35–49.

25. See J. Kocka, "1945: Neubeginn oder Restauration?" in C. Stern and H. A. Winkler, eds., *Wendepunkte deutscher Geschichte 1848–1945* (Frankfurt, 1979), 141–68; now above all M. Broszat et al., eds., *Von Stalingrad zur Währungsreform: Zur Sozialgeschichte des Umbruchs in Deutschland* (Munich, 1988), esp. xxv–xxxi.

Bibliography of Works on the Historians' Debate and Related Topics

Compiled by Gregory Pass

Abraham, David. *The Collapse of the Weimar Republic.* 2d. ed. New York, 1981.

Alltagsgeschichte der NS-Zeit: Neue Perspektive oder Trivialisierung? Kolloquien des Instituts für Zeitgeschichte. Munich, 1984.

Artz, Heinz. "Zur Abgrenzung von Kriegsverbrechen und NS-Verbrechen." In *NS-Prozesse: Nach 25 Jahren Strafverfolgung.* Edited by Adalbert Rücker. Karlsruhe, 1971.

Ash, Timothy Garton. "Germany after Bitburg." *New Republic,* July 15/22, 1985, 15–17. Reprinted in *Bitburg,* edited by Geoffrey Hartman.

Auffermann, Verena. "Fragen nach politischer Kultur: Zu den 13. Römerberg-Gesprächen in Frankfurt." *Süddeutsche Zeitung,* 13 June, 1986.

Augstein, Rudolf. "Auf die schiefe Ebene zur Republik." *Der Spiegel* 2 (January 1985).

———. "Die neue Auschwitz-Lüge." *Der Spiegel,* 6 October 1986. Reprinted in *Gegen der Versuch,* edited by Hilmar Hoffman.

Bade, Rolf. "Die Wende im Verständnis des Nationalsozialismus: Von der Harmonisierung zur Verharmlosung." *Bremer Lehrer Zeitung,* February 1987.

Barkin, Kenneth D. "From Uniformity to Pluralism: German Historical Writing since World War I." *German Life and Letters* 34 (1980–81): 234–47.

Bartov, Omer. "Historians on the Eastern Front: Andreas Hillgruber and Germany's Tragedy." *Tel Aviver Jahrbuch für deutsche Geschichte* 16 (1987): 325–45.

———. *The Eastern Front, 1941–45: German Troops and the Barbarization of Warfare.* London, 1986.

Benz, Wolfgang. "Judenvernichtung aus Notwehr? Die Legenden um Theodore N. Kaufmann." *Vierteljahrshefte für Zeitgeschichte* 29 (1981): 615–30.

Berghahn, Volker R. "Die Fischer Kontroverse—15 Jahre danach." *Geschichte und Gesellschaft* 6 (1980): 403–19.

———. "West German Historiography between Continuity and Change: Some Cross-Cultural Comparisons." *German Life and Letters* 34 (1980–81): 248–59.

———. "Geschichtswissenschaft und Grosse Politik." *Aus Politik und Zeitgeschichte (Beilage zur Wochenzeitung Das Parlament),* B11/87, 14 March 1987, 25–37.

Blackbourn, David. *Populists and Patricians: Essays in Modern German History.* London, 1987.

Blackbourn, David, and Geoff Eley. *The Peculiarities of German History*. Oxford, 1984.

Bodemann, Michal. "Die 'Überwölbung' von Auschwitz: Der jüdische Faktor in der Mythologie der Wende-Republik." *Ästhetik und Kommunikation: Beiträge zur politischen Erziehung* 15, 56 (1984).

Bölling, Rainer. "Nationalsozialismus und Geschichtsbewußtsein: Bericht über eine Essener Ringvorlesung." *Geschichtsdidaktik* 2 (1987): 194–97.

Bossmann, Dieter. *"Was ich über Adolf Hitler gehört habe: Folgen eines Tabus: Auszüge aus Schüleraufsätzen von heute*. Frankfurt, 1977.

Bower, Tom. *Blind Eye to Murder*. London, 1981.

Broszat, Martin. "Hitler and the Genesis of the 'Final Solution': An Assessment of David Irving's Thesis." *Yad Vashem Studies* 13 (1979). Also in *Aspects of the Third Reich*, edited by H. W. Koch.

———. *Nach Hitler: Der schwierige Umgang mit unserer Geschichte: Beiträge von Martin Broszat*. Edited by Hermann Graml and Klaus-Dietmar Henke. Munich, 1986.

———. "Die Ambivalenz der Forderung nach mehr Geschichtsbewusstsein." In *Gegen den Versuch*, edited by Hilmer Hoffmann. Frankfurt, 1987.

Broszat, Martin, Elke Fröhlich, and Falk Wiesmann. *Bayern in der NS-Zeit*. 6 vols. Munich, 1977–83.

Brüggemeier, Franz, and Jürgen Kocka. *"Geschichte von unten, Geschichte von innen': Kontroversen um die Alltagsgeschichte*. Fernuniversität Hagen, 1985.

Brumlik, Mischa, et al., eds. *Jüdisches Leben in Deutschland seit 1945*. Frankfurt am Main, 1986.

Bundeszentrale für politische Bildung. *Rückschau nach 30 Jahren: Hitlers Machtergreifung in der Sicht deutscher und ausländischer Historiker*. Bonn, 1963.

Burleigh, Michael. *Germany Turns Eastwards: A Study of Ostforschung in the Third Reich*. Cambridge, 1988.

Conze, Werner, and M. R. Lepsius, eds. *Sozialgeschichte der Bundesrepublik Deutschland*. Stuttgart, 1983.

Craig, Gordon A. "The War of the German Historians." *New York Review of Books*, 15 January 1987, 16–19.

Dahrendorf, Ralf. *Society and Democracy in Germany*. London, 1967.

———. "Zur politischen Kultur der Bundesrepublik." *Merkur*, January 1987.

"Debate: David Abraham's *The Collapse of the Weimar Republic*." *Central European History* 17 (1984): 159–293.

Diner, Dan. "The Historians' Controversy: Limits to the Historicization of National Socialism." *Tikkun* 2, 1 (1987): 74–78.

———. *Ist der Nationalsozialismus Geschichte? Zu Historisierung und Historikerstreit*. Frankfurt, 1987.

Ditt, Karl. *"Es ist Zeit für die ganze Wahrheit" (K. V. Dohnanyi): Aufarbeitung der NS-Zeit in Hamburg: Die nicht veröffentlichte Senatsbroschüre*. Hamburg, 1985.

Draper, Theodore. "Neoconservative History." *New York Review of Books*, 16 January 1986, 5–15.

Dregger, Alfred. "Im Wortlaut: 'Beleidigung meines Bruders': Offener Brief an 53 US Senatoren." *Frankfurter Rundschau*, 23 April 1985.

———. "Aus der Rede zum Volkstrauertag: 'Alle Toten verdienen die gleiche Ehrfurcht." *Frankfurter Allgemeine Zeitung*, 17 November 1986.

Eley, Geoff. "Recent Work in Modern German History." *Historical Journal* 23 (1980): 463–79.

————. *From Unification to Nazism: Reinterpreting the German Past.* Boston, 1985.

Epstein, Helen. *Die Kinder des Holocaust. Gespräche mit Söhnen und Töchtern von Überlebenden.* Munich, 1987.

Erdmann, Karl Dietrich, and Schulze, Hagen, eds. *Weimar: Selbstpreisgabe einer Demokratie.* Düsseldorf, 1980.

Erler, G. *Geschichtswende? Entsorgungsversuche zur deutschen Geschichte.* Freiburg, 1987.

Eschenhagen, Wieland, ed. *Die neue deutsche Ideologie: Einsprüche gegen die Entsorgung der Vergangenheit.* Darmstadt, 1988.

Evans, Richard J. "The New Nationalism and the Old History: Perspectives on the West German Historikerstreit." *Journal of Modern History* 59 (December 1987): 761–97.

————. *Rethinking German History: Nineteenth-Century Germany and the Origins of the Third Reich.* London, 1987.

————. *In Hitler's Shadow: West German Historians and the Attempt to Escape from the Nazi Past.* New York, 1989.

Faulenbach, Bernd. "NS-Interpretation und Zeitklima. Zum Wandel in der Aufarbeitung der jüngsten Vergangenheit." *Aus Politik und Zeitgeschichte*, B 22/87, 30 May 1987, 19–30.

Faulenbach, Bernd, and Rainer Bölling. *Geschichtsbewusstsein und historisch–politische Bildung in der Bundesrepublik Deutschland: Beiträge zum "Historikerstreit."* Düsseldorf, 1988.

Fest, Joachim. "Sieg und Niederlage." *FAZ*, 20 April 1985.

Fischer, Fritz. *From Kaiserreich to Third Reich: Elements of Continuity in German History.* London, 1986.

Fischer, Joschka. "Wir Kinder der Kapitulanten." *Die Zeit* 19, 10 May 1985, 146–64.

Friedländer, Saul. "Some German Struggles with Memory." In *Bitburg*, edited by Geoffrey Hartmann.

Fülberth, G. "Ein Philosoph blamiert die Historiker." *Deutsche Volkszeitung* 26, September 1986.

Funke, Hajo. "Bitburg, Jews, and Germans: A Case Study of Anti-Jewish Sentiment in Germany during May, 1985." *New German Critique* 38 (Spring/Summer 1986): 57–72.

Gall, Lothar, Klaus Hildebrand, et al. *Überlegungen und Vorschläge zur Errichtung eines Hauses der Geschichte der Bundesrepublik Deutschland in Bonn.* Bonn, 1984.

Geiss, Imanuel. "Auschwitz, 'asiatische Tat.'" *Der Spiegel*, 20 October 1986.

Gerstenberger, Heide, and Dorothea Schmidt, eds. *Normalität oder Normalisierung? Geschichtswerkstätten und Faschismusanalyse.* Münster, 1987.

Geschichtswerkstatt Berlin. *Die Nation als Ausstellungsstück: Planungen, Kritik und Utopien zu den Museumsgründungen in Bonn und Berlin.* Geschichtswerkstatt 11. Hamburg, 1987.

Giesselmann, Roland. *Reader zur Historikerdebatte.* Bielefeld University. Unpublished dossier.

Gilbert, Martin. *The Holocaust: The Jewish Tragedy.* London and New York, 1986.

Gill, Ulrich, and Winfried Steffani, eds. *Eine Rede und ihre Wirkung: Die Rede des Bundespräsidenten Richard von Weizsäcker vom 8. Mai 1985.* Berlin, 1986.

Gordon, Sarah. *Hitler, Germans and the "Jewish Question."* Princeton, 1984.

Grab, W. "Kritische Bemerkungen zur nationalen Apologetik Joachim Fests, Ernst Noltes und Andreas Hillgrubers." *1999* 2 (1987).

Graf, William. "Anti-Communism in the Federal Republic of Germany." *Socialist Register.* London, 1984.

Grebing, Helga, et al. *Von der Verdrängung zur Bagatellisierung: Aspekte des sogenannten Historikerstreits.* Hanover, 1988.

Groh, Dieter. "Le 'sonderweg' de l'histoire allemande: Mythe ou réalité?" *Annales: ESC* 38 (1983): 1166–87.

Grünberg, Kurt. "Folgen nationalsozialistischer Verfolgung bei jüdischen Nachkommen Überlebender in der Bundesrepublik Deutschland. *Psyche* 41 (1987): 492–507.

Habermas, Jürgen. "Von öffentlichen Gebrauch der Historie: Das offizielle Selbstverständnis in der Bundesrepublik bricht auf." *Die Zeit,* 7 November 1986.

————. *Eine Art Schadensabwicklung.* Frankfurt am Main, 1987.

Häusermann, Titus, ed. *Die Bundesrepublik und die deutsche Geschichte.* Stuttgart, 1987.

Hagen, William W. *Germans, Poles and Jews: The Nationality Conflict in the Prussian East, 1772–1914.* Chicago, 1980.

Hartman, Geoffrey, ed. *Bitburg in Moral and Political Perspective.* Bloomington, 1986.

Haug, Wolfgang Fritz. *Von hilflosen Antifaschismus zur Gnade der späten Geburt.* Berlin, 1987.

Heer, Hannes, and Ullrich Volker, eds. *Geschichte entdecken.* Reinbeck bei Hamburg, 1985.

Hennig, Eike. "Raus aus der politischen Kraft der Mitte! Bemerkungen zur Kritik der neokonservativen Geschichtspolitik." *Gewerkschaftliche Monatshefte* 3 (1987): 160–70.

————. *Zum Historikerstreit: Was heisst und zu welchem Ende studiert man Geschichte?* Frankfurt, 1988.

Herwig, Holger. "Andreas Hillgruber: Historian of 'Grossmachtpolitik,' 1871–1945." *Central European History* 15 (1982): 186–98.

Heuss, A. *Versagen und Verhängnis: Vom Ruin deutscher Geschichte und ihres Verständnisses.* Berlin, 1984.

Hildebrand, Klaus. "Wer dem Abgrund entrinnen will, muß ihn aufs genaueste ausloten: Ist die neue deutsche Geschichtsschreibung revisionistisch?" *Die Welt,* 22 November 1986.

————, ed. *Wem gehört die deutsche Geschichte? Deutschlands Weg vom alten Europa in die europäische Moderne.* Cologne, 1987.

Hillgruber, Andreas. "Die 'Endlösung' und das deutsche Ostimperium als Kernstück des rassenideologischen Programms des Nationalsozialismus." In *Hitler, Deutschland und die Mächte,* edited by Manfred Funke. Düsseldorf, 1975.

————. "Die ideologisch-dogmatische Grundlage der nationalsozialistischen Politik der Ausrottung der Juden in den besetzten Gebieten der Sowjetunion und ihre Durchführung, 1941–44." *German Studies Review* 2 (1979): 264–96.

————. "Jürgen Habermas, Karl-Heinz Janssen und die Aufklärung Anno 1986." *Geschichte in Wissenschaft und Unterricht* 37 (December 1986).

————. *Zweierlei Untergang: Die Zerschlagung des Deutschen Reiches und das Ende des europäischen Judentums.* Berlin, 1986.

Hirsch, Martin. "Anlass, Verlauf und Ergebnis der Verjährungsdebatten im Deutschen Bundestag." In *Vergangenheitsbewältigung durch Strafverfahren? NS-Prozesse in der Bundesrepublik Deutschland*, edited by Jürgen Webe, and Peter Steinbach. Munich, 1984.

Hirschfeld, Gerhard, ed. *The Policies of Genocide: Jews and Soviet Prisoners of War in Nazi Germany*. London, 1986.

"The Historikerstreit." Special issue of *German Politics and Society* 13 (February 1988). Center for European Studies, Harvard University.

Hoffman, Hilmar, ed. *Gegen den Versuch, Vergangenheit zu verbiegen: Eine Diskussion um politische Kultur in der Bundesrepublik aus Anlass der Frankfurter Römerberggespräche 1986*. Frankfurt, 1987.

Hörster-Philipps, U. "Kernfrage des bundesdeutschen Historikerstreits." *Deutsche Volkszeitung* 12 (December 1986).

Iggers, George. *The Conception of History: The National Tradition of Historical Thought from Herder to the Present*. Revised edition. Middleton, Conn., 1983.

————. *New Directions in European Historiography*. Revised edition. London, 1985.

————, ed. *The Social History of Politics: Critical Perspectives in West German Historical Writing since 1945*. Leamington Spa, 1985.

Iggers, George, and Harold T. Parker, eds. *International Handbook of Historical Studies: Contemporary Research and Theory*. Westport, Conn., 1979.

Jäckel, E. "Verantwortung übernehmen heißt nicht unterwürfig sein." *Frankfurter Rundschau*, 6 June 1987.

Jäger, Wolfgang. *Historische Forschung und politische Kultur in Deutschland: Die Debatte 1914–1980 über den Ausbruch des Ersten Weltkrieges*. Göttingen, 1984.

Janssen, Karl-Heinz. "Als ein Volk ohne Schatten?" *Die Zeit* 48, 21 November 1986.

Kampe, Norbert. "Normalizing the Holocaust? The Recent Historian's Debate in the Federal Republic of Germany." *Holocaust and Genocide Studies* 2 (1987): 61–80.

Kater, Michael H. "The Burden of the Past: Problems of Modern Historiography of Physicians and Medicine in Germany." *German Studies Review* 10 (February 1987): 31–56.

Kaye, Harvey J. "The Use and Abuse of the Past: The New Right and the Crisis of History." In *Socialist Register 1987*, edited by Ralph Miliband et al. London, 1987.

Kennedy, Paul M. "The Decline of Nationalistic History in the West, 1900–1970." *Journal of Contemporary History* 6, no. 1 (1973): 77–100.

Kershaw, Ian. "'Normality' and Genocide: The Problem of 'Historicization,'" In *The Nazi Dictatorship: Problems and Perspectives on Interpretation*. 2d. edition. London, 1989.

Klönne, A. "Historiker-Debatte und 'Kulturrevolution von rechs." *Blätter für deutsche und internationale Politik*, H. 3.

Knight, Robert. "The Waldheim Context: Austria and Nazism." *Times Literary Supplement*, 3 October 1986, 1003–4.

Koch, H. W., ed. *Aspects of the Third Reich*. London, 1985.

Kocka, Jürgen. "Der 'deutsche Sonderweg' in der Diskussion." *German Studies Review* 5 (1982): 365–79.

————. "Klassen oder Kultur? Durchbrüche und Sackgassen in der Alltagsgeschichte." *Merkur* 36 (1982): 955–65.

————. "Die deutsche Geschichte soll ins Museum." *Geschichte und Gessellschaft* 11 (1985): 59–66.

————. "Drittes Reich: Die Reihen fast geschlossen." *Die Zeit* 42, 14 October 1985.

————. "German History Before Hitler: The Debate About The German 'Sonderweg'." *Journal of Contemporary History* 23 (1988).

————. "Geschichtswerkstätten und Historikerstreit." *TAZ*, 26 January 1988.

Kosiek, R. *Historikerstreit und Geschichtsrevision.* Tübingen, 1987.

Kramer, Dieter. "Die Diskussion der 'Römerberg-Gespräche' 1986." In *Gegen den Versuch,* edited by Hilman Hoffmann. Frankfurt, 1987.

Kramer, Jane. "Letter from Europe." *The New Yorker,* 12 October 1987, 130–44.

————. *The Europeans.* New York, 1988.

Krausnick, Helmut, and Hans-Heinrich Wilhem. *Die Truppe des Weltanschauungskrieges: Die Einsatzgruppen der Sicherheitspolizei und des SD 1938–1942.* Stuttgart, 1981.

Kuhn, A. "Wem gehört die deutsche Geschichte?" *Blätter für deutsche und internationale Politik* 32 (1987): 25–32.

Kühnl, Reinhard. *Das Dritte Reich in der Presse der Bundesrepublik.* Frankfurt, 1966.

————. *Die von F. J. Strauß repräsentierten politischen Kräfte und ihr Verhältnis zum Faschismus.* Cologne, 1980.

————, ed. *Streit ums Geschichtsbild. Die "Historiker-Debatte," Dokumentation, Darstellung und Kritik.* Cologne, 1987.

————, ed. "Vergangenheit, die nicht vergeht." In *Die "Historiker-Debatte": Dokumentation, Darstellung und Kritik.* Cologne, 1987.

Kulka, Otto Dov. "Die deutsche Geschichtsschreibung über den Nationalsozialismus und die Endlösung: Tendenzen und Entwicklungsphasen 1924–1984." *Historische Zeitschrift* 240 (1985): 599–640.

Landeszentrale für politische Bildung, ed. *Streitfall Deutsche Geschichte: Geschichts- und Gegenwartsbewusstsein in den 80er Jahren.* Nordrhein-Westfalen, Essen, 1988.

Laqueur, Walter. *Germany Today: A Personal Report.* London, 1985.

Leggewie, Claus. "Frankreichs kollektives Gedächtnis und der Nationalsozialismus." In *Ist der Nationalsozialismus Geschichte? Zu Historisierung und Historikerstreit,* edited by Dan Diner. Frankfurt, 1987.

————. *Der Geist steht rechts: Ausflüge in die Denkfabriken der Wende.* Berlin, 1987.

Levkov, Ilya, ed. *Bitburg and Beyond: Encounters in American, German and Jewish History.* New York, 1987.

Luks, L. "Bolschewismus, Faschismus, Nationalsozialismus: Verwandte Gegner?" *Geschichte und Gesellschaft* 14 (1988).

Lübbe, Hermann. "Der Nationalsozialismus im Deutschen Nachkriegsbewusstein." *Historische Zeitschrift* 236 (1983): 579–99.

Maier, Charles. *The Unmasterable Past: History, Holocaust, and German National Identity.* Cambridge, Mass., 1988.

Markham, James M. "German Book Sets Off New Holocaust Debate." *New York Times,* 6 September 1986, 14.

Markovits, Andrei S. "Germans and Jews: An Uneasy Relationship Continues." *Jewish Frontier,* April 1984.

————. "Was ist das 'Deutsche' an den Grünen? Vergangenheitsaufarbeitung als Voraussetzung politischer Zukunftsbewältigung." In *Die Grünen: Letzte Wahl?* edited by Otto Kallscheuer. Berlin, 1986.

Mason, Tim. "Intention and Explanation: A Current Controversy about the Interpretation of National Socialism." In *Der 'Führerstaat': Mythos und Realität,* edited by Gerhard Hirschfeld and Lothar Kettenacker. Stuttgart, 1981.

Mayer, Arno. *Why Did The Heavens Not Darken? The "Final Solution" in History.* New York, 1988.

Medick, Hans. "Missionäre im Ruderboot? Ethnologische Erkenntnisweisen als Herausforderung an die Sozialgeschichte." *Geschichte und Gesellschaft* 10 (1984): 295–319.

Meier, Christian. "Gesucht: Ein modus vivendi mit uns selbst." *Rheinischer Merkur,* 10 October 1986.

———. *40 Jahre nach Auschwitz: Deutsche Geschichtserinnerung heute.* Munich, 1987.

Melnik, S. "Annotierte ausgewählte Bibliographie zur Historikerdebatte." *Liberal* 29 (1987): 85–95.

Merhav, Meir. "Honouring Evil." In *Bitburg,* edited by Geoffrey Hartman. Bloomington, 1986.

Meushel, Sigrid. "The Search for 'Normality' in the Relationship between Germans and Jews." *New German Critique* 38 (1986).

Miller, Judith. "Erasing the Past: Europe's Amnesia about the Holocaust." *New York Times Magazine,* 16 November 1986.

Miller, S. "'Wende'-Zeichen auf dem Gebeit der Geschichte." *Neue Gesellschaft/ Frankfurter Hefte* 9 (1986).

Moeller, Robert G. "The Kaiserreich Recast? Continuity and Change in Modern German Historiography." *Journal of Social History* 17 (1984): 655–83.

Mommsen, Hans. "Neues Geschichtsbewusstsein und Relativierung des Nationalsozialismus." *Blätter für deutsche und internationle Politik* 31, 10 (October 1986): 5–18.

———. "Verordnete Geschichtsbilder? Historische Museumpläne der Bundesregierung." *Gewerkschaftliche Monatshefte* 1 (1986).

———. "Aufarbeitung und Verdrängung des Dritten Reiches im westdeutschen Geschichtsbewusstsein." *Gewerkschaftliche Monatshefte* 3 (1987): 129–41.

———. *Auf der Suche nach historischer Normalität: Beiträge zum Geschichtsbildstreit in der Bundesrepublik.* Berlin, 1987.

———. "The Realization of the Unthinkable: The 'Final Solution of the Jewish Question' in the Third Reich." In *The Policies of Genocide,* edited by Gerhard Hirschfeld. London, 1987.

———. "Das Ressentiment als Wissenschaft: Anmerkungen zu Ernst Noltes 'Der europäische Bürgerkrieg 1917–1945.'" *Geschichte und Gesellschaft* 14 (1988): 495–540.

Moses, John A. *The Politics of Illusion: The Fischer Controversy in German Historiography.* London, 1975.

New German Critique. 19–21 (1980). Special issue: "Germans and Jews."

———. 37 (Winter 1986). [On the "German Question."]

———. 38 (1986). "Special Issue on the German-Jewish Controversy."

———. 44 (Spring/Summer 1988). "Special Issue on the Historikerstreit."

Niethammer, Lutz, ed. *"Die Jahre weiß man nicht, wo man die heute hinsetzen soll": Faschismuserfahrungen im Ruhrgebiet.* Bonn, 1986.

Niethammer, Lutz, and Alexander von Plato. eds. *Lebensgeschichte und Sozialstruktur im Ruhrgebiet 1930–1960.* 3 vols. Bonn, 1986.

Nipperday, Thomas. *Nachdenken über die Deutsche Geschichte: Essays.* Munich, 1986.

Noelle-Neumann, Elisabeth, and Renate Köcher. *Die verletzte Nation: Über den Versuch der Deutschen, ihren Charakter zu ändern.* Stuttgart, 1987.

Nolte, Ernst. *Marxism, Fascism, Cold War*. Atlantic Highlands, N.J., 1982.

―――. *Marxismus und Industrielle Revolution*. Munich, 1983.

―――. "Between Myth and Revisionism? The Third Reich in the Perspective of the 1980s." In *Aspects of the Third Reich*, edited by H. W. Koch. London, 1985.

―――. "Philophische Geschichtsschreibung heute? *Historische Zeitschrift* 252 (1986).

―――. *Der europäische Bürgerkrieg 1917–1945: Nationalsozialismus und Bolschewismus*. Berlin, 1987.

―――. *Das Vergehen der Vergangenheit: Antwort an meine Kritiker im sogenannten Historikerstreit*. Berlin, 1987.

Opitz, R. *Faschismus und Neofaschismus*. Frankfurt, 1984.

Pätzold, H. "Gewonnenem und Erstrebtem: Zur Historikerdebatte." *Blätter für deutsche und internationale Politik* 12 (1986): 1452–65.

Paul, Gerhard, and Bernhard Schössig, eds. *Die andere Geschichte*. Cologne, 1985.

Peukert, Detlev. "Alltag und Barbarei—zur Normalität des Dritten Reiches." In *Ist der Nationalsozialismus Geschichte?* edited by Dan Diner. Frankfurt, 1987.

―――. *Inside Nazi Germany: Conformity and Opposition in Everyday Life*. New Haven, 1987.

Pfeiffer, Hermannus. *Die FAZ: Nachforschungen über ein Zentralorgan*. Cologne, 1988.

Pietrow, B. "Deutschland im Juni 1941–ein Opfer sowjetischer Aggression? Zur Kontroverse über die Präventivkriegsthese." *Geschichte und Gesellschaft* 14, 1 (1988).

Postone, Moishel. "Anti-Semitism and National Socialism: Notes on the German Reaction to 'Holocaust.'" *New German Critique* (Winter 1980).

Puhle, Hans-Jürgen. "Deutscher Sonderweg: Kontroverse um eine vermeintliche Legende." *Journal für Geschichte* (1981).

―――. "Die neue Ruhelosigkeit: Michael Stürmers nationalpolitischer Revisionismus." *Geschichte und Gesellschaft* 13 (1987): 382–99.

Puhle, Hans-Jürgen, and Stürmer, Michael. *Two Lectures in Modern German History*. Edited by George Iggers. Amherst, 1978.

Pulzer, Peter. "Erasing the Past: German Historians Debate the Holocaust." *Patterns of Prejudice* 21 (1987): 3–14.

―――. "Germany Searches for a Less Traumatic Past." *Listener* 117, 25 June 1987, 16–18.

―――. *The Rise of Political Antisemitism in Germany and Austria*. Revised edition. Cambridge, Mass., 1988.

Rabe, K.-K., ed. *Von Oggersheim bis Oberschlesien: Union und Vertriebenenverbände im politischen Gleichklang: Eine Dokumentation*. Bornheim-Merten, 1985.

Recker, Marie-Louise. *Nationalsozialistische Sozialpolitik im Krieg*. Munich, 1985.

Rudolph, Hermann. "Falsche Fronten?" *Süddeutsche Zeitung*, 4–5 October 1986.

Rusconi, Gian Enrico. "Italien und der deutsche 'Historikerstreit.'" In *Ist der Nationalsozialismus Geschichte? Zu Historisierung und Historikerstreit*, edited by Dan Diner. Frankfurt, 1987.

Schieder, Wolfgang. "Der Nationalsozialismus im Fehlurteil philosophischer Geschichtsschreibung: Zur Methode von Ernst Nolte's 'Europäischen Bürgerkrieg.'" *Geschichte und Gesellschaft* 15 (1989): 89–114.

Schleier, H. "Zum idealistischen Historismus in der bürgerlichen deutschen Geschichtswissenschaft." *Jahrbuch für Geschichte* 28 (1983): 133–54.

Schlögel, Karl. *Die Mitte liegt ostwärts: Die Deutschen, der verlorene Osten und Mitteleuropa*. Berlin, 1986.

Schneider, Peter. "Hitler's Shadow: On Being a Self-Conscious German." *Harper's Magazine*, September 1987, 499–54.

——. "Im Teufelskreis der Schuld." *Die Zeit*, 27 March 1987.

Schreiber, Gerhard. *Hitler: Interpretationen 1923–1983*. Darmstadt, 1984.

Schulze, Hagen. "Auf der Suche nach einer deutschen Identität: Ein Gespräch mit Adalbert Reif." *Börsenblatt für den deutschen Buchhandel* 42 (1986): 690–95.

——. *Wir sind, was wir geoworden sind: Vom Nutzen der Geschichte für die deutsche Gegenwart*. Munich, 1987.

Seidel, Gill. *The Holocaust Denial: Antisemitism, Racism, and the New Right*. London, 1986.

Senfft, Heinrich. *Der Blick züruck: Hinter den Fassaden des Historikerstreits*. Nördlingen, 1989.

Sheehan, James J. "What Is German History? Reflections on the Role of the Nation in German History and Historiography." *Journal of Modern History* 53 (1981): 1–23.

Shlaes, Amity. "More History." *The American Spectator*, April 1987, 30–32.

Sichrovsky, Peter. *Born Guilty: Children of Nazi Families*. New York, 1989.

Speitkamp, W. "Die Historikerkontroverse und der Holocaust." *Geschichtsdidaktik* 12 (1987): 216–28.

Steinbach, Peter. "Nationalsozialistische Gewaltverbrechen in der deutschen öffentlichkeit nach 1945." In *Vergangenheitsbewältigung durch Strafverfahren? NS-Prozesse in der Bundesrepublik Deutschland*. Edited by Jürgen Weber and Peter Steinbach. Munich, 1984.

——. "Unbestechlich und unabhängig: Andreas Hillgrubers Essays über 'Zweierlei Untergang.'" *Frankfurter Allgemeine Zeitung*, 8 July 1986.

Strauss, Franz-Josef. "Im Wortlaut: 'Mehr aufrechter Gang': Passagen einer Rede." *Frankfurter Rundschau*, 14 January 1987.

Strauss, H. A. "Antisemitismus und Holocaust als Epochenproblem." *Aus Politik und Zeitgeschichte*, B 11/87, 14 March 1987, 15–23.

Streit, Christian. *Keine Kameraden: Die Wehrmacht und die sowjetischen Kriegsgefangenen, 1941–1945*. Stuttgart, 1978.

Stürmer, Michael. "Wem gehört die deutsche Geschichte? National-politisches Profil in Ostberlin." *Neue Züricher Zeitung*, 22/23 May 1982.

——. "Eine Anklage, die sich selbst ihre Belege fabriziert." *Frankfurter Allgemeine Zeitung*, 16 August 1986.

——. *Dissonanzen des Fortschritts: Essays über Geschichte und Politik in Deutschland*. Munich, 1986.

——. "Weder verträgen noch bewältigen: Geschichte und Geschichtsbewusstsein der Deutschen." *Schweizer Monatshefte* 66, September 1986, 689–94.

——. *Deutsche Fragen: Oder die Suche nach der Staatsräson*. Munich, 1988.

Sudholt, Gert. *Antigermanismus: Eine Streitschrift zu Dachau und zum "Auschwitz-Gesetz."* Berg, 1986.

Thamer, H.-U. "Der Nationalsozialismus in der deutschen Geschichte: Anmerkungen zum Historiker-Streit." *Geschichte, Politik und ihre Didaktik* 13 (1986): 142–47.

Wehler, Hans-Ulrich. "'Deutscher Sonderweg' oder allgemeine Probleme des westischen Kapitalismus?" *Merkur* 35 (1981): 477–87.

——. "30. Januar 1933—ein halbes Jahrhundert danach." *Aus Politik und Zeitgeschichte* 4–5 (1983).

————. "Historiography in Germany Today." In *Observations on "The Spiritual Situation of the Age"*, edited by Jürgen Habermas. Cambridge, Mass., 1984.

————. *Preussen ist wieder chic*. Frankfurt, 1984.

————. "Königsweg zu neuen Ufern oder Irrgarten der Illusionen? Die westdeutsche Alltagsgeschichte: Geschichte 'von innen' und 'von unten.'" In *"Geschichte von unten-Geschichte von innen": Kontroversen um die Alltagsgeschichte*. Edited by F. J. Brüggemeier and J. Kocka. Fernuniversität Hagen, 1985.

————. *Entsorgung der deutschen Vergangenheit: Ein polemischer Essay zum Historikerstreit*. Munich, 1988. English edition forthcoming.

Weidenfeld, Werner, ed. *Die Identität der deutschen: Fragen, Positionen, Perspectiven*. Munich, 1984.

————. "Am Pulsschlag der verletzten Nation: Was die Bundesbürger hoffen und fürchten." *Die Zeit*, 10 April 1987.

Weizsäcker, Richard von. *A Voice from Germany*. London, 1985.

Winkler, Heinrich August. "Der deutsche Sonderweg: Eine Nachlese." *Merkur* 35 (1981): 793–804.

Winkler, Karen J. "German Scholars Sharply Divided over Place of Holocaust in History." *The Chronicle of Higher Education*, 27 May 1987, 4–7.

Yad Vashem Studies 19 (1988). [Special number on *Historikerstreit*.]

Zang, Gert. *Die unaufhaltsame Annäherung an das Einzelne: Reflexionen über den theoretischen und praktischen Nutzen der Regional- und Alltagsgeschichte*. Konstanz, 1985.

Zipes, Jack, and Andrei Markovits. *Jews in Postwar Germany*.

Zipes, Jack, and Anson Rabinach, eds. *Germans and Jews since the Holocaust: The Changing Situation*. New York and London, 1986.

List of Contributors

Peter Baldwin is assistant professor of history at Harvard University.

Wolfgang Benz is a researcher at the Institut für Zeitgeschichte in Munich.

Martin Broszat was professor and director of the Institut für Zeitgeschichte in Munich until his death in late 1989.

Dan Diner is professor of history at the University of Essen.

Saul Friedländer is professor of history at the University of Tel Aviv and at the University of California, Los Angeles.

Jürgen Kocka is professor of history at the Free University of Berlin.

Otto Dov Kulka is professor of history at the Hebrew University of Jerusalem.

Charles S. Maier is professor of history at Harvard University.

Andrei S. Markovits is associate professor of political science at Boston University.

Hans Mommsen is professor of history at the University of Bochum.

Mary Nolan is associate professor of history at New York University.

Gregory Pass is a doctoral candidate in the History Department at Harvard University.

Anson Rabinbach is associate professor of history at the Cooper Union, New York.

Hagen Schulze is professor of history at the Free University of Berlin.

Hans-Ulrich Wehler is professor of history at the University of Bielefeld.

Credits

Hagen Schulze, "Explaining the 'German Catastrophe': The Use and Abuse of Historical Explanations," translated by Thomas Ertman from "Die 'Deutsche Katastrophe' erklären: Von Nützen und Nachteil historischer Erklärungsmodelle," in Dan Diner, ed., *Ist der Nationalsozialismus Geschichte?* 89–101.

Wolfgang Benz, "Warding Off the Past: Is This a Problem Only for Historians and Moralists?" translated by Bill Templer from "Die Abwehr der Vergangenheit: Ein Problem nur für Historiker und Moralisten?" in Dan Diner, ed., *Ist der Nationalsozialismus Geschichte?* 17–33.

Hans-Ulrich Wehler, "Unburdening the German Past? A Preliminary Assessment," translated by Thomas Ertman from "Ein Zwischenbilanz," chap. 6 of *Entsorgung der deutschen Vergangenheit? Ein polemischer Essay zum "Historikerstreit,"* © 1988 by C. H. Beck'sche Verlagsbuchhandlung (Oscar Beck), Munich.

Mary Nolan, "The *Historikerstreit* and Social History," reprinted by permission from *New German Critique* 44 (Spring/Summer 1988): 51–80.

Dan Diner, "Negative Symbiosis: Germans and Jews after Auschwitz," translated by Thomas Ertman from "Negative Symbiose: Deutsche und Juden nach Auschwitz," in Dan Diner, ed., *Ist der Nationalsozialismus Geschichte?* 185–97.

Andrei S. Markovits, "Coping with the Past: The West German Labor Movement and the Left," first presented at the Conference "Coping with the Past: Germany and Austria after 1945," held at Northwestern University, Evanston, Illinois, May 1–3, 1987.

Jürgen Kocka, "German Identity and Historical Comparison: After the Historikerstreit," translated by Thomas Ertman from an edited version of "Deutsche Identität und historischer Vergleich: Nach dem 'Historikerstreit,'" in *Aus Politik und Zeitgeschichte* B 40–41/88 (30 September 1988), 15, 21–28.